THE TEXT OF THE
NEW TESTAMENT

THE TEXT OF THE
NEW TESTAMENT

Its Transmission, Corruption, and
Restoration

BY

BRUCE M. METZGER

Professor of New Testament Language and Literature
Princeton Theological Seminary

SECOND EDITION

1968
OXFORD UNIVERSITY PRESS
NEW YORK AND OXFORD

© OXFORD UNIVERSITY PRESS 1968
Seventh printing, 1980
FIRST EDITION 1964
SECOND EDITION 1968

18 19 20

Preface

THE necessity of applying textual criticism to the books of the New Testament arises from two circumstances: (*a*) none of the original documents is extant, and (*b*) the existing copies differ from one another. The textual critic seeks to ascertain from the divergent copies which form of the text should be regarded as most nearly conforming to the original. In some cases the evidence will be found to be so evenly divided that it is extremely difficult to decide between two variant readings. In other instances, however, the critic can arrive at a decision based on more or less compelling reasons for preferring one reading and rejecting another.

It is the purpose of this book to supply the student with information concerning both the science and the art of textual criticism as applied to the New Testament. The science of textual criticism deals with (*a*) the making and transmission of ancient manuscripts, (*b*) the description of the most important witnesses to the New Testament text, and (*c*) the history of the textual criticism of the New Testament as reflected in the succession of printed editions of the Greek Testament. The art of textual criticism refers to the application of reasoned considerations in choosing among variant readings. The results of the practice of textual criticism have differed from one generation to another, partly because the balance in the quantity and the quality of witnesses available has gradually altered owing to the acquisition of additional manuscripts, and partly because theories and procedures of evaluating textual evidence have varied over the years. In Part Three of the volume the author has attempted to provide a succinct account of the several schools of textual methodology, indicating at the same time what in his view is the most satisfactory critical procedure for beginners to follow.

The author gratefully acknowledges the courtesy of the following for granting permission to reproduce specimen folios and diagrams of manuscripts: Bibliothèque Bodmer, the Bodleian Library, the British Museum, the Cambridge University

Press, Dr. W. H. P. Hatch, Macmillan & Co., Ltd., and the Speer Library of Princeton Theological Seminary.

Finally, I should like to express my gratitude to the Delegates of the Oxford University Press for their acceptance of my book for publication. I am also indebted to the readers of the Press for their customary care and painstaking vigilance in the reading of the proofs.

BRUCE M. METZGER

Princeton, New Jersey
August 1963

Preface to the Second Edition

DURING the four years that have elapsed since the initial publication of this book in 1964, a great amount of textual research has continued to come from the presses in both Europe and America. References to some of these publications were included in the German translation of the volume issued in 1966 under the title *Der Text des Neuen Testaments; Einführung in die neutestamentliche Textkritik* (Kohlhammer Verlag, Stuttgart). The second printing of the English edition provides opportunity to introduce a variety of small alterations throughout the volume as well as to include references to more than one hundred and fifty books and articles dealing with Greek manuscripts, early versions, and textual studies of recently discovered witnesses to the text of the New Testament. In order not to disturb the pagination, most of the new material has been placed at the close of the book (pp. 261–73), to which the reader's attention is directed by appropriate cross references.

BRUCE M. METZGER

February 1968

Contents

Contents

List of Plates

(at end)

List of Figures

PART ONE

The Materials for the Textual Criticism of the New Testament

I

The Making of Ancient Books

UNTIL the invention of printing with movable type in the fifteenth century the text of the New Testament—and, indeed, the text of every ancient record—could be transmitted only by laboriously copying it letter by letter and word by word. The consideration, therefore, of the processes involved in the making and transcribing of manuscripts is of the utmost importance to the historian of ancient culture in general and to the student of the New Testament in particular. The following sections deal with those aspects of Greek palaeography[1] that bear upon the textual criticism of the New Testament.

I. THE MATERIALS OF ANCIENT BOOKS

Clay tablets, stone, bone, wood, leather, various metals, potsherds (ostraca), papyrus, and parchment (vellum) were all used in antiquity to receive writing. Among these several materials, the student of the New Testament is interested chiefly in the last two, for almost all New Testament manuscripts are made of either papyrus or parchment.

The manufacture of papyrus was a flourishing business in Egypt, for the papyrus plant grew plentifully in the shallow waters of the Nile at the delta (cf. Job viii. 11, 'Can papyrus grow where there is no marsh?'). About 12 or 15 feet in height, the stem of the plant, which was triangular in cross-section and as thick as a man's wrist, was cut into sections about a foot long. Each section was split open lengthwise and the pith cut into thin strips. A layer of these was placed on a flat surface, all the

---

[1] Standard works on Greek palaeography include, for example, Viktor Gardthausen, *Griechische Palaeographie*, 2 vols., 2te Aufl. (Leipzig, 1911–13); E. M. Thompson, *An Introduction to Greek and Latin Palaeography* (Oxford, 1912); A. Sigalas, Ἱστορία τῆς Ἑλληνικῆς Γραφῆς (Thessaloniki, 1934); L. Gonzaga da Fonseca, S.J., *Epitome introductionis in palaeographiam Graecam (Biblicam)*, ed. altera (Rome, 1944); and B. A. van Groningen, *Short Manual of Greek Palaeography* (Leiden, 1940; 3rd ed., 1963). For additional bibliography, see the present writer's article 'Palaeography' in *Encyclopedia Americana*, xxi (1958), pp. 163–6. See below, p. 261.

fibres running in the same direction, and on top another layer was laid, with the fibres running at right angles to the lower layer. The two layers were then pressed together until they formed one fabric—a fabric which, though now so brittle that it can sometimes be crumbled into powder, once had a strength nearly equal to that of good paper.

The manufacture of parchment for writing purposes has an interesting history. According to Pliny the Elder (in his *Natural History*, xiii. 21 f.), it was King Eumenes of Pergamum, a city in Mysia of Asia Minor, who promoted the preparation and use of parchment. This ruler (probably Eumenes II, who ruled from 197 to 159 B.C.) planned to found a library in his city which would rival the famous library of Alexandria. This ambition did not please Ptolemy of Egypt (probably Ptolemy Epiphanes, 205–182 B.C.), who thereupon put an embargo on the export of papyrus sections. It was this embargo which forced Eumenes to develop the production of vellum, which from the place of its origin received the Greek name περγαμηνή (whence our English word 'parchment' is derived). Whatever may be thought of the details of this story—actually leather (parchment) was used for books long before Eumenes—the gist of it is probably true, namely that a high quality of parchment was developed at Pergamum, and that the city became famous in the manufacture and export of this kind of writing material, eventually giving its name to the product.

Parchment or vellum (the two words are often used interchangeably, but exact writers restrict the word 'vellum' to describe a finer, superior quality of parchment) was made from the skins of cattle, sheep, goats, and antelopes, and especially from the young of these animals. After the hair had been removed by scraping, the skins were washed, smoothed with pumice, and dressed with chalk. De luxe editions, according to St. Jerome, who did not approve of such extravagance,[1] were

---

[1] In his famous letter to Eustochium, Jerome inveighs against anomalous extravagance: 'Parchments are dyed purple, gold is melted into lettering, manuscripts are decked with jewels, while Christ lies at the door naked and dying' (*Epist.* xxii. 32; cf. also Jerome's preface to the Book of Job, and see Evaristo Arns, *La Technique du livre d'après Saint Jérôme* [Paris, 1953]). Writing to a correspondent named Laeta, who has asked how she ought to rear her young daughter, he advises, 'Let her treasures be not gems or silks, but manuscripts of the holy Scriptures; and in these let her think less of gilding and Babylonian parchment and arabesque patterns, than of correctness and accurate punctuation' (*Epist.* cvii. 12). For a list of extant

made of vellum dyed a deep purple and written with gold and silver inks. Ordinary editions were written with black or brown ink and had decorative headings and initial letters coloured with blue or yellow or (most often) red ink—whence the word 'rubric', from *ruber*, the Latin for 'red'.

Vellum or parchment continued to be generally used until the late Middle Ages. At that time paper, which was made of cotton, hemp, or flax, having been introduced into Europe from China by Arabian traders, became popular and supplanted other writing materials. (See below, p. 261.)

II. THE FORMS OF ANCIENT BOOKS[1]

In the Graeco-Roman world literary works were customarily published in the format of a scroll, made of papyrus or parchment. The papyrus roll or scroll was made by gluing together, side by side, separate sheets of papyrus and then winding the long strip around a stick, thus producing a volume (a word derived from the Latin *volumen*, 'something rolled up'). The length of such a papyrus roll was limited by considerations of convenience in handling the roll; the normal Greek literary roll seldom exceeded 35 feet in length.[2] Ancient authors therefore would divide a long literary work into several 'books', each of which could be accommodated in one roll. The two longest books in the New Testament—the Gospel of Luke and the Book of Acts—would each have filled an ordinary papyrus roll of

purple manuscripts of the Greek and Latin Bible, as well as a discussion of the special skills required to produce a *codex aureus purpureus*, see E. A. Lowe in *Studies in Art and Literature for Belle da Costa Greene*, ed. by Dorothy Miner (Princeton, 1954), pp. 266–8.

[1] See F. G. Kenyon, *Books and Readers in Ancient Greece and Rome* (Oxford, 1932; 2nd ed., 1951); Henry A. Sanders, 'The Beginnings of the Modern Book', *Michigan Alumnus Review*, xliv (1938), pp. 95–111; C. C. McCown, 'Codex and Roll in the New Testament', *Harvard Theological Review*, xxxiv (1941), pp. 219–50; id., 'The Earliest Christian Books', *Biblical Archaeologist*, vi (1943), pp. 21–31; Frank W. Beare, 'Books and Publication in the Ancient World', *University of Toronto Quarterly*, xiv (1945), pp. 150–67; H. L. Pinner, *The World of Books in Classical Antiquity* (Leiden, 1948); C. H. Roberts, 'The Codex', *Proceedings of the British Academy*, xl (1954), pp. 169–204; and Robert Devreesse, *Introduction à l'étude des manuscrits grecs* (Paris, 1954). See below, p. 261.

[2] Callimachus, the learned cataloguer of books in the great library at Alexandria, was accustomed to say, 'A big book is a big nuisance' (μέγα βιβλίον μέγα κακόν). Ceremonial copies of the Egyptian Book of the Dead have been found which measure more than 100 feet in length, but these were not meant to be read but to be buried in the tomb of a rich owner.

31 or 32 feet in length. Doubtless this is one of the reasons why Luke–Acts was issued in two volumes instead of one.

On the roll thus formed the writing was arranged in a series of columns, each about 2 or 3 inches wide. The height of the columns, which ran parallel to the stick on which the roll was wound, varied, of course, with the height of the original papyrus sheets. Sometimes, but not very often, the roll was written on both sides (see Rev. v. 1); this was called an opisthograph.

The roll was relatively inconvenient to use. The reader had to employ both hands, unrolling the scroll with one hand and rolling it up with the other as the reading proceeded. Moreover, the Christian community soon discovered how laborious it was to try to find specific passages in their sacred books when they were written in roll-form. Early in the second century (or perhaps even at the close of the first century) the codex, or leaf-form of book, began to come into extensive use in the Church. A codex was made by folding one or more sheets of papyrus in the middle and sewing them together. Christians found that this form had a number of advantages over the roll: (*a*) it permitted all four Gospels or all the Epistles of Paul to be bound into one book, a format which was impossible so long as the roll was used; (*b*) it facilitated the consultation of proof-texts; (*c*) it was better adapted to receiving writing on both sides of the page, thus keeping the cost of production down. The suggestion may well be true[1] that it was Gentile Christians who early adopted the codex-form for their Scriptures, instead of the roll-form, as part of a deliberate attempt to differentiate the usage of the Church from that of the synagogue, which was accustomed to transmit the Old Testament on scrolls.

The advantages of parchment over papyrus for the making of books seem obvious to us today. It was a much tougher and more lasting material than the more fragile papyrus. Moreover, parchment leaves could receive writing without difficulty on both sides, whereas the vertical direction of the fibres on the 'reverse' side of a sheet of papyrus made that side somewhat less satisfactory than the other as a writing surface. On the other hand, parchment also had its defects. For example, the edges of parchment leaves are apt to become puckered and uneven.

---

[1] See Peter Katz, 'The Early Christians' Use of Codices instead of Rolls', *Journal of Theological Studies*, xliv (1945), pp. 63–65. See below, p. 261.

Furthermore, according to the observation of Galen, the famous Greek physician of the second century A.D., parchment, which is shiny, strains the eyes more than does papyrus, which does not reflect so much light.

Eusebius, the noted Christian scholar of Caesarea in Palestine, included in his *Life of Constantine* information concerning an imperial request for fifty parchment manuscripts. About A.D. 331, when Constantine wished to secure copies of the Scriptures for the new churches which he proposed to build in Constantinople, he wrote to Eusebius requesting him to arrange without delay for the production of 'fifty copies of the sacred Scriptures . . . to be written on fine parchment in a legible manner, and in a convenient portable form, by professional scribes (καλλιγράφοι) thoroughly accomplished in their art'.[1] These orders, Eusebius continues, 'were followed by the immediate execution of the work itself, which we sent him in magnificent and elaborately bound volumes of threefold and fourfold forms'.[2]

The suggestion has been made by several scholars that the two oldest parchment manuscripts of the Bible which are in existence today, namely codex Vaticanus and codex Sinaiticus (see Chapter II for descriptions of these manuscripts), may have been among those ordered by Constantine. It has been pointed out that Eusebius' curious expression, 'volumes of threefold and fourfold forms', agrees with the circumstance that these two codices have respectively three columns and four columns on each page. There are, however, one or two indications which

---

[1] Eusebius, *Life of Constantine*, iv. 36.

[2] The Greek text of the concluding clause (ἐν πολυτελῶς ἠσκημένοις τεύχεσιν τρισσὰ καὶ τετρασσὰ διαπεμψάντων ἡμῶν) is difficult to interpret, and the words τρισσὰ καὶ τετρασσά have been taken in widely different senses. Thus it has been suggested that the words refer to codices which were composed of quires of three or four double leaves; that they were polyglot Bibles in three or four languages; that they were harmonies of three or four Gospels; that copies were sent off to Constantine three or four at a time; that each Bible was in three or four parts; or that the pages had three or four columns of script. Each of these interpretations involves more or less serious difficulties; perhaps the least unsatisfactory interpretation is the one mentioned last. For discussions of the problems involved, see Kirsopp Lake, 'The Sinaitic and Vatican Manuscripts and the Copies sent by Eusebius to Constantinople', *Harvard Theological Review*, xi (1918), pp. 32–35; J. H. Ropes, *The Text of Acts* (= *The Beginnings of Christianity*, part I, vol. iii; London, 1926), pp. xxxvi ff.; Carl Wendel, 'Der Bibel-Auftrag Kaiser Konstantins', *Zentralblatt für Bibliothekswesen*, lvi (1939), pp. 165–75; and T. C. Skeat, 'The Use of Dictation in Ancient Book-Production', *Proceedings of the British Academy*, xlii (1956), pp. 196 f.

point to Egypt as the place of origin of codex Vaticanus, and the type of text found in both codices is unlike that used by Eusebius. The most that can be said with certainty, therefore, is that codices Vaticanus and Sinaiticus are doubtless like those which Constantine ordered Eusebius to have copied.

III. ANCIENT SCRIBES AND THEIR HANDIWORK

In writing on papyrus the scribe was accustomed to utilize the horizontal fibres on the recto side of the sheet as guide lines for his script. Before writing on parchment he would score the surface with a blunt-pointed instrument, drawing not only horizontal lines but two or more vertical lines as well, thus marking the margins of each column of writing. In many manuscripts these guide lines are still visible, as are also the pinpricks which the scribe made first in order to guide him in ruling the vellum.[1] Different schools of scribes employed various procedures of ruling, and occasionally it is possible for the modern scholar to identify the place of origin of a newly discovered manuscript by comparing its ruling pattern (as it is called) with those in manuscripts whose place of origin is known.[2] Since the hair side of vellum is darker than the flesh side, it was found that the most pleasing effect upon the reader was obtained only when the separate sheets were not indiscriminately gathered together in quires, but when the hair side of one page faced the hair side of the opposite page, and the flesh side faced the flesh side, wherever the book was opened.[3]

In antiquity two styles of Greek handwriting were in general

---

[1] There is even a science of pinpricks! See E. K. Rand, 'Prickings in a Manuscript of Orleans', *Transactions and Proceedings of the American Philological Association*, lxx (1939), pp. 327–41; and L. W. Jones, ' "Pin Pricks" at the Morgan Library', ibid., pp. 318–26; 'Where are the Prickings?', op. cit., lxxii (1944), pp. 71–86; 'Pricking Manuscripts: the Instruments and their Significance', *Speculum, a Journal of Mediaeval Studies*, xxi (1946), pp. 389–403; and 'Prickings as Clues to Date and Origin: the Eighth Century', *Medievalia et humanistica*, xiv (1962), pp. 15–22. Rand dealt earlier with various methods of ruling manuscripts in vogue during the Middle Ages; see his study entitled 'How Many Leaves at a Time?' in *Palaeographica Latina*, v (1927), pp. 52–78.

[2] For a list of several hundred different ruling patterns, see Kirsopp and Silva Lake, *Dated Greek Minuscule Manuscripts to the Year 1200 A.D.* (Boston, 1934–45). See below, p. 261.

[3] This characteristic feature of parchment codices was discovered towards the end of the last century by Caspar R. Gregory; see his article 'The Quires in Greek Manuscripts', *American Journal of Philology*, vii (1886), pp. 27–32.

use. The cursive or 'running' hand, which could be written rapidly, was employed for non-literary, everyday documents, such as letters, accounts, receipts, petitions, deeds, and the like. Contractions and abbreviations of frequently recurring words (such as the definite article and certain prepositions) were common. Literary works, on the other hand, were written in a more formal style of handwriting, called uncials.[1] This 'bookhand' was characterized by more deliberate and carefully executed letters, each one separate from the others, somewhat like our capital letters. Some of the most beautiful specimens of Greek handwriting are certain classical and Biblical manuscripts dating from the third to the sixth century. In the course of time, however, the style of the book-hand began to deteriorate, and uncials became thick and clumsy. Then, about the beginning of the ninth century, a reform in handwriting was initiated, and a script of smaller letters in a running hand, called minuscules,[2] was created for the production of books.[3] This modified form of the cursive script became popular almost at once throughout the Greek world, though some liturgical books continued for one or two centuries to be written in uncial script. Thus manuscripts

---

[1] The word 'uncial' is derived from the Latin *uncia*, meaning 'a twelfth part' of anything. Apparently the term came to be applied to letters which occupied roughly about one-twelfth of an ordinary line of writing. Cf. W. H. P. Hatch, 'The Origin and Meaning of the Term "Uncial"', *Classical Philology*, xxx (1935), pp. 247–54.

[2] The word 'minuscule' is derived from the Latin *minusculus*, meaning 'rather small'; it was used because the letters designated by this term are usually smaller than capitals and uncials.

[3] The credit for initiating the reform in Greek handwriting has been commonly attributed to scholarly monks at the monastery of the Studium in Constantinople (see, for example, G. Zereteli, 'Wo ist das Tetraevangelium von Porphyrius Uspenskij aus dem Jahre 835 entstanden?', *Byzantinische Zeitschrift*, ix [1900], pp. 649–53, and T. W. Allen, 'The Origin of the Greek Minuscule Hand', *Journal of Hellenic Studies*, xl [1920], pp. 1–12), but recently it has been argued that the perfecting of minuscule script for book production was the work of humanistic scholars who were involved in the revival of culture at Constantinople during the second epoch of iconoclasm (see Bertrand Hemmerdinger, *Essai sur l'histoire du texte de Thucydide* [Paris, 1955], pp. 33–39).

It may be mentioned that the earliest known minuscule Greek manuscript bearing a date is a copy of the four Gospels, now in the Public Library of Leningrad, with its all-important colophon dated 7 May 6343 (= A.D. 835) by the monk Nicolaus, later abbot of the Studium. This manuscript has raised problems for scholars; palaeographically the handwriting appears to be too mature and fully developed to stand at the beginning of the minuscule period, yet no forerunners have been recognized among extant manuscripts. For a discussion, see Aubrey Diller, 'A Companion to the Uspenski Gospels', *Byzantinische Zeitschrift*, xlix (1956), pp. 332–5.

fall into two rather well-defined groups, the earlier being written in uncial letters (see Fig. 1) and the later in minuscules (see Fig. 2).

FIG. 1. Greek Uncial Script (from codex Sinaiticus, 4th cent.)
(actual width of each column about 2¼ in.)

Col. a, Matt. xiii. 5–10, αλλα δε επεσεν ε|πι τα πετρωδη ο|που ουκ ειχεν γην | πολλην και ευθε|ως εξανετιλεν δι|α το μη εχιν βαθος | γης ηλιου δε ανα|τιλαντος εκαυμα|τισθη και δια το | μη εχειν ριζαν ε|ξηρανθη | αλλα δε επεσεν ε|πι τας ακανθας | και ανεβησαν αι | ακανθαι και επνι|ξαν αυτα | αλλα δε επεσεν ε|πι την γην την κα|λην και εδιδου | καρπον ο μεν ε|κατον ο δε εξηκον|τα ο δε $\overline{\lambda}$ ο εχων | ωτα [insert ακουειν from the left-hand margin] ακουετω | και προσελθοντες ‖ col. b, Matt. xiii. 14–16 και αναπληρου|ται αυτοις η προ|φητια ησαϊου η | λεγουσα ακοη | ακουσετε και ου | μη συνητε και βλε|ποντες βλε|ψητε και ου μη ϊ|δητε επαχυνθη | γαρ η καρδια του | λαου τουτου και | τοις ωσιν αυτων | βαρεως ηκουσαν | και τους οφθαλ|μους αυτων εκαμ|μυσαν μηποτε | ιδωσιν τοις ο|φθαλμοις και τοις | ωσιν [αυτων between the lines] ακουσωσιν | και τη καρδια συνω|σιν και επιστρε|ψωσιν και ιασομε | αυτους | ϋμων δε μακαρι. The Eusebian canon numerals (see pp. 24 f. below) stand between the columns $\left(\dfrac{\overline{\rho\lambda\delta}}{\epsilon} = \dfrac{134}{5}\right)$.

The advantages of using minuscule script are obvious. Minuscule letters, as their name suggests, are smaller than uncials, and thus the writing is more compact. Hence, when the minuscule hand was used, less parchment was required and therefore the book was more economical. Furthermore, a literary work could be produced which was less bulky and therefore easier to handle than a larger manuscript. Moreover, it was possible to write minuscule letters more rapidly than uncials, and consequently books could be produced more quickly and more

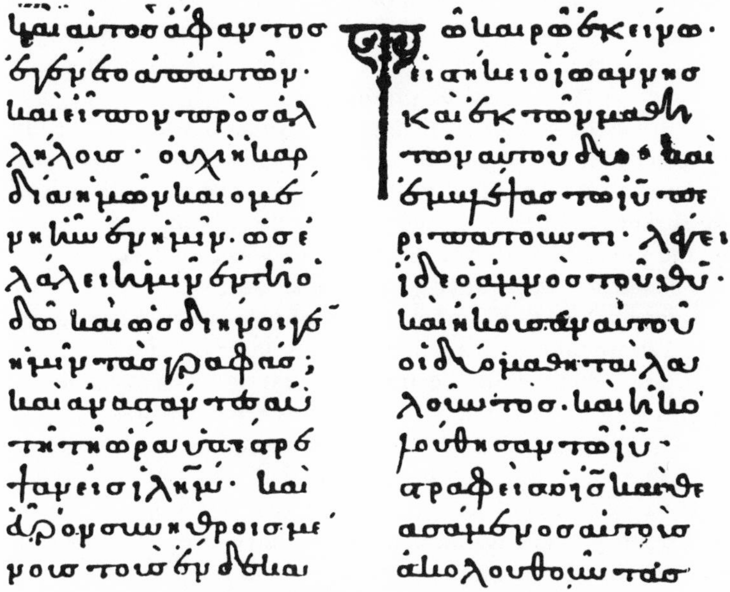

FIG. 2. Greek Minuscule Script (from lectionary 303, 12th or 13th cent.)
(actual width of each column about 3¼ in.)

Col. a, Luke xxiv. 31–33, καὶ αὐτὸς ἄφαντος | ἐγένετο ἀπ' αὐτῶν· | καὶ εἶπον πρὸς ἀλ|λήλους· οὐχὶ ἡ καρ|δία ἡμῶν καιομέ|νη ἦν ἐν ἡμῖν. ὡς ἐ|λάλει ἡμῖν ἐν τῇ ὁ|δῷ καὶ ὡς διήνοιγεν | ἡμῖν τὰς γραφάς; | καὶ ἀναστάντες αὐ|τῇ τῇ ὥρα ὑπέστρε|ψαν εἰς ἱ[ερουσα]-λήμ· καὶ | εὗρον συνηθροισμέ|νους τοὺς ἕνδεκα || col. b, John i. 35–38, Τῷ καιρῷ ἐκείνω· | εἰστήκει ὁ ἰωάννης | καὶ ἐκ τῶν μαθη|τῶν αὐτοῦ δύο· καὶ | ἐμβλέψας τῷ ἱ[ησο]ῦ πε|ριπατοῦντι· λέγει· | ἴδε ὁ ἀμνὸς τοῦ θ[εο]ῦ· | καὶ ἤκουσαν αὐτοῦ | οἱ δύο μαθηταὶ λα|λοῦντος. καὶ ἠκο|λούθησαν τῷ ἱ[ησο]ῦ· | στραφεὶς ὁ ἱ[ησοῦ]ς καὶ θε|ασάμενος αὐτοὺς | ἀκολουθοῦντας.

cheaply. It is easy to understand that this change in the style of script had a profound effect upon the textual tradition of the Greek Bible. Now the possession of copies of the Scriptures (and of other literary works) was placed within reach of persons of limited means. When literary works were copied almost exclusively in the uncial script, such persons were obliged to get along

without many books. Thus the minuscule hand was an important factor in the dissemination of culture in general and of the
Scriptures in particular. The minuscule manuscripts of the New
Testament outnumber the uncial manuscripts by more than ten
to one, and although one must make allowance for the greater
antiquity of the uncial style (and consequently the greater
likelihood of the destruction of uncial manuscripts through the
ravages of time), very much of the disparity in the number of
the survivors must be due to the increased ease with which the
minuscule copies could be produced.

In times of economic depression, when the cost of vellum
increased, the parchment of an older manuscript would be used
over again. The original writing was scraped and washed off,
the surface re-smoothed, and the new literary material written
on the salvaged material. Such a book was called a palimpsest
(which means 're-scraped', from πάλιν and ψάω). One of the
half-dozen or so most important parchment manuscripts of the
New Testament is such a palimpsest; its name is codex Ephraemi
rescriptus. Written in the fifth century, it was erased in the
twelfth century and many of the sheets rewritten with the text
of a Greek translation of thirty-eight treatises or sermons by
St. Ephraem, a Syrian Church Father of the fourth century.
By the application of certain chemical reagents and with the use
of the ultraviolet-ray lamp, scholars have been able to read
much of the almost obliterated underwriting, although the task
of deciphering it is most trying to the eyes.

In A.D. 692 the council in Trullo (also called the Quinisext
Council) issued a canon (no. 68) condemning the practice of
using parchment from manuscripts of the Scriptures for other
purposes. Despite the canon and the penalty of excommunication for one year, the practice must have continued, for of the
250 uncial manuscripts of the New Testament known today,
52 are palimpsests.[1]

Instead of writing *on* the lines, as we do today, ancient scribes
would ordinarily write the Greek letters pendent from the lines,
that is, hanging underneath the lines. Usually no spaces were

[1] Besides codex Ephraemi they are the following: P^e (= 024), P^{apr} (= 025),
Q (= 026), R (= 027), Z (= 035), Ξ (= 040), 048, 062, 064, 065, 066, 067, 068,
072, 078, 079, 086, 088, 093, 094, 096, 097, 098, 0103, 0104, 0116, 0120, 0130,
0132, 0133, 0134, 0135, 0158, 0159, 0161, 0168, 0196, 0197, 0208, 0209, 0225, 0229,
0233, 0240, 0245, 0246, 0247, 0248, 0249, and 0250. See below, pp. 261–2.

left between words or sentences (this kind of writing is called *scriptio continua*), and until about the eighth century punctuation was used only sporadically.[1] At times, of course, the meaning of a sentence would be ambiguous because the division into words was uncertain. In English, for example, GODISNOWHERE will be read with totally different meanings by an atheist and by a theist ('God is nowhere' and 'God is now here'). It must not be thought, however, that such ambiguities occur very often in Greek.[2] In that language it is the rule, with very few exceptions, that native Greek words can end only in a vowel (or a diphthong) or in one of three consonants, *ν*, *ρ*, and *s*. Furthermore, it should not be supposed that *scriptio continua* presented exceptional difficulties in reading, for apparently it was customary in antiquity to read aloud, even when one was alone.[3] Thus, despite the absence of spaces between words, by pronouncing to oneself what was read, syllable by syllable, one soon became used to reading *scriptio continua*.[4]

Christian scribes developed a system of contractions for

---

[1] Word-division, however, is occasionally found in school and liturgical texts, and scattered examples of punctuation, by point or spacing or a combination of both, are preserved in papyri from the third century B.C. onward.

[2] Examples in the New Testament include the following. In Mark x. 40 according to most editors Jesus says, '. . . but it is for those for whom it has been prepared' (ἀλλ' οἷς ἡτοίμασται). This can also be read ἄλλοις ἡτοίμασται, which means 'it has been prepared for others'. In Rom. vii. 14 οἴδαμεν may be divided οἶδα μέν. In I Tim. iii. 16 καὶ ὁμολογουμένως μέγα ἐστίν . . . may be taken as καὶ ὁμολογοῦμεν ὡς μέγα ἐστίν.

[3] Besides scattered evidence from classical antiquity (collected by Josef Balogh, 'Voces paginarum', *Philologus*, lxxxii [1927], pp. 84–109, 202–31; also published separately), the statement in Acts viii. 30 that Philip 'heard' the Ethiopian treasurer reading from Isaiah the prophet implies that he had been reading aloud to himself. Compare also the close of 2 Maccabees: 'Here I will end my story. If it is well told and to the point, that is what I myself desired; if it is poorly done and mediocre, that was the best I could do. For just as it is harmful to drink wine alone, or, again, to drink water alone, while wine mixed with water is sweet and delicious and enhances one's enjoyment, so also the style of the story delights the ears of those who read the work' (xv. 37–39). See also G. L. Hendrickson, 'Ancient Reading', *Classical Journal*, xxv (1929), pp. 182–96; H. J. Chaytor, 'The Medieval Reader and Textual Criticism', *Bulletin of the John Rylands Library*, xxvi (1941–2), pp. 49–56; and Eugene S. McCartney, 'Notes on Reading and Praying Audibly', *Classical Philology*, lxiii (1948), pp. 184–7. For a discussion of reading aloud κατὰ διαστολήν, see W. G. Rutherford, *A Chapter in the History of Annotation* (= *Scholia Aristophanica*, vol. iii, London, 1905), pp. 168 ff. See below, p. 262.

[4] The experience of Hermas, who says he copied a little scroll of heavenly origin 'letter by letter, for I could not make out the syllables' (*Vision*, II. i. 4), suggests that the normal method of copying books was by syllables.

certain 'sacred' words. These *nomina sacra*, as they are called today, include such frequently occurring nouns as θεός, κύριος, Ἰησοῦς, Χριστός, and υἱός (which were contracted by writing only the first and last letters); πνεῦμα, Δαυίδ, σταυρός, and μήτηρ (contracted by writing only the first two and the last letters); πατήρ, Ἰσραήλ, and σωτήρ (of which the first and the last two letters were written); and ἄνθρωπος, Ἰερουσαλήμ, and οὐρανός (of which the first and last syllables were written). In order to draw the reader's attention to the presence of a *nomen sacrum* the scribe would place a horizontal line above the contraction.[1]

In the earlier ages of the Church, Biblical manuscripts were produced by individual Christians who wished to provide for themselves or for local congregations copies of one or more books of the New Testament. Because the number of Christians increased rapidly during the first centuries, many additional copies of the Scriptures were sought by new converts and new churches. As a result, speed of production sometimes outran accuracy of execution. Furthermore, in preparing translations or versions for persons who knew no Greek, it occurred more than once (as Augustine complained) that 'anyone who happened to gain possession of a Greek manuscript and who imagined that he had some facility in both Latin and Greek, however slight that might be, dared to make a translation' (*De doctr. Chr.* II. xi. 16).

When, however, in the fourth century Christianity received official sanction from the State, it became more usual for commercial book manufacturers, or scriptoria, to produce copies of the books of the New Testament. Sitting in the workroom of a scriptorium, several trained scribes, Christian or non-Christian, each equipped with parchment, pens, and ink, would write a copy of the book being reproduced as the reader, or lector, slowly read aloud the text of the exemplar.[2] In this way as many

[1] The standard work of Ludwig Traube, *Nomina Sacra: Versuch einer Geschichte der christlichen Kürzung* (Munich, 1907), is now supplemented by the additional data collected by A. H. R. E. Paap, *Nomina Sacra in the Greek Papyri of the First Five Centuries A.D.: the Sources and Some Deductions* (Leiden, 1959). Traube had fewer than forty Greek papyri available; Paap cites evidence from 421 papyri of the first five centuries of the Christian era. According to C. H. Roberts, the origin of the distinctively Christian custom of contracting the *nomina sacra* lies in the first century (*The* [London] *Times Literary Supplement*, 10 Mar. 1961, p. 160).

[2] See especially T. C. Skeat, 'The Use of Dictation in Ancient Book-Production', *Proceedings of the British Academy*, xlii (1956), pp. 179–208.

copies could be produced simultaneously as scribes were working in the scriptorium. It is easy to understand how in such a method of reproduction errors of transcription would almost inevitably occur. Sometimes the scribe would be momentarily inattentive or, because of a cough or other noise, would not clearly hear the lector. Furthermore, when the lector read aloud a word which could be spelled in different ways (as in English, for example, the words 'great' and 'grate', or 'there' and 'their'), the scribe would have to determine which word belonged in that particular context—and sometimes he wrote down the wrong word. (For examples of such mistakes, see pp. 190–2 below.)

In order to ensure greater accuracy, books produced in scriptoria were commonly checked over by a corrector (διορθωτής) specially trained to rectify mistakes in copying. His annotations in the manuscript can usually be detected today from differences in styles of handwriting or tints of ink.

Scribes who were hired by a scriptorium to do a certain piece of work would be paid in accord with the number of lines which they wrote. The standard length of line was originally a line of poetry, either a Homeric hexameter or an iambic trimeter. When prose works were copied, a line called a stichos, having sixteen (or sometimes fifteen) syllables, was frequently used as a measure for determining the market price of a manuscript. A price-fixing edict issued in A.D. 301 by the Emperor Diocletian set the wages of scribes at the rate of 25 denarii for 100 lines in writing of the first quality, and of 20 denarii for the same number of lines in writing of the second quality (what the difference was between the two qualities of writing is not mentioned).[1] According to the computation of Rendel Harris, the cost of producing one complete Bible, such as codex Sinaiticus, would have come to about 30,000 denarii—a sizeable sum notwithstanding steadily rising inflation.[2]

The application of stichometric reckoning served also as a

[1] *De pretiis rerum venalium* ('Concerning the Prices of Things Sold'), vii. 39 f., published in *Corpus Inscriptionum Latinarum*, iii. 831; see E. R. Graser in Tenney Frank's *An Economic Survey of Ancient Rome*, vol. v (Baltimore, 1940), p. 342.

[2] See Rendel Harris, *New Testament Autographs*, being a Supplement to the *American Journal of Philology*, no. 12 (Baltimore, 1882), p. 23. It is difficult to estimate the exact equivalent in modern currency. Some measure of comparison may be had, however, when it is known that in the preceding century under Caracalla (211–17) a legionary was paid a *stipendium* of 750 denarii per year in addition to his maintenance.

rough and ready check on the general accuracy of a manuscript, for obviously a document which was short of the total number of stichoi was a defective copy. On the other hand, such calculations were far from being foolproof safeguards to the purity of the text, for only longer interpolations or omissions would be likely to be disclosed by counting stichoi. In manuscripts of the Gospels which supply stichometric information, the most frequently appearing statistics are the round numbers 2,600 for Matthew, 1,600 for Mark, 2,800 for Luke, and 2,300 for John. More precise figures, found in several manuscripts, are 2,560, 1,616, 2,750, and 2,024 respectively for the four Gospels, which imply, for example, the presence of xvi. 9–20 in Mark and the absence of vii. 53–viii. 11 in John.

Later, during the Byzantine period, copies of books were produced by monks. In monasteries there was much less pressure than in a commercial scriptorium to produce many copies at one time, and so, instead of writing at the dictation of a lector, individual monks, often working separately in their cells, would prepare copies of the Scriptures or other books either for themselves or for some benefactor to the monastery. Such a method of multiplying copies was not open to the same kinds of errors involved in the dictation method. But another set of circumstances operated to make absolute accuracy difficult to secure. The act of copying entails four fundamental operations: (1) the reading to oneself (in antiquity no doubt reading half-aloud) of a line or a clause of the text to be copied, (2) the retaining of this material in one's memory, (3) the dictating of this material to oneself (either silently or half-aloud), and (4) the movement of the hand in executing the copy. Though several of these steps are executed almost simultaneously, there was enough opportunity for the mind of a weary or half-awake scribe to play tricks that resulted in committing the most atrocious blunders (for examples, see pp. 193–5 below).

Besides various psychological causes of errors, physiological and external causes also conspired to make absolute accuracy extremely difficult to attain. One must bear in mind that the act of copying was in itself arduous and fatiguing, both because of the effort of sustained attention which it demanded as well as because of the cramped position of various muscles of the body. Though it seems strange to us today, in antiquity it was not customary to sit at a table or a desk while writing. Both literary[1] and artistic[2] evidence suggests that until the early Middle Ages it was customary for scribes either to stand (while making relatively brief notes), or to sit on a stool or bench (or even on the ground), holding their scroll or codex on their knees (see Plates I and VII).[3] It goes without saying that such a posture was more tiring than sitting at a desk or writing-table—though the latter must have been tiring enough to scribes thus occupied six hours a day[4] month after month.

Something of the drudgery of copying manuscripts can be learned from the colophons, or notes, which scribes not infrequently placed at the close of their books. A typical colophon found in many non-Biblical manuscripts reveals in no uncertain terms what every scribe experienced: 'He who does not know how to write supposes it to be no labour; but though only three fingers write, the whole body labours.' A traditional formula appearing at the close of many manuscripts describes the physiological effects of prolonged labour at copying: 'Writing bows

[1] An interesting piece of literary evidence is found in a colophon, dating from about the third century A.D., attached to a papyrus scroll containing portions of the third and fourth books of the *Iliad* (edited by H. J. M. Milne, *Catalogue of the Literary Papyri in the British Museum* [London, 1927], pp. 21–22). According to the reading proposed by Wifstrand, the first two lines of the colophon are as follows: Ἐγὼ κορωνίς εἰμι γραμμάτων φύλαξ· κάλαμός μ' ἔγραψε δεξιὰ χεὶρ καὶ γόνυ, i.e. because the scribe held the sheet of papyrus on his lap while he wrote, it could be said that the knee as well as the stylus and the right hand co-operated in producing what was written; cf. Albert Wifstrand, 'Ein metrischer Kolophon in einem Homeruspapyrus', *Hermes*, lxviii (1933), pp. 468–72.

[2] For a variety of artistic evidence bearing on the posture of scribes while writing, see the plates in A. M. Friend, Jr., 'The Portraits of the Evangelists in Greek and Latin Manuscripts', *Art Studies*, v (1927), pp. 115–47, and vii (1929), pp. 3–29; W. H. P. Hatch, *Greek and Syrian Miniatures in Jerusalem* (Cambridge, Massachusetts, 1931); and B. M. Metzger, 'When Did Scribes Begin to Use Writing Desks?', in *Akten des XI. internationalen Byzantinisten-Kongresses, 1958* (Munich, 1960), pp. 355–62. For a discussion of a miniature in the Rossano Gospels depicting the Trial of Jesus (see Plate VII), which suggests that it was customary for stenographers in a law court to stand while writing, even though a table was available, see William C. Loerke, 'The Miniatures of the Trial in the Rossano Gospels', *Art Bulletin*, xliii (1961), pp. 171–95. See below, p. 262.

[3] The so-called writing-tables found at Qumran, which have been built up by the archaeologists to the height of tables today, were originally but 20 inches high, too low to serve as writing-desks; see the present writer's discussion, 'The Furniture of the Scriptorium at Qumran', *Revue de Qumrân*, i (1958–9), pp. 509–15.

[4] See the anonymous complaint, dating perhaps from the ninth century, quoted by Falconer Madan in his *Books in Manuscript* (London, 1893), p. 37: 'Ardua scriptorum prae cunctis artibus ars est: | Difficilis labor est, durus quoque flectere colla, | Et membranas *bis ternas* sulcare per horas.'

one's back, thrusts the ribs into one's stomach, and fosters a
general debility of the body.' In an Armenian manuscript of the
Gospels a colophon complains that a heavy snowstorm was
raging outside and that the scribe's ink froze, his hand became
numb, and the pen fell from his fingers! It is not surprising that
a frequently recurring colophon in manuscripts of many kinds
is the following comparison: 'As travellers rejoice to see their
home country, so also is the end of a book to those who toil [in
writing].' Other manuscripts close with an expression of gratitude: 'The end of the book; thanks be to God!'

Upon more mature reflection, however, many scribes doubtless judged the rewards of copying the Scriptures to outweigh
the discomforts they experienced during the long hours of writing. Thus Cassiodorus, that remarkable rhetorician-philosopher
and Prime Minister to the Ostrogothic princes of Italy, who later
became a monk and founded the monastery of Vivarium, noted for
its school of Latin palaeography, dilates upon the spiritual
compensations gained by the faithful scribe:

> By reading the divine Scriptures [the scribe] wholesomely instructs
> his own mind, and by copying the precepts of the Lord he spreads
> them far and wide. What happy application, what praiseworthy
> industry, to preach unto men by means of the hand, to untie the
> tongue by means of the fingers, to bring quiet salvation to mortals,
> and to fight the Devil's insidious wiles with pen and ink! For every
> word of the Lord written by the scribe is a wound inflicted on Satan.
> And so, though seated in one spot, the scribe traverses diverse lands
> through the dissemination of what he has written. . . . Man multi-
> plies the heavenly words, and in a certain metaphorical sense, if I
> may dare so to speak, three fingers are made to express the utterances
> of the Holy Trinity. O sight glorious to those who contemplate it
> carefully! The fast-travelling reed-pen writes down the holy words
> and thus avenges the malice of the Wicked One, who caused a reed
> to be used to smite the head of the Lord during his Passion.[1]

In view of the difficulties involved in transcribing ancient
books, it is the more remarkable how high was the degree of
achievement of most scribes. The fact is that in most manuscripts
the size of the letters and the ductus of the script remain sur-
prisingly uniform throughout even a lengthy document.

[1] *Cassiodori Senatoris Institutiones*, edited from the manuscripts by R. A. B. Mynors
(Oxford, 1937), I. xxx. 1.

In order to secure a high degree of efficiency and accuracy, certain rules pertaining to the work of scribes were developed and enforced in monastic scriptoria. The following are examples of such regulations prepared for the renowned monastery of the Studium at Constantinople. About A.D. 800 the abbot of this monastery, Theodore the Studite, who was himself highly skilled in writing an elegant Greek hand, included in his rules for the monastery severe punishments for monks who were not careful in copying manuscripts.[1] A diet of bread and water was the penalty set for the scribe who became so much interested in the subject-matter of what he was copying that he neglected his task of copying. Monks had to keep their parchment leaves neat and clean, on penalty of 130 penances. If anyone should take without permission another's quaternion (that is, the ruled and folded sheets of parchment), fifty penances were prescribed. If anyone should make more glue than he could use at one time, and it should harden, he must do fifty penances. If a scribe broke his pen in a fit of temper (perhaps after having made some accidental blunder near the close of an otherwise perfectly copied sheet), he had to do thirty penances.

Added note on colophons

Besides the several colophons quoted above, which directly or indirectly witness to the difficulties involved in transcribing a book, there are many other kinds of colophons. Some provide the name of the scribe, and occasionally the place and date of writing. Obviously such information is of the greatest value to the palaeographer in tracing the background and family relationships of manuscripts.[2]

Some colophons are in the form of a blessing or prayer, or an invitation to the reader to offer such a prayer; e.g. 'Whoever says, 'God bless the soul of the scribe'', God will bless his soul.' The following prayer is found at the close of a Psalter copied in the year 862:

---

[1] The text of these rules is in Migne, *Patrologia Graeca*, xcix. 1739 f. For a modern biography of Theodore, see Alice Gardner's *Theodore of Studium, his Life and Times* (London, 1905).

[2] For a list of the names of Greek scribes, see Marie Vogel and Viktor Gardthausen, *Die griechischen Schreiber des Mittelalters und der Renaissance* (Leipzig, 1909).

ἔλεος τῷ γράψαντι, κύριε,
σοφία τοῖς ἀναγινώσκουσι,
χάρις τοῖς ἀκούουσι,
σωτηρία τοῖς κεκτημένοις· ἀμήν.

(Mercy be to him who wrote, O Lord, wisdom to those who read, grace to those who hear, salvation to those who own [this codex]. Amen.)

An extended prayer at the end of a Coptic–Arabic manuscript of the Gospels contains the following:

... O reader, in spiritual love forgive me, and pardon the daring of him who wrote, and turn his errors into some mystic good. ... There is no scribe who will not pass away, but what his hands have written will remain for ever. Write nothing with thy hand but that which thou wilt be pleased to see at the resurrection. ... May the Lord God Jesus Christ cause this holy copy to avail for the saving of the soul of the wretched man who wrote it.[1]

In some manuscripts one finds curse colophons, which were intended to serve as the equivalent of modern theft insurance. For example, in a twelfth- or thirteenth-century Greek lectionary of the Gospels, now in the library of Princeton Theological Seminary (see Fig. 2), there is a colophon stating that the volume was donated to the church of St. Saba at Alexandria; the colophon continues: 'No one therefore has authority from God to take it away under any condition, and whoever transgresses this will be under the wrath of the eternal Word of God, whose power is great. Gregory, Patriarch by the grace of God, wrote this.'[2]

Less formal are the conversational jottings which occasionally stand at the close of a manuscript or in the margins of folios throughout a document. Though scribes were forbidden to talk to one another in the scriptorium, the more irrepressible found devious ways to communicate with each other. One such means was to jot remarks on the margin of the page being transcribed and to show it to one's neighbour. The margins of a ninth-century Latin manuscript of Cassiodorus' commentary on the Psalms

[1] [George Horner,] *The Coptic Version of the New Testament in the Northern Dialect, otherwise called Memphitic and Bohairic*, i (Oxford, 1898), pp. cxlvi f.

[2] For other curse colophons, see Lawrence S. Thomson's interesting article, 'A Cursory Survey of Maledictions', *Bulletin of the New York Public Library*, lvi (1952), pp. 55–74.

contain a variety of commonplace remarks written in Irish.
For example: 'It is cold today.' 'That is natural; it is winter.'
'The lamp gives a bad light.' 'It is time for us to begin to do
some work.' 'Well, this vellum is certainly heavy!' 'Well, I call
this vellum thin!' 'I feel quite dull today; I don't know what's
wrong with me.'[1]

How did it happen that the head of the scriptorium allowed
his monks to disfigure a manuscript with such trivialities? One
may perhaps conjecture that the manuscript was written in a
continental monastery where the authorities knew no Irish and
therefore the scribes from Ireland felt they could play pranks
with impunity. When asked what he had written the scribe
might point to some pious sentences in Latin in the top margins
of preceding pages and say, 'Merely the Irish equivalents of
sentences like these!'[2]

In order to ensure accuracy in transcription, authors would
sometimes add at the close of their literary works an adjuration
directed to future copyists. So, for example, Irenaeus attached to
the close of his treatise *On the Ogdoad* the following note:

> I adjure you who shall copy out this book, by our Lord Jesus
> Christ and by his glorious advent when he comes to judge the living
> and the dead, that you compare what you transcribe, and correct it
> carefully against this manuscript from which you copy; and also that
> you transcribe this adjuration and insert it in the copy.[3]

IV. 'HELPS FOR READERS' IN NEW TESTAMENT MANUSCRIPTS

Many manuscripts of the New Testament are provided with
a variety of what may be called 'helps for readers', that is, aids to
assist in the private as well as public reading of the Scriptures.
This material originated in various places and at various times.

---

[1] The Irish text, with a German translation, is given by Kuno Meyer in his
article, 'Neu aufgefundene altirische Glossen', *Zeitschrift für celtische Philologie*, viii
(1912), pp. 173–7. For many other colophons and notes in Greek and Latin manuscripts, see W. Wattenbach, *Das Schriftwesen im Mittelalter*, 3te Aufl. (Leipzig, 1896),
pp. 491–534, and Viktor Gardthausen, *Griechische Palaeographie*, 2te Aufl., ii (Leipzig, 1913), pp. 424 ff.

[2] For other instances of conversation written in the margins of manuscripts, see
W. M. Lindsay, *Early Irish Minuscule Script* (Oxford, 1910), p. 42.

[3] *Apud* Eusebius, *Hist. Eccl.* v. xx. 2. Compare the warning given in Rev. xxii. 18,
and see W. C. van Unnik, 'De la règle Μήτε προσθεῖναι μήτε ἀφελεῖν dans l'histoire
du canon', *Vigiliae Christianae*, iii (1949), pp. 1–36.

It was handed on from generation to generation, and, as would be expected, it grew in volume with the passage of time. The following is an enumeration of some of these aids found in Greek manuscripts.[1]

I. CHAPTER DIVISIONS (κεφάλαια)

The oldest system of capitulation which is known to us is that preserved in the margins of codex Vaticanus (B) of the fourth century. In this manuscript there are 170 sections in Matthew, 62 in Mark, 152 in Luke, and 50 in John. Another system of chapter divisions is found in codex Alexandrinus (A) of the fifth century as well as in most other Greek manuscripts. According to this capitulation in Matthew there are 68 κεφάλαια, in Mark 48, in Luke 83, and in John 18. It is to be noted that in no case does the first chapter stand at the beginning of a book, probably because of the custom of scribes to refer to the opening section of a book as the προοίμιον or preface. Thus κεφ. α' of Mark begins at Mark i. 23.

For the Book of Acts several systems of chapter divisions are current in the manuscripts. Codex Vaticanus has two sets of capitulation, one of thirty-six chapters and the other of sixty-nine chapters. According to the opinion of Hatch, the chapter numbers of the former system were inserted in the margin of the manuscript by a very early hand—perhaps by the διορθωτής or possibly by the scribe himself—and the other system of chapter numbers was added somewhat later by another scribe.[2] In codex Sinaiticus of the fourth century the system of sixty-nine chapters was added by someone to the first part of Acts (chaps. i–xv), but for some unknown reason it was not continued to the end of the book.

Most other Greek manuscripts of Acts have a system of forty κεφάλαια. In some manuscripts the division of Acts into sections was carried still further, twenty-four of the forty chapters being subdivided into smaller sections (ὑποδιαιρέσεις). There were forty-eight such smaller subdivisions, making a total of eighty-

---

[1] For a discussion of the accessories in Latin manuscripts of the Bible, see [Donatien De Bruyne,] *Sommaires, divisions et rubriques de la Bible latine* (Namur, 1914), *Préfaces de la Bible latine* (Namur, 1920), and Patrick McGurk, *Latin Gospel Books from A.D. 400 to A.D. 800* (Paris and Brussels, 1961).

[2] W. H. P. Hatch, 'Euthalius', *The Twentieth Century Encyclopedia of Religious Knowledge*, i (Grand Rapids, 1955), p. 400.

eight κεφάλαια and ὑποδιαιρέσεις. It was inevitable that the distinction between the larger and smaller sections would be confused, and in some manuscripts they are numbered consecutively throughout the book.

Both the Pauline and the Catholic Epistles were also divided into chapters, and many of these were subdivided into smaller sections.[1] Codex Vaticanus has two sets of chapter divisions for the Epistles, an earlier and a later system. In the Pauline Epistles the earlier division enumerates the chapters consecutively throughout the whole corpus (for the clue which this provides regarding an ancestor of Vaticanus, see p. 48 below).

The Book of Revelation was supplied with a highly artificial system of divisions. At the latter part of the sixth century Archbishop Andrew of Caesarea in Cappadocia wrote a commentary on the book which gives a 'spiritual' exegesis. Instead of asking what material was in the book, and into how many parts it could most appropriately be divided, he divided the book into twenty-four λόγοι, or discourses, because of the twenty-four elders sitting on thrones about the throne of God (Rev. iv. 4). He further reflected that the nature of each of the twenty-four elders was tripartite (σῶμα, ψυχή, and πνεῦμα), and therefore divided each λόγος into three κεφάλαια, making a total of seventy-two chapters for the entire book.

2. TITLES OF CHAPTERS (τίτλοι)

Each of the κεφάλαια of the system found in codex Alexandrinus and in most other later manuscripts is provided with a τίτλος. This is a summary-heading placed in the margin and describing the contents of the chapter (see Plate VIII). These titles customarily begin with the word 'about' or 'concerning', and are not infrequently written with red ink. Thus κεφ. α' of John, which begins at ii. 1, has the title, 'Concerning the marriage at Cana' (περὶ τοῦ ἐν Κανὰ γάμου).[2] All of the τίτλοι for one book are frequently drawn up in a list and placed before that book as a summary-outline of what follows.

---

[1] For information regarding the number of each of these divisions in each of the Epistles, see W. H. P. Hatch, *Facsimiles and Descriptions of Minuscule Manuscripts of the New Testament* (Cambridge, Massachusetts, 1951), p. 25. See below, p. 262.

[2] For a complete list of τίτλοι, see H. von Soden, *Die Schriften des Neuen Testaments in ihrer ältesten erreichbaren Textgestalt*, I. i (Berlin, 1902), pp. 405 ff.

3. EUSEBIAN CANONS

An ingenious system was devised by Eusebius of Caesarea to aid one in locating parallel passages in the Gospels. Apparently his system was found to be highly useful, for it appears in a great number of manuscripts of the Gospels in Greek, as well as in Latin, Syriac, Coptic, Gothic, Armenian, and other versions.

The synopsis or harmony was prepared as follows. Each Gospel was divided into longer or shorter sections, depending upon the relation of each section to one or more parallels in the other Gospels. These sections were numbered consecutively throughout each Gospel (there are 355 in Matthew, 233 in Mark, 342 in Luke, and 232 in John). Then Eusebius prepared ten tables or canons ($\kappa\alpha\nu\acute{o}\nu\epsilon s$), the first containing references by numerals to parallel passages found in all four Gospels; the second to passages common to Matthew, Mark, and Luke; the third to passages common to Matthew, Luke, and John; and so on, until almost all possible combinations of Gospels were exhausted.[1] The final table gives references to matter peculiar to each Gospel alone. These tables of numerals, written out in columns, customarily occupy the opening pages of Gospel manuscripts.[2] Then, in the margin of the Gospel text of the manuscript, alongside or beneath the numeral of the consecutive sections, was written the numeral of the canon table in which that section could be found. For example, if while reading the Gospel according to John one came upon the statement, 'For Jesus himself testified that a prophet has no honour in his own country' (iv. 44), and wished to consult the parallels, he would see in the margin the numerals $\frac{\overline{\lambda\epsilon}}{\alpha}$ ($=\frac{35}{1}$). By turning to the first canon table and running his eye down the column of numerals referring to sections in John, he would find 35. In the horizontal line opposite this numeral he would then find the numeral 142 standing in the column of sections of Matthew, 51 in Mark, and 21 in Luke. Since, as was said above, the sections

[1] There is no table of references to sections in Mark, Luke, and John; nor of references to sections in Mark and John.

[2] The bare lists of numerals soon attracted the attention of artists, who ornamented the spaces between with decorative columns, arches, architraves, birds, flowers, &c.; see Plate XII*b*, and Carl Nordenfalk, *Die spätantiken Kanontafeln : Kunstgeschichtliche Studien über die Eusebianische Evangelien-Konkordanz in den vier ersten Jahrhunderten ihrer Geschichte*, 2 vols. (Göteborg, 1938). See below, p. 262.

in each Gospel are numbered consecutively, it is an easy matter to find in the other three Gospels each of the sections that contain the parallels to the statement in John.

For the added convenience of the user, in some manuscripts the numerals referring to the sections which are parallel to the passage on any given page are provided in the lower margin of the page (see Plates VIII and XII*b*), so that one can turn at once to the appropriate sections in the other Gospels.

Eusebius explained his ingenious system in a letter to a fellow Christian named Carpianus, and a copy of this letter appears with the canon tables on the opening folios of many Gospel manuscripts.[1] Several twentieth-century editions of the Greek Testament are provided with the Eusebian canon tables and numbers, which thus continue to be of service to present-day readers of the Gospels.

4. HYPOTHESES, BIOI, EUTHALIAN APPARATUS

The hypothesis (ὑπόθεσις, Latin *argumentum*) is a prologue or brief introduction to a book, supplying the reader with a certain amount of information concerning the author, content, and circumstances of composition of the particular book. The form and content of such hypotheses are often conventional and stereotyped. In some manuscripts the hypotheses for the Gospels are ascribed to Eusebius, but more often they are anonymous. Anti-Marcionite Gospel prologues are extant in Latin manuscripts from the fifth to the tenth century. The Marcionite prologues to the (ten) Pauline Epistles were taken over practically unaltered by the Roman Catholic Church for the Latin Vulgate.[2]

A longer statement of traditional information concerning the life of each evangelist (called his βίος) sometimes appears with the hypothesis. The lives are attributed to an otherwise unknown Dorotheus of Tyre or to Sophronius, the Patriarch of Jerusalem in the first half of the seventh century.

Several different prologues which define the word 'gospel' and provide general information about all four Gospels

[1] An English translation of Eusebius' letter was published by Harold H. Oliver in *Novum Testamentum*, iii (1959), pp. 138–45. See below, p. 262.

[2] For a survey of recent investigations concerning the Marcionite prologues, see B. M. Metzger in *The Text, Canon, and Principal Versions of the Bible*, ed. by E. E. Flack and B. M. Metzger (Grand Rapids, 1956), pp. 24 ff.

collectively occur in various manuscripts. Besides lists of the twelve apostles, the traditional names of the seventy[-two] disciples in Luke x. 1 ff. are given on the authority of Dorotheus and Epiphanius.

For the Book of Acts several different hypotheses are current; some are anonymous and others are taken from Chrysostom's commentary and homilies on Acts. For Acts and the Epistles a considerable apparatus of auxiliary materials circulated under the name of Euthalius or Evagrius.[1] Besides chapter divisions and hypotheses, these included a lengthy sketch of the life, writings, and chronology of the apostle Paul; a brief statement of the martyrdom of Paul; a table of Old Testament quotations in the Epistles; a list of places at which the Epistles were thought to be written; and a list of the names associated with Paul's in the headings to the Epistles. How much of this supplementary material was drawn up by Euthalius and how much was added later is not known.

5. SUPERSCRIPTIONS AND SUBSCRIPTIONS

In the oldest manuscripts of the New Testament the titles of the several books are short and simple, e.g. *KATA MAΘΘAION* or *ΠΡΟС ΡΩΜΑΙΟΥС*. But in later centuries these titles became longer and more complex (see p. 205 below).

The subscriptions appended to the end of the books were originally (like the titles) brief and simple, merely indicating the close of the book. As time passed these became more elaborate, and often included traditional information regarding the place at which the book was thought to be written and sometimes the name of the amanuensis. The King James version includes the subscriptions to the Pauline Epistles.

6. PUNCTUATION

As was mentioned above, the earliest manuscripts have very little punctuation. The Bodmer papyri and the Chester Beatty

---

[1] Scholarly opinion as to who this Euthalius or Evagrius was and when he lived has vacillated widely; see, for example, J. A. Robinson, *Euthaliana* (Cambridge, 1895); E. von Dobschütz, 'Euthaliusstudien', *Zeitschrift für Kirchengeschichte*, xxix (1899), pp. 107–54; H. von Soden, op. cit., i. i (1902), pp. 637–82; C. H. Turner in Hastings's *Dictionary of the Bible*, extra vol. (1904), pp. 524–9; G. Bardy in *Supplément au Dictionnaire de la Bible*, ii (1934), cols. 1215–18; G. Zuntz, 'Euthalius = Euzoius?', *Vigiliae Christianae*, vii (1953), pp. 16–22; and W. H. P. Hatch (in footnote 2 on p. 22 above).

papyri (see pp. 36–42 below) have only an occasional mark of punctuation,[1] as do also the early uncial manuscripts. A diaeresis is sometimes placed over an initial iota or upsilon. During the sixth and seventh centuries scribes began to use punctuation marks more liberally, though the sign of interrogation is rarely found before the ninth century. Gradually the earlier sporadic and somewhat haphazard usage gave way to a fuller and more or less consistent style. In addition to the usual marks of punctuation a syllable divider was often inserted after non-Greek proper names, as in such sequences as that in Matt. i. 2, *ABPAAM˙EΓENNHCEN*, where it stands to warn the reader against dividing it *a-braa-me-gen-nē-sen*.

7. GLOSSES, SCHOLIA, COMMENTARIES, CATENAE, ONOMASTICA

Glosses are brief explanations of difficult words or phrases. They were usually written in the margin of manuscripts, though occasionally they were placed between the lines. In the latter case a Greek manuscript might be 'glossed' throughout with a Latin interlinear, and a Latin manuscript with an Anglo-Saxon interlinear.

Scholia are interpretative remarks of a teacher placed beside the text in order to instruct the reader. When scholia are systematically developed in order to elucidate continuously the entire text, rather than being merely random notes on certain passages, the work is called a commentary. Scholia and commentaries are sometimes placed in the margins around the Scripture text and sometimes interspersed between sections of the Scripture text (see Plate IX). In uncial manuscripts the explanatory materials are usually in minuscule script, though in codex Zacynthius (*Ξ*) of the seventh or eighth century the commentary is written in uncials. When the text is in minuscules, occasionally the scholia are in small uncials.

Catenae are literally 'chains' of comments extracted from older ecclesiastical writers. The identity of the original commentator is indicated by prefixing the abbreviation of his name, though through carelessness this mark of identification is sometimes missing.

---

[1] For a list of papyri which have marks of punctuation, see Guilelmus Flock, *De graecorum interpunctionibus* (Diss. Bonn, 1908), pp. 14 ff.

Onomastica are philological aids which purport to give the meaning and etymology of proper names. Like so much of ancient etymological lore—preserved, for example, throughout the works of Philo and in Plato's *Cratylus*—these explanations almost always are arbitrary and fanciful.

8. ARTISTIC ADORNMENT

In addition to an ornamental headpiece at the beginning of a book and illuminated initials, the Greeks of the Byzantine period sought to assist the reader in understanding the significance of the Scriptures by providing pictures of various kinds.[1] Some are portraits of Christ and of his apostles, and others depict scenes or events that are narrated in the New Testament (see Plate VII). The portraits of the Evangelists fall into two main classes, those in which the figures are standing and those in which they are sitting. From a comparison with Hellenistic representations of ancient Greek poets and philosophers it appears that Christian artists, who had no knowledge of the likenesses of the Evangelists, adopted and adapted familiar portraits of pagan authors in contemporary art. According to the investigations of A. M. Friend, Jr.,[2] all the early Christian portraits of the Evangelists go back to two main sets of four portraits each: one set was of four philosophers, Plato, Aristotle, Zeno, and Epicurus, and the other set was of four playwrights, Euripides, Sophocles, Aristophanes, and Menander.

The earliest New Testament manuscripts which contain miniatures are two de luxe copies on purple vellum of the sixth century, namely codex Sinopensis (O) and codex Rossanensis (Σ; see pp. 55 and 59 below). In the course of time custom and tradition came to dictate the proper form and colours which artists should use in painting the several cycles of Biblical scenes and characters. These traditional directives are given in the Byzantine Painters' Manual compiled by Dionysius, a monk

[1] For reproductions of representative miniatures, see W. H. P. Hatch, *Greek and Syrian Miniatures in Jerusalem* (Cambridge, Massachusetts, 1931); E. J. Goodspeed, D. W. Riddle, and H. R. Willoughby, *The Rockefeller McCormick New Testament* (Chicago, 1932); E. C. Colwell and H. R. Willoughby, *The Four Gospels of Karahissar* (Chicago, 1936); and H. R. Willoughby and E. C. Colwell, *The Elizabeth Day McCormick Apocalypse* (Chicago, 1940). For a general introduction, see David Diringer, *The Illuminated Book, its History and Production* (New York, 1958).

[2] 'The Portraits of the Evangelists in Greek and Latin Manuscripts', *Art Studies*, v (1927), pp. 115–46, and vii (1929), pp. 3–29.

of Fourna d'Agrapha.[1] Unfortunately, New Testament scholars
have not yet availed themselves of the evidence supplied by
artistic adornment in the investigation of family relationships of
Byzantine manuscripts.[2]

9. COLA AND COMMATA

The helps mentioned above were designed chiefly to assist
private readers of Scripture; the following helps were intended
to provide aid for the public reading of Scripture lessons in
services of worship.

The practice of writing treatises in short lines according to
the sense antedated its application to Christian writings. Some
of the orations of Demosthenes and Cicero were transcribed in
this manner to assist the reader in making the correct inflection
and the proper pauses. It was also applied to the Septuagint
Greek text of the poetical books of the Old Testament,[3] and
when Jerome translated the Prophets into Latin he arranged
the text colometrically.[4] Each sense-line consisted of a single
clause (κῶλον) or a single phrase (κόμμα).[5]

Several bilingual Greek and Latin manuscripts of the Gospels,
Acts, and Epistles have the text colometrically arranged; these

---

[1] Edited by Athanasios Papadopoulos-Kérameus, *Manuel d'iconographie chrétienne* ... (St.-Pétersbourg, 1909).

[2] For suggestions regarding the relationship between picture criticism and
textual criticism, see Kurt Weitzmann, *Illustrations in Roll and Codex, a Study of the
Origin and Method of Text Illustration* (Princeton, 1947), pp. 182–92.

[3] One of the earliest examples of a portion of the Septuagint arranged in cola is
the second- (or third-)century Bodleian fragment of the Psalms edited by J. W. B.
Barns and G. D. Kilpatrick (*Proceedings of the British Academy*, xliii [1957],
pp. 229–32).

[4] Jerome, *Preface to Isaiah* (Migne, *Patrologia Latina*, xxviii. 825).

[5] In antiquity rhetoricians defined a comma as any combination of words that
makes a total of not more than eight syllables, while they required from a colon a
combination of at least nine, though not exceeding sixteen; see James A. Kleist,
S.J., 'Colometry and the New Testament', *Classical Bulletin*, iv (1928), pp. 26 f.
Kleist remarks that 'these figures will not seem arbitrary if we bear in mind that the
average length of a hexameter is sixteen syllables, and that the average speaker does
not easily go beyond sixteen syllables without renewing his breath.... In writing
colometrically, the one great purpose agreed upon by all ancient rhetoricians is to
enable the reader to read intelligently, and properly to husband his breath in
speaking. The all-essential thing is that both colon and comma, when taken by
themselves, make sense and admit of proper breathing. But essential as this requirement is, it is also a source of arbitrariness of interpretation. How much, after all, or
how little is required to make sense? How much can be uttered in one breath?
Here, as elsewhere, *quot capita, tot sententiae*, and *unusquisque in suo sensu abundat.*'
See Plate VI*a* for an example of unusually short lines.

include codex Bezae (D; see Plate V), codex Claromontanus (D[p]), and codex Coislinianus or Euthalianus (H[p]), all dating from about the sixth century. According to the recent investigations of N. A. Dahl, the original edition from which these copies were derived 'must have been a product of ancient book-publishing of high standards, in some way connected with the traditions of the library at Caesarea'.[1]

10. NEUMES

Neumes are Byzantine musical notes which assisted the lector in chanting or cantillating the Scripture lesson. They appear first in codices of the seventh or eighth century, but whether they were contemporary with the text of the manuscript or were added later it is difficult to determine. Their form is that of hooks, dots, and oblique strokes (see Plate XI), and they are usually written with red (or green) ink above the words to be sung.[2]

11. LECTIONARY EQUIPMENT

Following the custom of the synagogue, according to which portions of the Law and the Prophets were read at divine service each Sabbath day, the Christian Church adopted the practice of reading passages from the New Testament books at services of worship. A regular system of lessons from the Gospels and Epistles was developed, and the custom arose of arranging these according to a fixed order of Sundays and other holy days of the Christian year. In order to assist the lector in finding the beginning (ἀρχή) and the end (τέλος) of the lesson, several of the later uncial manuscripts were provided with the abbreviations ἀρχ and τέλ, inserted either in the margin or between the lines of the text (see Plate VIII). Lection notes, indicating that a given passage is to be read on a certain day, were sometimes written

[1] Quoted from a summary of a paper entitled 'Bilingual Editions of the Pauline Letters', read by Nils A. Dahl at the annual meeting of the Society of Biblical Literature and Exegesis held at St. Louis in 1961.

[2] See especially H. J. W. Tillyard, *Handbook of the Middle Byzantine Musical Notation* (*Monumenta Musicae Byzantinae*, Subsidia, I. i; Copenhagen, 1935); Carsten Höeg, *La Notation ekphonétique* (*Monumenta Musicae Byzantinae*, Subsidia, I. ii; Copenhagen, 1935; and E. G. Wellesz, *A History of Byzantine Music and Hymnography*, 2nd ed. (Oxford, 1961). See below, p. 262.

in the margin with red ink. A list of all these passages is occasionally given at the close (or at the beginning) of a codex.

For the added convenience of the reader, lectionary manuscripts were prepared which present in proper sequence (beginning with Easter) the text of the several passages of Scripture appointed to be read on Sundays, Saturdays, and, in some cases, on week-days throughout the year. Such lectionaries are called synaxaria (see Plate X). Another service book is the menologion, which supplies Scripture lessons for feast days, saints' days, and the like, starting with the first of September, the beginning of the civil year. It is noteworthy that substantially the same choice of Scripture passages in lectionary manuscripts dating from the seventh or eighth century is still followed by the Greek Orthodox Church today.

Scholars have only recently begun to appreciate the importance of lectionary manuscripts in tracing the history of the text of the New Testament during the Byzantine period.[1] Inasmuch as the form of the citation of the Scriptures in official liturgical books always tends to be conservative and almost archaic,[2] lectionaries are valuable in preserving a type of text that is frequently much older than the actual age of the manuscript might lead one to suspect.

V. STATISTICS OF GREEK MANUSCRIPTS OF THE NEW TESTAMENT[3]

It is customary to classify the Greek manuscripts of the New Testament into several categories, partly according to the material from which they are made, partly according to their script, and partly according to the use for which they were intended.

[1] For an introduction to the study of New Testament Greek lectionaries, see Ernest C. Colwell and Donald W. Riddle, *Prolegomena to the Study of the Lectionary Text of the Gospels* (Chicago, 1933). See below, p. 262.

[2] Thus, for example, in the Anglican Book of Common Prayer the Psalter and the Canticles from Luke are still in the translation of the Great Bible of 1539, despite repeated proposals to make them conform to the King James version of 1611.

[3] Prof. Kurt Aland of Münster, who currently assigns official numbers to newly discovered Greek manuscripts of the New Testament, graciously supplied the present writer (in a letter dated 11 July 1962) with information regarding the total number of New Testament papyri, uncials, minuscules, and lectionaries. For further information reference may be made to Aland's recent volume, *Kurzgefaßte Liste der griechischen Handschriften des Neuen Testaments: 1. Gesamtübersicht* (Berlin, 1963).

At first editors of the New Testament used cumbersome titles to designate the Greek manuscripts. These titles were usually derived from the names of the owners or the libraries possessing the manuscripts. Since no one system was agreed upon by all editors, and since manuscripts would change owners and locations, it was exceedingly confusing to compare the evidence in one critical apparatus with that in another. The first step in the direction of standardization of nomenclature was taken by a Swiss scholar, Johann Jakob Wettstein, who, in his handsome two-volume edition of the Greek Testament published at Amsterdam in 1751–2, employed capital letters to designate uncial manuscripts and Arabic numerals to designate minuscule manuscripts. The system now in general use was elaborated at the end of the nineteenth century by Caspar René Gregory, a native Philadelphian who, after receiving his theological training at Princeton, went to Germany where he became Professor of New Testament at the University of Leipzig in 1889. Building upon Wettstein's system, Gregory devised several other categories of the materials. Thus the manuscripts made of papyrus are listed separately from those made of parchment. Each of them is commonly referred to by the Gothic or Old English letter 𝔭 followed by a small superior numeral. At the time of this writing (1967), a total of eighty-one Greek papyri of the New Testament have been assigned official numbers by Gregory and his successors.

Following Wettstein's system, the uncial manuscripts which have been known for the longest time are commonly designated in a critical apparatus by capital letters of the Latin and Greek alphabets, and by one Hebrew letter (א, aleph). Since, however, the number of known uncial manuscripts came to exceed the number of letters in the Latin, Greek, and Hebrew alphabets combined, Gregory assigned to each uncial manuscript an Arabic numeral preceded by a zero. Thus far 266 uncial manuscripts have been catalogued. The minuscule manuscripts, which, as was mentioned above, are referred to by Arabic numbers, now total 2,754. (See below, p. 262.)

A subsidiary class of Greek manuscripts, involving both uncial and minuscule manuscripts (though the latter by far predominate in number), is devoted to lectionaries. As was mentioned earlier, these are church reading books containing the text of selections of the Scriptures appointed to be read on the several days of the ecclesiastical and the civil year, comprising, respectively, the synaxarion and the menologion. Although 2,135 lectionaries of the Greek New Testament have been catalogued, only comparatively few have been critically studied.[1] In the Gregory system of designating manuscripts, lectionaries are indicated by the letter '*l*' followed by an Arabic numeral. Thus '*l*' alone designates a Gospel lectionary; '*l*ᵃ' designates a lectionary of the Acts and the Epistles; and '*l*⁺ᵃ' designates a lectionary containing lessons from Gospels, Acts, and Epistles. (The Greek lectionary contains no lessons from the Book of Revelation.)

Two other forms of New Testament witnesses may be described with only a few words. Short portions of six New Testament books have been preserved on ostraca, or broken pieces of pottery used by the poorest people as writing material. Twenty-five of these have been catalogued, and are sometimes referred to by the Gothic or Old English letter 𝔒 followed by a superior numeral. Finally, a curious but unimportant source of our knowledge of the Greek text of the New Testament consists of a number of talismans, or good-luck charms. These amulets range in date from the fourth to the twelfth or thirteenth century and are made of vellum, papyrus, potsherd, and wood. The superstitious use of talismans, so prevalent in the ancient world, was scarcely less popular among the faithful than among the pagans—if we may judge from repeated remonstrances against them issued by ecclesiastical authorities.[2] Four of those catalogued contain the Lord's Prayer and five others include scattered verses from other parts of the Old and New Testaments. They are sometimes referred to by the letter 𝔗 followed by a superior numeral.

In evaluating the significance of these statistics of the amount

[1] Scholars at the University of Chicago have been sponsoring the study of this long-neglected source of information regarding the text of the New Testament; see the series of monographs published under the general title, 'Studies in the Lectionary Text of the Greek New Testament', begun by E. C. Colwell and D. W. Riddle, and now edited by A. Wikgren. See below, pp. 262–3.

[2] Thus, in addition to remonstrances by Eusebius and Augustine, the Synod of Laodicea issued a separate canon proscribing the manufacture and use of amulets: '. . . and those who wear such we command to be cast out of the Church'. For these and other references, see the annotations on a papyrus fever amulet edited by the present writer in *Papyri in the Princeton University Collections*, iii (Princeton, 1942), pp. 78 f. See below, p. 263.

of Greek evidence for the text of the New Testament, one should consider, by way of contrast, the number of manuscripts which preserve the text of the ancient classics. Homer's *Iliad*, for example, the 'bible' of the ancient Greeks, is preserved in 457 papyri, 2 uncial manuscripts, and 188 minuscule manuscripts.[1] Among the tragedians the witnesses to Euripides are the most abundant; his extant works are preserved in 54 papyri and 276 parchment manuscripts, almost all of the latter dating from the Byzantine period.[2]

The works of several ancient authors are preserved to us by the thinnest possible thread of transmission. For example, the compendious history of Rome by Velleius Paterculus survived to modern times in only one incomplete manuscript, from which the *editio princeps* was made—and this lone manuscript was lost in the seventeenth century after being copied by Beatus Rhenanus at Amerbach. Even the *Annals* of the famous historian Tacitus is extant, so far as the first six books are concerned, in but a single manuscript, dating from the ninth century. In 1870 the only known manuscript of the *Epistle to Diognetus*, an early Christian composition which editors usually include in the corpus of Apostolic Fathers, perished in a fire at the municipal library in Strasbourg. In contrast with these figures, the textual critic of the New Testament is embarrassed by the wealth of his material.[3] Furthermore, the work of many an ancient author has been preserved only in manuscripts which date

---

[1] For a list of papyri of the *Iliad*, see H. J. Mette, 'Neue Homer-Papyri', *Revue de philologie*, xxix (1955), pp. 193–9, 202–4, and *Lustrum*, i (1956), p. 9, Anm. 1; for a list of uncial and minuscule manuscripts, see T. W. Allen, *Homeri Ilias*, vol. i (Oxford, 1931). See below, p. 263.

[2] For a list of papyri of Euripides, see Roger A. Pack, *The Greek and Latin Literary Texts from Greco-Roman Egypt* (Ann Arbor, 1952), pp. 23 ff.; for a list of the Byzantine manuscripts, see Alexander Turyn, *The Byzantine Manuscript Tradition of the Tragedies of Euripides* (= *Illinois Studies in Language and Literature*, vol. xlv; Urbana, 1957).

[3] Lest, however, the wrong impression be conveyed from the statistics given above regarding the total number of Greek manuscripts of the New Testament, it should be pointed out that most of the papyri are relatively fragmentary and that only about fifty manuscripts (of which codex Sinaiticus is the only uncial manuscript) contain the entire New Testament. The great majority of the other manuscripts contain the four Gospels. The Book of Revelation is the least well-attested part of the New Testament, being preserved in about 300 Greek manuscripts. Of this number only ten are uncial manuscripts (namely ℵ, A, C, P, 046, 051, 052, 0163, 0169, and 0207), and three of these ten comprise only a single leaf each (the last three mentioned).

from the Middle Ages (sometimes the late Middle Ages), far removed from the time at which he lived and wrote. On the contrary, the time between the composition of the books of the New Testament and the earliest extant copies is relatively brief. Instead of the lapse of a millennium or more, as is the case of not a few classical authors, several papyrus manuscripts of portions of the New Testament are extant which were copied within a century or so after the composition of the original documents.

II

Important Witnesses to the Text of the New Testament

THREE classes of witnesses are available for ascertaining the text of the New Testament; they are the Greek manuscripts, the ancient translations into other languages, and the quotations from the New Testament made by early ecclesiastical writers. Something must be said now about certain individual witnesses in each of these three classes of evidence.

I. GREEK MANUSCRIPTS OF THE NEW TESTAMENT

Of the approximately 5,000 Greek manuscripts which contain all or part of the New Testament, the following are among the most important. They are listed here under the usual categories of (1) papyri, (2) uncials, and (3) minuscules; within each of these groups the sequence is that of the Gregory system of numeration. In the descriptions of these manuscripts reference is frequently made to various types of text, such as the Alexandrian, the Western, the Caesarean, and the Koine or Byzantine forms of text; for information concerning the significance of such terminology, see pp. 212–18 below. The name of the editor or collator is given for those manuscripts which have been published individually; it is to be understood that a more or less full conspectus of readings of the other manuscripts mentioned here may be found in the standard *apparatus critici*.

1. IMPORTANT GREEK PAPYRI OF THE NEW TESTAMENT[1]

Two of the most important collections of papyrus manuscripts of the New Testament were acquired in 1930–1 by Mr. (now Sir) Chester Beatty of London and by M. Martin Bodmer of Geneva in about 1955–6. The former collection is now in the

---

[1] For a list of all known Greek papyri of the New Testament, see the Appendix, pp. 247–55 below.

Beatty Museum in a suburb of Dublin and has been edited, with introductions and discussions, by Sir Frederic G. Kenyon.[1]

𝔭⁴⁵. The first of the Chester Beatty Biblical papyri, to which the siglum 𝔭⁴⁵ has been assigned, comprises portions of thirty leaves of a papyrus book formed by a succession of quires of only two leaves. Originally the codex consisted of about 220 leaves, each measuring about 10 by 8 inches, and contained all four Gospels and the Acts. Today Matthew and John are the least well preserved, each being represented by only two fragmentary leaves. Six leaves of Mark, seven of Luke, and thirteen of Acts remain of these books. Several small fragments of the codex, originally comprising a leaf from Matthew, have turned up in a collection of papyri at Vienna.[2]

The manuscript is dated by the editor in the first half of the third century. The type of New Testament text which it preserves in Mark is nearer to the Caesarean family than to either the Alexandrian or the Western text-types. In the other Gospels (where the Caesarean text has not yet been fully established) it is also intermediate between Alexandrian and Western. In Acts it is decidedly nearer the Alexandrian and has none of the major variants characteristic of the Western text of this book, though it has some of the minor ones.

𝔭⁴⁶. The second Chester Beatty Biblical papyrus, designated 𝔭⁴⁶, comprises eighty-six leaves (all slightly mutilated) of a single-quire[3] papyrus codex, measuring originally about 11 by 6½ inches, which contained on 104 leaves ten Epistles of Paul in the following order: Romans, Hebrews, 1 and 2 Corinthians, Ephesians, Galatians, Philippians, Colossians, 1 and 2 Thessalonians. Slightly earlier than 𝔭⁴⁵ it dates from about the year 200. Today portions of Romans and 1 Thessalonians, and 2 Thessalonians in its entirety, are lacking. The Pastoral Epistles were probably never included in the codex, for there does not appear to

---

[1] *The Chester Beatty Biblical Papyri, Descriptions and Texts* ... (London, 1933–7).

[2] Edited by Hans Gerstinger, 'Ein Fragment des Chester Beatty-Evangelienkodex in der Papyrussammlung der Nationalbibliothek in Wien', *Aegyptus*, xiii (1933), pp. 67–72.

[3] Three and possibly four of the Beatty Biblical papyri are single-quire manuscripts. For a discussion of this form of codex, see Campbell Bonner's introduction to his *Papyrus Codex of the Shepherd of Hermas* (Ann Arbor, 1934), pp. 7–12. More recently several other examples of single-quire codices have come to light, including the Michigan Gospel of John in Fayyumic Coptic and twelve of the thirteen Gnostic manuscripts from Nag Hammadi.

be room for them on the leaves missing at the end. (Since it is a single-quire codex, the number of leaves lacking at both ends can be computed more or less accurately.) Thirty of the eighty-six surviving leaves are in the library at the University of Michigan.[1]

It will be observed that, in addition to the reversal of the present order of Galatians and Ephesians, the anonymous Epistle to the Hebrews is included among the Pauline Epistles, which are arranged in a general order of their decreasing lengths. 𝔭46 is noteworthy, likewise, in that the doxology to Romans, which in many of the earlier manuscripts stands at the end of chapter xiv, is here placed at the end of chapter xv (see Plate II).[2] In general the papyrus is closer to the Alexandrian than to the Western type of text.

𝔭47. The third Chester Beatty Biblical papyrus of the New Testament, designated 𝔭47, comprises ten slightly mutilated leaves of a codex, measuring about 9½ by 5½ inches, of the Book of Revelation. Of the original codex, estimated to have been thirty-two leaves in length, only the middle portion remains, containing the text of ix. 10–xvii. 2. It dates from the middle or latter part of the third century. In general the text of 𝔭47 agrees more often with that of codex Sinaiticus than with any other, though it often shows a remarkable independence.

𝔭52. Measuring only 2½ by 3½ inches and containing but a few verses from the Fourth Gospel (xviii. 31–33, 37–38), this papyrus fragment is the oldest copy of any portion of the New Testament known to be in existence today. Although it had been acquired in Egypt by Bernard P. Grenfell as long ago as 1920, it remained unnoticed among hundreds of similar shreds of papyri until 1934. In that year C. H. Roberts, Fellow of St. John's College, Oxford, while sorting over the unpublished papyri belonging to the John Rylands Library at Manchester, recognized that this scrap preserves several sentences from John's Gospel. Without waiting to edit the fragment along with

---

[1] Edited by Henry A. Sanders, *A Third-Century Papyrus Codex of the Epistles of Paul* (Ann Arbor, 1935). See below, p. 263.

[2] This papyrus, however, contrary to common opinion, is not alone in placing Hebrews immediately following Romans; in six minuscule manuscripts and in a Syrian canon composed about A.D. 400 Hebrews occupies this position; see W. H. P. Hatch, 'The Position of Hebrews in the Canon of the New Testament', *Harvard Theological Review*, xxix (1936), pp. 133–51.

others of a miscellaneous nature, he immediately published a booklet setting forth a description of the fragment, its text, and a discussion of its significance.[1]

On the basis of the style of the script, Roberts dated the fragment in the first half of the second century. Though not all scholars are convinced that it can be dated within so narrow a range, such eminent palaeographers as Sir Frederic G. Kenyon, W. Schubart, Sir Harold I. Bell, Adolf Deissmann, Ulrich Wilcken, and W. H. P. Hatch have expressed themselves as being in agreement with Roberts's judgement.[2]

Although the extent of the verses preserved is so slight, in one respect this tiny scrap of papyrus possesses quite as much evidential value as would the complete codex. Just as Robinson Crusoe, seeing but a single footprint in the sand, concluded that another human being, with two feet, was present on the island with him, so 𝔭⁵² proves the existence and· use of the Fourth Gospel during the first half of the second century in a provincial town along the Nile, far removed from its traditional place of composition (Ephesus in Asia Minor). Had this little fragment been known during the middle of the past century, that school of New Testament criticism which was inspired by the brilliant Tübingen professor, Ferdinand Christian Baur, could not have argued that the Fourth Gospel was not composed until about the year 160.

𝔭⁶⁶. The most important discoveries of New Testament manuscripts since the purchase of the Chester Beatty papyri are the acquisitions made by the Genevan bibliophile and humanist, M. Martin Bodmer, founder of the Bodmer Library of World Literature at Cologny, a suburb of Geneva. One of the oldest considerable portions of the Greek New Testament is a papyrus codex of the Gospel of John, the Bodmer Papyrus II, which was published in 1956 by Victor Martin, Professor of Classical

---

[1] C. H. Roberts, *An Unpublished Fragment of the Fourth Gospel in the John Rylands Library* (Manchester, 1935). This was republished, with slight alterations, in the *Bulletin of the John Rylands Library*, xx (1936), pp. 45–55, and again, with critical notes and bibliography of reviews and opinions expressed by other scholars, in the *Catalogue of the Greek and Latin Papyri in the John Rylands Library*, iii (Manchester, 1938), pp. 1–3.

[2] Deissmann was convinced that 𝔭⁵² was written well within the reign of Hadrian (A.D. 117–38) and perhaps even during the time of Trajan (A.D. 98–117); see his article, 'Ein Evangelienblatt aus den Tagen Hadrians', *Deutsche allgemeine Zeitung*, Nr. 564 (3 Dec. 1935); Eng. trans. in *British Weekly*, 12 Dec. 1935, p. 219.

Philology at the University of Geneva. According to its editor, the manuscript dates from about A.D. 200.[1] It measures about 6 by 5½ inches and consists of six quires, of which 104 pages remain. These contain the text of John i. 1–vi. 11 and vi. 35b–xiv. 15. Subsequently fragments of forty-six other pages of the same codex were also acquired by M. Bodmer, and were edited as a *Supplément* by Martin (1958).[2] Since most of these fragments are small, some of them mere scraps, the amount of text of John xiv–xxi which has been preserved is not great.

The text of 𝔭⁶⁶ is a mixed text, with elements which are typically Alexandrian and Western. It is noteworthy that the manuscript contains about four hundred and forty alterations, introduced between lines, over erasures, and in the margins. Most of them appear to be the scribe's corrections of his own hasty blunders, though others seem to imply the use of a different exemplar. Several passages present unique readings that previously had not been found in any other manuscript. In xiii. 5 a picturesque word is used in connexion with the washing of the disciples' feet; according to 𝔭⁶⁶ Jesus took not a 'basin' ($\nu\iota\pi\tau\hat{\eta}\rho\alpha$) but a 'foot-basin' ($\pi\omega\delta\omega\nu\iota\pi\tau\hat{\eta}\rho\alpha$). In vii. 52 the presence of the definite article in a difficult passage now supports what scholars had long thought was the required sense, namely 'Search [the Scriptures] and you will see that *the* prophet does not rise from Galilee'.

𝔭⁷². What is the earliest known copy of the Epistle of Jude and the two Epistles of Peter is contained in another papyrus codex that was acquired by M. Bodmer and edited by Michel Testuz (1959). This manuscript, which the editor dates in the third century, contains a miscellaneous assortment of documents in the following order: the Nativity of Mary, the apocryphal correspondence of Paul to the Corinthians, the eleventh Ode of Solomon, the Epistle of Jude, Melito's Homily on the Passover, a fragment of a hymn, the Apology of Phileas, Psalms

---

[1] Herbert Hunger, the director of the papyrological collections in the National Library at Vienna, dates 𝔭⁶⁶ earlier, in the middle if not even in the first half of the second century; see his article, 'Zur Datierung des Papyrus Bodmer II (P66)', *Anzeiger der österreichischen Akademie der Wissenschaften*, phil.-hist. Kl., 1960, Nr. 4, pp. 12–33.

[2] A new edition of the *Supplément*, augmented and corrected, was published in 1962 with the assistance of J. W. B. Barns of Oxford, accompanied by a photographic reproduction of the entire manuscript (chs. i–xxi). For still further emendations, see Barns, 'Papyrus Bodmer II, Some Corrections and Remarks', *Muséon*, lxxv (1962), pp. 327–9. See below, p. 263.

xxxiii and xxxiv, and the two Epistles of Peter. Because of the relatively small size of the codex (it measures 6 by 5¾ inches), the editor concludes that it was made for private usage and not for reading in church services. Apparently four scribes took part in producing the manuscript. The textual affinities of its text of 1 Peter belong definitely with the Alexandrian group, and particularly with codex Alexandrinus. (See below, p. 263.)

𝔭⁷⁴. The Bodmer Papyrus XVII, edited by Rodolphe Kasser in 1961, is a rather voluminous papyrus codex dating from the seventh century. Originally the manuscript contained 264 pages, each measuring about 13 by 8 inches. Today it is in a poor state of preservation, and contains, with many lacunae, portions of the Book of Acts, James, 1 and 2 Peter, 1, 2, and 3 John, and Jude. The type of text which it preserves agrees frequently with Alexandrian witnesses. (See below, pp. 263–4.)

𝔭⁷⁵. Still another early Biblical manuscript acquired by M. Bodmer is a single-quire codex of Luke and John. It originally contained about 144 pages, each measuring 10¼ by 5⅛ inches, of which 102 have survived, either in whole or in part. The script is a clear and carefully executed uncial, somewhat like that of 𝔭⁴⁵, though with a less pronounced ductus. The editors, Victor Martin and Rodolphe Kasser, date this copy between A.D. 175 and 225. It is thus the earliest known copy of the Gospel according to Luke and one of the earliest of the Gospel according to John. The orthography of the name 'John' varies in a curious manner. In Luke it is invariably written with a single ν (’Ιωάνης), and the same orthography appears at the beginning of the Gospel according to John. At John i. 26, however, a second ν is added between the lines above the α and the ν (as also at x. 40), and thereafter the geminated form appears everywhere except at iii. 27, where, perhaps because of a distraction, the scribe reverted to his former spelling.

The textual significance of this newly acquired witness is hard to overestimate, presenting, as it does, a form of text very similar to that of Vaticanus (see below, p. 264). Occasionally it is the only known Greek witness which agrees with the Sahidic in supporting several interesting readings. Thus, at John x. 7, instead of the traditional text, 'I am the door of the sheep', 𝔭⁷⁵ replaces 'door' (ἡ θύρα) by 'shepherd' (ὁ ποιμήν). What is still more remarkable is the addition at Luke xvi. 19, where in

Jesus' account of the Rich Man and Lazarus this new witness inserts after πλούσιος the words ὀνόματι Νευης (see Plate III). The Sahidic version agrees with a rather widespread tradition among ancient catechists of the Coptic Church that the name of the Rich Man was 'Nineveh', a name which had become the symbol of dissolute riches. Obviously the scribe of 𝔭⁷⁵ was acquainted with this tradition and by accidental haplography wrote 'Neve' for 'Nineveh' (Νευης for Νινευης).[1]

2. IMPORTANT GREEK UNCIAL MANUSCRIPTS OF THE NEW TESTAMENT

א. Primacy of position in the list of New Testament manuscripts is customarily given to the fourth-century codex of the Greek Bible which was discovered about the middle of the nineteenth century by Dr. Constantin von Tischendorf at the monastery of St. Catharine on Mount Sinai. Hence this manuscript is known as codex Sinaiticus. It once contained the entire Bible written in a carefully executed uncial hand (see Fig. 1) and arranged with four columns per page, measuring about 15 by 13½ inches. Today parts of the Old Testament have perished, but fortunately the entire New Testament has survived. In fact, codex Sinaiticus is the only known complete copy of the Greek New Testament in uncial script.

The story of its discovery makes a fascinating tale, and deserves to be told in some detail. In 1844, when he was not yet

---

[1] It was probably the *horror vacui* which led more than one reader to provide a name for the anonymous Rich Man. Toward the close of the fourth century Priscillian, a highly educated layman who revived certain Manichean errors in southern Spain, gave the name Finees to the Rich Man, perhaps because in the Old Testament Eleazar [compare 'Lazarus'] and Phinehas are associated. (The only manuscript extant of Prisc. *Tract.* xi [ed. G. Schepps, p. 91] reads Fineet, with the *t* cancelled and *s* written above.)

The widespread use of 'Dives' as the name of the Rich Man is, of course, to be accounted for by the rendering of the passage in the Latin Vulgate: 'Homo quidam erat dives et . . . .' Among the literature on the subject, see A. Harnack, 'Der Name des reichen Mannes in Luc 16, 19', *Texte und Untersuchungen*, xiii (1) (1895), pp. 75–78; J. Rendel Harris, 'On Certain Obscure Names in the New Testament', *Expositor*, 6th ser., i (1900), pp. 161–77, 304–8, especially pp. 175–7; Hugo Gressmann, *Vom reichen Mann und armen Lazarus: eine literargeschichtliche Studie (Abhandlungen der preussischen Akademie der Wissenschaften*, phil.-hist. Kl., 1918): A. Meyer, 'Namen der Namenlosen', in E. Hennecke, *Neutestamentliche Apokryphen*, 2te Aufl. (Tübingen, 1924), pp. 78–81; L. Th. Lefort, 'Le Nom du mauvais riche (Lc 16. 19) et la tradition copte', *Zeitschrift für die neutestamentliche Wissenschaft*, xxxvii (1938), pp. 65–72; and Henry J. Cadbury, 'A Proper Name for Dives', *Journal of Biblical Literature*, lxxxi (1962), pp. 399–402. See also footnote 3 on p. 188 below.

thirty years of age, Tischendorf, a *Privatdozent* in the University of Leipzig, began an extensive journey through the Near East in search of Biblical manuscripts. While visiting the monastery of St. Catharine at Mount Sinai, he chanced to see some leaves of parchment in a waste-basket full of papers destined to light the oven of the monastery. On examination these proved to be part of a copy of the Septuagint version of the Old Testament, written in an early Greek uncial script. He retrieved from the basket no fewer than forty-three such leaves, and the monk casually remarked that two basket loads of similarly discarded leaves had already been burned up! Later, when Tischendorf was shown other portions of the same codex (containing all of Isaiah and 1 and 4 Maccabees), he warned the monks that such things were too valuable to be used to stoke their fires. The forty-three leaves which he was permitted to keep contained portions of 1 Chronicles, Jeremiah, Nehemiah, and Esther, and upon returning to Europe he deposited them in the university library at Leipzig, where they still remain. In 1846 he published their contents, naming them the codex Frederico-Augustanus (in honour of the King of Saxony, Frederick Augustus, the discoverer's sovereign and patron).

In 1853 Tischendorf revisited the monastery of St. Catharine, hoping to acquire other portions of the same manuscript. The excitement which he had displayed on the occasion of his discovery during his first visit had made the monks cautious, and he could learn nothing further about the manuscript. In 1859 his travels took him back once more to Mount Sinai, this time under the patronage of the Czar of Russia, Alexander II. The day before he was scheduled to leave he presented to the steward of the monastery a copy of the edition of the Septuagint which he had recently published in Leipzig. Thereupon the steward remarked that he too had a copy of the Septuagint, and produced from a closet in his cell a manuscript wrapped in a red cloth. There before the astonished scholar's eyes lay the treasure which he had been longing to see. Concealing his feelings, Tischendorf casually asked permission to look at it further that evening. Permission was granted, and upon retiring to his room Tischendorf stayed up all night in the joy of studying the manuscript—for, as he declared in his diary (which as a scholar he kept in Latin), *quippe dormire nefas videbatur* ('it really seemed a sacrilege to sleep')! He soon found that the document contained much more than he had even hoped; for not only was most of the Old Testament there, but also the New Testament was intact and in excellent condition, with the addition of two early Christian works of the second century, the Epistle of Barnabas (previously known only through a very poor Latin translation) and a large portion of the Shepherd of Hermas, hitherto known only by title.

The next morning Tischendorf tried to buy the manuscript, but without success. Then he asked to be allowed to take it to Cairo to study; but the monk in charge of the altar plate objected, and so he had to leave without it.

Later, while in Cairo, where the monks of Sinai have also a small monastery, Tischendorf importuned the abbot of the monastery of St. Catharine, who happened to be in Cairo at the time, to send for the document. Thereupon swift Bedouin messengers were sent to fetch the manuscript to Cairo, and it was agreed that Tischendorf would be allowed to have it quire by quire (i.e. eight leaves at a time) to copy it. Two Germans who happened to be in Cairo and who knew some Greek, an apothecary and a bookseller, helped him transcribe the manuscript, and Tischendorf revised carefully what they copied. In two months they transcribed 110,000 lines of text.

The next stage of the negotiations involved what may be called euphemistically 'ecclesiastical diplomacy'. At that time the highest place of authority among the monks of Sinai was vacant. Tischendorf suggested that it would be to their advantage if they would make a gift to the Czar of Russia, whose influence, as protector of the Greek Church, they desired in connexion with the election of the new abbot—and what could be more appropriate as a gift than this ancient Greek manuscript! After prolonged negotiations the precious codex was delivered to Tischendorf for publication at Leipzig and for presentation to the Czar in the name of the monks. In the East a gift demands a return (compare Genesis xxiii, where Ephron 'gives' Abraham a field for a burying plot, but nevertheless Abraham pays him 400 shekels of silver for it). In return for the manuscript the Czar presented to the monastery a silver shrine for St. Catharine, sent a gift of 7,000 roubles for the library at Sinai and a gift of 2,000 roubles for the monks in Cairo, and conferred several Russian decorations (similar to honorary degrees) on the authorities of the monastery. In 1862, on the one-thousandth anniversary of the founding of the Russian Empire, the text of the manuscript was published in magnificent style at the expense of the Czar in four folio volumes, being printed at Leipzig with type cast for the purpose so as to resemble the characters of the manuscript, which it represents line for line with the greatest attainable accuracy.[1]

The definitive publication of the codex was made in the twentieth century when the Oxford University Press issued a facsimile from photographs taken by Professor Kirsopp Lake (New Testament, 1911; Old Testament, 1922). After the revolutions in Russia, the U.S.S.R., not being interested in the Bible and being in need of money, negotiated with the Trustees of the British Museum for the sale of the codex for £100,000 (then slightly more than $500,000). The British Government guaranteed one-half the sum, while the other half was raised by popular subscription, contributions being made by interested Americans as well as individuals and congregations throughout Britain. Just before Christmas Day, 1933, the manuscript was carried under guard into the British Museum. A most thorough palaeographical study of the manuscript was then undertaken by H. J. M. Milne and T. C. Skeat of the staff of the Museum, and their results were published in a volume entitled *Scribes and Correctors of Codex Sinaiticus* (London, 1938).[2] Additional information regarding the manuscript was brought to light. For example, the application of a new technique in manuscript study, the use of ultraviolet-ray lamps, enabled Milne and Skeat to discover that when the original scribe finished writing John xxi. 24 he drew two decorative lines (called a coronis) at

[1] Certain aspects of the negotiations leading to the transfer of the codex to the Czar's possession are open to an interpretation that reflects adversely upon Tischendorf's candour and good faith with the monks at St. Catharine's. For a recent account intended to exculpate him of blame, see Erhard Lauch's article, 'Nichts gegen Tischendorf', in *Bekenntnis zur Kirche: Festgabe für Ernst Sommerlath zum 70. Geburtstag* (Berlin, *c.* 1961), pp. 15–24; for an account that includes a hitherto unknown receipt given by Tischendorf to the authorities at the monastery promising to return the manuscript from St. Petersburg 'to the Holy Confraternity of Sinai at its earliest request', see Ihor Ševčenko's article, 'New Documents on Tischendorf and the Codex Sinaiticus', published in the journal *Scriptorium*, xviii (1964), pp. 55–80. [2] See below, p. 264.

the lower part of the column of writing and then appended a
subscription signifying that the text of the Gospel of John was
finished. (Similar decorative lines and subscriptions appear elsewhere in the manuscript at the end of books.) Later the same
scribe washed the vellum and added the concluding verse (vs. 25),
repeating the coronis and subscription at a correspondingly
lower position (see Plate IV).

The type of text witnessed by Sinaiticus belongs in general
to the Alexandrian group, but it also has a definite strain of the
Western type of readings. Before the manuscript left the scriptorium it was gone over by several scribes who did the work of
a διορθωτής (corrector). Readings for which they are responsible
for introducing are designated in a critical apparatus by the
siglum ℵª. At a later date (probably some time about the sixth
or seventh century) a group of correctors working at Caesarea
entered a large number of alterations into the text of both Old
and New Testaments. These readings, designated by the siglum
ℵ^ca or ℵ^cb, represent a thoroughgoing effort to correct the text to
a different standard, which according to a colophon at the end of
the books of Esdras and Esther is stated to have been 'a very
ancient manuscript that had been corrected by the hand of the
holy martyr Pamphilus'.[1]

A. This handsome codex, dating from about the fifth century,
contains the Old Testament, except for several mutilations, and
most of the New Testament (the whole of Matthew's Gospel as
far as xxv. 6 is lost, as well as the leaves which originally contained John vi. 50–viii. 52 and 2 Cor. iv. 13–xii. 6). It was presented in 1627 by Cyril Lucar, Patriarch of Constantinople, to
King Charles I of England. Today it rests along with codex
Sinaiticus in one of the prominent show-cases in the Department
of Manuscripts of the British Museum. A photographic reproduction of the codex was published in 1879–83 by the British
Museum, under the supervision of E. Maunde Thompson. Subsequently F. G. Kenyon edited a reduced facsimile of the New
Testament (1909) and of parts of the Old Testament.

---

[1] Pamphilus of Caesarea, who was martyred A.D. 309, devoted many years in
hunting for and obtaining possession of books illustrative of the Scriptures from all
parts of the world (Jerome, *Epist.* xxxiv). His library, which was especially rich in
Biblical codices, was catalogued by Eusebius himself (*Hist. Eccl.* vi. 32). Among its
priceless treasures were the Hexapla and the Tetrapla of Origen in the original
copies.

The quality of the text preserved in codex Alexandrinus varies in different parts of the New Testament. In the Gospels it is the oldest example of the Byzantine type of text, which is generally regarded as an inferior form of text. In the rest of the New Testament (which may have been copied by the scribe from a different exemplar from that which he employed for the text of the Gospels), it ranks along with B and ℵ as representative of the Alexandrian type of text. (See below, p. 264.)

B. One of the most valuable of all the manuscripts of the Greek Bible is codex Vaticanus. As its name indicates, it is in the great Vatican Library at Rome, which has been its home since some date prior to 1475, when it was mentioned in the first catalogue made of the treasures of the library. For some reason which has never been fully explained, during a large part of the nineteenth century the authorities of the library put continual obstacles in the way of scholars who wished to study it in detail. It was not until 1889–90 that a complete photographic facsimile of the whole manuscript, edited by Giuseppe Cozza-Luzi, made its contents available to all. Another facsimile edition of the New Testament was issued at Milan in 1904. (See below, p. 264.)

The manuscript was written about the middle of the fourth century and contained both Testaments as well as the books of the Apocrypha, with the exception of the books of Maccabees. Today there are three lacunae in the codex: at the beginning almost forty-six chapters of Genesis are missing; a section of some thirty Psalms is lost; and the concluding pages (from Heb. ix. 14 onwards, including 1 and 2 Timothy, Titus, Philemon, and Revelation) are gone.

The writing is in small and delicate uncials, perfectly simple and unadorned. Unfortunately, the beauty of the original writing has been spoiled by a later corrector, who traced over every letter afresh, omitting only those letters and words which he believed to be incorrect. The complete absence of ornamentation from Vaticanus has generally been taken as an indication that it is slightly older than codex Sinaiticus. On the other hand, some scholars believe that these two manuscripts were originally among the fifty copies of the Scriptures which the Emperor Constantine commissioned Eusebius to have written (see pp. 7–8 above). Indeed, T. C. Skeat of the

British Museum has suggested to the present writer that codex Vaticanus was a 'reject' among the fifty copies, for it is deficient in the Eusebian canon tables, has many corrections by different scribes, and, as was mentioned above, lacks the books of Maccabees apparently through an oversight. Whether 'reject' or not, however, the text which it contains has been regarded by many scholars as an excellent representative of the Alexandrian text-type of the New Testament.

In common with other manuscripts of the New Testament, the Scripture text of Vaticanus is divided into what may be called chapters. The system of division, however, appears to be more ancient than that current in other early parchment copies of the New Testament. For example, in the Epistles no notice is taken of 2 Peter, and therefore the system of divisions appears to date from a time when this Epistle was not regarded as canonical. Furthermore, the Epistles of Paul have chapter numbers that do not begin afresh with each Epistle (as is customary in other manuscripts), but continue in one series from Romans onwards. In this manuscript the Epistle to the Hebrews follows the Thessalonian Epistles; nevertheless, the sequence of the chapter numbers discloses that in an ancestor of Vaticanus Hebrews stood immediately after Galatians (compare the sequence of Epistles in 𝔭⁴⁶).[1]

C. Codex Ephraemi is the name given to a fifth-century manuscript of the Greek Bible that, as was mentioned in Chapter I, was erased during the twelfth century and many of its sheets rewritten with the text of a Greek translation of thirty-eight ascetical treatises or sermons by St. Ephraem, a

---

[1] In codex Vaticanus the Epistle to the Galatians concludes with the 58th chapter, whereas the next Epistle, that to the Ephesians, commences with the 70th chapter, and then the numbers continue regularly through Philippians, Colossians, 1 and 2 Thessalonians, ending with the 93rd chapter. Following 2 Thessalonians stands Hebrews, which begins with the 59th chapter, and proceeds with the 60th, 61st, 62nd, 63rd, and 64th chapter, as far as Heb. ix. 14, where the manuscript breaks off, the remaining part being lost. It is clear from the sequence of chapter divisions that in an ancestor of Vaticanus Hebrews stood after Galatians, and that the scribe of Vaticanus copied mechanically the chapter numerals even though they no longer were appropriate after Galatians.

Since the present sequence of the New Testament books in codex Vaticanus agrees with the list included in Athanasius' Thirty-Ninth Festal Letter (which was written A.D. 367), it has sometimes been supposed that the manuscript was perhaps 'made by Alexandrian scribes for the Emperor Constans during Athanasius' stay in Rome in 340' (Berthold Altaner [and] Alfred Stuiber, *Patrologie; Leben, Schriften und Lehre der Kirchenväter*, 7te Aufl. [Freiburg, 1966], p. 277).

Syrian Church Father of the fourth century. By the application of chemical reagents and by dint of painstaking labour, Tischendorf was able to decipher the almost totally obliterated underwriting of this palimpsest.[1] Only sixty-four leaves are left of the Old Testament, and of the New Testament there are 145 leaves (about five-eighths of the number which must have been originally required), containing portions of every book except 2 Thessalonians and 2 John.

Though the document dates from the fifth century, its text is of less importance than one might have assumed from its age. It seems to be compounded from all the major text-types, agreeing frequently with the later Koine or Byzantine type, which most scholars regard as the least valuable type of New Testament text. Two correctors, referred to as C^2 or C^b and C^3 or C^c, have made corrections in the manuscript. The former probably lived in Palestine in the sixth century, and the latter seems to have done his work in Constantinople in the ninth century.

D. Different in several respects from all the manuscripts mentioned above is codex Bezae (also known as codex Cantabrigiensis), which was presented in 1581 to the library at Cambridge University by Theodore Beza, the celebrated French scholar who became the successor of Calvin as leader of the Genevan Church. Dating from the fifth or possibly sixth century,[2] this codex contains most of the text of the four Gospels and Acts, with a small fragment of 3 John. The text is presented in Greek and in Latin, the two languages facing each other on opposite pages, the Greek being on the left, the Latin on the right. Each page contains a single column of text, which is not written straight ahead but is divided into κῶλα, that is, lines of varying length with the object of making the pauses in sense come at the end of lines. The Gospels stand in the so-called Western order, with the two apostles first and the two companions of the apostles following (Matthew, John, Luke, and Mark). In each book the first three lines are in red letters, and red ink and black ink alternate in the lines of the subscriptions at the close of each book. In 1864 F. H. Scrivener published a careful edition of the manuscript, with full annotations, and in 1899 the Cambridge

---

[1] A list of corrections of Tischendorf's edition (Leipzig, 1843), based on a fresh examination of the manuscript, was published by Robert W. Lyon in *New Testament Studies*, v (1958–9), pp. 266–72.   [2] See below, p. 264.

University Press issued a handsome facsimile reproduction of the entire manuscript.[1]

No known manuscript has so many and such remarkable variations from what is usually taken to be the normal New Testament text. Codex Bezae's special characteristic is the free addition (and occasional omission) of words, sentences, and even incidents. Thus in Luke vi this manuscript has verse 5 after verse 10, and between verses 4 and 6 it contains the following account: 'On the same day, seeing one working on the Sabbath day, he [Jesus] said to him, "Man, if you know what you are doing, you are blessed; but if you do not know, you are accursed and a transgressor of the law" ' (see Plate V). Although this sentence, which is found in no other manuscript, cannot be regarded as part of the original text of Luke, it may well embody a first-century tradition, one of the 'many other things which Jesus did' but which were not written in the Gospels (see John xxi. 25). In the Lucan account of the Last Supper (xxii. 15–20) this manuscript (along with some Latin and Syriac witnesses) omits the latter part of verse 19 and the whole of 20, thus removing all mention of the second cup, and leaving the order of institution inverted (Cup–Bread). In Luke xxiii. 53 there is the additional information that Joseph of Arimathea, after laying the body of Jesus in his rock-hewn tomb, 'put before the tomb a [great] stone which twenty men could scarcely roll'.

Codex Bezae is the principal authority, being supported by one other uncial, *Φ*, the Old Latin and Curetonian Syriac versions, and by a few copies of the Vulgate, in inserting after Matt. xx. 28 the long passage:

But seek to increase from that which is small, and to become less from that which is greater. When you enter into a house and are summoned to dine, do not sit down at the prominent places, lest perchance a man more honourable than you come in afterwards, and he who invited you come and say to you, 'Go down lower'; and you shall be ashamed. But if you sit down in the inferior place, and one inferior to you come in, then he that invited you will say to you, 'Go up higher'; and this will be advantageous for you.[2]

---

[1] A convenient presentation of the distinctive text of codex Bezae (collated against the Gebhardt–Tischendorf edition of the New Testament) was given by Eberhard Nestle in his *Novi Testamenti supplementum* (Leipzig, 1896), pp. 7–66.

[2] It may be mentioned that English translations of codex Bezae have been published by William Whiston (*The Primitive New Testament* [London, 1745]) and by

It is particularly in the Acts of the Apostles that Bezae differs markedly from other witnesses, being nearly one-tenth longer than the text generally received. Thus in Acts xii. 10 this document refers to the seven steps from the prison where Peter was kept down to the street. In xix. 9 it adds the detail that in Ephesus Paul preached daily in the lecture hall of Tyrannus 'from eleven o'clock to four', that is, at that time of day when the rhetorician Tyrannus would normally not hold his own sessions. In the Decree which the Apostolic Council at Jerusalem issued about A.D. 50, this manuscript omits from the list of four prohibitions the clause 'and from what is strangled', and adds at the close (Acts xv. 20 and 29) the negative Golden Rule.

These examples will be sufficient to indicate the characteristic freedom of what is called the Western text, of which codex Bezae is the principal representative. More study has been expended upon this manuscript, particularly where the Greek text differs from the parallel Latin text and where one or both differ from other witnesses, than has been devoted to any other New Testament witness.[1] There is still no unanimity of opinion regarding the many problems which the manuscript raises.

D^p. The symbol D^p (sometimes called D_2) refers to the sixth-century[2] codex Claromontanus, which contains only the Pauline Epistles (including Hebrews). Like codex Bezae (which lacks the Pauline Epistles), D^p is a bilingual Greek and Latin manuscript, having the Greek on the left-hand page and the text arranged in lines of irregular length corresponding to the pauses in the sense. The work of at least nine different correctors has been identified; the fourth of these added accent and breathing marks in the ninth century. Like codex Bezae, the type of text in this manuscript is distinctly Western; it should be noted, however, that Western readings in the Epistles are not so striking as those in the Gospels and Acts. An edition of the manuscript was published by Tischendorf in 1852.

Johannes Greber (*The New Testament: a New Translation and Explanation Based on the Oldest Manuscripts* [New York, 1937]). J. M. Wilson published *The Acts of the Apostles, Translated from the Codex Bezae* . . . (London, 1923). See below, p. 264.

[1] See, for example, A. F. J. Klijn, *A Survey of the Researches into the Western Text of the Gospels and Acts* (Utrecht, [1949]), continued in *Novum Testamentum*, iii (1959), pp. 1–27, 161–74. Happily there is now available a complete *Concordance to the Distinctive Greek Text of Codex Bezae*, compiled by James D. Yoder (Leiden and Grand Rapids, 1961).   [2] See below, p. 264.

E. Codex Basiliensis, dating from the eighth century, contains the four Gospels on 318 leaves. It is now, as its name indicates, in the library of the University of Basle, Switzerland. It has a Byzantine type of text. (See p. 264 and Plate VIII.)

E^a (also called E$_2$). Formerly in the possession of Archbishop Laud, codex Laudianus 35 of the Bodleian Library at Oxford dates from the late sixth or early seventh century. It contains the Book of Acts in Latin and Greek, arranged in very short lines of only one to three words each with the Latin in the left-hand column. The text exhibits a mixture of types of text, sometimes agreeing with codex Bezae but more often with the Byzantine type. It is the earliest known manuscript which contains Acts viii. 37 (the Ethiopian's confession of faith; see Plate VI*a*). An edition of the manuscript was published by Tischendorf in 1870.

E^p (also called E$_3$). Codex Sangermanensis, now in Leningrad, contains the Pauline Epistles in Greek and Latin on opposite pages. It was copied in the ninth or tenth century from codex Claromontanus, and therefore is of no independent value.

F. Codex Boreelianus, since 1830 in the University Library of Utrecht, once belonged to Johannes Boreel, Dutch Ambassador at the Court of James I of England. It contains the four Gospels (with large lacunae), and dates from the ninth century. Its text is typically Byzantine.

F^p (also called F$_2$). Codex Augiensis, of the ninth century, contains the Pauline Epistles in double columns of Greek and Latin (Hebrews is given in Latin only). The manuscript once belonged to the monastery of Reichenau near Constance, which was known as Augia Maior; today it is in the library of Trinity College, Cambridge. Its text, which was published by F. H. A. Scrivener in 1859, is of the Western type.

G. Codex Wolfii A, also called codex Harleianus, of the tenth century, contains the four Gospels with many lacunae. It was brought from the East by Andrew E. Seidel in the seventeenth century and was acquired by J. C. Wolf, who published extracts of it in 1723. Later it became part of the library of Robert Harley, and is now in the British Museum. Its text is Byzantine.

G^p (also called G$_3$). Codex Boernerianus, once owned by the Leipzig professor C. F. Börner, is now at Dresden. Dating from the ninth century, it contains the Pauline Epistles in Greek, with a literalistic Latin translation between the lines. After

Philemon there stands the superscription for the Epistle to the Laodiceans, but the text of this apocryphal Epistle is not present. In type of text it is closely akin to F^p, and both of them probably go back one or two generations to a common archetype.[1] In many respects it resembles the St. Gall MS. *Δ*, and is thought to have been written in the monastery of St. Gall by some of the Irish monks who emigrated to those parts. At the foot of one of the leaves (fol. 23) are eight lines of Irish verse which refer to making a pilgrimage to Rome:

> To come to Rome, [to come to Rome,]
> Much of trouble, little of profit,
> The thing thou seekest here,
> If thou bring not with thee, thou findest not.[2]

H. Codex Wolfii B was brought from the East with G, and passed with it into the possession of J. C. Wolf. Its subsequent history is unknown until 1838, when it was acquired by the public library at Hamburg. Dating from the ninth or tenth century, it contains the four Gospels with many lacunae. The text is of the Byzantine type.

H^a (also called H$_2$). Codex Mutinensis, a ninth-century copy of Acts (lacking about seven chapters), is in the Grand Ducal Library at Modena. The text is of the Byzantine type.

H^p (also called H$_3$). Codex Coislinianus is an important codex of the Pauline Epistles written in a very large hand with only a few words in each line. The text is Alexandrian. Dating from the sixth century, it came into the possession of the monastery of the Laura on Mount Athos, where, after it began to be dilapidated, its leaves were used to supply materials for the binding of several other volumes. Forty-one leaves are known to exist today, divided among libraries at Paris, Leningrad, Moscow, Kiev, Turin, and Mount Athos. A note appended to the Epistle to Titus states that it was corrected from the copy in the library of Caesarea, written by the hand of the holy Pamphilus himself. The text is arranged according to the colometrical edition of the Epistles prepared by Euthalius (or Evagrius), which is found in several other manuscripts (see p. 26 above).

[1] See W. H. P. Hatch, 'On the Relationship of Codex Augiensis and Codex Boernerianus of the Pauline Epistles', *Harvard Studies in Classical Philology*, lx (1951), pp. 187–99.

[2] For the entire text, see F. H. A. Scrivener, *A Plain Introduction to the Criticism of the New Testament*, 4th ed., i (1894), p. 180, n. 2.

I. The Washington manuscript of the Pauline Epistles, in the Freer Museum at the Smithsonian Institution, originally contained about 210 leaves, of which only 84 survive in fragmentary condition. Dating from the fifth or sixth century, it contains portions of all the Pauline Epistles except Romans (the Epistle to the Hebrews follows 2 Thessalonians). The text, which was edited by H. A. Sanders in 1921, is a good representative of the Alexandrian group, agreeing more closely with ℵ and A than with B.

K. Codex Cyprius, dating from the ninth or tenth century, is a complete copy of the four Gospels with a typically Byzantine type of text.

K^{ap} (also called K₂). Codex Mosquensis is a ninth- or tenth-century manuscript of the Acts, the Catholic Epistles, and the Pauline Epistles (including Hebrews). The text, which is written in uncial script, is separated into paragraphs by comments, written in minuscule script. At the foot of the page are scholia, attributed to John Chrysostom (see Plate IX). The text is a form of von Soden's *I*-text (see p. 141 below).

L. Codex Regius is an eighth-century codex of the Gospels, nearly complete, now in the Bibliothèque Nationale at Paris. It was edited by Tischendorf in 1846. Though badly written by a scribe who committed many ignorant blunders, its type of text is good, agreeing very frequently with codex Vaticanus (B). Its most notable feature is the presence of two endings to the Gospel according to Mark. The second of these is the traditional verses 9–20, but the first is a shorter ending, which is also found in a small number of other witnesses. This shorter ending reads as follows: 'But they [the women] reported briefly to Peter and those with him all that they had been told. And after this, Jesus himself sent out by means of them, from east to west, the sacred and imperishable proclamation of eternal salvation.'

L^{ap} (also called L₂). Codex Angelicus, now in the Angelican Library at Rome, is a ninth-century copy of the Acts, Catholic Epistles, and Pauline Epistles. Its text is mainly Byzantine.

M. Codex Campianus, containing the four Gospels, is now in the Bibliothèque Nationale at Paris. It dates from the ninth century, and contains a text that is mainly Byzantine, but with admixture of Caesarean readings as well.

N. One of the de luxe parchment manuscripts is codex Purpureus Petropolitanus, written in the sixth century in silver letters upon purple vellum, with gold ink for the contractions of the names of God and Jesus. Originally containing the four Gospels on approximately 462 leaves, it was dismembered about the twelfth century, possibly by Crusaders, and its leaves were carried far and wide. Today 182 leaves are in the Imperial Library at Leningrad, 33 at Patmos, 6 in the Vatican Library, 4 in the British Museum, 2 at Vienna, 1 in private possession at Lerma, Italy, 1 in the Byzantine Museum, Athens, and 1 in the Pierpont Morgan Library, New York.[1] The text belongs predominantly to the Byzantine type, but it preserves a number of readings of earlier types; B. H. Streeter regarded it (along with three other purple manuscripts, Σ, O, and Φ) as a weak member of the Caesarean text.[2]

O. Codex Sinopensis is a de luxe edition, written in the sixth century with gold ink on purple vellum, of which forty-three leaves of the Gospel according to Matthew survive (mainly chs. xiii–xxiv), as well as five miniatures. It was acquired at Sinope in Asia Minor by a French officer in 1899, and is now in the Bibliothèque Nationale at Paris. Its text, which was edited by Henri Omont in 1901, is a tertiary witness to the Caesarean type of text.

P^{apr} (also called P$_2$). Codex Porphyrianus, now in Leningrad, a palimpsest dating from the ninth century, is one of the very few uncial manuscripts that include the Book of Revelation (see n. 3 on p. 34 above). In addition it contains the Book of Acts and the Catholic and Pauline Epistles, though with lacunae. The upper writing, which is dated in the year 1301, consists of the commentary of Euthalius on the Acts and the Pauline Epistles, together with the Biblical text. Tischendorf edited the manuscript in 1865–9. According to von Soden, in Acts the text is Koine with sporadic *I*-readings, and in the other books it is Alexandrian. According to Schmid, however, in Revelation its text is a secondary development of a basic Andreas type of text.

R. Codex Nitriensis, now in the British Museum, is·a palimpsest containing parts of Luke in a fine large hand of the sixth century, over which the Syriac treatise of Severus of Antioch

---

[1] These last two leaves have recently been edited for the first time by Stanley Rypins in the *Journal of Biblical Literature*, lxxv (1956), pp. 27–39.

[2] B. H. Streeter, 'Codices 157, 1071 and the Caesarean Text', *Quantulacumque, Studies Presented to Kirsopp Lake* (London, 1937), pp. 149–50.

against Johannes Grammaticus was written in the eighth or ninth century. The same manuscript also contains a palimpsest of 4,000 lines of Homer's *Iliad*. Along with more than 500 other manuscripts it was brought to England in 1847 from the monastery of St. Mary the Mother of God, in the Nitrian Desert, 70 miles north-west of Cairo. According to von Soden, the text belongs to his *I* (i.e. Western) type of text. Tischendorf edited the text in 1857.

S. This is one of the earliest dated Greek manuscripts of the Gospels; a colophon states that it was written by a monk named Michael in the year of the world 6457 (= A.D. 949). It is now in the Vatican Library (no. 354). The text-type is Byzantine.

S^{ap}. Codex Athous, of the Laura of St. Athanasius, contains the Acts, Catholic Epistles and Romans, and portions of 1 and 2 Corinthians and Ephesians. Dating from the eighth or ninth century, its text-type is Byzantine.

T. Codex Borgianus, at the Collegium de Propaganda Fide in Rome, is a valuable Graeco-Sahidic manuscript of the fifth century.[1] Unfortunately, it is fragmentary, preserving only 179 verses of Luke xxii–xxiii and John vi–viii. The text is very close to that represented by codex Vaticanus (B).

V. Codex Mosquensis, formerly of the monastery of Vatopedi on Mount Athos and now in Moscow, is a copy of the four Gospels, nearly complete, dating from the eighth or ninth century. The manuscript is written in uncials down to John viii. 39, where it breaks off, and from that point the text is continued in a minuscule hand of the thirteenth century. The text-type of the manuscript is Byzantine.

W. Among the more important uncial manuscripts discovered during the twentieth century is a codex of the four Gospels acquired by Mr. Charles L. Freer of Detroit in 1906 and now in the Freer Museum of the Smithsonian Institution in Washington, D.C. It dates from the late fourth or early fifth century and, like codex Bezae, contains the Gospels in the so-called Western order (Matthew, John, Luke, and Mark). Each of the two leaves which serve as covers has two painted panels depicting two of the Evangelists; these miniatures are thought to date from about the seventh or eighth century. The type of text in this manu-

---

[1] The text of the fragment of John was edited by A. A. Georgi, *Fragmentum Evangelii S. Johannis Graecum Copto-Sahidicum* . . . (Rome, 1789).

script is curiously variegated, as though copied from several manuscripts of different families of text. In Matthew and Luke viii. 13–xxiv. 53 the text is of the common Byzantine variety, but in Mark i. 1–v. 30 it is Western, resembling the Old Latin; Mark v. 31–xvi. 20 is Caesarean, akin to $\mathfrak{p}^{45}$; and Luke i. 1–viii. 12 and John v. 12–xxi. 25 are Alexandrian. The text of John i. 1–v. 11, which fills a quire that was added about the seventh century, presumably to replace one which was damaged, is a mixed text with some Alexandrian and a few Western readings. In the opinion of its editor, Henry A. Sanders, this stratification of different kinds of text is to be explained by the theory that the codex goes back to an ancestor made up of fragments from different manuscripts of the Gospels pieced together after the attempt of the Emperor Diocletian to crush Christianity by destroying its sacred books.

One of the most noteworthy of the variant readings in codex W is a remarkable insertion near the close of the Gospel according to Mark, part of which was known to Jerome, who declares that it was present 'in certain copies and especially in Greek codices'. Following the reference to the appearance of the risen Christ, who upbraided the eleven 'for their unbelief and hardness of heart, because they had not believed those who saw him after he had risen' (Mark xvi. 14), the text proceeds immediately with the following addition:

And they excused themselves, saying, 'This age of lawlessness and unbelief is under Satan, who does not allow the truth and power of God to prevail over the unclean things of the spirits.[1] Therefore reveal thy righteousness now'—thus they spoke to Christ. And Christ replied to them, 'The term of years for Satan's power has been fulfilled, but other terrible things draw near. And for those who have sinned I was delivered over to death, that they may return to the truth and sin no more; that they may inherit the spiritual and incorruptible glory of righteousness which is in heaven.'[2]

X. Codex Monacensis, now in the University Library at Munich, contains portions of the four Gospels in the order Matthew, John, Luke, and Mark. It dates from the latter part

---

[1] Or, 'does not allow what lies under the unclean spirits to understand the truth and power of God'.

[2] The text of this passage, with notes and commentary, was edited by Caspar René Gregory in *Das Freer-Logion* (Leipzig, 1908).

of the ninth or from the tenth century. Except in Mark the text is interspersed with a patristic commentary, which is written in a contemporary minuscule hand. Though its text is mainly of the Byzantine type, it also contains occasional readings of an earlier type, akin to the Alexandrian text-type.

Z. Codex Dublinensis is an interesting palimpsest in the library of Trinity College, Dublin. It consists of thirty-two leaves and preserves 295 verses of Matthew in large and broad uncials of the sixth (or possibly even fifth) century. The text agrees chiefly with that of codex Sinaiticus. The manuscript was edited by T. K. Abbott in 1880.

Δ. Codex Sangallensis is a ninth-century Graeco-Latin manuscript, the Latin version being written between the lines of the Greek (see Plate XIIIa). It contains the four Gospels complete with the exception of John xix. 17–35. In Mark its text belongs to the Alexandrian type, similar to that of L; in the other Gospels, however, it belongs to the ordinary Koine or Byzantine type. The manuscript was edited by H. C. M. Rettig in 1836.

Θ. Codex Koridethi is the name given to a manuscript of the Gospels which was discovered in the church of Sts. Kerykos and Julitta at Koridethi, located in the Caucasian Mountains near the Caspian Sea; it is now at Tiflis, the capital of the Soviet Socialist Republic of Georgia. Θ is written in a rough, inelegant hand, by a scribe who clearly was not familiar with Greek. Its editors, Gustav Beermann and C. R. Gregory, date the manuscript in the ninth century. In Matthew, Luke, and John the text is similar to the type of text in most Byzantine manuscripts, but in Mark it is quite different; here it is akin to the type of text which Origen and Eusebius used in the third and fourth century at Caesarea.

Λ. Codex Tischendorfianus III, now in the Bodleian Library at Oxford, contains the text of Luke and John in a ninth-century hand characterized by sloping Slavonic uncials. Its text is mainly Byzantine. At the close of the Gospels stands the so-called 'Jerusalem colophon' (see the description of MS. 157 below).

Ξ. One of the most interesting palimpsest manuscripts is codex Zacynthius, a fragmentary codex preserving the greater part of Luke i. 1–xi. 33. It was brought from the isle of Zante in 1821 and is today in the library of the British and Foreign

Bible Society in London. It is the earliest known New Testament manuscript that is provided with a marginal commentary, and it is the only one which has both text and commentary in uncial script. This commentary, which surrounds the single column of the Gospel text on three sides, is a catena of quotations from the exegetical writings of nine Church Fathers. The type of text is Alexandrian, akin to that of codex Vaticanus (B), and it has the same system of chapter divisions, which is peculiar to these two uncial manuscripts and to codex 579. Written in the seventh or eighth century,[1] it was erased in the twelfth or thirteenth century, and the sheets were re-used to receive the text of a Gospel lectionary. It was edited by S. P. Tregelles in 1861.

Π. Codex Petropolitanus is a copy of the four Gospels, almost complete (it lacks seventy-seven verses of Matthew and John). Dating from the ninth century, it contains a Byzantine type of text, being the head of a sub-family which is akin to, but not descended from, codex Alexandrinus. (See below, pp. 264–5.)

Σ. Codex Rossanensis, containing Matthew and Mark, is written on thin vellum stained purple, in silver letters, the first three lines of each Gospel being in gold. Dating from the sixth century, it is the earliest known copy of Scripture which is adorned with contemporary miniatures in water-colours, seventeen in number.[2] These include the raising of Lazarus, the driving of the traders out of the temple, the ten virgins, the entry into Jerusalem, the foot-washing, the last supper, and Jesus before Pilate (see Plate VII). Its text (which was edited by O. von Gebhardt in 1883) is closely akin to that of N, agreeing frequently with the Byzantine type of text, but with certain Caesarean readings as well. The manuscript belongs to the Archbishop of Rossano, at the southern end of Italy.

Φ. Codex Beratinus of the sixth century is (like manuscripts

---

[1] W. H. P. Hatch has argued for a sixth-century date ('The Redating of Two Important Uncial Manuscripts of the Gospels—Codex Zacynthius and Codex Cyprius', *Quantulacumque*, pp. 333–8), but most scholars who have examined the manuscript prefer a later date; see J. H. Greenlee, 'The Catena of Codex Zacynthius', *Biblica*, xl (1959), pp. 992–1001.

[2] A study of the manuscript in its artistic aspects, with photographic reproductions of all the miniatures, was published by A. Haseloff, *Codex Purpureus Rossanensis* (Berlin and Leipzig, 1898). Another reproduction, with the plates in colour, was edited by A. Muñoz, *Il codice purpureo di Rossano* (Rome, 1907). For its textual affinities, see William Sanday in *Studia Biblica*, i (Oxford, 1885), pp. 103–12.

N, O, and *Σ*) a de luxe purple vellum manuscript written with silver ink. It contains only Matthew and Mark, with several considerable lacunae, and is in the possession of the church of St. George at Berat in Albania. Its text (which was edited by P. Batiffol in 1887) is generally of the Koine type, but it contains the long Western addition after Matt. xx. 28, already quoted as occurring in D. According to Streeter the manuscript is a tertiary witness to the Caesarean text.

Ψ. Codex Athous Laurae, as its name implies, is a manuscript in the monastery of the Laura on Mount Athos. Dating from about the eighth or ninth century, it contains the Gospels (from Mark ix onwards), Acts, the Catholic Epistles (in the unusual order of Peter, James, John, and Jude), the Pauline Epistles, and Hebrews (except one leaf of the last). It agrees with L in giving the shorter ending of Mark before the longer one. According to Kirsopp Lake[1] its text in Mark is an early one, with readings both Alexandrian and Western, but chiefly akin to the group *א*, C, L, and *Δ*. The other Gospels are predominantly Byzantine with a somewhat larger proportion of Alexandrian readings than in *Δ*.

Ω. Codex Athous Dionysiou, a complete copy of the four Gospels (except Luke i. 15–28) in the monastery of Dionysius on Mount Athos, dates from the eighth or ninth century. Von Soden classed it as one of the three oldest of the manuscripts which in his opinion present the earliest variety of the Koine or Byzantine text. A collation made by Mary W. Winslow was published in 1932 by Kirsopp Lake and Silva New.[2]

046. Codex Vaticanus 2066, dating from the eighth or ninth century, contains the Book of Revelation between treatises of Basil and Gregory of Nyssa. Previously it was designated B^r or B₂, which gave rise to confusion with the famous codex Vaticanus (B). In text-type it is related to minuscules 61 and 69, with a form of text that differs from the early uncials as well as the later ecclesiastical text.

0171. This numeral is given to two parchment fragments from Egypt dating from the fourth century and containing Luke

---

[1] Lake published the text of Mark and a collation of Luke, John, and Colossians in *Studia Biblica et Ecclesiastica*, v (Oxford, 1903), pp. 94–131.
[2] Kirsopp Lake and Silva New, *Six Collations of New Testament Manuscripts* (*Harvard Theological Studies*, xvii; Cambridge, Massachusetts, 1932), pp. 3–25.

xxi. 45–47, 50–53, and xxii. 44–56, 61–63. According to La-grange it is an important witness in Egypt to the Western text.[1]

0220. This third- or fourth-century parchment leaf of Romans (iv. 5–v. 3 and v. 8–13) was purchased at Cairo in 1950 by Dr. Leland C. Wyman, Professor of Biology at Boston University. The importance of 0220 lies in its agreement with codex Vaticanus everywhere except in v. 1, where it apparently reads the indicative ἔχομεν.[2]

3. IMPORTANT GREEK MINUSCULE MANUSCRIPTS OF THE NEW TESTAMENT

The more important minuscule manuscripts of the New Testament include the following. In several cases scholars have discovered that certain manuscripts exhibit such striking similarities of text-type as to suggest a close 'family' relationship.

Fam. 1. Early in the twentieth century Kirsopp Lake[3] identified a family of witnesses that includes manuscripts 1, 118, 131, and 209, all of which date from the twelfth to the fourteenth centuries. Textual analysis of the Gospel according to Mark indicates that the type of text preserved in these minuscules often agrees with that of codex Θ and appears to go back to the type of text current in Caesarea in the third and fourth centuries.

Fam. 13. In 1868 a professor of Latin at Dublin University, William Hugh Ferrar, discovered that four medieval manuscripts, namely 13, 69, 124, and 346, were closely related textually. His collations were published posthumously in 1877 by his friend and colleague, T. K. Abbott. It is known today that this group (the Ferrar group) comprises about a dozen members (including manuscripts 230, 543, 788, 826, 828, 983, 1689, and 1709). They were copied between the eleventh and fifteenth centuries, and are descendants of an archetype which came either from Calabria in southern Italy or from Sicily.[4] One of the noteworthy features of these manuscripts is that they have the section about the adulterous woman (John vii. 53–viii. 11), not

---

[1] The text is edited in *Pubblicazioni della Società Italiana, Papiri Greci e Latini*, i (Florence, 1912), pp. 2–4, and ii (1913), pp. 22–25.

[2] The leaf was edited by W. H. P. Hatch in the *Harvard Theological Review*, xlv (1952), pp. 81–85. [3] In *Texts and Studies*, vii (2) (Cambridge, 1902).

[4] See Robert Devreesse, *Les Manuscrits grecs de l'Italie méridionale* (*histoire, classement, paléographie*) (= *Studi e testi*, clxxxiii, Città del Vaticano, 1955).

in the Fourth Gospel, but after Luke xxi. 38. Like fam. 1, this family also has affinities with the Caesarean type of text.[1]

MS. 28. This eleventh-century copy of the four Gospels (with lacunae) is carelessly written but contains many noteworthy readings, especially in Mark, where its text is akin to the Caesarean type of text. It is in the Bibliothèque Nationale at Paris; a collation was published by the Lakes.[2]

MS. 33. Since the time of J. G. Eichhorn in the early nineteenth century, MS. 33 has often been called 'the Queen of the cursives'. Now in the Bibliothèque Nationale at Paris, it is an important minuscule codex, containing the entire New Testament except the Book of Revelation and dating from the ninth or possibly tenth century. It is an excellent representative of the Alexandrian type of text, but it shows also the influence of the Koine or Byzantine type, particularly in Acts and the Pauline Epistles.

MS. 61. This manuscript of the entire New Testament, dating from the late fifteenth or early sixteenth century, now at Trinity College, Dublin, has more importance historically than intrinsically. It is the first Greek manuscript discovered which contains the passage relating to the Three Heavenly Witnesses (1 John v. 7–8). It was on the basis of this single, late witness that Erasmus was compelled to insert this certainly spurious passage into the text of 1 John. The manuscript, which is remarkably fresh and clean throughout (except for the two pages containing 1 John v, which are soiled from repeated examination of this passage), gives every appearance of having been produced expressly for the purpose of confuting Erasmus. (See below, p. 101.)

MS. 69. Containing the entire New Testament, this manuscript was copied in the fifteenth century by a Greek named Emmanuel, from Constantinople, who worked for Archbishop Neville of York about 1468.[3] Written partly on vellum and partly on paper, it is an important member of fam. 13 (and was edited by T. K. Abbott with other members of that family). The manuscript is now in the Museum of Leicester, England.

---

[1] Kirsopp and Silva Lake, *Family 13* (*The Ferrar Group*) (*Studies and Documents*, xi, London and Philadelphia, 1941). See below, p. 265.

[2] The collation was published in their monograph, *Family 13*, pp. 117–54.

[3] M. R. James, *Journal of Theological Studies*, v (1904), pp. 445–7; xi (1910), pp. 291–2; and xii (1911), pp. 465–6. See below, p. 265.

MS. 81. Written in the year A.D. 1044, this manuscript, now in the British Museum, is one of the most important of all minuscule manuscripts. It contains the text of Acts in a form which agrees frequently with the Alexandrian type of text. It was collated by Scrivener.[1]

MS. 157. This is a handsome twelfth-century codex of the Gospels, now in the Vatican Library, written for the Emperor John II Comnenus (1118–43). Its text-type resembles that of MS. 33, and was thought by Streeter to belong to the Caesarean text.[2] A colophon, which is also found in a dozen other manuscripts (Λ, 20, 164, 215, 262, 300, 376, 428, 565, 686, 718, and 1071), states that it was copied and corrected 'from the ancient manuscripts at Jerusalem'. This colophon is repeated after each of the four Gospels. A collation of the manuscript was published by H. C. Hoskier.[3]

MS. 383. This is a thirteenth-century codex of the Acts and Epistles (Catholic and Pauline) in the Bodleian Library at Oxford. It was collated by August Pott for his volume, *Der abendländische Text der Apostelgeschichte und die Wir-Quelle* (Leipzig, 1900), pp. 78–88, and was used by A. C. Clark in his reconstruction of the Western text of Acts.

MS. 565. One of the most beautiful of all known manuscripts, 565 is now in the public library at Leningrad. It is a de luxe copy of the Gospels, written in gold letters on purple vellum during the ninth or tenth century.[4] In Mark it is an ally of Θ in support of the Caesarean text. At the close of Mark it contains the so-called 'Jerusalem colophon' (see the description of codex 157).

MS. 579. This is a thirteenth-century copy of the Gospels in Paris.[5] In Matthew its text belongs to the late Byzantine group, but in the other Gospels it preserves an extremely good

---

[1] F. H. Scrivener, *An Exact Transcript of the Codex Augiensis . . . to which is added a Full Collation of Fifty Manuscripts* (Cambridge, 1859).

[2] See the article cited in n. 2 on p. 55 above.

[3] *Journal of Theological Studies*, xiv (1913), pp. 78 ff., 242 ff., 359 ff.

[4] The text of Mark and a collation of Matthew, Luke, and John were published by Johannes Belsheim in *Christiania Videnskabs-Selskabs Forhandlinger*, 1885, Nr. 9. Corrections of Belsheim's edition were included by H. S. Cronin in *Texts and Studies*, v (4) (Cambridge, 1899), pp. 106–8.

[5] Alfred Schmidtke published an edition of Mark, Luke, and John in his *Die Evangelien eines alten Uncialcodex (BN-Text) nach einer Abschrift des dreizehnten Jahrhunderts* (Leipzig, 1903).

Alexandrian text which often agrees with B, ℵ, and L. Like MS. L, it contains the double ending of Mark.

MS. 614. A thirteenth-century codex of Acts and the Epistles (Pauline and Catholic) from Corfu, MS. 614 is now in the Ambrosian Library at Milan. It contains a large number of pre-Byzantine readings, many of them of the Western type of text.[1]

MS. 700. This eleventh- or twelfth-century codex of the Gospels, now in the British Museum, diverges 2,724 times from the Textus Receptus, and has besides 270 readings peculiar to itself.[2] Along with one other Greek manuscript (no. 162) it has the remarkable reading in the Lucan form of the Lord's Prayer, 'Thy Holy Spirit come upon us and cleanse us', instead of 'Thy kingdom come' (xi. 2). This was also the text of the Lord's Prayer known to Marcion and Gregory of Nyssa.[3]

MS. 892. This is a ninth- or tenth-century codex of the four Gospels, acquired by the British Museum in 1887.[4] It contains many remarkable readings of an early type, belonging chiefly to the Alexandrian text. Von Soden observed that the scribe of 892 preserved the divisions in pages and lines of its uncial parent.

MS. 1071. This twelfth-century copy of the four Gospels, now in the Laura on Mount Athos, contains the so-called 'Jerusalem colophon' referred to above in the description of codex 157.[5] Streeter classified its text as a tertiary witness to the Caesarean type of text.

MS. 1241. MS. 1241, containing the whole New Testament except the Book of Revelation, dates from the twelfth or thirteenth century.[6] In the Gospels its text agrees frequently with

[1] An edition prepared by A. V. Valentine-Richards was published posthumously, with an introduction by J. M. Creed (Cambridge, 1934).

[2] A collation was published by H. C. Hoskier in *A Full Account and Collation of the Greek Cursive Codex Evangelium 604* (London, 1890).

[3] For what can be said in support of the opinion that this variant reading stood in the original text of Luke, see Robert Leaney in *Novum Testamentum*, i (1956), pp. 103–11; for a statement of the view that this form of the Lord's Prayer represents a modification of the usual form for use at special services (such as ordination), see the present writer's discussion in the *Twentieth Century Encyclopedia of Religious Knowledge*, ii (1955), pp. 673 f.

[4] A collation was published by J. R. Harris in the *Journal of Biblical Literature*, ix (1890), pp. 31–59.

[5] A collation of Mark and of several chapters from the other Gospels was published by Kirsopp Lake in *Studia Biblica et Ecclesiastica*, v (Oxford, 1903), pp. 140–8.

[6] A collation of the Gospels was published by Kirsopp Lake in the volume mentioned in n. 2, p. 60 above.

C, L, *Δ*, *Ψ*, and 33. According to Kirsopp Lake, in Matthew and Mark its text shows a larger infusion of Byzantine readings than in Luke and John.

Fam. 1424. Codex 1424 is a ninth- or tenth-century copy of the entire New Testament, written by a monk named Sabas in the sequence of Gospels, Acts, Catholic Epistles, Revelation, and Pauline Epistles. All the books except Revelation are supplied with a commentary, which is written in the margins. Formerly in the monastery at Drama (Turkish Kosinitza) in Greece, it was probably taken thence to western Europe after the Balkan wars of 1912–13. It was bought by Dr. L. Franklin Gruber, president of the Chicago Lutheran Theological Seminary at Maywood, Illinois, and bequeathed at his death to the Seminary library. According to von Soden its text in the Gospels belongs to his I^ϕ-group, which Streeter renamed fam. 1424 and classified as a tertiary witness to the Caesarean text. In addition to MS. 1424, which is the oldest minuscule of the family, the other members of the family are M, 7, 27, 71, 115 (Matt., Mark), 160 (Matt., Mark), 179 (Matt., Mark), 185 (Luke, John), 267, 349, 517, 659, 692 (Matt., Mark), 827 (Matt., Mark), 945, 954, 990 (Matt., Mark), 1010, 1082 (Matt., Mark), 1188 (Luke, John), 1194, 1207, 1223, 1293, 1391, 1402 (Matt., Mark), 1606, 1675, and 2191 (Matt., Mark).

MS. 1739. Containing the Acts and the Epistles, this tenth-century manuscript was discovered at Mount Athos in 1879 by E. von der Goltz, and is usually known by his name.[1] It is of extreme importance because it contains a number of marginal notes taken from the writings of Irenaeus, Clement, Origen, Eusebius, and Basil. Since nothing is more recent than Basil, who lived from A.D. 329 to 379, it appears that the ancestor of this manuscript was written by a scribe toward the close of the fourth century. A colophon indicates that for the Pauline Epistles the scribe followed a manuscript which contained an Origenian text. It is, however, not of the Caesarean type but presents a relatively pure form of the Alexandrian type of text.

MS. 2053. This is a thirteenth-century manuscript at Messina, containing the text of the Book of Revelation with Oecumenius' commentary on it. Along with codices A, C, and 2344, it is

---

[1] A collation made by Morton S. Enslin was published in the volume mentioned in n. 2, p. 60 above.

(according to Schmid[1]) one of the best sources for the text of the Apocalypse, superior even to 𝔭⁴⁷ and ℵ.

MS. 2344. An eleventh-century codex now in the Bibliothèque Nationale at Paris, MS. 2344 contains Acts, the Catholic Epistles, Pauline Epistles, and Revelation (where it agrees frequently with MS. 2053), besides parts of the Old Testament.

4. OTHER NOTEWORTHY MANUSCRIPTS

Manuscripts which are noteworthy because of their external format include the following. An uncial copy of the four Gospels,[2] no. 047, dating from the ninth or tenth century and now at Princeton University Library, has the writing on each page arranged in the form of a cross; that is, the lines comprising the top third of the column and those of the bottom third are about one-half the length of the lines comprising the middle section of the column.

Codex 16, a fourteenth-century copy of the four Gospels in Greek and Latin, formerly in the possession of Catherine de Medici and now in the Bibliothèque Nationale at Paris, is written in four colours of ink according to the contents. The general run of the narrative is in vermilion; the words of Jesus, the genealogy of Jesus, and the words of angels are in crimson; the words quoted from the Old Testament, as well as those of the disciples, Zachariah, Elizabeth, Mary, Simeon, and John the Baptist, are in blue; and the words of the Pharisees, the centurion, Judas Iscariot, and the devil are in black. The words of the shepherds are also in black, but this may well have been an oversight.

One of the smallest Greek manuscripts containing the four Gospels is MS. 461, now in the public library at Leningrad. There are 344 leaves, each of which measures $6\frac{3}{8}$ by $3\frac{7}{8}$ inches; the single column of writing occupies an area of about $4\frac{1}{2}$ by $2\frac{3}{8}$ inches. This manuscript is noteworthy also because it is the earliest dated Greek minuscule manuscript known to exist, having been copied in A.D. 835.[3]

---

[1] Josef Schmid, *Studien zur Geschichte des griechischen Apokalypse-Textes:* 2. Teil, *Die alten Stämme* (Munich, 1955), p. 24.

[2] Collated by William Sanday, *Revue biblique,* iv (1895), pp. 201–13.

[3] The earliest known Biblical manuscript which bears a date is apparently a palimpsest fragment of Isaiah in Syriac, written A.D. 459–60, now in the British Museum; for a description of it, see E. Tisserant, 'Le plus ancien manuscrit

Even more tiny must have been the vellum codex of the Book of Revelation of which only one leaf is extant (MS. 0169, now in the library of Princeton Theological Seminary; see Plate VI*b*). Discovered at Oxyrhynchus in Egypt and dating from the fourth century, the page measures only 3¾ by 2⅞ inches—truly a pocket edition![1]

What is without doubt the largest Biblical codex is the so-called codex Gigas ('the giant codex'), now at Stockholm, which when lying open measures about 40 inches across the two pages and 36 inches high (see pp. 74 f. below). It is said that the hides of 160 asses were required for its production.

II. ANCIENT VERSIONS OF THE NEW TESTAMENT[2]

The earliest versions of the New Testament were prepared by missionaries to assist in the propagation of the Christian faith among peoples whose native tongue was Syriac, Latin, or Coptic. Besides being of great value to the Biblical exegete as he traces the history of the interpretation of the Scriptures, these versions are of no less importance to the textual critic in view of their origin in the second and third centuries. At the same time, however, it must be observed that there are certain limitations in the use of versions for the textual criticism of the New Testament. Not only were some of the translations prepared by persons who had an imperfect command of Greek,[3] but certain

biblique daté', *Revue biblique*, viii (1911), pp. 85–92. For an early dated Greek uncial manuscript, see the description of codex S.

[1] One of the smallest Latin codices of the Gospels, measuring 5 by 4 inches and furnished with illuminations, is described by Françoise Henry, 'An Irish Manuscript in the British Museum (Add. 40618)', *Journal of the Royal Society of Antiquaries of Ireland*, lxxxvii (1957), pp. 147-66. Eight other examples of small books are discussed by Patrick McGurk in his article 'The Irish Pocket Gospel Book', *Sacris Erudiri*, viii (1956), pp. 249-70. These manuscripts, all of which date from the seventh to the ninth century, are written in a very small script, with a large number of abbreviations. They are also distinguished by a capricious and irregular use of one, two, or three columns to the page for the same manuscript, and by all sorts of fanciful arrangements of the text on the page. See below, p. 265.

[2] For the history of scholarly research on the early versions, reference may be made to Arthur Vööbus, *Early Versions of the New Testament, Manuscript Studies* (Stockholm, 1954), and, more briefly, the chapter on 'The Evidence of the Versions for the Text of the New Testament' by the present writer in *New Testament Manuscript Studies*, ed. by Parvis and Wikgren (Chicago, 1950). See below, p. 265.

[3] Cf. St. Augustine's complaint of early translators of the Bible into Latin, that 'no sooner did anyone gain possession of a Greek manuscript, and imagine himself to have any facility in both languages (however slight that might be), than he made bold to translate it' (*De doctr. Christ.* II. xi [16]).

features of Greek syntax and vocabulary cannot be conveyed in
a translation. For example, Latin has no definite article; Syriac
cannot distinguish between the Greek aorist and perfect tenses;
Coptic lacks the passive voice and must use a circumlocution.
In some cases, therefore, the testimony of these versions is ambiguous. As for other questions, however, such as whether or not
a given phrase or sentence was present in the Greek exemplar
from which the translation was made, the evidence of the versions is clear and valuable.[1]

The study of the early versions of the New Testament is complicated by the circumstance that various persons made various translations from various Greek manuscripts. Furthermore,
copies of a translation in a certain language were sometimes
corrected one against the other or against Greek manuscripts
other than the ones from which the translation was originally
made. Thus the reconstruction of a critical edition of an ancient
version is often more complicated than the editing of the original Greek text itself. On the other hand, however, in tracing
the internal history of a version the scholar has the advantage
of divergent renderings (*Übersetzungsfarbe*) to aid him. Greek
text-types can be differentiated by variant readings alone,
whereas in manuscripts of the versions the same Greek reading
may be represented by different renderings. By means of such
variant renderings as well as variant readings, the several
stages in the evolution of a version may be traced in the manuscript tradition.

The most significant of the early versions of the New Testament are the following.

I. THE SYRIAC VERSIONS

Scholars have distinguished five different Syriac versions of
all or part of the New Testament. They are the Old Syriac, the
Peshitta (or common version), the Philoxenian, the Harclean,
and the Palestinian Syriac version.

(*a*) *The Old Syriac version* of the four Gospels is preserved today in two manuscripts, both of which have large gaps. They
are (1) a parchment manuscript now in the British Museum,

---

[1] See A. F. J. Klijn, 'The Value of the Versions for the Textual Criticism of the
New Testament', translated by H. H. Oliver in *The Bible Translator*, viii (1957),
pp. 127–30. See below, p. 265.

written in a clear and beautiful Estrangela hand (see Plate XIIa);
it was edited by William Cureton in 1858 and is usually referred
to as Syr^c; and (2) a palimpsest manuscript which Mrs. Agnes
Smith Lewis discovered in the monastery of St. Catharine on
Mount Sinai in 1892; it is called Syr^s. Though these manuscripts were copied in about the fifth and fourth centuries
respectively, the form of text which they preserve dates from the
close of the second or beginning of the third century. When the
two manuscripts are compared it is seen that the Sinaitic Syriac
represents a slightly earlier form of text than does the Curetonian, even though in some places it may have corruptions which
the Curetonian has escaped. How far the text of the separated
Gospels was influenced by the Gospel Harmony which Tatian
prepared about A.D. 170 (see pp. 89–92 below) has been much
debated. In general the Old Syriac version is a representative of
the Western type of text.

The Old Syriac version of Acts and the Pauline Epistles has
not survived *in extenso*; we know it only through citations
made by Eastern Fathers. In the case of Acts, F. C. Conybeare
reconstructed Ephraem's commentary from Armenian sources,
of which a Latin translation is published in J. H. Ropes's *The
Text of Acts* (London, 1926), pp. 373–453. Ephraem's text of
the Pauline Epistles was reconstructed by Joseph Molitor, *Der
Paulustext des hl. Ephräm (Monumenta biblica et ecclesiastica*, vol. iv,
Rome, 1938).

Editions: William Cureton, *Remains of a Very Antient Recension of the
Four Gospels in Syriac* . . . (London, 1858); F. Crawford Burkitt,
*Evangelion da-Mepharreshe: the Curetonian Version of the Four Gospels,
with the Readings of the Sinai-Palimpsest* . . ., 2 vols. (Cambridge, 1904);
Agnes Smith Lewis, *The Old Syriac Gospels* . . . (London, 1910);
Arthur Hjelt, *Syrus Sinaiticus* (Helsingfors, 1930) [photographic
facsimile].

(*b*) *The Peshitta version, or Syriac Vulgate*, of the New Testament
(Syr^p) was prepared about the beginning of the fifth century,
probably in order to supplant the divergent, competing Old
Syriac translations. It contains only twenty-two books; 2 Peter,
2 and 3 John, Jude, and Revelation were not translated. Until recently scholars thought that Rabbula, Bishop of Edessa
(A.D. 411–31), was responsible for the Peshitta, but it is more
likely that his revision marked an intermediate stage between the

F

Old Syriac text and the final form of the Peshitta.[1] Because the Peshitta was accepted as the standard version of the Scriptures by both Eastern and Western branches of Syrian Christendom, one must conclude that it had attained some degree of status prior to the split in the Syrian Church in A.D. 431.

More than 350 manuscripts of the Peshitta New Testament are known today, several of which date from the fifth and sixth centuries. The text of the Peshitta has been transmitted with remarkable fidelity, so that very few significant variants exist among the witnesses. The textual complexion of the Peshitta version has not yet been satisfactorily investigated, but apparently it represents the work of several hands in various parts of the New Testament. In the Gospels it is closer to the Byzantine type of text than in Acts, where it presents many striking agreements with the Western text.

Editions: P. E. Pusey and G. H. Gwilliam, *Tetraevangelium sanctum iuxta simplicem Syrorum versionem ad fidem codicum* . . . (Oxford, 1901) [based on forty-two manuscripts; with a critical apparatus and a Latin translation]; *The New Testament in Syriac* (London, 1905–20) [published by the British and Foreign Bible Society; the Gospels are reprinted from Pusey and Gwilliam's text (without apparatus), and the rest of the New Testament was edited by Gwilliam and J. Gwynn].

(c) *The Philoxenian and/or Harclean version(s)*. One of the most confused and confusing tangles of textual criticism involves the unravelling of the Philoxenian and/or Harclean version(s), usually abbreviated Syr^ph and Syr^h. The scanty evidence in several colophons found in certain Harclean manuscripts has been interpreted in quite different ways. On the one hand, it has been held that the Syriac version produced in A.D. 508 for Philoxenus, Bishop of Mabbug, by Polycarp his chorepiscopus was re-issued in 616 by Thomas of Harkel (Heraclea), Bishop of Mabbug, who merely added marginal notes derived from two or three Greek manuscripts. On the other hand, it has been held that the Philoxenian version was thoroughly revised by Thomas, who also added in the margin certain readings which he considered to be important but not worthy of inclusion in the text. In other words, according to the first view, there is but one version which was republished with variant readings noted in

[1] See Arthur Vööbus, *Studies in the History of the Gospel Text in Syriac* (Louvain, 1951).

the margin; according to the second, there are two separate versions entirely, the later one being provided with marginalia. It is not necessary to attempt to decide this complicated problem here; in any case during the sixth century, for the first time in the history of the Syriac-speaking Churches, the minor Catholic Epistles and Revelation were translated into Syriac. The Harclean apparatus of Acts is the second most important witness to the Western text, being surpassed in this respect only by codex Bezae.

Editions: Joseph White, *Sacrorum Evangeliorum Versio Syriaca Philoxeniana* (Oxford, 1778); id., *Actuum Apostolorum et Epistolarum tam Catholicarum quam Paulinarum Versio Syriaca Philoxeniana* (Oxford, 1799–1803); R. L. Bensly, *The Harklean Version of the Epistle to the Hebrews, Chap. XI. 28–XIII. 25* (Cambridge, 1889); John Gwynn, *The Apocalypse of St. John, in a Syriac Version Hitherto Unknown . . .* (Dublin and London, 1897); id., *Remnants of the Later Syriac Versions of the Bible . . . The Four Minor Catholic Epistles in the Original Philoxenian Version . . . and John VII. 52–VIII. 12 . . .* (London and Oxford, 1909). [The text of the Apocalypse and of the minor Catholic Epistles is included in the British and Foreign Bible Society's edition of the Peshitta.]

(*d*) *The Palestinian Syriac version.* The translation into Christian Palestinian Syriac (i.e. Aramaic) is known chiefly from a lectionary of the Gospels, preserved in three manuscripts dating from the eleventh and twelfth centuries. In addition fragments of the Gospels, in a continuous text, are extant, as well as scraps of Acts and of several of the Pauline Epistles. When this version (abbreviated Syr[pal]) was made has been much disputed, but most scholars think that it dates from about the fifth century. Apparently it is based on a Greek text of the Caesarean type, and is quite independent of the other Syriac versions.

Editions: Agnes Smith Lewis and Margaret Dunlop Gibson, *The Palestinian Syriac Lectionary of the Gospels* (London, 1899); Agnes Smith Lewis, *Codex Climaci rescriptus* (*Horae semiticae*, viii, Cambridge, 1908) [contains fragments of the Gospels, Acts, and Pauline Epistles]; for other fragments, see Cyril Moss, *Catalogue of Syriac Printed Books and Related Literature in the British Museum* (London, 1962), to which should be added Nina V. Pigulevskaya, *Katalog siriĭskikh rukopiseĭ Leningrada* (= *Palestinskiĭ sbornik*, issued by the Akademiya Nauk S.S.S.R., vi [69], 1960, pp. 3–230). See below, p. 265.

2. THE LATIN VERSIONS

When and where it was that the earliest attempts were made to translate the Bible into Latin has been much disputed. In the opinion of most scholars today the Gospels were first rendered into Latin during the last quarter of the second century in North Africa, where Carthage had become enamoured of Roman culture. Not long afterward translations were also made in Italy, Gaul, and elsewhere. The wooden and literalistic style that characterizes many of these renderings suggests that early copies were made in the form of interlinear renderings of the Greek (compare Plate XIII*a*). (See below, p. 265.)

(*a*) *The Old Latin version(s)*. During the third century many Old Latin versions circulated in North Africa and Europe, including distinctive versions which were current in Italy, Gaul, and Spain. Divergent renderings of the same verse (e.g. at Luke xxiv. 4–5 there are at least twenty-seven variant readings in the Old Latin manuscripts that have survived) bear out Jerome's complaint to Pope Damasus that there were almost as many versions as manuscripts (*tot enim sunt exemplaria paene quot codices*).[1]

No codex of the entire Old Latin Bible is extant. The Gospels are represented by about thirty-two mutilated manuscripts, besides a number of fragments. About a dozen manuscripts of Acts are extant. There are four manuscripts and several fragments of the Pauline Epistles but only one complete manuscript and several fragments of the Apocalypse. These witnesses date from the fourth century to the thirteenth century, thus proving that the Old Latin version was still copied long after it had gone out of general use. The Old Latin manuscripts are designated in a critical apparatus by small letters of the Latin alphabet.[2]

The textual complexion of the Old Latin version(s) is typically Western. As a rule the form of the Old Latin current in Africa presents the greater divergencies from the Greek, and that current in Europe the smaller.

The most important witnesses of the Old Latin versions are the following (grouped according to the African and European types of text).

---

[1] See St. Jerome's preface (*Novum opus*) to his translation of the four Gospels.
[2] For a complete list, see Bonifatius Fischer, *Vetus Latina*: i, *Verzeichnis der Sigel* (Freiburg, 1949), or Teófilo Ayuso Marazuela, *La Vetus Latina Hispana*: i, *Prolegómenos* (Madrid, 1953), pp. 224–7.

African Old Latin manuscripts

e. Codex Palatinus, designated by the symbol *e*, is a fifth-century manuscript containing portions of the four Gospels, written with silver ink on purple parchment. Though the type of text in *e* is basically African, it has been strongly europeanized. Augustine probably employed a Gospel text of this kind before A.D. 400.

h. The symbol *h* is given to the fragmentary sixth-century manuscript known as the Fleury palimpsest, which contains about one-quarter of Acts, besides portions of the Catholic Epistles and the Book of Revelation. The manuscript contains many scribal errors, and the rendering into Latin is often very free; for example, the narrative of Paul's voyage, Acts xxviii. 1–13, appears to be a corrupt form of an abridgement made by the translator.

k. The most important witness to the African Old Latin is codex Bobbiensis, to which the symbol *k* has been assigned. Unfortunately, it is quite fragmentary, containing only about half of Matthew and Mark. It was copied about A.D. 400 in Africa and brought to the Irish monastery of Bobbio in northern Italy, where it was preserved for many centuries until it found a home in the National Library at Turin, where it is now. Its form of text agrees very closely with the quotations made by St. Cyprian of Carthage (about A.D. 250). According to E. A. Lowe[1] *k* shows palaeographical marks of having been copied from a second-century papyrus. It is noteworthy that *k* contains the intermediate ending of the Gospel according to Mark (see pp. 226–9 below).

European Old Latin manuscripts

a. What is probably the oldest European manuscript of the Gospels is codex Vercellensis (known by the symbol *a*), kept in the cathedral treasure room at Vercelli in northern Italy. According to an old tradition it was written by the hand of St. Eusebius, Bishop of Vercelli, who was martyred in 370 or 371. Next to *k* it is the most important Old Latin manuscript of the Gospels.

b. Codex Veronensis (*b*), in the possession of the Chapter

---

[1] Reported by D. Plooij in the *Bulletin of the Bezan Club*, xi (1936), p. 11.

Library of the cathedral at Verona, Italy, is a purple parchment manuscript written in the fifth century with silver and occasionally gold ink. It contains the four Gospels (almost in their entirety) in the order of Matthew, John, Luke, and Mark. According to Burkitt's opinion it represents the type of text which Jerome used as the basis of the Vulgate.

c. Codex Colbertinus, written in the twelfth century, probably in southern France, is now in the Bibliothèque Nationale at Paris, and contains the four Gospels in a mixed form of text. Clear traces of African readings persist in what is generally a European Old Latin text contaminated here and there by Jerome's Vulgate.

d. The Latin side of the fifth- or sixth-century bilingual codex Bezae (D), though corrected here and there from the Greek side, preserves an ancient form of Old Latin text. Since *d* agrees occasionally with readings of *k* and of *a* when all other authorities differ, it witnesses to a text that was current no later than the first half of the third century, and may be earlier still.

*ff*². Codex Corbiensis is a mutilated copy of the four Gospels, of the fifth or sixth century, formerly belonging to the monastery of Corbey, near Amiens, and now in the Bibliothèque Nationale at Paris. It contains a form of text akin to that preserved in *a* and *b*.

gig. What is undoubtedly one of the largest manuscripts in the world is appropriately named codex Gigas (the 'giant').[1] Each page measures about 20 inches wide and 36 inches high, and when the codex lies open it makes an impressive sight. Written in the early part of the thirteenth century at the Benedictine monastery of Podlažic in Bohemia, it was later acquired by the Imperial Treasury in Prague. When the Swedish army conquered the city in 1648, it was brought to Sweden and presented to the Royal Library in Stockholm the following year.

In addition to the text of the entire Bible in Latin, the 'giant' manuscript contains Isidore of Seville's *Etymologiae* (a general encyclopedia in twenty books), a Latin translation of Flavius Josephus' *Antiquities of the Jews*, Cosmas of Prague's *Chronicle of Bohemia*, as well as other works. It is sometimes called the Devil's Bible (*Djävulsbibeln*) because fol. 290 contains a huge picture of that potentate in garish colours, with horns, forked tongue, and

---

[1] For a description of the manuscript and its contents, see B. Dudík, *Forschungen in Schweden für Mährens Geschichte* (Brünn, 1852), pp. 207–35.

claws on fingers and toes (see Plate XIII*b*). According to legend the scribe was a monk who had been confined to his cell for some breach of monastic discipline and who, by way of penance, finished the manuscript in a single night with the aid of the devil, whom he had summoned to help him.

Codex Gigas is of importance to textual critics because the Book of Acts and the Book of Revelation preserve a form of Old Latin text which agrees with the scriptural quotations made by Lucifer of Cagliari (in Sardinia) about the middle of the fourth century.

m. This symbol is used to refer to a patristic collection of Biblical passages arranged by topics to illustrate special points of conduct. The treatise is frequently called *Speculum* (the Latin word meaning 'mirror' [for conduct]), and is preserved in a number of manuscripts, of which the oldest is of the eighth or ninth century. The scriptural quotations are in a Spanish form of the African Old Latin text, agreeing (in the Catholic Epistles) almost *ad litteram* with the quotations of Priscillian, who in 385 was condemned at Treves for magic (*maleficium*) and executed— the first person to be.put to death by the Church.

Editions: The more important manuscripts of the Old Latin Bible have been published in two series entitled *Old Latin Biblical Texts*, 7 vols. (Oxford, 1883 onwards) and *Collectanea biblica latina*, 8 vols. so far (Rome, 1912 onwards). The most satisfactory edition of the Old Latin texts of the Gospels is the series entitled *Itala: das Neue Testament in altlateinischer Überlieferung*, begun by Adolf Jülicher and continued by W. Matzkow and Kurt Aland. The Vetus-Latina-Institut at the monastery of Beuron in Württemberg, Germany, under the leadership of Fr. Bonifatius Fischer, has begun to issue fascicles of an edition entitled *Vetus Latina: die Reste der altlateinischen Bibel*. This ambitious project seeks to assemble from manuscripts and quotations made by Church Fathers all the evidence of the Latin Bible as it circulated prior to the revision undertaken by St. Jerome. According to information received from the director of the project, considerably more than one million quotations from both Testaments have been thus far collected and filed. See below, p. 266.

(*b*) *The Latin Vulgate.* Toward the close of the fourth century the limitations and imperfections of the Old Latin versions became evident to the leaders of the Roman Church. It is not surprising that about A.D. 382 Pope Damasus requested the most capable Biblical scholar then living, Sophronius Eusebius Hieronymus, known today as St. Jerome, to undertake a revision of the Latin Bible. Within a year or so Jerome was able to present Damasus with the first-fruits of his work—a revision of the text of the four Gospels, where the variations had been extreme. In a covering letter he explains the principles which he followed: he used a relatively good Latin text as the basis for his revision, and compared it with some old Greek manuscripts. He emphasizes that he treated the current Latin text as conservatively as possible, and changed it only where the meaning was distorted. Though we do not have the Latin manuscripts which Jerome chose as the basis of his work, it appears that they belonged to the European form of the Old Latin (perhaps they were similar to manuscript *b*). The Greek manuscripts apparently belonged to the Alexandrian type of text.

When and how thoroughly Jerome revised the rest of the New Testament has been much debated. Several scholars (De Bruyne, Cavallera, B. Fischer) have argued that Jerome had nothing to do with the making of the Vulgate text of the rest of the New Testament, but that, by a curious twist of literary history, the work of some other translator came to be circulated as Jerome's work. The commonly accepted view, however, rests upon the natural interpretation of what Jerome says about his work of revision. In either case, it is apparent that the rest of the New Testament was revised in a much more cursory manner than were the Gospels. (See below, pp. 266–7.)

It was inevitable that, in the course of the transmission of the text of Jerome's revision, scribes would corrupt his original work, sometimes by careless transcription and sometimes by deliberate conflation with copies of the Old Latin versions. In order to purify Jerome's text a number of recensions or editions were produced during the Middle Ages; notable among these were the successive efforts of Alcuin, Theodulf, Lanfranc, and Stephen Harding. Unfortunately, however, each of these attempts to restore Jerome's original version resulted eventually in still further textual corruption through mixture of the several types of Vulgate text which had come to be associated with various European centres of scholarship. As a result, the more than 8,000 Vulgate manuscripts which are extant today exhibit the greatest amount of cross-contamination of textual types.

The most noteworthy of these manuscripts include the following (they are usually denoted by capital letters or sometimes by the first syllable of their names).

A. Codex Amiatinus, in the Laurentian Library at Florence, is a magnificent manuscript containing the whole Bible. It was written by order of Ceolfrid, Abbot of Jarrow and Wearmouth, and sent by him as a gift to Pope Gregory in 716. Many scholars regard it as the best manuscript of the Vulgate. (See Plate I*b*.)

C. Codex Cavensis, dating from the ninth century, is in the La Cava monastery near Salerno. It contains the whole Bible and is one of the chief representatives of the Spanish group of manuscripts.

D. Codex Dublinensis, or the Book of Armagh, is at Trinity College, Dublin. Dating from the eighth or ninth century, it contains the whole New Testament as well as the apocryphal Epistle of Paul to the Laodiceans. It presents the Irish type of Vulgate text, which is characterized by small additions and insertions. Here and there it shows signs of having been corrected from Greek manuscripts akin to the Ferrar group (fam. 13). (See below, p. 267.)

F. Codex Fuldensis, now in the Landesbibliothek at Fulda, was written between A.D. 541 and 546 at Capua by order of Victor, the bishop of that see, and was corrected by him personally. It contains the whole New Testament, together with the apocryphal Epistle to the Laodiceans. The Gospels are arranged in a single, consecutive narrative, in imitation of Tatian's Diatessaron (see pp. 89–91 below). Its text, which is very good, is akin to that of codex Amiatinus.

M. Codex Mediolanensis, in the Ambrosian Library at Milan, is a Gospels manuscript of the early sixth century. In the judgement of Wordsworth and White it ranks with Amiatinus and Fuldensis as one of the best witnesses of the Vulgate.

Y. The celebrated Lindisfarne Gospels, of about A.D. 700, now in the British Museum, is a beautifully executed codex, adorned with Celtic-Saxon illumination. It is furnished with an Anglo-Saxon interlinear gloss—the earliest form of the Gospels in the ancestor of English. Its text is closely akin to that of Amiatinus.

Z. Codex Harleianus, formerly in the Royal Library at Paris, was stolen from there, as it seems, by Jean Aymon in 1707 and sold to Robert Harley, who deposited it in the British Museum. It is a beautifully written copy of the Gospels, dating from the sixth or seventh century.

Σ. Codex Sangallensis, the oldest known manuscript of the Vulgate Gospels, was written in Italy probably towards the close of the fifth century.[1] More than half of it survives at the monastery of St. Gall and in other libraries. Unfortunately, Wordsworth and White overlooked this important manuscript in preparing their edition of the Vulgate.

P. What has been called one of the finest, if not *the* finest of purple manuscripts in existence is the Golden Gospels now in the J. Pierpont Morgan Library, New York. Written entirely in letters of burnished gold on purple parchment, this sumptuous codex contains a Vulgate Latin text with Northumbrian and Irish affinities. Previously thought to date from the close of the seventh or the beginning of the eighth century, it has lately been assigned to the tenth century.[2]

Editions: The decision of the Council of Trent (1546) to prepare an authentic edition of the Latin Scriptures was finally taken up by Pope Sixtus V, who authorized its publication in 1590. The Sixtine Vulgate was issued with a papal bull threatening the major excommunication for violators of the commands that variant readings should not be printed in subsequent editions, and that the edition must not be modified. (According to Steinmüller,[3] however, this bull 'today is commonly recognized as not having been properly and canonically promulgated'.) In 1592, after the death of Sixtus, Pope Clement VIII called in all the copies he could find and issued another authentic edition—differing from the former in some 4,900 variants! This latter edition remains the official Latin Bible text of the Roman Catholic Church to the present day. See below, p. 267.

Since 1907 work has been going forward among Benedictine scholars on a revised edition of the Latin Vulgate; most of the Old Testament volumes have now been published. Another project involving a critical edition of the New Testament, with an apparatus,

[1] Lowe thinks that it may have been copied 'possibly during the lifetime of Jerome'; see E. A. Lowe, *Codices Latini Antiquiores*, vii (Oxford, 1956), p. 41.

[2] The earlier date was advocated by Wattenbach, de Rossi, Gregory, and its editor, H. C. Hoskier, *The Golden Latin Gospels in the Library of J. Pierpont Morgan* (New York, 1910); the later date was recently proposed by E. A. Lowe in 'The Morgan Golden Gospels: The Date and Origin of the Manuscript', *Studies in Art and Literature for Belle da Costa Greene*, ed. by Dorothy Miner (Princeton, 1954), pp. 266–79.

[3] John E. Steinmüller, *A Companion to Scripture Studies*, i (New York, 1941), p. 192.

was published at Oxford by a group of Anglican scholars. Begun by Bishop John Wordsworth and H. J. White, the first volume, containing the text of the four Gospels, was issued in 1899; the last volume, containing the Book of Revelation, was completed by H. F. D. Sparks in 1954. For a judicious appraisal of the adequacy of the Oxford Vulgate (the volume containing the Gospels suffered particularly from the editors' inexperience), see Bonifatius Fischer in *Zeitschrift für die neutestamentliche Wissenschaft*, xlvi (1955), pp. 178–96.

3. THE COPTIC VERSIONS

Coptic is the latest form of the ancient Egyptian language, which until Christian times was written in hieroglyphs and their two derivatives, hieratic and demotic script. In the first centuries of the Christian era the language came to be written in Greek uncials, with the addition of seven characters taken from demotic.

During the early Christian period the old Egyptian language was represented in at least half a dozen dialectal forms throughout Egypt, differing from one another chiefly in phonetics but also to some extent in vocabulary and syntax as well. In the southern part of the country, called Upper Egypt, the Sahidic dialect prevailed from Thebes to the south. Around the delta in the northern part of Egypt, called Lower Egypt, the Bohairic dialect was used along with Greek. At various settlements along the Nile between these two parts of the country there developed intermediate dialects, chiefly the Fayyumic (formerly known as Bashmuric), Memphitic (or Middle Egyptian), Achmimic, and sub-Achmimic (used south of Asyut).

Of these dialects the Sahidic and the Bohairic are the most important for the study of early versions of the Bible. About the beginning of the third century portions of the New Testament were translated into Sahidic, and within the following century most of the books of the New Testament became available in that dialect. Indeed, to judge on the basis of widely divergent Sahidic texts, some parts of the Scriptures were translated at various times by independent translators. In general the Sahidic version agrees with the Alexandrian form of text, but in the Gospels and Acts it has many Western readings. Unfortunately, when Horner prepared his edition of this version only fragmentary manuscripts were available.[1] Subsequently the Pierpont

---

[1] What has been thought to be the oldest Sahidic manuscript of those used by Horner is a papyrus codex containing portions of Deuteronomy, Jonah, and the

Morgan Library in New York acquired a large collection of Coptic manuscripts, most of which are complete. Among them is a Sahidic tetraevangelium (Morgan MS. 569) dating from the eighth or ninth century and preserving Matthew, Mark, and John in their entirety; Luke lacks fourteen leaves. The collection of manuscripts is now available in photographic reproduction in fifty-six folio volumes prepared by Henri Hyvernat. Mr. A. Chester Beatty also acquired three Sahidic manuscripts dating from about the sixth or seventh century. One of them (codex B) contains the Acts of the Apostles, followed by the Gospel according to John (see Plate XIV*a*); another (codex A) preserves the Pauline Epistles, followed by the Fourth Gospel. The third codex is fragmentary and contains the text of Psalms i–l with the first chapter of Matthew. Thompson published an edition of the text of the Beatty Acts and Pauline Epistles, with a collation of the text of John against Horner's edition.

The Bohairic version appears to be somewhat later than the Sahidic version. It survives in many manuscripts, almost all of them of a very late date (the earliest complete Gospel codex still extant was copied A.D. 1174). Recently M. Bodmer acquired an early papyrus codex containing most of the Gospel of John and the opening chapters of Genesis in Bohairic.[1] Although the first few folios are badly mutilated, beginning at about the middle of the fourth chapter of John the text is much better preserved. The editor, Rodolphe Kasser, is inclined to date the manuscript in the fourth century. It is of interest that passages which textual scholars have regarded as critically suspect (such as the statement about the angel's moving the water in John v. 3b–4, and the *pericope de adultera*, vii. 53–viii. 11) are not present in this manuscript. The Greek prototype of the Bohairic version appears to be closely related to the Alexandrian text-type.

Acts of the Apostles (B.M. Or. 7594), ed. by E. A. W. Budge, *Coptic Biblical Texts in the Dialect of Upper Egypt* (London, 1912). Fol. 108ᵛ contains a section written in Coptic but in a cursive Greek hand which Kenyon assigned (Introduction, p. lxiii) to about the middle of the fourth century. Ad. Hebbelynck, however, raised questions about the unity and the age of the manuscript (*Muséon*, xxxiv [1921], pp. 71–80), and H. Hyvernat thought a case could be made for dating it in the sixth century (quoted by Lagrange, *Critique textuelle*, ii [Paris, 1935], p. 324, n. 2). Sir Herbert Thompson, it should be added, accepted Kenyon's fourth-century dating (*The Coptic Version of the Acts of the Apostles* . . . [Cambridge, 1932], p. xxi).

[1] The only other early manuscript of the New Testament in Bohairic (actually it is semi-Bohairic) is a fourth- or early fifth-century parchment fragment of Philippians, edited by Paul E. Kahle in *Muséon*, lxiii (1950), pp. 147–57.

Among the scattered manuscripts that preserve portions of the New Testament in the Fayyumic dialect, one of the earliest is a papyrus codex, now at the University of Michigan, which contains John vi. 11–xv. 11 (with lacunae). According to its editor, Mrs. Elinor M. Husselman, the manuscript dates from the early part of the fourth century. In textual affinities it agrees roughly twice as often with the Sahidic version as it does with the Bohairic.

The most significant representative of the sub-Achmimic version is a papyrus codex containing the Gospel of John. In the opinion of its editor, Sir Herbert Thompson, the manuscript dates from about A.D. 350–75. Like the Sahidic version, with which it is related, the version appears to be a representative of the Alexandrian type of text.

Editions: [George Horner,] *The Coptic Version of the New Testament in the Northern Dialect, otherwise called Memphitic and Bohairic . . .*, 4 vols. (Oxford, 1898–1905); id., *The Coptic Version of the New Testament in the Southern Dialect, otherwise called Sahidic and Thebaic . . .*, 7 vols. (Oxford, 1911–24) [each with a literal English translation]; Henri Hyvernat, *Bybliothecae Pierpont Morgan Codices Coptici, photographice expressi . . .* (Rome, 1922), 56 vols. in 63 [the contents are indexed in Winifred Kammerer, *A Coptic Bibliography* (Ann Arbor, 1950), pp. 33 f.]; Herbert Thompson, *The Gospel of St. John According to the Earliest Coptic Manuscript* (London, 1924) [sub-Achmimic dialect]; id., *The Coptic Version of the Acts of the Apostles and the Pauline Epistles in the Sahidic Dialect* (Cambridge, 1932) [Chester Beatty MSS.]; Rodolphe Kasser, *Évangile de Jean et Genèse I–IV*, 2 (Louvain, 1958) [Bodmer MS.]; Elinor M. Husselman, *The Gospel of John in Fayumic Coptic (P. Mich. inv. 3521)* (Ann Arbor, 1962). For lists of all published manuscripts and fragments of the Coptic versions, see A. Vaschalde in *Revue biblique*, N.S., xvi (1919), pp. 220–43, 513–31; xxix (1920), pp. 91–106, 241–58; xxx (1921), pp. 237–46; xxxi (1922), pp. 81–88, 234–58; *Muséon*, xliii (1930), pp. 409–31; xlv (1932), pp. 117–56; xlvi (1933), pp. 299–313; and W. C. Till, *Bulletin of the John Rylands Library*, xlii (1959), pp. 220–40. A list of all known Coptic fragments (whether Biblical or not) down to the sixth century is included by Paul E. Kahle in his *Bala'izah*, i (London, 1954), pp. 269–78. See below, pp. 267–8.

4. THE GOTHIC VERSION

Shortly after the middle of the fourth century, Ulfilas, often called the apostle to the Goths, translated the Bible from Greek into Gothic. For this purpose he created the Gothic alphabet and reduced the spoken language to written form. The Gothic version is the earliest known literary monument in a Germanic dialect.

The most nearly complete of the half-dozen extant Gothic manuscripts (all of which are fragmentary) is a de luxe copy dating from the fifth or sixth century and now in the University Library at Uppsala. It contains portions of all four Gospels, which stand in the so-called Western order (Matthew, John, Luke, and Mark). It is written on purple vellum in large letters of silver ink, whence the name which is commonly given to this manuscript, codex Argenteus, i.e. the 'silver codex' (see Plate XII*b*). The initial lines of the Gospels and the first line of every section of text are in gold letters. All the other manuscripts of the Gothic New Testament, with the exception of a vellum leaf from a bilingual Gothic–Latin codex, are palimpsests.

Ulfilas' translation is remarkably faithful to the original, frequently to the point of being literalistic. For the basis of his version Ulfilas used that form of Greek text which was current in Byzantium about A.D. 350, belonging to the early Koine type of text. Western readings, particularly in the Pauline Epistles, were subsequently introduced from Old Latin manuscripts.

Editions: Wilhelm Streitberg, *Die gotische Bibel*, 2te Aufl. (Heidelberg, 1919; reprinted with additions, 5th ed. 1965) [Gothic and reconstructed Greek text on opposite pages]; *Codex Argenteus Upsaliensis, jussu senatus universitatis phototypice editus* (Upsaliae, 1927).

5. THE ARMENIAN VERSION

Sometimes called 'the Queen of the versions', the Armenian version is generally regarded as one of the most beautiful and accurate of all early translations of the Bible (see Plate XIV*b*). With the exception of the Latin Vulgate, more manuscripts of this version are extant than of any other early version; Rhodes has catalogued 1,244 copies of all or part of the New Testament, and it is known that several hundred more are in libraries within the Soviet Union. Traditions differ regarding its origin. According to Bishop Koriun (died *c.* 450) and the historian Lazar of Pharb (*c.* 500), it was St. Mesrop (died A.D. 439), a soldier who became a Christian missionary, who created a new alphabet and, with the help of the Catholicus Sahak (Isaac the Great, 390–439), translated the version from the Greek text. On the other hand, Moses of Chorion, the nephew and disciple of St. Mesrop, says that Sahak made it from the Syriac text. Both views, with various modifications, have found defenders among modern scholars. There is some reason to think that the earliest Armenian version of the Gospels circulated in the form of a Harmony, distantly related to Tatian's Diatessaron.

The earliest Armenian version appears to have undergone a revision prior to the eighth century. Whether the Greek text which served as the basis for the revision was predominantly Caesarean or Koine in textual type is a question which has not yet been satisfactorily answered. In any case, the text of Matthew and Mark in many Armenian manuscripts and even in Zohrab's printed edition appears to be strongly Caesarean in character.

Editions: There is no satisfactory critical edition; the edition most frequently used was prepared by the Mechitarist Yovhan Zohrabian (Venice, 1789; whole Bible 1805). The oldest known manuscript, a tetraevangelium copied A.D. 887, was photographically reproduced by G. Khalatheants (Moscow, 1899). For other manuscripts, see Erroll F. Rhodes, *An Annotated List of Armenian New Testament Manuscripts* (Tokyo, 1959).

6. THE GEORGIAN VERSION

Of all the early versions of the New Testament, probably the least well known among Western scholars is the Georgian version. The people of Caucasian Georgia, that rough, mountainous district between the Black Sea and the Caspian Sea, received the Gospel during the first half of the fourth century. The time and circumstances of the translation of the New Testament into Georgian, an agglutinative language not known to be related to any other, are hidden in the mists of legend. Like the Armenian version, it is an important witness to the Caesarean type of text. (See below, p. 268.)

Among the oldest known Gospel manuscripts are the Adysh manuscript of A.D. 897, the Opiza manuscript of 913, and the Tbet' manuscript of 995. In most *apparatus critici* the Adysh manuscript is cited as Geo[1], and the testimony of the other two as Geo[2] (A and B).

Editions: *The Old Georgian Version of the Gospel of Mark* . . ., edited with a Latin translation by Robert P. Blake (Paris, 1929); *Matthew* (Paris, 1933); *John*, edited by Blake and Maurice Brière (Paris, 1950); *Luke*, edited by Brière (Paris, 1955); Joseph Molitor, 'Das Adysh-Tetraevangelium. Neu übersetzt und mit altgeorgischen Paralleltexten verglichen', *Oriens Christianus*, xxxvii (1953), pp. 33–55; xxxviii (1954), pp. 11–40; xxxix (1955), pp. 1–32; xl (1956), pp. 1–15; xli (1957), pp. 1–21; xlii (1958), pp. 1–18; xliii (1959), pp. 1–16; G. Garitte, *L'ancienne version géorgienne des Actes des Apôtres d'après deux manuscrits de Sinaï* (Louvain, 1955). See below, p. 268.

7. THE ETHIOPIC VERSION

Scholars differ on the question of the date of the origin of the Ethiopic version; some argue for a date as early as the fourth century, while others attribute it to the sixth or seventh century. Opinion also differs as to whether the translators made use of a Greek or Syriac original. In any case, it is a curious fact that in the Epistles of Paul the version frequently agrees with $\mathfrak{p}^{46}$ with little or no other support. The version also shows evidence of later contamination from Coptic and Arabic texts. Thus the Ethiopic text eventually became a conglomerate with quite disparate elements standing side by side. The analyses which have been made of the earlier form of the Ethiopic version disclose a mixed type of text, predominantly Byzantine in complexion, but with occasional agreement with certain early Greek witnesses ($\mathfrak{p}^{46}$ and B) against all other witnesses. The little that is known of this version so far as the New Testament is concerned (the Old Testament has been studied more thoroughly) suggests that it deserves far more attention than it has received heretofore. The earliest known manuscript, a codex of the four Gospels, dates from the thirteenth century; most other manuscripts are of the fifteenth and succeeding centuries.

Editions: The *editio princeps* of the Ethiopic New Testament was published by three Abyssinian monks, who issued their work in two volumes under the pseudonym Petrus Ethyops (Rome, 1548–9). This text was reprinted, with a Latin translation, in Brian Walton's Polyglot Bible (1657). Other more recent editions, made for modern missionary purposes, were edited by T. Pell Platt (London, 1826), re-edited by F. Prätorius (Leipzig, 1899; reprinted 1914), and F. da Bassano (Asmara, 1920). The readings of the *editio princeps* are referred to by using the siglum Eth[ro].

8. THE OLD SLAVONIC VERSION

With the exception of St. Jerome, more is known of the life and work of SS. Cyril and Methodius, the apostles to the Slavs, than of any other translators of an ancient version of the Bible. Sons of a wealthy official in Salonica, they are credited with the creation of the Glagolitic alphabet, as well as the so-called Cyrillic alphabet. Soon after the middle of the ninth century they began the translation of the Gospels (probably in the form of a Greek lectionary) into Old Bulgarian, commonly called Old Slavonic. The version belongs basically, as one would expect, to the Byzantine type of text, but it also contains not a few earlier readings of the Western and Caesarean types.[1]

Editions: Josef Vajs, *Evangelium sv. Matouše, text rekonstruovaný* (Prague, 1935) [with the reconstructed underlying Greek text printed on opposite pages]; . . . *Marka* (Prague, 1935); . . . *Lukáše* (Prague, 1936); . . . *Jana* (Prague, 1936).

9. OTHER ANCIENT VERSIONS

Subsequent to the rise of Islam, various books of the New Testament were translated into Arabic from Greek, Syriac, Coptic (several dialects), Latin, and from combinations of these. During the thirteenth century two revisions were made of the Arabic version (or versions) current at Alexandria. As a consequence of such a tangled background the study of the Arabic versions is exceedingly complicated, and many problems remain to be solved.

Fragments of the Nubian[2] and the Sogdian versions were edited at the beginning of the twentieth century, but as yet no thorough analysis has been made of their texts. The Anglo-Saxon version was translated from the Latin Vulgate. Four complete manuscripts and five fragmentary manuscripts of the Gospels are known; these date from the eleventh to the thirteenth centuries. The famous Lindisfarne Gospels (see p. 77 above) and the Rushworth Gospels, Latin manuscripts which were written toward the close of the seventh century, have had interlinear Anglo-Saxon glosses added three centuries later.

---

[1] For a survey of research on the Old Slavonic version, see B. M. Metzger, *Chapters in the History of New Testament Textual Criticism* (Leiden and Grand Rapids, 1963), pp. 73–96.   [2] See below, p. 268.

Two versions of the Gospels in Old Persian were published in the seventeenth and eighteenth centuries, but unfortunately next to no attention has been given them by modern textual critics, despite the suggestion by Kirsopp Lake that one of them shows traces of Caesarean readings.[1]

III. PATRISTIC QUOTATIONS FROM THE NEW TESTAMENT

Besides textual evidence derived from New Testament Greek manuscripts and from early versions, the textual critic has available the numerous scriptural quotations included in the commentaries, sermons, and other treatises written by early Church Fathers.[2] Indeed, so extensive are these citations that if all other sources for our knowledge of the text of the New Testament were destroyed, they would be sufficient alone for the reconstruction of practically the entire New Testament.

The importance of patristic quotations lies in the circumstance that they serve to localize and date readings and types of text in Greek manuscripts and versions. For example, since the quotations which Cyprian, Bishop of Carthage in North Africa about A.D. 250, includes in his letters agree almost always with the form of text preserved in the Old Latin manuscript *k*, scholars have correctly concluded that this fourth- or fifth-century manuscript is a descendant of a copy current about 250 in North Africa. Occasionally it happens that a patristic writer specifically cites one or more variant readings present in manuscripts existing in his day. Such information is of the utmost importance in providing proof of the currency of such variant readings at a given time and place.[3]

On the other hand, however, before the textual critic can use patristic evidence with confidence, he must determine whether

[1] For a survey of literature on these so-called secondary versions, see the present writer's chapter in M. M. Parvis and A. P. Wikgren, eds., *New Testament Manuscript Studies* (Chicago, 1950), pp. 25–68. To the literature cited there on the Anglo-Saxon version may be added N. R. Ker's *Catalogue of Manuscripts Containing Anglo-Saxon* (Oxford, 1957). See below, p. 268.

[2] For recent discussions of the significance of the patristic witnesses for the New Testament text, see R. P. Casey's essay in M. M. Parvis and A. P. Wikgren, eds., *New Testament Manuscript Studies* (Chicago, 1950), pp. 69–80; and M.-E. Boismard, 'Critique textuelle et citations patristiques', *Revue biblique*, lvii (1950), pp. 388–408.

[3] For a list of two dozen such passages in the works of Origen, reference may be made to the present writer's contribution to *Biblical and Patristic Studies in Memory of Robert Pierce Casey*, ed. by J. N. Birdsall and R. W. Thomson (Freiburg, 1963), pp. 78–95.

the true text of the ecclesiastical writer has been transmitted. As in the case of New Testament manuscripts, so also the treatises of the Fathers have been modified in the course of copying. The scribe was always tempted to assimilate scriptural quotations in the Fathers to the form of text which was current in the later manuscripts of the New Testament—a text which the scribes might well know by heart.[1] When the manuscripts of a Father differ in a given passage, it is usually safest to adopt the one which diverges from the later ecclesiastical text (the Textus Receptus or the Vulgate).

After the true text of the Patristic author has been recovered, the further question must be raised whether the writer intended to quote the scriptural passage verbatim or merely to paraphrase it. If one is assured that the Father makes a bona fide quotation and not a mere allusion, the problem remains whether he quoted it after consulting the passage in a manuscript or whether he relied on his memory. The former is more probable in the case of longer quotations, whereas shorter quotations were often made from memory.[2] Furthermore, if the Father quotes the same passage more than once, it often happens that he does so in divergent forms. Origen is notorious in this regard, for he seldom quotes a passage twice in precisely the same words.[3] Moreover,

---

[1] The requirements of memorizing portions of the Scriptures as prerequisite for ordination to the deaconate and the priesthood are specified in a Coptic ostracon edited by Crum. According to the ostracon, Samuel, Jacob, and Aaron, who applied to Bishop Abraham to be ordained as deacons, were required 'to master the Gospel according to John and learn it by heart by the end of Pentecost and to recite it'. Aphou, Bishop of Oxyrhynchus, is said to have required a deacon at ordination to know twenty-five Psalms, two Epistles of Paul, and a portion of a Gospel by heart; a priest had to know, in addition, portions of Deuteronomy, Proverbs, and Isaiah (W. E. Crum, *Coptic Ostraca from the Collections of the Egypt Exploration Fund* [London, 1902], p. 9, no. 29). According to the Rules of St. Pachomius, applicants for entrance into the monastery were required to know twenty Psalms or two Epistles of Paul, or a portion of some other part of Scripture (*Regulae Monasticae S. Pachomii*, ed. by P. B. Albers, p. 41; see also Richard Reitzenstein, *Historia Monachorum*, pp. 61 f., 162 ff.).

[2] According to Preuschen, 'the briefer the citation is, the greater is the probability that it represents the text favoured by Origen; the more extensive the citation is, so much the more doubtful is it whether we can recognize in it the text of Origen' (Erwin Preuschen, 'Bibelcitate bei Origenes', *Zeitschrift für die neutestamentliche Wissenschaft*, iv [1903], pp. 71 f.).

[3] The memory can play strange tricks when one quotes even the most familiar passages. 'Dr. Salmon adduces from E. Abbot (*Authorship of the Fourth Gospel*, p. 39) a remarkable instance of this in no less a person than Jeremy Taylor, who quotes the text "Except a man be born again he cannot see the kingdom of God" nine times,

while dictating to one of his several amanuenses, Origen would sometimes refer merely to a few catchwords in the Scripture passage which had come to his mind as an illustration of his argument; later the amanuensis would hunt out the passage in a Biblical manuscript and insert its words at the appropriate place in Origen's treatise.[1] Differences among the longer quotations could therefore arise, depending upon which of several available copies of the Scriptures the amanuensis may have consulted. Despite these difficulties which attend the determination and evaluation of patristic evidence for the New Testament text, this kind of evidence is of such great importance in tracing the history of the transmission of the text that the labour of refining the ore from the dross is well worth the effort.

The following is a list of several of the more important Church Fathers whose writings contain numerous quotations from the New Testament.[2]

Ambrose of Milan, d. 397
Ambrosiaster [= Pseudo-Ambrose] of Rome, second half of fourth century
Athanasius, Bishop of Alexandria, d. 373
Augustine, Bishop of Hippo, d. 430
Chrysostom, Bishop of Constantinople, d. 407
Clement of Alexandria, d. *c.* 212
Cyprian, Bishop of Carthage, d. 258
Cyril of Alexandria, d. 444
Didymus of Alexandria, d. *c.* 398
Ephraem the Syrian, d. 373
Epiphanius, Bishop of Salamis, d. 403
Eusebius, Bishop of Caesarea, d. 339 or 340
Gregory of Nazianzus in Cappadocia, d. 389 or 390
Gregory of Nyssa in Cappadocia, d. 394
Hilary of Poitiers, d. 367
Hippolytus of Rome, d. 235
Irenaeus, Bishop of Lyons, d. *c.* 202

yet only twice in the same form, and never once correctly' (F. G. Kenyon, *Handbook to the Textual Criticism of the New Testament*, 2nd ed., 1912, p. 245).

[1] For several such passages in Origen's commentary on John, see Preuschen in *Die griechischen christlichen Schriftsteller*, Origenes, iv, pp. lxxxix ff.

[2] For information concerning the literary contributions of these Fathers, as well as bibliographical references to editions and monographs, see Berthold Altaner, *Patrology* (New York, 1960), and the more extensive work by Johannes Quasten, *Patrology* (Westminster, Md., 1950 ff.), of which three of the four projected volumes have already appeared.

Isidore of Pelusium, d. *c.* 435
Jerome [= Hieronymus], d. 419 or 420
Justin Martyr, d. *c.* 165
Lucifer of Calaris (Cagliari), d. 370 or 371
Marcion, flourished at Rome, *c.* 150–60
Origen of Alexandria and Caesarea, d. 253 or 254
Pelagius, fourth–fifth century
Primasius, Bishop of Hadrumentum, d. soon after 552
Pseudo-Hieronymus, fifth–sixth century
Rufinus of Aquileia, d. 410
Tatian, flourished *c.* 170
Tertullian of Carthage, d. after 220
Theodore of Mopsuestia in Cilicia, d. 428

Among these writers one of the more controversial figures was Tatian, a Syrian from Mesopotamia, known chiefly for his Diatessaron, or Harmony of the four Gospels. Combining distinctive phrases preserved by only one Evangelist with those preserved by another, he arranged the several sections of the Gospels into a single narrative. Omitting only a very few sections (such as the genealogies of Jesus in Matthew and in Luke, the former of which traces Jesus' lineage from Abraham onwards, and the latter of which traces it backwards to Adam), Tatian managed to preserve practically the entire contents of the separate Gospels woven into one. The name by which it came to be known is 'Diatessaron',[1] derived from the Greek phrase διὰ τεσσάρων, meaning 'through [the] four [Gospels]'.

Tatian's Harmony soon became popular, particularly in the East. As late as the fifth century Theodoret, who became Bishop of Cyrrhus or Cyrus on the Euphrates in upper Syria in A.D. 423, found that many copies of the Diatessaron were in use within his diocese. But because Tatian had become heretical in his later life, and because Theodoret believed that orthodox Christians were in danger of being corrupted by using Tatian's work, he destroyed all of the copies of the Diatessaron that he could find (totalling about 200) and put in their place the separate Gospels of the four Evangelists.[2]

---

[1] Victor of Capua's reference (in codex Fuldensis; see p. 77 above) to Tatian's work as a *Diapente* is not a *lapsus calami*, as some have thought, but is to be explained as the application to the Harmony of a musical term that involves four intervals; see Franco Bolgiani, *Vittore di Capua e il 'Diatessaron'* (*Memorie dell'Accademia delle Scienze di Torino*, Classe di scienze morali, storiche e filologiche, Serie 4ᵃ, n. 2; 1962).   [2] Theodoret, *Treatise on Heresies*, i. 20.

As a result of the zeal of Bishop Theodoret, and doubtless of others like him, no complete copy of Tatian's Diatessaron is extant today. In 1933 a small fragment of parchment containing a portion of the Diatessaron in Greek was unearthed by archaeologists on the site of the ancient Roman fortress-town of Dura-Europos on the lower Euphrates. It is known that this town fell to the Persians under King Shapur I in A.D. 256–7, and therefore the fragment must antedate that event.[1] The text which is preserved contains the narrative of the coming of Joseph of Arimathea for the body of Jesus. A literal translation will show how words and phrases from all four Gospels have been woven together. Since the left-hand margin of the vellum has suffered damage, the first half-dozen or so letters at the beginning of each line are lacking. They can be restored, however, with almost perfect confidence. In the following rendering the restorations are enclosed within square brackets and the modern Scripture references (which are not, of course, in the fragment) are enclosed within parentheses.

[. . . the mother of the sons of Zebed]ee (Matt. xxvii. 56) and Salome (Mark xv. 40) and the wives [of those who] had followed him from [Galile]e to see the crucified (Luke xxiii. 49b–c). And [the da]y was Preparation; the Sabbath was daw[ning] (Luke xxiii. 54). And when it was evening (Matt. xxvii. 57), on the Prep[aration], that is, the day before the Sabbath (Mark xv. 42), [there came] up a man (Matt. xxvii. 57), be[ing] a member of the council (Luke xxiii. 50), from Arimathea (Matt. xxvii. 57), a c[i]ty of [Jude]a (Luke xxiii. 51), by name Jo[seph] (Matt. xxvii. 57), good and ri[ghteous] (Luke xxiii. 50), being a disciple of Jesus, but se[cret]ly, for fear of the [Jew]s (John xix. 38). And he (Matt. xxvii. 57) was looking for [the] k[ingdom] of God (Luke xxiii. 51b). This man [had] not [con]sented to [their] p[urpose] (Luke xxiii. 51a). . . .

It is evident that Tatian went about composing his Diatessaron with great diligence. Probably he worked from four separate manuscripts, one of each of the Gospels, and, as he wove together phrases, now from this Gospel and now that, he would no doubt cross out those phrases in the manuscripts from which he was copying. Otherwise it is difficult to understand how he

---

[1] The fragment was edited by Carl H. Kraeling in *Studies and Documents*, vol. iii (London, 1935). See below, p. 269.

was able to put together so successfully a cento of very short phrases from four separate documents.

The most spectacular reading preserved in this fragment is near the beginning. Although it rests partly on a restoration, and although none of the secondary translations of Tatian which were known hitherto exhibits the reading, it is probable that Tatian referred to 'the wives of those who had followed' Jesus from Galilee. This statement and the implications which it conveys are without parallel in the text of the separate Gospels in any other manuscript or version.

In addition to the Greek fragment, portions of Tatian's Harmony are known through the quotations from it which certain early Syrian Church Fathers included in their homilies and other treatises, particularly in the commentary that St. Ephraem of the fourth century wrote on the Diatessaron. Until recently this commentary was available only in an Armenian translation, preserved in two manuscripts that were copied A.D. 1195. In 1957 announcement was made of the acquisition by Sir Chester Beatty of a Syriac manuscript containing about three-fifths of Ephraem's treatise.[1] The manuscript, which dates from the late fifth or early sixth century, has been edited by Dom Louis Leloir,[2] who previously prepared a careful edition and translation of the commentary in its Armenian form. Several harmonies in other languages (Arabic and Persian in the East, and Latin, Medieval Dutch, Old English, and Old Italian in the West) show more or less dependence, either in form or in text, upon Tatian's pioneering work.

How much contamination the Diatessaron has exerted on the transmission of the text of the separate Gospels has been variously estimated. Not many scholars today agree with the extreme views of Hermann von Soden and Anton Baumstark, who thought that they detected the presence of Tatianic influence on a great number of Eastern and Western manuscripts

---

[1] For a description and a preliminary discussion of the manuscript, see Dom Louis Leloir, 'L'Originale syriaque du commentaire de S. Éphrem sur le Diatessaron', *Biblica*, xl (1959), pp. 959–70 (= *Studia Biblica et Orientalia*, ii, pp. 391–402). Tjitze Baarda has edited a brief quotation of Ephraem's Commentary which is included in a Nestorian manuscript brought to Rome in 1869 ('A Syriac Fragment of Mar Ephraem's Commentary on the Diatessaron', *New Testament Studies*, viii [1962], pp. 287–300).

[2] *Saint Éphrem, Commentaire de l'Évangile concordant, texte syriaque (Manuscrit Chester Beatty 709)*, (Dublin, 1963). See below, p. 269.

of the Gospels. It is doubtless true, however, that not a few instances of harmonization of the text of the Gospels in certain witnesses (notably the Western witnesses) are to be ascribed to Tatian's influence.[1]

---

[1] For a recent summary of the history of research on Tatian's Diatessaron, reference may be made to B. M. Metzger's *Chapters in the History of New Testament Textual Criticism* (Leiden and Grand Rapids, 1963), pp. 97–120. See below, p. 269.

PART TWO

The History of
New Testament Textual Criticism
as reflected in Printed Editions
of the Greek Testament

III

The Pre-critical Period:
The Origin and Dominance of the
Textus Receptus

I. FROM XIMENES AND ERASMUS TO THE ELZEVIRS

JOHANNES GUTENBERG'S invention of printing by using movable type had the most momentous consequences for Western culture and civilization. Now copies of books could be reproduced more rapidly, more cheaply, and with a higher degree of accuracy than had ever been possible previously. Quite appropriately, the first major product of Gutenberg's press was a magnificent edition of the Bible. The text was Jerome's Latin Vulgate, and the volume was published at Mayence (Mainz) between 1450 and 1456. During the next fifty years at least one hundred editions of the Latin Bible were issued by various printing houses. In 1488 the first edition of the complete Hebrew Old Testament came from the Soncino press in Lombardy. Before 1500 Bibles had been printed in several of the principal vernacular languages of Western Europe—Bohemian (Czech), French, German, and Italian.

But, except for several short extracts,[1] the Greek New Testament had to wait until 1514 to come from the press. Why was there so long a delay? Two reasons may be suggested which help to account for the lapse of some sixty years from Gutenberg's invention to the first printed Greek Testament.

In the first place, the production of fonts of Greek type necessary for a book of any considerable size was both difficult and expensive.[2] The attempt was made to reproduce in print the

---

[1] In 1481 the Greek text of the hymns of Zachariah and Elizabeth (Luke i) was printed at Milan in an appendix to a Greek Psalter. In 1504 the first six chapters of John in Greek (taken from a Gospel lectionary, and retaining the rubrics) were printed at Venice in a book containing a Latin translation of the Poems of Gregory Nazianzen. In 1514 John i. 1–14 in Greek was reprinted at Tübingen.

[2] The first book with continuous Greek type was a grammar of the Greek language entitled *Erotemata*, written by Constantine Lascaris and published at

appearance of minuscule Greek handwriting, with its numerous alternative forms of the same letter, as well as its many combinations of two or more letters (ligatures).[1] Instead, therefore, of producing type for merely the twenty-four letters of the Greek alphabet, printers prepared about 200 different characters. (Subsequently these variant forms of the same letters were abandoned, until today there remain only the two forms of the lower-case sigma, σ and ς.)

The principal cause which retarded the publication of the Greek text of the New Testament was doubtless the prestige of Jerome's Latin Vulgate. Translations into the vernacular languages were not derogatory to the supremacy of the Latin text from which they were derived. But the publication of the Greek New Testament offered to any scholar acquainted with both languages a tool with which to criticize and correct the official Latin Bible of the Church.

At length, however, in 1514 the first printed Greek New Testament came from the press, as part of a Polyglot Bible. Planned in 1502 by the cardinal primate of Spain, Francisco Ximenes de Cisneros (1437–1517), this magnificent edition of the Hebrew, Aramaic, Greek, and Latin texts was printed at the university town of Alcalá (called Complutum in Latin). Known as the Complutensian Polyglot,[2] the project was under the editorial care of several scholars, of whom Diego Lopez de Zuñiga (Stunica) is perhaps best known.[3] Volume v, containing

---

Milan in 1476; see Richard P. Breaden, 'The First Book Printed in Greek', *Bulletin of the New York Public Library*, li (1947), pp. 586–92. Before 1476 several editions of Latin classics and Church Fathers had appeared containing occasional Greek words and phrases. The honour of being the first to print Greek goes either to Johann Fust and Peter Schoeffer for their edition of Cicero's *De officiis* and *Paradoxa*, published at Mainz in 1465, or to Conrad Sweynheym and Arnoldus Pannartz for their volume of Lactantius' *Opera*, issued at Subiaco, Italy, on 30 Oct. 1465. See Victor Scholderer, *Greek Printing Types, 1465–1927* (London, 1927), p. 1. See below, p. 269.

[1] For a list of many of the ligatures used in incunabula, see the *Style Manual* of the United States Government Printing Office (Washington, 1945), pp. 316–18, or Georg F. von Ostermann, *Manual of Foreign Languages* (New York, 1952), pp. 105–8.

[2] Of the original 600 sets which were printed, the locations of ninety-seven are known today; see James P. R. Lyell, *Cardinal Ximenes* (London, 1917), and Mariano Revilla Rico, *La Políglota de Alcalá, estudio histórico-crítico* (Madrid, 1917).

[3] One of the less well-known collaborators in the project, who nevertheless played an important role in the preparation of the Greek text of the Septuagint and of the New Testament for the Polyglot, was Demetrius Ducas, a Greek from Crete whom Ximenes brought to Alcalá to teach in his Academy and to edit Greek books; see the account concerning Ducas in Deno J. Geanakoplos, *Greek Scholars in Venice:*

the New Testament and a Greek glossary with Latin equivalents, was printed first, its colophon bearing the date 10 January 1514. Volume vi, the appendix, containing a Hebrew lexicon and an elementary Hebrew grammar, was printed next, in 1515. The four volumes of the Old Testament appeared last, the colophon of volume iv bearing the date 10 July 1517. The sanction of Pope Leo X, printed in volume i, was not obtained until 22 March 1520, but it appears that for some reason the Polyglot was not actually circulated (that is, published) until about 1522.

The four volumes which contain the Old Testament present the Hebrew text, the Latin Vulgate, and the Greek Septuagint in three columns side by side on each page, together with the Aramaic Targum of Onkelos for the Pentateuch at the foot of the page, accompanied by a Latin translation. The Greek type used in the New Testament volume is modelled after the style of the handwriting in manuscripts of about the eleventh or twelfth century, and is very bold and elegant (see Plate XVI).[1] It is printed without rough or smooth breathing marks and is accented according to a system never heard of before or since: monosyllables have no accent, while the tone syllable in other words is marked with a simple *apex*, resembling the Greek acute accent mark. Each word or group of Greek words is coded to the adjacent column of the Latin Vulgate by small supralinear roman letters, thus assisting readers with little Greek to find the equivalent words in each column. The Septuagint is printed with the familiar cursive style of Greek characters popularized by Aldus Manutius, the famous Venetian printer.

What Greek manuscripts lie behind the text of the Complutensian New Testament has never been satisfactorily

---

Studies in the Dissemination of Greek Learning from Byzantium to Western Europe (Cambridge, Massachusetts, 1962), pp. 238 ff.

[1] According to Scholderer, the unknown designer of the Greek font of type used in the Complutensian New Testament incorporated certain features of Nicolas Jenson's Greek font, which was put in use in 1471. 'In fact, it [the Greek of the Complutensian New Testament] is the last and most beautiful example of the Jensonian class of type, carrying it to the limit of its possibilities, and is fairly entitled to its generally acknowledged position as the king of all Greek founts, although its full perfection was not disclosed until the present century, when Robert Proctor completed a revival of the lower-case in an enlarged copy by adding a full set of capitals adapted to it. The Greek of the Complutensian New Testament remains the only original contribution of Spain to Hellenic typography' (Scholderer, op. cit., p. 10).

ascertained.[1] In his dedication to Pope Leo X, after mentioning the pains which he had taken to secure Latin, Greek, and Hebrew manuscripts, Ximenes continues: 'For Greek copies indeed we are indebted to your Holiness, who sent us most kindly from the Apostolic Library very ancient codices, both of the Old and the New Testament; which have aided us very much in this undertaking.'[2]

Though the Complutensian text was the first Greek New Testament to be printed, the first Greek New Testament to be published (that is, put on the market) was the edition prepared by the famous Dutch scholar and humanist Desiderius Erasmus of Rotterdam (1469–1536). It cannot be determined exactly when Erasmus first decided to prepare an edition of the Greek Testament, but on a visit to Basle in August 1514 he discussed (probably not for the first time) the possibility of such a volume with the well-known publisher Johann Froben. Their negotiations seem to have been broken off for a time, but were resumed in April 1515 while Erasmus was on a visit at the University of Cambridge. It was then that Froben importuned him through a mutual friend, Beatus Rhenanus, to undertake immediately an edition of the New Testament. Doubtless Froben had heard of the forthcoming Spanish Polyglot Bible and, sensing that the market was ready for an edition of the Greek New Testament, wished to capitalize upon that demand before Ximenes' work would be finished and authorized for publication. Froben's proposal, which was accompanied by a promise to pay Erasmus

[1] See, for example, Franz Delitzsch, *Studien zur Entstehungsgeschichte der Polyglottenbibel des Cardinals Ximenes* (Programm, Leipzig, 1871; also published [in German] at London under the title, *Studies on the Complutensian Polyglott*, 1872); Samuel Berger, *La Bible au seizième siècle* (Paris, 1879), pp. 51–58; Delitzsch, *Fortgesetzte Studien zur Entstehungsgeschichte der Complutensischen Polyglottenbibel* (Programm, Leipzig, 1886); and M. Goguel, 'Le Texte et les éditions du Nouveau Testament grec', *Revue de l'histoire des religions*, lxxxii (1920), pp. 14–18.

[2] Some have doubted the truth of this statement, for Leo had been elected Pope less than a year before the New Testament volume was finished and therefore (so it is argued) could hardly have sent manuscripts in time to be useful (see Marvin R. Vincent, *A History of the Textual Criticism of the New Testament* [New York, 1899], p. 50). One should observe, however, that Ximenes does not explicitly say that the manuscripts were sent during Leo's pontificate; it is altogether possible, as Hug suggested long ago, that they had been sent during the pontificate of the previous Pope, Julius II, through the intervention of the Cardinal de Medici, who had great influence over Julius and who in turn succeeded him to the Papal throne (J. L. Hug, *Einleitung in die Schriften des Neuen Testaments* [Stuttgart und Tübingen, 1826], § 55).

as much as anyone else might offer for such a job (*se daturum pollicetur, quantum alius quisquam*), apparently came at an opportune moment. Going to Basle again in July of 1515, Erasmus hoped to find Greek manuscripts sufficiently good to be sent to the printer as copy to be set up in type along with his own Latin translation, on which he had been working intermittently for several years. To his vexation the only manuscripts available on the spur of the moment required a certain amount of correcting before they could be used as printer's copy. (See below, p. 269.)

The printing began on 2 October 1515, and in a remarkably short time (1 March 1516) the entire edition was finished, a large folio volume of about 1,000 pages which, as Erasmus himself declared later, was 'precipitated rather than edited' (*praecipitatum verius quam editum*). Owing to the haste in production, the volume contains hundreds of typographical errors; in fact, Scrivener once declared, '[It] is in that respect the most faulty book I know.'[1] Since Erasmus could not find a manuscript which contained the entire Greek Testament, he utilized several for various parts of the New Testament. For most of the text he relied on two rather inferior manuscripts from a monastic library at Basle, one of the Gospels (see Plate XV) and one of the Acts and Epistles, both dating from about the twelfth century.[2] Erasmus compared them with two or three others of the same books and entered occasional corrections for the printer in the margins or between the lines of the Greek script.[3] For the Book of Revelation he had but one manuscript, dating from the twelfth century, which he had borrowed from his friend Reuchlin. Unfortunately, this manuscript lacked the final leaf, which had contained the last six verses of the book. For these verses, as well as a few other passages throughout the book where the Greek text of the Apocalypse and the adjoining Greek commentary with which the manuscript was supplied are so mixed up as to be almost indistinguishable,

[1] F. H. A. Scrivener, *A Plain Introduction to the Criticism of the New Testament*, 4th ed., ii (London, 1894), p. 185.

[2] Though some have dated the manuscript of the Gospels in the fifteenth century (so Scrivener [doubtfully], Kenyon, and von Dobschütz), Gregory, Eberhard Nestle, von Soden, and Clark assign it to the twelfth.

[3] These corrections are described by Kenneth W. Clark, 'The Erasmian Notes in Codex 2', in *Studia Evangelica*, ed. by K. Aland, F. L. Cross, *et al.* (= *Texte und Untersuchungen*, lxxiii; Berlin, 1959), pp. 749–56. See also C. C. Tarelli, 'Erasmus's Manuscripts of the Gospels', *Journal of Theological Studies*, xliv (1943), pp. 155–62.

Erasmus depended upon the Latin Vulgate, translating this text into Greek. As would be expected from such a procedure, here and there in Erasmus' self-made Greek text are readings which have never been found in any known Greek manuscript—but which are still perpetuated today in printings of the so-called Textus Receptus of the Greek New Testament.[1]

Even in other parts of the New Testament Erasmus occasionally introduced into his Greek text material taken from the Latin Vulgate. Thus in Acts ix. 6, the question which Paul asks at the time of his conversion on the Damascus road, 'And he trembling and astonished said, Lord, what wilt thou have me to do?', was frankly interpolated by Erasmus from the Latin Vulgate. This addition, which is found in no Greek manuscript at this passage (though it appears in the parallel account of Acts xxii. 10), became part of the Textus Receptus, from which the King James version was made in 1611.

The reception accorded Erasmus' edition, the first published Greek New Testament, was mixed. On the one hand, it found many purchasers throughout Europe. Within three years a second edition was called for, and the total number of copies of the 1516 and 1519 editions amounted to 3,300. The second edition became the basis of Luther's German translation.[2] On the other hand, in certain circles Erasmus' work was received with suspicion and even outright hostility. His elegant Latin translation, differing in many respects from the wording of Jerome's Vulgate, was regarded as a presumptuous innovation. Particularly objectionable were the brief annotations in which Erasmus sought to justify his translation. He included among the philological notes not a few caustic comments aimed at the corrupt lives of many of the priests. In the words of J. A. Froude, 'The clergy's skins were tender from long impunity. They

[1] For example ἀκαθάρτητος (Rev. xvii. 4; there is, however, no such word in the Greek language as ἀκαθάρτης, meaning 'uncleanness'); ὀρθρινός (xxii. 16); ἐλθέ twice, ἐλθέτω (xxii. 17); συμμαρτυροῦμαι γάρ . . . ἐπιτιθῇ πρὸς ταῦτα (xxii. 18); ἀφαιρῇ βίβλου . . . ἀφαιρήσει (future for ἀφελεῖ!!), βίβλου (second occurrence) (xxii. 19); ὑμῶν (xxii. 21).

[2] It has often been debated how far Luther's translation rests on the Greek text. In recent times H. Dibbelt (*Archiv für Reformationsgeschichte*, xxxviii [1941], pp. 300–30) has maintained that the translation reflects only an occasional consultation of the Greek; on the other hand, H. Bornkamm (*Theologische Literaturzeitung*, lxxii [1947], pp. 23–28) holds that Luther translated from the combination of Greek and Latin texts in Erasmus' edition and from the Vulgate, which he had in his head. See below, p. 269.

shrieked from pulpit and platform, and made Europe ring with their clamour.'[1] As a result, 'universities, Cambridge and Oxford among them, forbade students to read Erasmus's writings or booksellers to sell them'.[2]

Among the criticisms levelled at Erasmus one of the most serious appeared to be the charge of Stunica, one of the editors of Ximenes' Complutensian Polyglot, that his text lacked part of the final chapter of 1 John, namely the Trinitarian statement concerning 'the Father, the Word, and the Holy Ghost: and these three are one. And there are three that bear witness in earth' (1 John v. 7–8, King James version). Erasmus replied that he had not found any Greek manuscript containing these words, though he had in the meanwhile examined several others besides those on which he relied when first preparing his text. In an unguarded moment Erasmus promised that he would insert the *Comma Johanneum*, as it is called, in future editions if a single Greek manuscript could be found that contained the passage. At length such a copy was found—or was made to order! As it now appears, the Greek manuscript had probably been written in Oxford about 1520 by a Franciscan friar named Froy (or Roy), who took the disputed words from the Latin Vulgate.[3] Erasmus stood by his promise and inserted the passage in his third edition (1522), but he indicates in a lengthy footnote his suspicions that the manuscript had been prepared expressly in order to confute him.[4]

Among the thousands of Greek manuscripts of the New Testament examined since the time of Erasmus, only three others are known to contain this spurious passage. They are Greg. 88, a twelfth-century manuscript which has the *Comma* written in the margin in a seventeenth-century hand; Tisch. ω 110, which is a sixteenth-century manuscript copy of the Complutensian Polyglot Greek text; and Greg. 629, dating from the fourteenth

---

[1] J. A. Froude, *Life and Letters of Erasmus* (New York, 1896), p. 127. See also August Bludau, *Die beiden ersten Erasmus-Ausgaben des Neuen Testaments und ihre Gegner* (Freiburg i. Br., 1902).

[2] Froude, op. cit., p. 138.

[3] See J. Rendel Harris, *The Origin of the Leicester Codex of the New Testament* (London, 1887), pp. 40–53; and C. H. Turner, *The Early Printed Editions of the Greek Testament* (Oxford, 1924), pp. 23–24.

[4] Today the codex (designated Greg. 61), which is in the library of Trinity College, Dublin, opens almost of its own accord at 1 John v—so often has it been consulted at this passage!

or, as Riggenbach has argued, from the latter half of the six-teenth century.[1] The oldest known citation of the *Comma* is in a fourth-century Latin treatise entitled *Liber apologeticus* (ch. 4), attributed either to Priscillian or to his follower, Bishop Instan-tius of Spain. The *Comma* probably originated as a piece of allegorical exegesis of the three witnesses and may have been written as a marginal gloss in a Latin manuscript of 1 John, whence it was taken into the text of the Old Latin Bible during the fifth century. The passage does not appear in manuscripts of the Latin Vulgate before about A.D. 800. In view of its in-clusion in the Clementine edition of the Latin Vulgate (1592), in 1897 the Holy Office in Rome, a high ecclesiastical congre-gation, made an authoritative pronouncement, approved and confirmed by Pope Leo XIII, that it is not safe to deny that this verse is an authentic part of St. John's Epistle.[2] Modern Roman Catholic scholars, however, recognize that the words do not be-long in the Greek Testament; for example, the four bilingual editions of the New Testament that were edited by Bover, Merk, Nolli, and Vogels include the words as part of the Vulgate text approved by the Council of Trent, but reject them from the Greek text that faces the Latin on the opposite page.[3]

Subsequently Erasmus issued a fourth and definitive edition (1527), which contains the text of the New Testament in three parallel columns, the Greek, the Latin Vulgate, and Erasmus' own Latin version. He had seen Ximenes' Polyglot Bible shortly after the publication of his own third edition in 1522, and wisely decided to avail himself of its generally superior text in the improvement of his own. In the Book of Revelation, for example, he altered his fourth edition in about ninety passages on the basis of the Complutensian text. A fifth edition, which appeared in 1535, discarded the Latin Vulgate but differs very little from the fourth as regards the Greek text.

Thus the text of Erasmus' Greek New Testament rests upon a half-dozen minuscule manuscripts. The oldest and best of these manuscripts (codex 1, a minuscule of the tenth century, which agrees often with the earlier uncial text) he used least, because he was afraid of its supposedly erratic text! Erasmus'

[1] *Das Comma Johanneum* (Gütersloh, 1928). [2] See below, p. 269.
[3] For a full discussion by a noted Roman Catholic textual scholar, see Teófilo Ayuso Marazuela, 'Nuevo estudio sobre el "Comma Ioanneum"', *Biblica*, xxviii (1947), pp. 83–112, 216–35; xxix (1948), pp. 52–76. See below, p. 270.

text is inferior in critical value to the Complutensian, yet because it was the first on the market and was available in a cheaper and more convenient form, it attained a much wider circulation and exercised a far greater influence than its rival, which had been in preparation from 1502 to 1514. In addition to Erasmus' five editions mentioned above, more than thirty unauthorized reprints are said to have appeared at Venice, Strasbourg, Basle, Paris, and other places.

Subsequent editors, though making a number of alterations in Erasmus' text, essentially reproduced this debased form of the Greek Testament. Having secured an undeserved pre-eminence, what came to be called the Textus Receptus of the New Testament resisted for 400 years all scholarly efforts to displace it in favour of an earlier and more accurate text. The highlights of this history are as follows.

The first edition of the whole Bible in Greek was published in three parts in February 1518 at Venice by the celebrated Aldine press. The New Testament, which is dedicated to Erasmus, follows the first edition of Erasmus so closely as to reproduce many typographical errors—even those which Erasmus had corrected in the list of errata!

A beautifully printed pocket-sized edition (its pages measure 3 by 4 inches) was produced in two volumes (616 pp., 475 pp.) by Ioannes Antonius de Nicolinis de Sabio at Venice in 1538. Its text, edited by Melchiorre Sessa, is curiously eclectic, depending now on Erasmus, now on the Aldine text, and occasionally departing from all previous editions.[1] Like several other early editions it contains in Greek certain 'helps for readers', such as lists of chapter headings, lives of the Evangelists, hypotheses (introductions) to the several books, and accounts of the journeys of Paul and of his martyrdom.[2]

The famous Parisian printer and publisher, Robert Estienne,

---

[1] For an analysis of the textual affinities of this extremely rare edition, see W. H. P. Hatch, 'An Early Edition of the New Testament in Greek', *Harvard Theological Review*, xxxiv (1941), pp. 69–78. The rarity of copies of the edition may be gauged from the statement of Reuss that after diligent search he was unable to locate a copy anywhere in the libraries of Germany. Hatch indicates that only seven copies of the complete edition, and one copy of volume ii, are known to exist today. (In addition to the copies mentioned by Hatch, the present writer subsequently acquired a copy of volume ii.)

[2] These 'helps for readers' were drawn from minuscule manuscripts of the New Testament; see pp. 25 f. above.

latinized as Stephanus (1503–59), issued four editions of the Greek Testament, three at Paris (1546, 1549, and 1550) and the last at Geneva (1551), where he spent his final years as a professed Protestant.[1] The three Parisian editions are most sumptuously printed, with type cast at the expense of the French Government. The handsome third edition, of folio size (8⅝ by 13 inches), is the first Greek Testament that has a critical apparatus; Stephanus entered on the inner margins of the pages variant readings from fourteen Greek codices as well as many readings from the Complutensian Polyglot. One of the manuscripts that he cited is the famous codex Bezae, which had been collated for him, he says, 'by friends in Italy'.

The text of Stephanus' editions of 1546 and 1549 was a compound of the Complutensian and Erasmian editions; the third edition (1550) approaches more closely the text of Erasmus' fourth and fifth editions. As it happened, Stephanus' third edition became for many persons, especially in England, the received or standard text of the Greek Testament.

Stephanus' fourth edition (1551), which contains two Latin versions (the Vulgate and that of Erasmus) printed on either side of the Greek text, is noteworthy because in it for the first time the text was divided into numbered verses. It has often been stated that Stephanus marked the verse divisions while journeying 'on horseback', and that some of the infelicitous divisions arose from the jogging of the horse that bumped his pen into the wrong places.[2] Stephanus' son does indeed assert that his father did the work while on a journey (*inter equitandum*) from Paris to Lyons, but the most natural inference is that the task was accomplished while resting at the inns along the road. (See below, p. 270.)

In 1553 Stephanus' folio edition of 1550 was reprinted in a small-sized volume (3⅜ by 5½ inches) by Jean Crispin (or Crespin), the French printer of Geneva, who published many editions of the Scriptures in various languages, including the second quarto English Geneva Bible of 1570. Crispin reproduced the text of Stephanus with only half a dozen minor alterations. The variant readings of the 1550 folio edition are

---

[1] See Elizabeth Armstrong, *Robert Estienne, Royal Printer: an Historical Study of the Elder Stephanus* (Cambridge, 1954), pp. 211 ff.

[2] So, for example, A. T. Robertson, *An Introduction to the Textual Criticism of the New Testament*, 2nd ed. (New York, 1928), p. 100.

also reproduced,[1] though without Stephanus' sigla referring to individual manuscripts. It was either Stephanus' folio edition or Crispin's pocket-sized reprint that William Whittingham and his fellow Protestant refugees from England utilized when they prepared their English translation of the New Testament (Geneva, 1557), the first English version to include variant readings in the margins.[2]

Théodore de Bèze (Beza, 1519–1605), the friend and successor of Calvin at Geneva and an eminent classical and Biblical scholar, published no fewer than nine editions of the Greek Testament between 1565 and 1604, and a tenth edition appeared posthumously in 1611. Only four of them, however, are independent editions (those of 1565, 1582, 1588–9, and 1598), the others being smaller-sized reprints. Accompanied by annotations and his own Latin version, as well as Jerome's Latin Vulgate, these editions contain a certain amount of textual information drawn from several Greek manuscripts which Beza had collated himself, as well as the Greek manuscripts collated by Henry Stephanus, son of Robert Stephanus. Noteworthy among Beza's own manuscript possessions were codex Bezae and codex Claromontanus, though he made relatively little use of them, for they deviated too far from the generally received text of the time. Beza seems also to have been the first scholar to collate the Syriac New Testament, which was published in 1569 by Emmanuel Tremellius. For Acts and 1 and 2 Corinthians he utilized information from the Arabic version put at his disposal by Franciscus Junius. Despite the variety of this additional textual evidence available to Beza, which is reflected chiefly in his annotations, the Greek text which he printed differs little from Stephanus' fourth edition of 1551. The importance of Beza's work lies in the extent to which his editions tended to popularize and to stereotype the Textus Receptus. The King James translators of 1611 made large use of Beza's editions of 1588–9 and 1598.

In 1624 the brothers Bonaventure and Abraham Elzevir,

---

[1] The variant reading at Luke xvii. 35, however, is introduced into Crispin's text itself.

[2] The translation, with minor alterations, and the variant readings were incorporated in the Geneva Bible of 1560; see the discussion of the variant readings in B. M. Metzger, 'The Influence of Codex Bezae upon the Geneva Bible of 1560', *New Testament Studies*, viii (1961), pp. 72–77.

two enterprising printers at Leiden,[1] published a small and convenient edition of the Greek Testament, the text of which was taken mainly from Beza's smaller 1565 edition. The preface to the second edition, which appeared in 1633, makes the boast that '[the reader has] the text which is now received by all, in which we give nothing changed or corrupted'.[2] Thus from what was a more or less casual phrase advertising the edition (what modern publishers might call a 'blurb'), there arose the designation 'Textus Receptus', or commonly received, standard text. Partly because of this catchword the form of the Greek text incorporated in the editions that Stephanus, Beza, and the Elzevirs had published succeeded in establishing itself as 'the only true text' of the New Testament, and was slavishly reprinted in hundreds of subsequent editions. It lies at the basis of the King James version and of all the principal Protestant translations in the languages of Europe prior to 1881. So superstitious has been the reverence accorded the Textus Receptus that in some cases attempts to criticize or emend it have been regarded as akin to sacrilege. Yet its textual basis is essentially a handful of late and haphazardly collected minuscule manuscripts, and in a dozen passages its reading is supported by no known Greek witness.

II. THE COLLECTION OF VARIANT READINGS

The next stage in the history of New Testament textual criticism is characterized by assiduous efforts to assemble variant readings from Greek manuscripts, versions, and Fathers. For almost two centuries scholars ransacked libraries and museums, in Europe as well as the Near East, for witnesses to the text of the New Testament. But almost all of the editors of the New Testament during this period were content to reprint the time-honoured but corrupt Textus Receptus, relegating the evidence for the earlier readings to the apparatus. An occasional brave soul who ventured to print a different form of Greek text was either condemned or ignored.

The first systematic collection of variant readings (those given in the margin of Stephanus' 1550 edition had been assembled

---

[1] The printing house of Elzevir (properly Elzevier), founded by Louis Elzevier (1540–1617), issued many beautiful editions of classical authors from 1595 to 1681.

[2] 'Textum ergo habes, nunc ab omnibus receptum: in quo nihil immutatum aut corruptum damus.'

somewhat at random) was included in the Polyglot Bible edited by Brian Walton (1600–61) and published at London in 1655–7 in six folio volumes. The fifth volume (1657) contains the New Testament in Greek, Latin (both the Vulgate and the version of Arius Montanus), Syriac, Ethiopic, Arabic, and (for the Gospels) Persian. The Greek text as well as each of the oriental versions is supplied with a literal translation into Latin. The Greek text is that of Stephanus' 1550 edition, with slight alterations. At the foot of the page are variant readings from codex Alexandrinus, which had recently been presented (1627) by Cyril Lucar, the Patriarch of Constantinople, to Charles I. In the sixth volume of the Polyglot, the Appendix, Walton included a critical apparatus, prepared by Archbishop Ussher, of variant readings derived from fifteen other authorities, to which were added the variants from Stephanus' margin.[1]

In 1675 Dr. John Fell (1625–86),[2] Dean of Christ Church and afterwards Bishop of Oxford, issued anonymously a small-sized volume (3¾ by 6½ inches), the first Greek Testament to be published at Oxford. The text, drawn from the Elzevir 1633 edition, was supplied with an apparatus in which Fell claimed to give variants from more than 100 manuscripts and ancient versions. Unfortunately, however, about twenty of these witnesses, including codex Vaticanus (B), are not cited individually, but only in statements concerning the total number of manuscripts which agree in any particular reading. For the first time evidence from the Gothic and Bohairic versions, supplied by T. Marshall, was also made available through Fell's apparatus.

About the time of the publication of Fell's edition, John Mill[3] (1645–1707), a fellow of Queen's College, Oxford, began his studies of New Testament textual criticism which were to come to fruition thirty years later in an epoch-making edition of the

---

[1] The London Polyglot was attacked by Dr. John Owen, the Puritan Dean of Christ Church, Oxford, in *Considerations on the Prolegomena and Appendix to the late Polyglotta* (1659), to which Walton made a prompt and sharp rejoinder, *The Considerator Considered* (1659). Walton's stature as a scholar and churchman was recognized at the Restoration, when he was appointed Bishop of Chester in 1660. In 1667 the London Polyglot had the distinction of being put on the Index Librorum Prohibitorum.

[2] This Dr. Fell is the theme of Thomas Brown's well-known quatrain (adapted from Martial, *Epig.* i. 32) beginning 'I do not love thee, Dr. Fell', &c.

[3] Or Mills, as the *Oxford Dictionary of the Christian Church* prefers, s.v.

Greek text, published exactly two weeks before his death at the age of sixty-two (23 June 1707).[1] Besides collecting all the evidence from Greek manuscripts, early versions, and Fathers that lay within his power to procure, Mill prefixed to his edition valuable prolegomena in which he dealt with the canon of the New Testament and the transmission of the New Testament text, described thirty-two printed editions of the Greek Testament and nearly 100 manuscripts, and discussed patristic citations from all the Fathers of any importance. Some idea of the extent and detail of the prolegomena may be had from the size of the index to the verses to which Mill makes reference in his discussion; these number 3,041 out of almost 8,000 verses in the whole New Testament. Despite the vast amount of solid learning embodied in his edition, however, Mill did not venture to form a text of his own, but reprinted Stephanus' text of 1550 without intentional variation.

In 1710 a reprint of Mill, with the prolegomena somewhat rearranged and with collations of twelve more manuscripts, was published at Amsterdam and Rotterdam by a Westphalian, Ludolf Küster. Küster's reprint also appeared, with a new title-page, at Leipzig in 1723 and again at Amsterdam in 1746.

As Walton's critical efforts had been attacked by Owen, so also Mill's monumental work came under fire from the controversial writer, Dr. Daniel Whitby, Rector of St. Edmund's, Salisbury. Alarmed by the great number of variant readings which Mill had collected—some 30,000 in all—Whitby argued that the authority of the holy Scriptures was in peril, and that the assembling of critical evidence was tantamount to tampering with the text.[2]

There were others, however, who, appreciating the textual evidence collected by Mill, attempted to embody in practical

[1] See Adam Fox, *John Mill and Richard Bentley, a Study of the Textual Criticism of the New Testament, 1675–1729* (Oxford, 1954).

[2] Daniel Whitby, *Examen variantium lectionum J. Millii* (London, 1709). The English Deist, Anthony Collins (1676–1729), did, in fact, appeal to the existence of so many variant readings as an argument against the authority of the Scriptures (*A Discourse of Freethinking* [London, 1713]). The extent to which such considerations might be pushed is disclosed in Dean Swift's satirical essay, *An Argument against the Abolition of Christianity*, in which he refers to a roué 'who had heard of a text brought for proof of the Trinity, which in an ancient manuscript was differently read; he thereupon immediately took the hint, and by a sudden deduction of a long *sorites*, most logically concluded: "Why, if it is as you say, I may safely whore and drink on, and defy the parson" ' (Jonathan Swift, *Works*, iii [Edinburgh, 1814], p. 199).

form the results of his honest critical endeavours. Between 1709 and 1719 Dr. Edward Wells (1667–1727), a mathematician and theological writer, published at Oxford, in ten parts, a Greek Testament with a variety of helps for the reader.[1] Wells deserted the Elzevir text 210 times, almost always agreeing with the judgement of nineteenth-century critical editors. Though Wells's edition was largely ignored by his contemporaries, history accords him the honour of being the first to edit a complete New Testament which abandoned the Textus Receptus in favour of readings from the more ancient manuscripts.

The name of Richard Bentley (1662–1742), Master of Trinity College, Cambridge, is famous in the annals of classical scholarship for his exposure of the spurious Epistles of Phalaris, for his critical editions of Horace and Terence, for his discovery of the use of the digamma in the Homeric poems, and generally for his skill in textual emendation. At an early age Bentley began to correspond with various scholars on the subject of a critical edition of the Greek and Latin New Testament. In 1720 he issued a six-page prospectus of *Proposals for Printing* such an edition, giving as a specimen of his proposed text the last chapter of Revelation in Greek and Latin.[2] Here Bentley abandoned the Textus Receptus in more than forty places.[3]

By following the oldest manuscripts of the Greek original and of Jerome's Vulgate, Bentley was confident that he could

[1] The content of Wells's edition may be seen from the lengthy descriptions on the title-pages, of which the following is a sample:

An Help for the more Easy and Clear Understanding of the Holy Scriptures: being the Two Sacred Treatises of St Luke, Viz. his Gospel and the Acts of the Apostles, Explained after the following Method, viz.
I. The Original or Greek Text amended, according to the Best and most Ancient Readings.
II. The Common English Translation rendered more Agreeable to the Original.
III. A Paraphrase, wherein not only the Difficult Expressions and Passages are explain'd, but also Each Treatise is divided into Proper Sections and Paragraphs: and withall it is observ'd, What Supplements to the Two Gospels of St Matthew and Mark are given us by St Luke in his Gospel. To the End of each Treatise is subjoin'd a Synopsis of the Contents therof.
IV. Annotations relating (as Occasion requires) to the Several Particulars. Oxford, 1719.

[2] For a reproduction of the pamphlet, see Caspar René Gregory, *Prolegomena* (being vol. iii of Tischendorf's *Novum Testamentum Graece*, ed. critica octava maior; Leipzig, 1884–94), pp. 231–40.

[3] Bentley's proposals were the occasion of an acrimonious controversy between Dr. Conyers Middleton and himself; for a summary of the points at issue, see James H. Monk, *The Life of Richard Bentley, D.D.*, 2nd ed., ii (London, 1833), pp. 130 ff.

restore the text of the New Testament as it stood in the fourth century. 'By taking two thousand errors out of the Pope's Vulgate [Bentley refers to Pope Clement's edition of 1592], and as many out of the Protestant Pope Stephen's [referring to Stephanus' Greek text of 1550], I can set out an edition of each in columns, without using any book under nine hundred years old, that shall so exactly agree, word for word, and order for order, that no two tallies, nor two indentures, can agree better.'[1] It is obvious that the Master of Trinity College was not inclined to underestimate his own abilities. In his *Proposals* he refers to the forthcoming edition as 'a κτῆμα ἐσαεί, a *charter*, a *Magna Charta*, to the whole Christian church; to last when all the ancient MSS. here quoted may be lost and extinguished'.

In order to finance the publication, subscriptions were solicited and about £2,000 collected from considerably more than 1,000 prospective purchasers of the edition. Despite the elaborate plans, however, and the amassing of new evidence from manuscripts and Fathers, the scheme came to naught, and after Bentley's death his literary executor returned the money to the subscribers.[2]

While Bentley was gathering materials for a definitive edition which would supplant the Textus Receptus, a Greek and English diglot in two volumes was published anonymously at London in 1729 with the title, *The New Testament in Greek and English. Containing the Original Text Corrected from the Authority of the Most Authentic Manuscripts: and a New Version Form'd agreeably to the Illustrations of the most Learned Commentators and Critics: with Notes and Various Readings, and a Copious Alphabetical Index.* The edition has several typographical peculiarities. In the Greek text the editor discards smooth breathing marks and accents, and at the close of questions he uses '?' instead of the Greek mark of interrogation (the semicolon). In the English translation, as well as in the explanatory notes, he begins sentences with a capital letter only at the beginning of a new paragraph.

The editor of this diglot edition was Daniel Mace, a Presbyterian minister at Newbury, who chose from Mill's apparatus those variant readings which seemed to him to be superior to the Textus Receptus. In a high proportion of these alterations Mace

---

[1] *Bentleii Critica Sacra*, ed. by A. A. Ellis (Cambridge, 1862), p. xv.
[2] See Fox, op. cit., pp. 105–26.

anticipated the opinions of much later scholars.[1] Likewise his English translation reveals a certain independent vigour, for Mace adopted many racy and colloquial expressions; for example, 'don't', 'can't', 'what's', and (words of Simon the Pharisee to Jesus, Luke vii. 40) 'master, said he, lets hear it.' Here and there he anticipated modern versions; for example, in Matt. vi. 27, instead of the King James reference to adding one cubit to one's stature, Mace renders, 'who by all his sollicitude can add one moment to his age?' (In Luke xii. 25 he translates, 'but which of you, with all his disquietude, can add one moment to the period of his life?') In footnotes and appended notes Mace gives reasons for his departure from the earlier traditional text and translation. Several of these notes indicate Mace's free and independent spirit. Thus, in his note on Σινα ορος εστιν εν τη Αραβια (Gal. iv. 25), he declares: 'This has all the marks of an interpolation: it is quite foreign to the argument, and serves only to perplex the apostle's reasoning, which without it appears very clear and coherent.' He dismisses Mill's argument (*Proleg.* 1306), based on the unanimity of manuscript evidence in its favour, with the contemptuous remark, 'as if there was any manuscript so old as COMMON SENSE' (p. 689), and prints the conjecture, το γαρ Αγαρ συστοιχει τη νυν Ιερουσαλημ. . . . In his extended discussion of the title of the Epistle to the Hebrews and the authorship of the Epistle, he writes: 'A very learned writer of our own thinks xiii. 23 a sufficient proof that Paul was the original author. as if no body could be acquainted with Timothy but Paul. which shows, that in order to understand the doctrine of MORAL EVIDENCE, that is, the doctrine of CHANCES, some other discipline and diet is necessary besides that of bearly chewing a few Hebrew roots' (p. 840).

Like the work of many other innovators, Mace's edition was either vehemently attacked or quietly ignored. In England Dr. Leonard Twells, Vicar of St. Mary's in Marlborough, issued in three parts *A Critical Examination of the late New Testament and Version of the New Testament: wherein the Editor's Corrupt Text, False Version, and fallacious Notes are Detected and Censur'd* (London, 1731–2),[2] and on the Continent scholars like Pritius,

---

[1] For a list of some of these, see Eduard Reuss, *Bibliotheca Novi Testamenti graeci* . . . (Brunsvigae, 1872), pp. 175 f.

[2] In Part I under the heading, 'False Renderings, and other foul Management

Baumgarten, and Masch rivalled Twells in their invective and abuse of Mace. But most theologians assumed an ostrich-like pose, and Mace's work was soon all but forgotten.[1]

With Johann Albrecht Bengel (1687–1752) we reach a new stage in the history of the textual criticism of the New Testament. While a student in theology at Tübingen his pietistic faith in the plenary inspiration of the Bible was disturbed by the 30,000 variants which had recently been published in Mill's edition of the Greek Testament, and he resolved to devote himself to the study of the transmission of the text. With characteristic energy and perseverance he procured all the editions, manuscripts, and early translations available to him. After extended study he came to the conclusion that the variant readings were fewer in number than might have been expected, and that they did not shake any article of evangelic doctrine.

In 1725, while teaching at the Lutheran preparatory school for ministerial candidates at Denkendorf, Bengel published an elaborate essay as a 'Forerunner' to his projected edition of the New Testament.[2] Here he laid down sound critical principles. He recognized that the witnesses to the text must not be counted but weighed, that is, classified in 'companies, families, tribes, nations'. He was accordingly the first to distinguish two great groups or 'nations' of manuscripts: the Asiatic, which originated from Constantinople and its environs and which included the manuscripts of more recent date; and the African, which he subdivided into two tribes, represented respectively by codex Alexandrinus and the Old Latin. For the weighing of variant readings Bengel formulated a canon of criticism that, in one form or other, has been approved by all textual critics since. It is based on the recognition that a scribe is more likely to make a difficult construction easier, than make more difficult what was already easy. Formulated in Bengel's pithy Latin it is, *proclivi scriptioni praestat ardua* ('the difficult is to be preferred to the easy reading').

---

favouring Arianism' (pp. 134–44), Twells lists fifteen examples of what he, in some cases with justice, regarded as biased translation.

[1] See now H. McLachlan's article, 'An Almost Forgotten Pioneer in New Testament Criticism', *Hibbert Journal*, xxxvii (1938–9), pp. 617–25.

[2] This essay is entitled 'Prodromus Novi Testamenti recte cauteque ordinandi' and was included as an appendix to his edition of *Chrysostomi libri VI de sacerdotio* (Denkendorf, 1725).

In 1734 Bengel published at Tübingen an edition of the Greek New Testament in a handsome quarto volume. He did not venture to correct the traditional Textus Receptus in accord with personal judgement, but followed (except in nineteen passages in the Book of Revelation) the self-imposed rule of not printing any reading which had not been previously published in an earlier printed edition. He indicated in the margin, however, his views of the relative value of the variant readings according to the following categories: α designates the original reading; β a reading which is better than that which is printed in the text; γ a reading just as good as that in the text; δ less good than the text; ϵ a very inferior reading to be rejected. Bengel also took great pains to standardize the punctuation of the New Testament and to divide it into paragraphs—features which later editors borrowed from his edition. More than half of the volume is devoted to three excursuses in which Bengel supplied a reasoned account of his principles of textual criticism, and an apparatus drawn from Mill's collations plus his own collations of twelve additional manuscripts.[1]

Though Bengel was a man whose personal piety and life of good works were known to all (he had been in charge of an orphan home at Halle) and whose orthodoxy of belief was acknowledged (he was Superintendent of the Evangelical church of Württemberg), he was treated as though he were an enemy of the holy Scriptures. So many persons impugned his motives and condemned his edition that he published in German, and then in Latin, a *Defence of the New Testament*. After Bengel's death his son-in-law, Philip David Burk, published in 1763 an enlarged edition of the *apparatus criticus*, along with several short pamphlets which Bengel had written to explain and defend his mature views on the correct methods of recovering the earliest form of the text of the New Testament.

Among those who collated manuscripts for Bentley was Johann Jakob Wettstein (1693–1754), a native of Basle. His taste for textual criticism showed itself early; when ordained to the ministry at the age of twenty he delivered an address on variant readings in the New Testament. His textual studies, however,

---

[1] A summary of his text-critical principles is available also in the preface to his celebrated commentary on the New Testament entitled *Gnomon Novi Testamenti* (sect. viii).

were interpreted by some as preparations for denying the doctrine of the divinity of Christ, and in 1730 he was deposed from his pastorate and driven into exile. He secured a position as professor of philosophy and Hebrew in the Arminian college at Amsterdam (in succession to the celebrated Jean Leclerc), and resumed his textual studies.¹ In 1751–2 the fruits of forty years of research appeared in his publication at Amsterdam of a magnificent edition of the Greek New Testament in two folio volumes. Though he printed the Elzevir text, he indicated in the margin those readings which he himself held to be correct. In an appendix entitled 'Animadversiones et cautiones ad examen Variarum Lectionum N. T. necessariae',² Wettstein sets forth a good deal of sound advice; for example, he states that *codices autem pondere, non numero estimandi sunt* (§ xviii fin., 'manuscripts must be evaluated by their weight, not by their number'). Despite his generally excellent theoretical views, Wettstein was somewhat haphazard in applying his rules. Furthermore, he came to advocate (largely, it seems, in opposition to Bengel) the quite untenable theory that all of the early Greek manuscripts have been contaminated by the Latin versions, and that consequently the later Greek manuscripts should be relied upon as preserving a more authentic text.

Wettstein's apparatus is the first in which the uncial manuscripts are regularly denoted by capital Roman letters, and the minuscule manuscripts (including lectionaries) by Arabic numerals—a system which has continued to be used to the present time. In addition to the textual material, Wettstein's edition provides a thesaurus of quotations from Greek, Latin, and rabbinical authors, illustrating the usage of words and phrases of the New Testament. Though his critical judgement was not as sound as Bengel's, his passion for the study of manuscripts, which took him on extensive journeys, resulted in the collation or recollation of about 100 manuscripts, and his commentary is still a valuable storehouse of classical, patristic, and rabbinical lore.³

¹ On Wettstein's wide-ranging lectures under the general rubric of 'philosophy', see C. L. Hulbert-Powell's biography, *John James Wettstein, 1693–1754* (London, 1938), pp. 196 f.

² Vol. ii, pp. 851–74, reproduced, with some condensation, from his anonymously published treatise *Prolegomena ad Novi Testamenti graeci editionem accuratissimam . . .* (Amsterdam, 1730), pp. 165–201.

³ In an appendix to his edition of the Greek Testament Wettstein published the

Though he published no edition of the Greek Testament, Johann Salomo Semler (1725–91), often regarded as the father of German rationalism, made noteworthy contributions to the science of textual criticism by his reprint of Wettstein's *Prolegomena*, with discerning comments of his own.[1] Adopting Bengel's system of classifying manuscripts by groups, Semler carried the process still further by assigning the origin of Bengel's Asiatic group (which he renamed Eastern) to the recension[2] prepared in the early fourth century by Lucian of Antioch, and the origin of Bengel's African group (Semler's Western or Egypto-Palestinian group) to Origen. Subsequently Semler expanded his textual researches and classified New Testament manuscripts in three recensions: (1) Alexandrian, derived from Origen and preserved in the Syriac, Bohairic, and Ethiopic versions; (2) Eastern, current in the Antiochian and Constantinopolitan Churches; and (3) Western, embodied in the Latin versions and Fathers. Later witnesses, he thought, were characterized by a mixture of all recensions.[3]

For the next important edition of the Greek Testament we must return to England, where William Bowyer, Jr. (1699–1777), was the third generation in a line of famous printers in London. Often regarded as 'the most learned English printer of whom we have any account',[4] Bowyer not only exercised a scholarly vigilance in printing a wide variety of volumes, but frequently contributed learned prefaces, annotations, and corrigenda to the works which passed through his publishing house. After his father and he had issued several editions of the Textus Receptus of the Greek Testament (in 1715, 1728, 1743, and 1760), Bowyer decided to produce a critical edition worthy of the reputation of his firm. In 1763 such an edition was issued in two volumes of duodecimo size. Bowyer constructed his text

editio princeps of the Syriac text of the two pseudo-Clementine epistles, *De virginitate*, with a Latin translation in parallel columns.

[1] J. S. Semler, *Wetstenii libelli ad crisin atque interpretationem Novi Testamenti* (Halle, 1764).

[2] Semler was the first to apply the term 'recension' to groups of New Testament witnesses (*Hermeneutische Vorbereitung*, iii (1) [Halle, 1765]). Properly a recension is the result of deliberate critical work by an editor; it is, however, often used in a loose sense as synonymous with 'family'.

[3] Semler, *Apparatus ad liberalem Novi Testamenti interpretationem* (Halle, 1767).

[4] S. Austin Allibone, *A Critical Dictionary of English Literature*, i (Philadelphia, 1871), p. 229.

largely by following the critical judgements which Wettstein had expressed in his marginal notes regarding the earliest form of text. By using square brackets Bowyer marked in his text not a few familiar passages which lack the support of good manuscripts; for example, he bracketed the doxology of the Lord's Prayer (Matt. vi. 13), the *pericope de adultera* (John vii. 53–viii. 11), the *comma Johanneum* (1 John v. 7–8), and single verses (such as Acts viii. 37 and xv. 34) and words throughout the New Testament. In other passages Bowyer departed from the Textus Receptus by introducing into his edition readings which the better manuscripts support.[1] In an appendix to the second volume Bowyer included nearly 200 pages of conjectural emendations on the New Testament, bearing on the text and punctuation of the New Testament.[2]

Another Englishman, Edward Harwood (1729–94), a Nonconformist minister, published at London in 1776 a two-volume edition of the New Testament which was, according to the statement on the title-page, 'Collated with the most approved Manuscripts; with Select Notes in English, critical and explanatory; and References to those Authors who have best illustrated the Sacred Writings. To which are added, a Catalogue of the principal Editions of the Greek Testament; and a List of the most esteemed Commentators and critics.' For the Gospels and Acts Harwood followed in the main the text of codex Bezae, and for the Pauline letters codex Claromontanus. Where these were not available he utilized other manuscripts, chiefly codex Alexandrinus.[3] In an analysis of 1,000 passages in the New

---

[1] For a selected list of these, along with other details of Bowyer's edition, reference may be made to the present writer's book, *Chapters in the History of New Testament Textual Criticism* (Leiden and Grand Rapids, 1963), pp. 155–60.

[2] A second edition of the *Conjectures*, with extensive additions, was published separately at London in 1772 with the following title, *Critical Conjectures and Observations on the New Testament, Collected from Various Authors, as Well in Regard to Words as Pointing: With the Reasons on Which Both are Founded*. This volume was translated into German by Joh. Chr. F. Schulz (2 vols., Leipzig, 1774–5). Two other editions, enlarged still further, were published posthumously at London, one in 1782 and the other in 1812, the latter from the annotated interleaved copy of Dr. Henry Owen.

[3] In his preface Harwood declares, 'Excepting typographical errors, which a moderate acquaintance with the language will easily enable the reader to correct, I persuade myself, that the Text of the inspired writers here exhibited will approve itself to every Scholar who is a judge of sacred criticism, to be as near to the original autograph of the Evangelists and Apostles as any hitherto published in the world. To accomplish this arduous design, I carefully read through the late Professor Wetstein's Greek Testament, published at Amsterdam in two Volumes in folio,

Testament, Reuss found that Harwood deserted the Textus Receptus more than 70 per cent. of the time, and in 643 passages agrees with the epoch-making critical edition of Lachmann, published in the nineteenth century (see pp. 124–6 below).

It is not surprising that, in a period when the Textus Receptus held sway and when only occasionally an independent spirit ventured to question its authority, the first Greek Testament to be published in America was the time-honoured Textus Receptus.[1] The printer of this edition, Isaiah Thomas, Jr. (1749–1831), was a typically enterprising and hard-working Yankee. Apprenticed to a printer at the age of six, after only six weeks of indifferent schooling, Thomas began his upward climb that resulted in his becoming a member of nearly every learned society in the country and the recipient of honorary degrees from Dartmouth and Allegheny colleges. His printing establishment issued over 900 different books, more than those of Benjamin Franklin, Hugh Gaine, and Matthew Carey, his nearest rivals. Indeed, owing to the excellence of his typographical work and the range and number of his imprints, Franklin called him 'the Baskerville of America'. Sensing that the market called for an edition of the Greek New Testament, Thomas secured the assistance of a scholarly minister, the Rev. Caleb Alexander,[2] and issued the *editio prima Americana* of the Greek New Testament. The volume, a small-sized duodecimo of 478 pages, was published at Worcester, Massachusetts, in April 1800.

scrupulously weighed the merit or demerit of the various lections there exhibited from a great multitude of Manuscripts of different value, and adopted only those which to my judgment appeared to be best authenticated: my meaning is, that I espoused only those which I verily believed to be the very words which the inspired authors originally wrote' (pp. viii–ix).

[1] The first Bible to be printed in America was the translation made by John Eliot into the Algonquin Indian language, published at Cambridge, Massachusetts, in 1661–3. The first Bible in a European language to be printed in America was Luther's German translation published in 1743 by Christoph Sauer in Germantown, Pennsylvania. The first Bible in English to be published in America came from the press of Robert Aitken at Philadelphia in 1782.

[2] Caleb Alexander (1755–1828), a native of Northfield, Massachusetts, was graduated from Yale College in 1777. During his pastorate at Mendon, a village not far from Worcester, Alexander found time to write two Latin grammars and a Greek grammar, the latter being published by Thomas with the title *Grammatical System of the Grecian Language* (Worcester, 1796). It was doubtless at this period that Thomas secured Alexander's services in supervising the preparation of a Greek New Testament.

The title-page states that the edition reproduces accurately the text of John Mill's edition (*juxta exemplar Joannis Millii accuratissime impressum*). This is, however, not entirely true to fact, for in more than a score of passages the editorial work of Alexander is discernible. According to Isaac H. Hall,[1] a comparison with editions issued by Beza and by the Elzevirs shows that Alexander, in eclectic fashion, occasionally chose a reading now from this edition and now from that. Externally the format of the volume bears many resemblances to Bowyer's editions of the Textus Receptus. In fact, the title-page of the Alexander–Thomas edition reproduces exactly, line for line, word for word, and style for style of type (except only as to date and names and place of publication), the title-page of Bowyer's edition of 1794.[2]

[1] Isaac H. Hall, *A Critical Bibliography of the Greek New Testament as Published in America* (Philadelphia, 1883), p. 11.

[2] For further information regarding the publisher and the text of this first American edition of the Greek Testament, see B. M. Metzger, 'Three Learned Printers and their Unsung Contributions to Biblical Scholarship', *Journal of Religion*, xxxii (1952), pp. 254–62.

IV

The Modern Critical Period:
From Griesbach to the Present

I. THE BEGINNINGS OF SCIENTIFIC TEXTUAL CRITICISM OF THE NEW TESTAMENT

DURING the latter part of the eighteenth century the German scholar Johann Jakob Griesbach (1745–1812) laid foundations for all subsequent work on the Greek text of the New Testament. A pupil of Semler's at Halle, Griesbach was Professor of New Testament at the University of Jena from 1775 until his death. After travelling in England, Holland, and France in order to collate manuscripts, he devoted special attention to the New Testament quotations in the Greek Fathers and to several versions of the New Testament which previously had been little studied, such as the Gothic, the Armenian, and the Philoxenian Syriac.

Griesbach also investigated the history of the transmission of the New Testament text in antiquity and further developed Bengel's and Semler's grouping of manuscripts in recensions. At first he was inclined to divide the extant materials into five or six different groups; he afterwards limited them to three, the Alexandrian, Western, and Byzantine recensions. The standard of the Alexandrian text he believed to be Origen, who, though writing many of his works in Palestine, was assumed to have brought with him into exile copies of the Scriptures similar to those used in his native city. To this group Griesbach assigned the uncial manuscripts C, L, and K, the minuscules 1, 13, 33, 69, 106, and 118, the Bohairic, Armenian, Ethiopic, and Harclean Syriac, and in addition to quotations of Origen, those of Clement of Alexandria, Eusebius, Cyril of Alexandria, and Isidore of Pelusium. To the Western group he assigned codex D, the Latin versions, and, in part, the Peshitta Syriac and the Arabic versions. The Constantinopolitan group, which he regarded as a later compilation from the other two, was represented by A (in the Gospels), and by the great mass of later uncial and minuscule manuscripts, as well as the larger proportion of patristic quotations.

Among the fifteen canons of textual criticism which Griesbach elaborated, the following (his first canon) may be given as a specimen:

The shorter reading (unless it lacks entirely the authority of the ancient and weighty witnesses) is to be preferred to the more verbose, for scribes were much more prone to add than to omit. They scarcely ever deliberately omitted anything, but they added many things; certainly they omitted some things by accident, but likewise not a few things have been added to the text by scribes through errors of the eye, ear, memory, imagination, and judgement. Particularly the shorter reading is to be preferred, even though according to the authority of the witnesses it may appear to be inferior to the other,—

(*a*) if at the same time it is more difficult, more obscure, ambiguous, elliptical, hebraizing, or solecistic;

(*b*) if the same thing is expressed with different phrases in various manuscripts;

(*c*) if the order of words varies;

(*d*) at the beginning of pericopes;

(*e*) if the longer reading savours of a gloss or interpretation, or agrees with the wording of parallel passages, or seems to have come from lectionaries.

But on the other hand the longer reading is to be preferred to the shorter (unless the latter appears in many good witnesses),—

(*a*) if the occasion of the omission can be attributed to homoeoteleuton;

(*b*) if that which was omitted could have seemed to the scribe to be obscure, harsh, superfluous, unusual, paradoxical, offensive to pious ears, erroneous, or in opposition to parallel passages;

(*c*) if that which is lacking could be lacking without harming the sense or the structure of the sentence, as for example incidental, brief propositions, and other matter the absence of which would be scarcely noticed by the scribe when re-reading what he had written;

(*d*) if the shorter reading is less in accord with the character, style, or scope of the author;

(*e*) if the shorter reading utterly lacks sense;

(*f*) if it is probable that the shorter reading has crept in from parallel passages or from lectionaries.

Griesbach showed great skill and tact in evaluating the evidence of variant readings. For example, his judgement, based on patristic and versional evidence, that the shorter form of the Lord's Prayer in Luke xi. 3–4 is to be preferred was remarkably confirmed a few years later when the readings of codex Vaticanus were published, for it was found that all of the omissions are supported by that early manuscript.

The importance of Griesbach for New Testament textual criticism can scarcely be overestimated. For the first time in Germany a scholar ventured to abandon the Textus Receptus at many places and to print the text of the New Testament in the form to which his investigations had brought him. Though at times Griesbach permitted himself to be led astray by a too mechanical adherence to his system of recensions,[1] his textual labours on the whole were characterized by caution and candour. His principal editions were published at Halle in 1775–7, at Halle and London in 1796–1806, and at Leipzig in 1803–7. Several editions of his text were also issued by enterprising printers in England, Scotland, and America. His influence was extended still further when his work was adopted as the basis of smaller manual editions issued on the Continent by Schott, Knapp, Tittmann, Hahn, and Theile.

Soon after the publication of Griesbach's first edition, several other scholars published collations which greatly increased the availability of evidence for the text of the New Testament from Greek manuscripts, the early versions, and the Church Fathers. Christian Friedrich Matthaei (1744–1811), professor first at Wittenberg and then at Moscow, where he taught classical literature, issued at Riga in twelve parts, between 1782 and 1788, an edition of the Greek text with the Latin Vulgate. His printed text is of little value because it is based on manuscripts of recent date, but his apparatus is valuable. Besides collating manuscripts at Dresden, Leipzig, and Göttingen, Matthaei sought out Biblical and patristic manuscripts in Moscow, originally brought to Russia from Mount Athos.[2] He made, for

---

[1] He was vehemently criticized for this and other reasons by Archbishop R. Laurence in his *Remarks on the Systematical Classification of Manuscripts adopted by Griesbach in his Edition of the New Testament* (Oxford, 1814; reprinted in the *Biblical Repertory*, edited by Charles Hodge, ii [1826], pp. 33–95). See below, p. 270.

[2] While in Russia Matthaei managed to steal a good many manuscripts of both the classics and the Fathers. Some of these he kept in his own library, while others

example, collations of thirty-four manuscripts of the homilies of John Chrysostom on the Gospels and the Pauline Epistles. In the second edition of his New Testament, without the Latin Vulgate (3 vols., 1803–7), Matthaei provides evidence from about thirty additional manuscripts. His edition is noteworthy as containing, apparently for the first time, evidence from the Slavic version of the New Testament. In an appendix to his edition of the Book of Revelation Matthaei lists ten Slavic manuscripts which he had examined; he contented himself, however, with collating the text of Revelation in the folio edition of the Slavic Bible published at Moscow in 1762. This evidence is given in Latin, the collation having been made against a manuscript of the Latin Vulgate at Moscow, codex Demidovianus.

Franz Karl Alter (1749–1804), a Jesuit of Silesia who became Professor of Greek at Vienna, published an edition of the Greek Testament in two volumes (Vienna, 1786–7), based on the text of a single manuscript in the Imperial Library at Vienna. In separate appendixes he cited evidence from twenty other Greek manuscripts, two Latin manuscripts, the Bohairic version (which David Wilkins had edited at Oxford in 1716), and four Slavic manuscripts. This is the first edition of the Greek New Testament which contains evidence from Slavic manuscripts themselves.

A still larger addition to the quantity of materials available to the textual critic was made through the efforts of four Danish scholars, Andreas Birch, Jacob G. C. Adler, D. G. Moldenhauer, and O. G. Tychsen, who were sent by the King of Denmark, Christian VII, to examine manuscripts in Italy, Spain, Germany, and other European countries. The results of their labours were published by Birch in a volume describing the then known Greek manuscripts of the New Testament,[1] and in four volumes of collations (Copenhagen, 1788–1801). The latter contain variant readings from 172 Greek manuscripts, and also evidence from two Syriac versions (the Philoxenian and Palestinian). Many of the manuscripts, however, were only partially

he sold or gave to various libraries and friends in Germany and Holland. For an account of his life with incriminating evidence of his brazen thievery, see Oscar von Gebhardt in *Centralblatt für Bibliothekswesen*, xv (1898), pp. 345–57, 393–420, 441–82, and 537–66.

[1] Andreas Birch, *Kritisk Beskrivelse over græske Haandskrifter af det Nye Testamente* (Copenhagen, 1785).

examined by Birch and his colleagues, including codex Vaticanus (B), readings of which now for the first time appeared in print.

About this time two Roman Catholic scholars gave, in different ways, an impetus to the textual criticism of the New Testament. Johann Leonhard Hug (1765–1846), professor at the University of Freiburg in Breisgau, developed the theory[1] that at about the beginning of the third century the several types of New Testament text degenerated rapidly and produced what is commonly called the Western text, which Hug called the κοινὴ ἔκδοσις (the common edition). Toward the middle of the third century, according to Hug, this edition was revised in Palestine by Origen, a revision adopted later by Jerome; in Egypt it was revised by Hesychius, and in Syria by Lucian, a presbyter of Antioch, both of which revisions Jerome condemned. Although Hug started from what was on the whole a true conception of the Western text and its manifold variations, his ingenious attempt to connect three recensions of the Septuagint (whose places of origin he believed assured) with three types of New Testament text failed.

Johannes Martin Augustinus Scholz (1794–1852), a pupil of Hug's and professor at the University of Bonn, travelled extensively throughout Europe and the Near East in order to draw up what was the first comprehensive listing of Greek manuscripts of the New Testament, adding 616 new manuscripts to those previously known. He was the first to emphasize the importance of ascertaining the geographical provenance represented by the several manuscripts, a point which B. H. Streeter was to elaborate in 1924 by his theory of 'local texts'. Unlike Streeter, who relied on the congruence of manuscript readings with patristic citations, Scholz was guided chiefly by certain external signs of provenance, such as details of palaeography, iconography, marginal notes, colophons, and evidence regarding local saints who were honoured in lectionaries.

After some tentative attempts at classifying manuscripts, Scholz came to adopt essentially Bengel's division into two families, which he called the Alexandrian and the Constantinopolitan. During his extensive examinations of minuscule

[1] J. L. Hug, *Einleitung in die Schriften des Neuen Testaments* (Stuttgart, 1808), §§ 22 ff.

manuscripts he was impressed by their general uniformity of text-type, a feature which he regarded as evidence of their superiority to the earlier Alexandrian type. Thus Scholz's two-volume edition of the Greek Testament (Leipzig, 1830–6) marked a retrogression in textual criticism toward the Textus Receptus; only here and there does it happen to contain readings supported by the earlier manuscripts, because the editor was inconsistent in the application of his critical theories. It is symptomatic of the low ebb to which appreciation of textual scholarship had sunk in England at this time that Scholz's edition was welcomed and praised by many British scholars, and its text was reprinted by Bagster in London in several editions. At a later date (1845) Scholz retracted his preference for the Byzantine text, and declared that, if a new edition of his Greek Testament were called for, he would receive into the text most of the Alexandrian readings which he had formerly placed in the margin.

II. THE OVERTHROW OF THE TEXTUS RECEPTUS

The first recognized scholar to break totally with the Textus Receptus was the celebrated classical and Germanic philologist of Berlin, Karl Lachmann (1793–1851), who published an edition of the Greek Testament which rests wholly upon the application of textual criticism in the evaluation of variant readings. Lachmann is famous for his editions of ancient classical authors, including Propertius, Catullus, Tibullus, Lucretius, as well as medieval epics and lyrics, such as the *Nibelungenlied*, Walther von der Vogelweide, and Wolfram von Eschenbach. He demonstrated how, by comparison of manuscripts, it is possible to draw inferences as to their lost ancestors or archetypes, their condition, and their pagination. In his most famous work, that on Lucretius, he showed that the peculiarities of the three chief manuscripts all derive from a single archetype, containing 302 pages of twenty-six lines to the page, and thus he was enabled to make various transpositions in the received text.

In editing the New Testament Lachmann's aim was not to reproduce the original text, which he believed to be an impossible task, but to present on purely documentary evidence, apart from any previously printed editions, the text current in Eastern

Christendom at the end of the fourth century (about A.D. 380). Using no minuscule manuscripts, he based his text on several of the earlier uncials, the Old Latin and Jerome's Vulgate, and the testimony of Irenaeus, Origen, Cyprian, Hilary, and Lucifer. After five years of work, in 1831 he published at Berlin an edition of the Greek text, with a list of passages where it differs from the Textus Receptus. Brackets are used to indicate words of doubtful textual authority. Instead of including in the edition itself an account of his methodology and the reasons that led him to reject the Textus Receptus, Lachmann chose to refer the reader to an article which he had published the previous year in a German periodical.[1] It is not surprising that theologians, even liberal ones like de Wette, generally misunderstood Lachmann's intentions and attacked him with considerable vehemence, coining such names of reproach as 'Bentley's ape' (*simia Bentleii*). In the preface to his second edition (2 vols., Berlin, 1842–50), Lachmann replied in kind, arrogantly twitting his critics for their blind preference for the familiar but corrupt later text to the earlier, purer form.

It was not always appreciated that Lachmann did not pretend to print the original text of the New Testament, but only a provisional one, namely that current in the fourth century, including even palpable scribal errors if sufficiently well attested. The weakness of the edition is the slender manuscript basis to which Lachmann restricted himself. According to Scrivener, 'Lachmann's text seldom rests on more than four Greek codices, very often on three, not infrequently on two; in Matt. vi. 20–viii. 5, and in 165 out of 405 verses of the Apocalypse, on but *one*.'[2] Despite such limitations, however, the judgement of most later scholars has agreed with Hort's evaluation of Lachmann and his work:

A new period began in 1831, when for the first time a text was constructed directly from the ancient documents without the intervention of any printed edition, and when the first systematic attempt was made to substitute scientific method for arbitrary choice in the discrimination of various readings. In both respects the editor,

---

[1] 'Rechenschaft über seine Ausgabe des Neuen Testaments', *Theologische Studien und Kritiken*, [iii] (1830), pp. 817–45.

[2] F. H. A. Scrivener, *A Plain Introduction to the Criticism of the New Testament* 4th ed., ii (London, 1894), p. 233.

Lachmann, rejoiced to declare that he was carrying out the principles and unfulfilled intentions of Bentley, as set forth in 1716 and 1720.[1]

The man to whom modern textual critics of the New Testament owe most is without doubt Lobegott Friedrich Constantin von Tischendorf (1815–74), who sought out and published more manuscripts and produced more critical editions of the Greek Bible than any other single scholar. Between 1841 and 1872 he prepared eight editions of the Greek Testament, some of which were reissued alone or with German or Latin versions, as well as twenty-two volumes of texts of Biblical manuscripts. The total number of his books and articles, most of them relating to Biblical criticism, exceeds 150.[2]

While studying theology at Leipzig from 1834 to 1838 young Tischendorf came under the influence of Johann G. B. Winer, whose grammar of New Testament Greek (1822) went through many editions and remained the standard for several generations. Winer infused in his student a passion to seek and to utilize the most ancient witnesses in reconstructing the purest form of the Greek Scriptures. To this task the young scholar dedicated himself; writing to his fiancée, he declared: 'I am confronted with a sacred task, the struggle to regain the original form of the New Testament.' At the age of twenty-five, supported by a small stipend from the Government of Saxony, Tischendorf began the laborious work of deciphering the palimpsest codex Ephraemi and certain other manuscripts in the Bibliothèque Nationale at Paris. Subsequently he visited libraries throughout Europe and the Near East searching for and examining manuscripts new and old. (For the story of his discovery of codex Sinaiticus, see pp. 42–45 above.)

Of Tischendorf's several editions of the Greek Testament the most important is the eighth (*editio octava critica maior*), issued in eleven parts, beginning in 1864, and published in two volumes (Leipzig, 1869–72). This was accompanied by a rich *apparatus criticus* in which Tischendorf assembled all of the variant read-

---

[1] Westcott and Hort, *The New Testament in the Original Greek*, [ii,] *Introduction* [and] *Appendix* (Cambridge, 1881), p. 13. See below, p. 270.

[2] See the biographical article on Tischendorf written by Caspar René Gregory in *Bibliotheca Sacra*, xxxiii (1876), pp. 153–93, containing a list of Tischendorf's publications.

ings which he or his predecessors had found in manuscripts, versions, and Fathers. Soon after the publication of the second volume a stroke of palsy prevented Tischendorf from continuing his labours. A third volume of valuable *Prolegomena* to the edition was prepared by Caspar René Gregory and issued in three parts (Leipzig, 1884, 1890, 1894).[1]

Tischendorf's claim to fame rests chiefly upon his indefatigable industry in assembling textual evidence; his use of that evidence in constructing his editions, however, was marked by a somewhat wooden adherence to a number of critical canons, as well as a certain arbitrariness in dealing with problems not covered by the canons. The text of his eighth edition differs (according to Eberhard Nestle) from the seventh edition in 3,572 places, and he has been accused of giving excessive weight to the evidence of codex Sinaiticus, which he had discovered between issuing the two editions.

In England the scholar who, at the middle of the nineteenth century, was most successful in drawing British preference away from the Textus Receptus was Samuel Prideaux Tregelles (1813–75). As a boy he had shown exceptional talent and intellectual curiosity, and while earning his livelihood at an ironworks managed to devote his spare time to learning Greek, Aramaic, Hebrew, and Welsh. While still in his early twenties, Tregelles began to form plans for a new critical edition of the New Testament. Having observed how persistently Scholz rejected the evidence of the earliest manuscripts, and being dissatisfied with the somewhat hesitating way in which Griesbach still clung to the Textus Receptus, he determined to employ his leisure time in preparing an edition based only on the evidence of the earliest witnesses. Without his knowing it, Tregelles developed critical principles that paralleled to a remarkable degree those of Lachmann. Thereafter he was engaged in the collation of Greek manuscripts, making extensive travels throughout Europe for the purpose. His careful and systematic examination of practically all the then known uncials and several of the important minuscules resulted in the correction of many erroneous citations made by previous editors. He also

---

[1] Gregory's volume of *Prolegomena*, with additions and corrections, was later published in German in three parts, entitled *Textkritik des Neuen Testamentes* (Leipzig, 1900–9).

examined afresh the New Testament quotations found in Greek Church Fathers down to Eusebius, as well as the ancient versions, and edited (1861) a palimpsest manuscript of the Gospel of Luke, codex Zacynthius (E), acquired in 1821 by the British and Foreign Bible Society. Before issuing any portion of his new text, however, Tregelles published a survey of earlier editions in which he set forth his own critical principles (*An Account of the Printed Text of the Greek New Testament* . . ., London, 1854); he also rewrote that portion of T. H. Horne's encyclopedic *Introduction to the Critical Study and Knowledge of the Holy Scriptures* which relates to the textual criticism of the New Testament (vol. iv, 10th ed., London, 1856).

Unlike Tischendorf, who hurried into print with another edition as soon as he had discovered some new manuscript evidence, Tregelles preferred to fix his full energy upon the final goal of a definitive text representing his mature judgement, and issued but one edition. This was published at London in six parts between 1857 and 1872. Disabled by a stroke of paralysis in 1870, he secured the assistance of B. W. Newton for the final fascicle. A volume of prolegomena compiled from Tregelles's other works, and containing many pages of *addenda et corrigenda*, was edited by F. J. A. Hort and A. W. Streane and published posthumously in 1879. In spite of poverty, opposition, and ill health, Tregelles overcame all difficulties and devoted a lifetime of meticulous labours upon the text of the New Testament as an act of worship, undertaken, as he declares in the preface, 'in the full belief that it would be for the service of God, by serving His Church'.

Though remembered primarily for his widely used commentary on the New Testament, Henry Alford (1810–71), Dean of Canterbury and author of several well-known hymns (among them 'Come, ye thankful people, come' and 'Ten thousand times ten thousand'), deserves mention here as an ardent advocate of the critical principles formulated by those who, like Lachmann, had worked for the 'demolition of the unworthy and pedantic reverence for the received text, which stood in the way of all chance of discovering the genuine word of God'.[1] In the successive editions of his commentary, Alford

---

[1] Henry Alford, *The Greek Testament, with a critically revised Text* . . ., new ed., i, (New York, 1881), p. 76 of the prolegomena.

set forth more and more fully the evidence of variant readings, and boldly printed that form of Greek text which he believed was supported by the earliest and best witnesses.

The year 1881 was marked by the publication of the most noteworthy critical edition of the Greek Testament ever produced by British scholarship. After working about twenty-eight years on this edition (from about 1853 to 1881), Brooke Foss Westcott (1825–1901), Canon of Peterborough and Regius Professor of Divinity at Cambridge (he was consecrated Bishop of Durham in 1890), and Fenton John Anthony Hort (1828–92), Hulsean Professor of Divinity at Cambridge, issued two volumes entitled, *The New Testament in the Original Greek*. Volume i contains the Greek text; volume ii comprises a valuable *Introduction* and *Appendix*, in which the critical principles followed by the two editors are set forth in detail by Hort, with the concurrence of his colleague, and certain problem passages are discussed.[1]

Unlike earlier editors, neither Westcott nor Hort was concerned to collate manuscripts, nor did they provide a critical apparatus. Rather, utilizing previous collections of variant readings, they refined the critical methodology developed by Griesbach, Lachmann, and others, and applied it rigorously, but with discrimination, to the witnesses to the text of the New Testament. The principles and procedures of criticism which they elaborated may be summarized as follows.

Hort begins the classic *Introduction* by discussing what he calls Internal Evidence of Readings.

The most rudimentary form of criticism [he writes] consists in dealing with each variation independently, and adopting at once in each case out of two or more variants that which looks most probable. . . . Internal Evidence of Readings is of two kinds, which cannot be too sharply distinguished from each other; appealing respectively to Intrinsic Probability, having reference to the author, and what may be called Transcriptional Probability, having reference to the copyists. In appealing to the first, we ask what an author is likely to have written: in appealing to the

---

[1] Occasionally, when the editors could not agree in certain details, the opinion of each is identified by his initials. The second edition of the second volume, published in 1896, contains some additional notes by F. C. Burkitt on the recently discovered Sinaitic Syriac manuscript.

second, we ask what copyists are likely to have made him seem to write.[1]

When, as sometimes happens, Intrinsic and Transcriptional Probabilities are in conflict, it is usually safer to make judgements on the basis of what Hort called the 'observed proclivities of average copyists' than on what one imagines the original author must have written.

In order to transcend the limitations inherent in a procedure based solely on Internal Evidence of Readings, the textual critic must also utilize Internal Evidence of Documents. When weighing the evidence in individual cases, one gains assurance by considering whether a witness is normally credible and trustworthy. Therefore, instead of being content with evaluating one reading after another, in isolation from each other, the critic should collect information regarding the character of individual manuscripts. If one finds that a given manuscript frequently supports certain readings which clearly commend themselves as original on the basis of probability, it is natural to prefer its readings in other instances when the Internal Evidence of Readings is not clear enough for a decision. Hort summarizes this point by enunciating the principle that 'knowledge of documents should precede final judgement upon readings'.[2]

The next step involves the examination of the relationship of the several witnesses to one another. Manuscripts may be grouped and considered from the standpoint of their genealogy. If, for example, of ten manuscripts nine agree against one, but the nine have a common original, the numerical preponderance counts for nothing. The clearest evidence in tracing the genealogy of witnesses is the presence of conflate readings, that is, readings which have arisen from the combination of elements which had existed previously in separate manuscripts. Here Hort enunciates another principle of criticism, that 'all trustworthy restoration of corrupted texts is founded on the study of their history, that is, of the relations of descent or affinity which connect the several documents'.[3]

Finally, in his discussion of methodology, Hort considers the Internal Evidence of Groups, which is in some sense inter-

---

[1] Westcott and Hort, op. cit., pp. 19–20.
[2] Ibid., p. 31.
[3] Ibid., p. 40.

mediate between Internal Evidence of Documents and Genealogical Evidence. Just as it is useful to determine the general
characteristics of a given manuscript by observing how often it
supports or rejects readings which have been previously evaluated individually on the basis of Internal Probability, so the
general characteristics of a given *group* of witnesses can be
determined and evaluated in relation to other groups.

The validity of inferences based on this procedure depends on
the genealogical principle that 'community of reading implies
community of origin'.[1] Such generalizations on the value of
groups of witnesses, in turn, assist the critic in coming to decisions in instances where mixture in the ancestry of manuscripts
makes it difficult to draw up a genealogical family tree.

The paragraphs above contain a summary of the critical
principles adopted and elaborated by Westcott and Hort. The
results of their application of these principles to the then known
New Testament manuscripts will now be briefly set forth.

On the basis of investigations as to relationships among the
witnesses to the text of the New Testament, Westcott and Hort
distinguished four principal types of text, which they called the
Syrian, the Western, the Alexandrian, and the Neutral.

(1) The latest of these four forms of text is the Syrian, which
is a mixed text resulting from a revision made by an editor or
editors in the fourth century who wished to produce a smooth,
easy, and complete text. This conflated text, the farthest removed from the originals, was taken to Constantinople, whence
it was disseminated widely throughout the Byzantine Empire.
It is best represented today by codex Alexandrinus (in the Gospels, not in Acts and the Epistles), the later uncial manuscripts,
and the great mass of minuscule manuscripts. The Textus Receptus is the latest form of the Syrian text.

Hort's classic description of the Syrian text is as follows:

> The qualities which the authors of the Syrian text seem to have
> most desired to impress on it are lucidity and completeness. They
> were evidently anxious to remove all stumbling-blocks out of the way
> of the ordinary reader, so far as this could be done without recourse
> to violent measures. They were apparently equally desirous that he
> should have the benefit of instructive matter contained in all the
> existing texts, provided it did not confuse the context or introduce

[1] Ibid., p. 60.

seeming contradictions. New omissions accordingly are rare, and
where they occur are usually found to contribute to apparent simplicity. New interpolations on the other hand are abundant, most
of them being due to harmonistic or other assimilation, fortunately
capricious and incomplete. Both in matter and in diction the Syrian
text is conspicuously a full text. It delights in pronouns, conjunctions, and expletives and supplied links of all kinds, as well as in more
considerable additions. As distinguished from the bold vigour of the
'Western' scribes, and the refined scholarship of the Alexandrians,
the spirit of its own corrections is at once sensible and feeble. Entirely
blameless on either literary or religious grounds as regards vulgarised
or unworthy diction, yet shewing no marks of either critical or spiritual insight, it presents the New Testament in a form smooth and
attractive, but appreciably impoverished in sense and force, more
fitted for cursory perusal or recitation than for repeated and diligent
study.[1]

(2) Of the remaining types of texts which Westcott and Hort
isolated, the so-called Western type is both ancient and widespread. It is preserved in certain bilingual uncial manuscripts,
notably codex Bezae of the Gospels and Acts (D) and codex
Claromontanus of the Epistles (D^p), in the Old Latin version(s),
and in the Curetonian Syriac. Its date of origin must have been
extremely early, perhaps before the middle of the second century. Marcion, Tatian, Justin, Irenaeus, Hippolytus, Tertullian, and Cyprian all made use to a greater or less extent of a
Western form of text.

One of the marked characteristics of the Western text, according to Hort, is a love of paraphrase:

Words, clauses, and even whole sentences were changed, omitted,
and inserted with astonishing freedom, wherever it seemed that the
meaning could be brought out with greater force and definiteness....
Another equally important characteristic is a disposition to enrich
the text at the cost of its purity by alterations or additions taken from
traditional and perhaps from apocryphal or other non-biblical
sources. [The Western text is also characterized by] the multiplication of genitive pronouns, but occasionally their suppression
where they appeared cumbrous; the insertion of objects, genitive,
dative, or accusative, after verbs used absolutely, the insertion of
conjunctions in sentences which had none, but occasionally their
excision where their force was not perceived and the form of the

---

[1] Westcott and Hort, op. cit., pp. 134 f.

sentence or context seemed to commend abruptness; free interchange of conjunctions; free interchange of the formulæ introduc-
tory to spoken words; free interchange of participle and finite verb
with two finite verbs connected by a conjunction; substitution of
compound verbs for simple as a rule, but conversely where the
compound verb of the true text was difficult or unusual; and substitution of aorists for imperfects as a rule, but with a few examples of
the converse. . . .

Another impulse of scribes abundantly exemplified in Western
readings is the fondness for assimilation. In its most obvious form
it is merely local, abolishing diversities of diction where the same
subject matter recurs as part of two or more neighbouring clauses
or verses, or correcting apparent defects of symmetry. But its most
dangerous work is 'harmonistic' corruption, that is, the partial or
total obliteration of differences in passages otherwise more or less
resembling each other.[1]

(3) The Alexandrian text, according to Westcott and Hort, is
preserved to a greater or less extent in codex Ephraemi (C),
codex Regius (L), codex 33, and the Coptic versions (especially
the Bohairic), as well as the quotations of the Alexandrian
Fathers, Clement, Origen, Dionysius, Didymus, and Cyril. Its
characteristic is that which might be expected from the influence
of a Greek literary centre—a delicate philological tact in correcting forms, syntax, and in subtle changes made in the interest of
attaining a greater degree of polish in language and style (such
as the rearrangement of the order of words to avoid hiatus).

(4) The Neutral text, as its question-begging name implies, is,
in the opinion of Westcott and Hort, the most free from later
corruption and mixture, and comes nearest to the text of the
autographs. It is best represented by codex Vaticanus (B), and
next by codex Sinaiticus (‫א‬). The concurrence of these two
manuscripts is very strong, and cannot be far from the original
text. With the exception of a few passages, which they specify,
Westcott and Hort declare:

It is our belief (1) that the readings of ‫א‬ B should be accepted
as the true readings until strong internal evidence is found to the
contrary, and (2) that no readings of ‫א‬ B can safely be rejected
absolutely, though it is sometimes right to place them only on an
alternative footing, especially where they receive no support from
Versions or Fathers.[2]

[1] Ibid., pp. 122–4.   [2] Ibid., p. 225.

The exceptions to their preference for the Neutral text are several passages which Westcott and Hort term 'Western non-interpolations'. They doubtless chose this cumbersome nomenclature simply because they could not bring themselves to refer directly to 'Neutral interpolations'—which is exactly what, on their own reconstruction, is involved in these readings. In several passages in the last three chapters of Luke, and one in Matthew,[1] the Western text is regarded by Westcott and Hort as preserving the original form of text. The reason they abandon the testimony of ℵ and B in these passages is that here the Western text, which normally is the fuller and more circumstantial form of text, has resisted (so they believe) the impulse to add material, whereas it is the Neutral text that presents the expanded reading.

In accord with Westcott and Hort's critical reconstruction, the relation of their four text-types to the autograph may be represented by the following stemma:

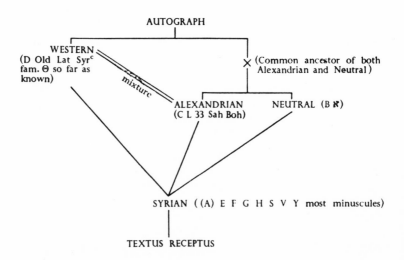

---

[1] The Western non-interpolations, which Westcott and Hort print within double brackets, are in Matt. xxvii. 49; Luke xxii. 19–20; xxiv. 3, 6, 12, 36, 40, 51, and 52. Nearly a score of other, somewhat similar passages throughout the Gospels form an intermediate class which, in their opinion, may also involve Western non-interpolations; see Westcott and Hort, op. cit., p. 176.

By way of retrospect and evaluation it may be said that scholars today generally agree that one of the chief contributions made by Westcott and Hort was their clear demonstration that the Syrian (or Byzantine) text is later than the other types of text. Three main types of evidence support this judgement: (1) the Syrian text contains combined or conflate readings which are clearly composed of elements current in earlier forms of text; (2) no ante-Nicene Father quotes a distinctively Syrian reading; and (3) when the Syrian readings are compared with the rival readings their claim to be regarded as original is found gradually to diminish, and at last to disappear.[1]

It was perhaps not surprising that Westcott and Hort's total rejection of the claims of the Textus Receptus to be the original text of the New Testament should have been viewed with alarm by many churchmen. During the closing decades of the nineteenth century the traditional text found a doughty defender in the person of John W. Burgon (1813–88), Dean of Chichester. He has been described as 'a High-churchman of the old school' who became notorious as 'a leading champion of lost causes and impossible beliefs; but the vehemence of his advocacy somewhat impaired its effect'.[2] His conservatism can be gauged from a sermon he preached at Oxford in 1884 in which he denounced the higher education of 'young women as young men' as 'a thing inexpedient and immodest'; the occasion was the admission of women to university examinations!

The publication in 1881 of the Revised Version of the King James or Authorized Version of 1611 aroused Burgon's indignation not only on the score of its unidiomatic English, but even more because the Revisers had adopted an underlying Greek text substantially identical with that of Westcott and Hort. In a series of three learned articles in the London *Quarterly Review*, which were reprinted in a volume entitled *The Revision Revised* (London, 1883), Burgon used every rhetorical device at his disposal to attack both the English Revision and the Greek Testament of Westcott and Hort. Burgon's argument was basically theological and speculative. As an ardent high-churchman he could not imagine that, if the words of Scripture had been dictated by the inspiration of the Holy Spirit, God would not

---

[1] Ibid., pp. 93–119.
[2] So the *Dictionary of National Biography*, suppl. vol. i, s.n.

have providentially prevented them from being seriously corrupted during the course of their transmission. Consequently it was inconceivable to Burgon that the Textus Receptus, which had been used by the Church for centuries, could be in need of the drastic revision which Westcott and Hort had administered to it. (See below, p. 270.)

What Burgon was apparently unable to comprehend was the force of the genealogical method, by which the later, conflated text is demonstrated to be secondary and corrupt. Instead of following the text of the few earlier manuscripts, Burgon preferred the readings supported by the majority of the later witnesses.[1] Consequently, so far from sharing Westcott and Hort's high regard for the testimony of codex Vaticanus and codex Sinaiticus, Burgon maintained that, with the single exception of D, which exhibits the wildest text of all, the two manuscripts honoured by Westcott and Hort are the most depraved. He assures his readers

without a particle of hesitation, that ℵ B D are three of *the most scandalously* corrupt copies extant:—exhibit *the most shamefully mutilated* texts which are anywhere to be met with:—have become, by whatever process (for their history is wholly unknown), the depositories of the largest amount of *fabricated readings*, ancient *blunders*, and *intentional perversions of Truth*,—which are discoverable in any known copies of the Word of GOD.[2]

[1] Burgon found an ally in Thomas R. Birks, Honorary Canon of Ely, in his *Essay on the Right Estimation of Manuscript Evidence in the Text of the New Testament* (London, 1878). Birks, who attempted to assign a mathematical weight to individual manuscripts, considered the later manuscripts in general to be more valuable than the earlier ones!

The anachronistic views of Burgon have been resuscitated recently by Edward F. Hills in his booklet, *The King James Version Defended! A Christian View of the New Testament Manuscripts* (Des Moines, 1956), in which the author outdoes Burgon in defending the Textus Receptus, arguing even for the genuineness of the *Comma Johanneum* of 1 John v. 7–8. See also Hills's introduction entitled 'Dean Burgon in the Light of Criticism' in the 1959 reprint of Burgon's book, *The Last Twelve Verses of the Gospel according to St. Mark Vindicated . . .* (first published in 1871).

[2] *The Revision Revised* (London, 1883), p. 16 (the italics are Burgon's).

At the suggestion of Prebendary Edward Miller, Burgon's literary executor, a debate was held at New College, Oxford, on 6 May 1897, when the position of Burgon was upheld by Miller, G. H. Gwilliam, and A. Bonus, against William Sanday, A. C. Headlam, and Willoughby C. Allen, who advocated the textual views of Westcott and Hort. One of the chief points of contention was the date of the Peshitta Syriac version of the New Testament. Miller maintained that this version, which is a witness to the Syrian type of text, goes back to the second century, and that therefore the Syrian type of text did not originate with Lucian and his con-

Two other British scholars, F. H. A. Scrivener and George Salmon, were also critical of Westcott and Hort's theories, but were far more temperate than Burgon in the expression of their dissent. The former objected to Hort's total rejection of the testimony of the Syrian text,[1] and the latter complained that more consideration should have been given to the weight of purely Western readings.[2]

This somewhat lengthy account of the work of Westcott and Hort may be concluded with the observation that the over-whelming consensus of scholarly opinion recognizes that their critical edition was truly epoch-making. They presented what is doubtless the oldest and purest text that could be attained with the means of information available in their day. Though the discovery of additional manuscripts has required the realignment of certain groups of witnesses,[3] the general validity of their critical principles and procedures is widely acknowledged by textual scholars today.

During his long and fruitful life Bernhard Weiss (1827–1918), Professor of New Testament Exegesis at Kiel and at Berlin, edited the New Testament in Greek (3 vols., Leipzig, 1894–1900; second, small ed., 3 vols., 1902–5). Primarily an exegete, Weiss brought to his task an extensive and detailed knowledge of the theological and literary problems of the text of the New Testament. Instead of grouping manuscript authorities and evaluating variants in terms of external support, Weiss discriminated among readings in accord with what he deemed to be the most appropriate meaning in the context. His procedure was to go through each New Testament book with a critical apparatus and to consider important textual variants,

temporaries at the beginning of the fourth century. Sanday acknowledged that the date of the Peshitta was 'the sheet anchor' of Miller's position, but was unable to produce convincing evidence for its later origin (*The Oxford Debate on the Textual Criticism of the New Testament* [London, 1897], p. 28).

A few years later F. C. Burkitt set forth evidence in his monograph, *St. Ephraim's Quotations from the Gospel* (Cambridge, 1901), showing that the New Testament quotations in the genuine works of Ephraem (d. 373) agree largely with the Old Syriac version and not with the Peshitta, and that therefore the latter appears to have been produced subsequently to Ephraem's lifetime.

[1] F. H. A. Scrivener, *A Plain Introduction to the Criticism of the New Testament*, 4th ed., ii (London, 1894), pp. 287 f.

[2] George Salmon, *Some Thoughts on the Textual Criticism of the New Testament* (London, 1897), pp. 129 ff.

[3] See pp. 214–17 below.

selecting in each case that reading which seemed to him to be justified, as Hort would have said, by intrinsic probability. While this procedure is certainly 'subjective' to an extreme, one must not suppose that other methods are entirely 'objective'. Even Westcott and Hort's criticism is subjective, for first they chose the method which they decided to follow, and then they judged that their so-called Neutral text is generally to be preferred above all other types of text.

After Weiss had edited his text by adopting the variants which he regarded as most appropriate to the author's style and theology, he drew up lists of different classes of error which he observed among the variant readings, and evaluated each of the chief Greek manuscripts in accordance with its relative freedom from such faults. The classes of error which he detected are: (*a*) harmonizations among the Gospels; (*b*) the interchange of words; (*c*) omissions and additions; (*d*) alterations of word order; and (*e*) orthographical variation. In assessing the degree of freedom of Greek manuscripts from these errors, Weiss decided that codex Vaticanus was the best. It is not surprising, therefore, that the general complexion of Weiss's edition is remarkably similar to that of Westcott and Hort, who relied so largely on codex Vaticanus. The importance of Weiss's text is not only that it represents the mature opinion of a great exegetical scholar who had given years of detailed consideration to the meaning of the text; it is important also because the results of his 'subjective' methodology confirm the results of scholars who followed a different procedure, sometimes regarded as more 'objective' because it started from the grouping of the manuscripts themselves.[1]

Though issued in 1910 (the text remained unchanged in the second edition, 1947) Alexander Souter's Greek New Testament represents the position of British textual scholarship as it was in 1881; the edition merely reproduces the Greek text that Archdeacon Edwin Palmer, a member of the New Testament panel of British translators, constructed as the text which inferentially lies behind the Revised Version of 1881. Taking the third edition of Stephanus (1550) as the basis of his edition, Palmer formed

---

[1] See C. R. Gregory, 'Bernhard Weiss and the New Testament', *American Journal of Theology*, i (1896), pp. 16–37, and Kirsopp Lake, 'Dr. Weiss's Text of the Gospels: the Thoughts of a Textual Critic on the Text of an Exegete', ibid. vii (1903), pp. 249–58.

a continuous text which represents the textual decisions of the Revisers. When, however, the English Revision was considered to represent correctly either of two competing readings, Palmer did not ordinarily alter the Textus Receptus. As a result the orthography, the spelling of proper names, and the typographical peculiarities or errors of Stephanus are, with a few exceptions, retained.

Souter's contribution in 1910 was the preparation of a selected critical apparatus to go with Palmer's text. The chief strength of this apparatus lies in the relatively full evidence which is quoted from the Church Fathers, particularly the Latin Fathers. In 1947 the apparatus was enlarged by the addition of evidence from the Chester Beatty papyri and other witnesses brought to light since 1910. As regards textual complexion, Souter's edition is closer to the Textus Receptus than is any other widely used Greek Testament today.[1]

The most monumental edition of the Greek New Testament that has appeared thus far in the twentieth century is von Soden's *Die Schriften des Neuen Testaments in ihrer ältesten erreichbaren Textgestalt hergestellt auf Grund ihrer Textgeschichte;* I. Teil, *Untersuchungen* (Berlin, 1902–10); II. Teil, *Text mit Apparat* (Göttingen, 1913).[2] Hermann Freiherr von Soden was born in 1852 at Cincinnati, Ohio, and died in 1914 as the result of a mishap that occurred while boarding a subway train in Berlin. Containing the results of prolonged investigation of the Greek minuscules and of intensive study of the history of the Greek text, von Soden's edition has nevertheless been described as 'a magnificent failure'.

Through the financial assistance of a friend, Miss Elise Koenigs, von Soden was enabled to send out a considerable number of research students and scholars to examine manuscripts in the libraries of Europe and the Near East. These

---

[1] On the basis of an analysis of eleven sample chapters scattered throughout the New Testament J. Harold Greenlee found that: Nestle's text differs from the Textus Receptus in 233 cases, Merk's text differs in 160 cases, Bover's text in 111 cases, Vogels's text in 67 cases, and Souter's in 47 cases. In terms of percentage, this means that Nestle differs from the Textus Receptus 496% in comparison with Souter! See Kurt Aland, who quotes Greenlee's statistics in his article 'The Position of New Testament Textual Criticism' in *Studia Evangelica*, ed. by Aland, F. L. Cross, et al. (= *Texte und Untersuchungen*, lxxiii, Berlin, 1959), p. 719. See below, p. 270.

[2] Von Soden also published a smaller edition (Handausgabe), entitled *Griechisches Neues Testament, Text mit kurzem Apparat* (Göttingen, 1913).

helpers secured partial or complete collations of an immense number of hitherto unexamined manuscripts. Utilizing this information, von Soden set forth his views regarding the history of the text in 2,203 pages of prolegomena, much of it printed in small type! Dissatisfied with the sigla previously used to designate uncial and minuscule manuscripts, he devised a new system of nomenclature which indicates the age, contents, and type of each manuscript. Though the system is ingenious, it is also so highly complicated[1] that most subsequent textual critics have refused to adopt it, preferring instead the old system, which was slightly revised by Gregory[2] in order to remove a number of anomalies. As a result, in order to make practical use of von Soden's apparatus, it is necessary to consult a 'key' to unlock the significance of what otherwise are meaningless hieroglyphs.[3]

Von Soden's classification of the text-types of manuscripts of the Gospels is based on considerations of their general textual

---

[1] Von Soden divides all known Greek manuscripts into three classes: (1) the δ-manuscripts, containing the whole New Testament ($\delta\iota\alpha\theta\eta\kappa\eta$), with or without the exception of the Book of Revelation; (2) the ε-manuscripts, containing the Gospels ($\epsilon\dot{\nu}\alpha\gamma\gamma\dot{\epsilon}\lambda\iota\sigma\nu$); (3) the α-manuscripts, containing Acts and the Epistles, with or without the Book of Revelation ($\dot{\alpha}\pi\dot{\sigma}\sigma\tau\sigma\lambda\sigma s$). Within each of these classes numbers are assigned in accord with the date and contents of each manuscript. The δ- and α-manuscripts, up to the close of the ninth century, are numbered 1–49; those of the tenth century, 50–90; for the following centuries numbers of three digits are used, and the numeral in the hundreds place indicates the century (thus, 146 is a manuscript of the eleventh century; 446, a manuscript of the fourteenth century). In δ-manuscripts the presence of the Book of Revelation is indicated by using 1–49 in each hundred and 50–99 for those without it (thus δ 421 would be a fourteenth-century manuscript containing the whole of the New Testament; δ 271 would be a twelfth-century manuscript containing all the books of the New Testament except the Apocalypse). Similarly, the contents of the α-manuscripts are indicated by a still more involved system of numerals. Since the ε-manuscripts are so very numerous, the system is modified by the addition of other digits.

Besides being intolerably complicated, von Soden's nomenclature tells more than one is likely to want to know—for what useful end is gained by being informed of the other New Testament books which a manuscript contains in addition to the book in which the given variant appears? Furthermore, the system permits the addition of only a limited number of newly found manuscripts, and makes no provision at all for the Greek lectionaries. Moreover, since opinion concerning the date of individual manuscripts may change, the elaborate provision to represent the age of a given document may well perpetuate what has come to be regarded as an error.

[2] Caspar René Gregory, *Die griechischen Handschriften des Neuen Testaments* (Leipzig, 1908).

[3] For convenient 'keys' to transpose von Soden's system of enumeration into the Gregory system, see Friedrich Krüger, *Schlüssel zu von Sodens Die Schriften des Neuen Testaments . . .* (Göttingen, 1927), and Benedikt Kraft, *Die Zeichen für die wichtigeren Handschriften des griechischen Neuen Testaments*, 3te Aufl. (Freiburg i. Br., 1955).

characteristics, on the form of the text of the *pericope de adultera*, and on the chapter divisions attached to them. Using these criteria, he divided the witnesses into three main groups, which he called the Koine, the Hesychian, and the Jerusalem recensions.

The K ($= Kοινή$) text is divided into about seventeen sub-groups, of which K^1 is the oldest and best form. Produced by Lucian of Antioch (martyred A.D. 312), this text, with various subsequent alterations, became the prevailing text throughout the Byzantine Church (Westcott and Hort's Syrian text).

The H ($= 'Hσύχιος$) text, which von Soden traced to Hesychius of Egypt, is preserved today in the old uncials (B, א, C, L, $Δ$, and $Ψ$), some minuscules (e.g. 33, 579, 892, and 1241), the Sahidic and Bohairic versions, and in the Alexandrian Fathers Athanasius, Didymus, Cyril, and others. It therefore includes what Westcott and Hort called the Neutral and the Alexandrian texts.

The I ($= 'Iεροσόλυμα$) text, deriving probably from Eusebius and Pamphilus of Caesarea in Palestine, is not preserved in substantial integrity in any outstanding manuscripts, but must be elicited from a number of authorities of mixed characteristics. The best witnesses in the Gospels are the uncials D and $Θ$ and the minuscules 28, 372, 565, and 700, but so diverse are the textual phenomena that von Soden was compelled to posit seventeen sub-groups of witnesses which are more or less closely related to this text.

According to von Soden these three recensions go back to a lost archetype, the I–H–K text, used by Origen, but already corrupted in the second century by Marcion, in the case of the Pauline Epistles, and by Tatian, in the case of the Gospels and Acts. The discovery and elimination of these corruptions brings us to the original text.

Among the principles which von Soden followed in constructing his text are the following:

(1) When the readings of the three great recensions are certain, the reading supported by two recensions is generally adopted.

(2) If two recensions have a reading which agrees with a parallel, the reading of the third which differs from the parallel is usually preferred.

(3) The reading supported by Tatian is at once open to the

suspicion of departing from the original text. Only in the event of two recensions agreeing with Tatian and the dissenting recension agreeing with a parallel is the latter to be adjudged secondary; and this remains the case even when the former reading also agrees with a parallel.

(4) When early, certainly mutually independent witnesses— even though they may be only patristic writers or versions— agree in a reading which differs from Tatian, this reading requires serious consideration for adoption even when all three recensions agree with Tatian.

While acknowledging the enormous amount of research which von Soden's edition represents, most scholars have criticized his methods and results in the following respects:[1]

(*a*) Since von Soden tends to give preference to readings supported by two of the three main texts, by this procedure the Koine type of text is elevated to a rank co-ordinate in importance with the other two texts. So far from regarding the Koine as an independent entity, however, most scholars today follow the view of Griesbach, Hort, and others, that this text is largely secondary and derivative from the others. As a consequence of von Soden's high estimate of the value of the Koine text, his edition approaches the Textus Receptus more closely than does any previous modern critical text.

(*b*) Though von Soden thought that his chief contribution to textual studies was the isolation and subdivision of his *I*-text, later scholars regard it as the least sound, for he includes in one text-type such heterogeneous elements as the Western witnesses, the Caesarean text, the Old Latin, and the Old Syriac, as well as witnesses which are mixed with the Koine text.

(*c*) While Marcion and Tatian undoubtedly had a certain corrupting influence upon the transmission of the New Testament text, von Soden assigned them an altogether disproportionate degree of importance in the contamination not only of the Latin and Syriac versions but of Greek witnesses as well.

(*d*) Though absolute accuracy in an extensive critical apparatus is probably unattainable, where von Soden's work can be

---

[1] See, for example, K. Lake in *Review of Theology and Philosophy*, iv (1908), pp. 201–17, 277–95; H. C. Hoskier in *Journal of Theological Studies*, xv (1914), pp. 307–26; Hans Lietzmann in *Zeitschrift für die neutestamentliche Wissenschaft*, xv (1914), pp. 323–31; and A. Souter in *Expositor*, 8th series, x (1915), pp. 429–44.

tested it has been found to contain a higher percentage of errors than is usually considered to be consistent with trustworthy scholarship.

Despite these and other justifiable criticisms which have been levelled against von Soden, his edition remains a monument of broad research and immense industry which, with the extensive prolegomena dealing with the history of the transmission of the text, must be taken into account by every serious textual critic.

The next three editions to be mentioned are the products of twentieth-century Roman Catholic scholarship. The edition prepared by Heinrich Joseph Vogels (Düsseldorf, 1920; with the Latin Vulgate, 1922; 4th ed., Freiburg i. Br., 1955) is closer to the Textus Receptus than the other two.[1] The editor provides a limited apparatus which, in addition to citing the principal uncial and minuscule manuscripts, is relatively full as regards evidence derived from the Old Latin materials and the Syriac versions.

Relying on von Soden's apparatus, but transposing von Soden's sigla to those of the Gregory system, and adding fresh manuscript evidence, Augustin Merk, S.J., published an edition of the Greek and Latin New Testament through the Pontifical Biblical Institute (Rome, 1933; 9th ed., 1964, with an Appendix of variant readings from recently discovered papyri).[2] The apparatus, which includes evidence from the several Tatianic witnesses, is drawn up so as to show family relationship among the witnesses. Unfortunately, however, Merk's citation of evidence is far from accurate,[3] and when his apparatus supplies evidence not available for verification in other publications, one hesitates to rely upon his testimony. In the construction of his Greek text, Merk departs farther from the Textus Receptus than do the other two Roman Catholic editors.

José Maria Bover, S.J., devoted his efforts over many years to the collection and evaluation of textual materials.[4] The Greek

[1] See footnote 1 on p. 139 above.

[2] Merk's text was reprinted by Gianfranco Nolli in his *Novum Testamentum graece et latine* (Rome, 1955). The footnotes of Nolli's edition supply the student with a limited number of text-critical, syntactical, and lexical aids.

[3] See, for example, H. G. Opitz's review in *Gnomon*, xii (1936), pp. 429–36, and G. D. Kilpatrick, 'Three Recent Editions of the Greek New Testament', *Journal of Theological Studies*, l (1949), pp. 145 ff.

[4] For a summary of Bover's textual investigations, see B. M. Metzger, *Chapters in the History of New Testament Textual Criticism* (Leiden and Grand Rapids, 1963), pp. 121–41.

text of his bilingual edition (Madrid, 1943; 4th ed., 1959), which is printed with the beautiful font of Greek type belonging to the Association Guillaume Budé, is an eclectic one, departing frequently from the Alexandrian type of text and approaching the Western or Caesarean type. The apparatus, which presents information concerning the textual opinions of six modern editors, supplies manuscript evidence for only the more important variants.

The most widely used pocket edition of the Greek Testament is that prepared by Eberhard Nestle (1851–1913) for the Württembergische Bibelanstalt (Stuttgart, 1898; 24th ed., by Erwin Nestle and Kurt Aland, 1960). Its text (since the 3rd ed., 1901) is based on a comparison of the texts edited by Tischendorf (1869–72), by Westcott and Hort (1881), and by Bernhard Weiss (1894–1900); where two of these three editions agree, this reading is printed by Nestle.[1] Thus the text of Nestle represents the state of nineteenth-century scholarship; its apparatus, however, which is a marvel of condensation, supplies with a high degree of accuracy a great amount of textual information, including many early witnesses that were discovered during the twentieth century.

In connexion with the sesquicentennial celebration of the British and Foreign Bible Society (1804–1954), a new edition of Eberhard Nestle's 1904 text was edited with an apparatus prepared by G. D. Kilpatrick with the help of Erwin Nestle and several other scholars (London, 1958). The text of the 1904 edition was changed in about twenty passages (of which eleven are listed in the introduction) and several alterations were made in orthography, accentuation, and the use of brackets. As regards the apparatus, the number of variants cited is substantially smaller than those in current editions of Nestle, but a certain amount of additional information is provided for the variants that are cited. (For comments on Kilpatrick's Greek text of the Diglot New Testament, privately circulated by the British and Foreign Bible Society, see pp. 177 f. below.)

In conclusion, reference should be made to the *apparatus*

---

[1] Since the 17th ed., however, a small number of variants which, according to widespread scholarly opinion, have strong claims to be original have been taken into the text against the majority of the three nineteenth-century editions.

criticus published by S. C. E. Legg at Oxford in 1935 and 1940. Choosing the Greek text of Westcott and Hort as the collating base, Legg supplied for Mark (1935) and for Matthew (1940) an enormous thesaurus of variant readings of Greek manuscripts, early versions, and patristic quotations. It is regrettable that Legg did not indicate in every case the editions of the versions and Fathers on which he relied. He has been criticized also for incomplete citation of evidence as well as occasional errors.[1] Despite such justifiable criticisms of faults which arise chiefly from the ambitious scope of Legg's project—a project which probably exceeded the capacity of any single scholar to accomplish—these two volumes present an extraordinary amount of textual information, surpassing any previous apparatus for Matthew and Mark.[2]

Shortly after the publication of the New Testament of the New English Bible (1961), requests were received by the Oxford and Cambridge University Presses to issue an edition of the Greek text that inferentially lies behind the new English version. R. V. G. Tasker, a member of the Panel of Translators of the N.E.B., was entrusted with the task of preparing the edition, which was published in 1964. In an Appendix Tasker cites manuscript evidence[3] for about 270 sets of variant readings that are represented in the margin of the N.E.B.[4]

In 1966, after a decade of work by an international Com-

---

[1] See, for example, E. C. Colwell, *Classical Philology*, xxxiii (1938), pp. 112–15; A. Souter, *Expository Times*, liii (1941), pp. 169 ff.; G. D. Kilpatrick, *Journal of Theological Studies*, xliii (1942), pp. 30–34; and T. W. Manson, ibid., pp. 83–92.

[2] In 1949 an international project was launched in order to pool the resources of textual scholars in Britain and America for the production of a comprehensive *apparatus criticus* of the Greek New Testament. Work is in progress on the Gospel of Luke. For a description of the aims of the project, see M. M. Parvis in *Crozer. Quarterly*, xxvii (1950), pp. 301–8; for a report of progress, see an article by E. C. Colwell *et al.* to appear in *Journal of Biblical Literature*, lxxxvii (1968).

[3] The very important Bodmer Papyri, however, are conspicuous by their absence, for most of them were published after the N.E.B. Panel had completed its work.

[4] For an evaluation of Tasker's edition, reference may be made to T. Gaumer, 'An Examination of Some Western Textual Variants Adopted in the Greek Text of the New English Bible', *The Bible Translator*, xvi (1965), pp. 184–9, and to the present writer's volume, *Historical and Literary Studies, Pagan, Jewish, and Christian* (Leiden and Grand Rapids, 1968), pp. 160 f.

mittee,[1] five Bible Societies[2] published an edition of the Greek New Testament designed for the use of Bible translators and students. The textual apparatus, which provides a relatively full citation of manuscript evidence, includes about 1440 sets of variant readings, chosen especially in view of their exegetical significance. There is also a punctuation apparatus that cites meaningful differences of punctuation in about 600 passages, drawn from five editions of the Greek New Testament and from ten translations in English, French, and German. A companion volume, providing a summary of the Committee's reasons for adopting one or another of the variant readings, has been prepared by the present writer, and is scheduled for publication toward the close of 1968.

The preceding survey of the more important printed editions of the Greek New Testament has referred to only a relatively small proportion of the total number of editions. No one knows exactly how many separate editions of the Greek Testament have come from the press since 1514, but it is undoubtedly a very great number indeed. Eduard Reuss of Strasbourg, who published a description of editions issued up to 1869, was able to enumerate 584 separate editions.[3] If one adds the re-editions, the variant editions, and some doubtful editions which Reuss mentions in part, the number amounts to 853. Furthermore, since Reuss's list is not complete for the more recent period which he covers, and since many editions have appeared since he published his volume, it is altogether probable that the 1,000 mark was passed early in the twentieth century.

[1] The members of the Committee are Kurt Aland of Münster, Matthew Black of St. Andrews, Allen Wikgren of Chicago, and the present writer. During the first four years of its v ork the Committee also included the Estonian scholar Arthur Vööbus. For the preparation of the second edition, scheduled to appear in 1968, the Committee was enlarged by the addition of Carlo M. Martini, S.J., of Rome.

[2] They are the American, British and Foreign, Dutch, Scottish, and Württemberg Societies. In 1967 the edition was published under the auspices of the United Bible Societies.

[3] Eduard Reuss, *Bibliotheca Novi Testamenti graeci cuius editiones ab initio typographiae ad nostram aetatem impressas quoquot reperiri potuerant* (Brunsvigae, 1872). For additions to Reuss's list, see Isaac H. Hall in Philip Schaff, *A Companion to the Greek Testament and the English Version*, 3rd ed. (New York, 1889), pp. 519–24.

PART THREE

The Application of Textual Criticism to the Text of the New Testament

V

The Origins of Textual Criticism
as a Scholarly Discipline

IKE so many disciplines that we take for granted in our
Western culture, textual criticism originated among the
Greeks. Its rise and development were connected with the
Homeric epics. Because the rhapsodists who recited portions of
the *Iliad* and the *Odyssey* in public would occasionally alter the
text to suit the special occasion or their own notion of an effec-
tive arrangement, there were many versions current even in
very early times. There subsequently grew up several 'City
Editions' of Homer, namely those which presumably were preserved by civic authority in various centres (traditionally, seven
centres) and from which private copies were made. Other special texts were made by Theagenes of Regium, by Stesimbrotus
of Thasos (*c.* 450 B.C.), and by Aristotle, who prepared a version
for his pupil Alexander the Great, usually called ἡ ἐκ τοῦ νάρθηκος
from the case in which it was kept (Plutarch, *Alex.* 8).

A more scientific criticism of the text of Homer was developed
in the Hellenistic Age. This critical study was pursued at the
famed library in Alexandria, which was reputed to have about
600,000 volumes,[1] and for which, according to tradition, the
Greek translation of the Old Testament, the so-called Septuagint, was made. The early directors of the library sought to provide ever more accurate editions of the Homeric poems. Shortly
before 274 B.C. the first of these scholarly librarians, Zenodotus
of Ephesus (*c.* 325–*c.* 234 B.C.), made a comparison of many manuscripts in order to restore the original text of both the *Iliad* and
the *Odyssey*. The corrections which Zenodotus made in the text
of Homer were of four kinds: (1) he eliminated verses which he
regarded as spurious; (2) he marked others as doubtful but left
them in his edition; (3) he transposed the order of verses; and
(4) he introduced new readings not generally current.

---

[1] See Edward A. Parsons, *The Alexandrian Library, Glory of the Hellenic World: Its
Rise, Antiquities, and Destructions* (Amsterdam, London, and New York, 1952).

One of the subsequent directors of the library was Aristophanes of Byzantium (*c.* 257–*c.* 180 B.C.), perhaps the most distinguished philologist of Greek antiquity, to whom is ascribed the invention of the Greek accent marks as well as other diacritical signs. In his edition of the *Iliad* and the *Odyssey* Aristophanes employed a variety of critical symbols to indicate his opinion of the state of the text thus marked. His greatest pupil was Aristarchus of Samothrace (*c.* 220–*c.* 144 B.C.), who, becoming his successor at the library, edited the works of half a dozen Greek authors and published two critical editions of the Homeric poems, supplementing the number of critical symbols which his predecessors had used.

Thus there was a fairly well-developed scholarly discipline of textual and literary criticism in antiquity, localized chiefly at Alexandria and directed primarily toward the epics of Homer. It is common knowledge that Philo Judaeus and many Church Fathers, influenced by the philological scholarship current at Alexandria, utilized in their interpretation of the Scriptures the methods of allegorical exegesis which had been applied to certain stories of the gods and goddesses included in the Homeric cycle. It is less widely appreciated—indeed, the question has seldom been raised—how far the methods of textual criticism current at Alexandria were adopted by scholars in the Church and applied to the text of the New Testament. The following is a brief summary of what can be learned from patristic sources relating to this subject.

Ironically enough, the earliest efforts[1] to ascertain the original text of the New Testament seem to have been made by those who were excommunicated as heretics by the authoritarian Bishop of Rome, Pope Victor (A.D. 187–98). It appears that a learned leather-merchant (σκυτεύς) named Theodotus, lately come from Byzantium to Rome, had been stung by certain criticisms which Galen, the famous Greek physician, had levelled against the philosophical *naïveté* of many Christians.[2] In an attempt to introduce improvements in the methodology of scriptural interpretation, Theodotus and his followers seem to have undertaken a critical recension of the Biblical text. Eusebius preserves a

---

[1] The alterations made by Marcion in the New Testament were motivated by doctrinal considerations rather than by an interest in textual criticism.

[2] See R. Walzer, *Galen on Jews and Christians* (Oxford, 1949), pp. 75 ff.

large excerpt of an almost contemporary pamphlet by an anonymous author directed against these philosophically minded Christians.[1] According to this author the Theodotians deserved to be condemned on three scores: (1) they were engrossed in the study of logic, mathematics, and empirical science ('Some of them, in fact, study the geometry of Euclid, and admire Aristotle and Theophrastus; and Galen perhaps is even worshipped by some of them'); (2) abjuring allegorizing, they practised strict grammatical exegesis; and (3) they applied textual criticism to the Septuagint and the Greek New Testament ('They did not fear to lay hands on the divine Scriptures, alleging that they had critically revised ($\delta\iota\omega\rho\theta\omega\kappa\epsilon\nu\alpha\iota$) them.... For they cannot deny that this audacious act is their own, seeing that the copies are written in their own hand, and they did not receive the Scriptures in this condition from their teachers, nor can they show any copies from which they made their emendations ($\delta\epsilon\hat{\iota}\xi\alpha\iota\ \dot{\alpha}\nu\tau\acute{\iota}\gamma\rho\alpha\phi\alpha$ $\ddot{o}\theta\epsilon\nu\ \alpha\dot{\upsilon}\tau\grave{\alpha}\ \mu\epsilon\tau\epsilon\gamma\rho\acute{\alpha}\psi\alpha\nu\tau o\ \mu\grave{\eta}\ \ddot{\epsilon}\chi\omega\sigma\iota\nu$)').[2] Unfortunately, nothing more is known of this early effort at textual criticism.

Not long after the Theodotians had been excommunicated, one of the most assiduous and erudite scholars of his age, Origen of Alexandria and Caesarea, began a text-critical study of the entire Old Testament in Hebrew and in several Greek translations. His resulting Hexapla, which must have required many years of the most painstaking labour, was a monumental tool that many patristic scholars consulted, in the famed library of Pamphilus at Caesarea, until its destruction in the seventh century during the Islamic conquest of the Near East.

The question whether Origen ever attempted to edit a critical text of the New Testament has been answered quite diversely by modern scholars;[3] it seems probable to the present writer that he did not extend his textual efforts to preparing a formal edition of the New Testament. At the same time, in all his

[1] Eusebius, *Hist. Eccl.* v. xxviii. 13–19 (the excerpt may be from Hippolytus of Rome's *Little Labyrinth*).

[2] For a discussion of this passage, see Hermann Schöne, 'Ein Einbruch der antiken Logik und Textkritik in die altchristliche Theologie', in *Pisciculi: Studien zur Religion und Kultur des Altertums; Franz Joseph Dölger ... dargeboten ...* (Münster in W., 1939), pp. 252–65.

[3] For a summary of these opinions, reference may be made to B. M. Metzger, 'Explicit References in the Works of Origen to Variant Readings in New Testament Manuscripts', in *Biblical and Patristic Studies in Memory of Robert Pierce Casey*, ed. by J. N. Birdsall and R. W. Thomson (Freiburg, 1963), pp. 78–95.

writings and particularly in his exegetical treatises, Origen reveals a certain solicitude for critical details in the Biblical text. He complains that 'the differences among the manuscripts [of the Gospels] have become great, either through the negligence of some copyists or through the perverse audacity of others; they either neglect to check over what they have transcribed, or, in the process of checking, they lengthen or shorten, as they please'.[1] Besides making comments of a general nature about the text, Origen sought out information (though he did not always utilize this information) concerning variant readings in Greek manuscripts of the New Testament. He observes, for example, that in Matthew's account (xviii. 1) of the disciples' question as to who is the greatest in the kingdom of heaven, according to some of the manuscripts the Evangelist prefixed the phrase ἐν ἐκείνῃ τῇ ὥρᾳ, whereas according to others the expression ἐν ἐκείνῃ τῇ ἡμέρᾳ appears.[2] Similarly, Origen notices the two readings in Heb. ii. 9, 'apart from God' (χωρὶς θεοῦ) and 'by the grace of God' (χάριτι θεοῦ), but is not interested in deciding between them, for he finds spiritual significance in both readings.

At other times Origen declared his preference among variant readings, but often his choice appears to be based on considerations other than those of a purely textual nature. Thus when he dismisses the reading 'Jesus Barabbas' in favour of simply 'Barabbas' (Matt. xxvii. 16–17), he does so because he thinks that the name 'Jesus' was never applied to evil-doers.[3] Again, Origen's well-known preference for the reading 'Bethabara' instead of 'Bethany' as the place of John's baptizing (John i. 28) was adopted on geographical and etymological grounds,[4] and the same reasons dictated his preference for 'Gergesa' rather than 'Gerasa' or 'Gadara' as the name of the place where the demons entered the herd of swine.[5] In a different category are instances where, because of some exegetical difficulty, Origen suggests that perhaps all of the manuscripts existing in his day may have become corrupt.[6]

---

[1] *Comm. in Matt.* xv. 14 (*Die griechischen christlichen Schriftsteller*, Origenes, x. 387. 28–388. 7, ed. Klostermann).

[2] *Comm. in Matt.* xiii. 14 (*G.C.S.*, Origenes, x. 213. 21 ff., ed. Klostermann).

[3] *In Matt. Comm. ser.* 121 (*G.C.S.*, Origenes, xi. 2. 255, 24 ff., ed. Klostermann).

[4] *Comm. in Joan.* vi. 40 (24) (*G.C.S.*, Origenes, iv. 149. 12 ff., ed. Preuschen).

[5] *Comm. in Joan.* vi. 41 (24) (*G.C.S.*, Origenes, iv. 150. 3 ff., ed. Preuschen).

[6] For examples, see the study mentioned in n. 3 on the preceding page.

Judged according to modern standards, St. Jerome (*c.* 347–420) was a more sagacious textual critic than Origen, well aware of the varieties of errors which arise in the transcription of manuscripts. He refers, for example, to the possibility of confusion of similar letters, confusion of abbreviations, accidents involving dittography and haplography, the metathesis of letters, assimilation, transpositions, and deliberate emendations by scribes.[1] Several explicit references will indicate his interest in text-critical details. In the preface to his revision of the Latin Gospels, addressed to Pope Damasus, who had requested that he undertake the work, Jerome declares that for the textual basis of the revision he has relied upon older Greek manuscripts. Again, in his letter to Minervius and Alexander,[2] two monks at Toulouse who had written to Jerome asking him to explain certain passages in Scripture, Jerome discusses several forms of the text of 1 Cor. xv. 51 ('We shall not all sleep, but we shall all be changed'). He indicates that he prefers the reading, 'We shall all sleep, but we shall not all be changed'. In his *Dialogue against the Pelagians*,[3] Jerome states that in certain copies, and especially in Greek codices, an extensive addition was to be found at the close of the Gospel according to Mark. Jerome does not tell us where he found these manuscripts, and no such copy was known until the twentieth century, when the passage turned up in a Greek manuscript which Mr. Charles L. Freer of Detroit had bought from an Arab dealer in Gizeh near Cairo (for the translation of this addition, see p. 57 above).

Though primarily a theologian, St. Augustine (354–430) showed on occasion a keen critical judgement in textual problems. Thus when considering the difficulty that Matthew (xxvii. 9) attributes a quotation to Jeremiah which actually appears in Zechariah, Augustine suggests that one should 'first take notice of the fact that this ascription of the passage to Jeremiah is not contained in all the manuscripts of the Gospels, and that some of them state simply that it was spoken "by the prophet". It is possible, therefore, to affirm that those manuscripts deserve rather to be followed which do not contain the

---

[1] For one or more examples from the works of Jerome illustrating each of these categories, see K. K. Hulley, 'Principles of Textual Criticism Known to St. Jerome', *Harvard Studies in Classical Philology*, lv (1944), pp. 87–109.

[2] *Epist.* 119 (Migne, *Patrologia Latina*, xxii. 966 ff.).

[3] *Dialog. contra Pelagianos*, ii. 15 (Migne, *P.L.* xxiii. 576).

name of Jeremiah. For these words were certainly spoken by a prophet, only that prophet was Zechariah. . . .' With commendable candour, however, Augustine declares that he is not altogether satisfied with this explanation, because 'a majority of manuscripts contain the name of Jeremiah, and those who have studied the Gospel with more than usual care in the Greek copies report that they have found it to stand so in the more ancient Greek exemplars'. Thereupon Augustine virtually enunciates the critical canon that the more difficult reading is to be preferred; he continues, 'I look also to this further consideration, namely that there was no reason why this name should have been added [subsequently to the true text] and a corruption thus created; whereas there was certainly an intelligible reason for erasing the name from so many of the manuscripts. For presumptuous inexperience (*audax imperitia*) might readily have done that, when perplexed with the problem presented by the circumstance that this passage cannot be found in Jeremiah.'[1]

On another occasion Augustine suggests that preference should be given to readings that are current in important sees, thus anticipating B. H. Streeter's theory of 'local texts' (see pp. 169–73 below). He writes: 'If the books of the New Testament are confusing in the variety of their Latin translations, they should certainly give place to the Greek versions, especially to those which are found among the more learned and diligent churches.'[2]

During the Middle Ages, when a knowledge of Greek was at a low ebb, text-critical efforts were now and then directed toward the purification of Jerome's Vulgate text. It was perhaps to be expected that this version, besides being corrupted with the usual types of error incident to all transcription, would once again incorporate certain Old Latin readings which Jerome had eliminated from his text. (For some of these attempts to purify Jerome's text, see p. 76 above.) The writings of such authors as Gilbert of Porrée and Peter Lombard contain sporadic comments, reflecting information derived from Jerome and Augustine, regarding the Greek lying behind such and such Latin renderings.[3]

---

[1] *De consensu Evangel.* iii. 7. 29 (Migne, *P.L.* xxxiv. 1174 f.).

[2] *De doctr. Christ.* ii. 15. 22 (Migne, *P.L.* xxxiv. 46), 'apud ecclesias doctiores et diligentiores'.

[3] See Arthur Landgraf, 'Zur Methode der biblischen Textkritik im 12. Jahrhundert', *Biblica*, x (1929), pp. 445–74. See below, p. 270.

At the time of the Renaissance and with the spread of the knowledge of ancient Greek, scholars began to correct the Latin Vulgate by the original Greek. In their Biblical annotations Erasmus and Beza not infrequently refer to variant readings in Greek manuscripts. As was mentioned in Chapter III, the first English Bible to contain the translation of variant readings from Greek manuscripts (including codex Bezae) was the Geneva Bible of 1560, prepared by William Whittingham and other English exiles residing at Geneva. This Bible has, for example, the negative Golden Rule in the margin opposite Acts xv. 29, as well as a literal translation of the Western variant at Acts xix. 9, that Paul preached daily at the school of Tyrannus 'from five a clocke unto ten'.[1]

The first scholar to make any use of all three classes of evidence for the text of the New Testament—that is, Greek manuscripts, the early versions, and quotations from the Fathers— was probably Francis Lucas of Bruges (Brugensis) in his *Notationes in sacra Biblia, quibus variantia . . . discutiuntur* (Antwerp, 1580). Toward the close of the seventeenth century the scientific foundations of New Testament criticism were laid in four monumental publications of Richard Simon (1638–1712), a French Catholic scholar far ahead of his day in Biblical research. The volumes are entitled *Histoire critique du texte du Nouveau Testament* (Rotterdam, 1689); Eng. trans., *Critical History of the Text of the New Testament*, 2 parts (London, 1689); *Histoire critique des versions du Nouveau Testament* (Rotterdam, 1690); Eng. trans., *Critical History of the Versions of the New Testament* (London, 1692); *Histoire critique des principaux commentateurs du Nouveau Testament*, 2 parts (Rotterdam, 1693); and *Nouvelles observations sur le texte et les versions du Nouveau Testament* (Paris, 1695). Disregarding the traditional and dogmatic presuppositions of his age, Simon examined critically the text of the Bible as a piece of literature. His works are full of acute observation and reasoning, and anticipate in detail many of the conclusions of scholars two and three centuries later.

---

[1] The Genevan translation of this verse is a literal rendering of the Greek; the equivalent according to the modern reckoning of time is 'from eleven o'clock to four'. For a score of other variant readings given in the margins of the Geneva Bible, see the article mentioned in n. 2 on p. 105 above.

VI

Modern Methods of Textual Criticism

I. THE CLASSICAL METHOD OF TEXTUAL CRITICISM

THE method of textual criticism which has been generally practised by editors of classical Greek and Latin texts involves two main processes, recension and emendation. Recension is the selection, after examination of all available material, of the most trustworthy evidence on which to base a text. Emendation is the attempt to eliminate the errors which are found even in the best manuscripts.[1]

The classical method of textual criticism arose during and after the Renaissance when attention was drawn to spurious papal decretals and when questions were raised regarding falsifications in Church history and in the credentials of certain religious orders. The critical acumen of scholars was sharpened likewise by the large number of forged texts that began to appear; for example, a single forger, Giovanni Nanni (alias Joannes Annius, 1432–1502), a Dominican monk of Viterbo, put forth seventeen spurious treatises attributed by him to ancient Greek and Latin authors.[2]

A more critical spirit in dealing with ecclesiastical documents found expression during the sixteenth century in the work of Matthias Flacius and the group of Lutheran scholars known as

---

[1] For a concise account of these two basic processes, see Paul Maas, *Textual Criticism* (Oxford, 1958). Other useful discussions of the classical procedures of textual criticism include the following: R. C. Jebb in *A Companion to Greek Studies*, ed. by Leonard Whibley (Cambridge, 1906), pp. 610–23; J. P. Postgate in *A Companion to Latin Studies*, ed. by J. E. Sandys (Cambridge, 1910), pp. 791–805; L. Havet, *Manuel de critique verbale appliquée aux textes latins* (Paris, 1911); F. W. Hall, *A Companion to Classical Texts* (Oxford, 1913), pp. 108–98; H. Kantorowicz, *Einführung in die Textkritik* (Leipzig, 1921); and L. Bieler, 'The Grammarian's Craft', in *Folia: Studies in the Christian Perpetuation of the Classics*, x (1956), pp. 3–42. See below, p. 271.

[2] Annius' volume, *De Commentariis antiquitatum* (Rome, 1498), includes the allegedly rediscovered writings of Xenophon, Berosus, Cato, Antoninus Pius, Manetho, Philo Judaeus, Caius Sempronius, and Myrsilus, all of which, Annius declared, he had found buried in the ground. See 'Nanni' in Pierre Bayle's *Dictionaire historique et critique*, and 'Annius' in J. S. Ersch and J. G. Gruber's *Allgemeine Encyclopädie*; cf. also James Farrer, *Literary Forgeries* (London, 1907), pp. 67–81.

the Magdeburg Centuriators, who were the first to write the history of the Church from a Protestant point of view. In 1675 the Jesuit scholar Daniel Papebroch aroused the hostility of the Benedictines by denying the authenticity of documents constituting the credentials of certain Benedictine monasteries. The learned Benedictine monks at St. Maur took up the challenge by founding the science of palaeography, which is the classification of manuscripts according to their age in the light of their handwriting and other indications. The first treatise to deal with the Latin palaeography of official documents was the monumental work of the Maurist Jean Mabillon (1632–1707) entitled *De re diplomatica* (Paris, 1681). The science was extended to Greek manuscripts by another Benedictine, Bernard de Montfaucon (1655–1741), in his *Palaeographica graeca* (Paris, 1708).

The application of critical methods in the editing of classical texts was developed principally by three German scholars, Friedrich Wolf (1759–1824), one of the founders of classical philology, Immanuel Bekker (1785–1871), and Karl Lachmann (1793–1851). Bekker devoted his long life to the preparation of critical editions of Greek texts. The transfer of many manuscripts to public libraries as a result of the upheaval following the French Revolution gave opportunity for extensive collation of manuscripts older than those which had previously been generally available. Bekker collated some 400 manuscripts, grouped existing manuscripts of an author into families where one was derived from another, and published sixty volumes of improved editions of Greek authors. As was mentioned earlier (p. 124 above), Lachmann went further than Bekker, showing how, by comparison of manuscripts, it is possible to draw inferences as to their lost ancestors or archetypes, their condition, and even their pagination.

The basic principle which underlies the process of constructing a stemma, or family tree, of manuscripts is that, *apart from accident, identity of reading implies identity of origin*. By way of example, suppose that there are seven manuscripts of an ancient book, and that in a certain paragraph three of them agree in lacking a sentence which is present in the other four manuscripts. From this circumstance we would deduce either that a common ancestor of the three had omitted the sentence, or that an ancestor of the four had added it. Suppose, moreover, that we find that the seven manuscripts frequently range themselves so that one of them (which we may designate A) stands apart, showing no great similarity to any of the other six, while B, C, and D, on the one hand, and E, F, and G, on the other hand, greatly resemble each other, though differing somewhat from the rest. We can express this by saying that B, C, and D form a family, descended from a hypothetical common ancestor which we may call *X*, and that E, F, and G form another family, descended from a hypothetical ancestor which we may call *Y*. The readings of *X* which can be deduced by comparing those of B C D will be of a higher antiquity and of greater authority than any of the readings in B or C or D taken singly. And the same may be said for the readings of *Y* when compared with those in E or F or G. Indeed, it is possible to go further: we may compare the readings of *X* and *Y* with each other, and with those of A, and thus deduce the readings of a still more remote ancestor which we may call *Z*, the hypothetical archetype of all the manuscripts. Thus the pedigree of all ten manuscripts (the seven extant and the three hypothetical) would be as follows:

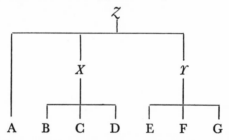

It follows that because B, C, and D may agree in a given reading against A, such a reading is not three times more likely to be correct than the reading in A. In fact it is obvious that, other things being equal, there is a fifty-fifty chance that either of the two readings may be correct, for where B, C, and D agree they represent a manuscript (*X*) which is as far removed from the archetype (*Z*) as is A. Thus, instead of merely counting the number of manuscripts supporting a given reading, the editor must weigh their significance in accord with their mutual relations to one another.

Often, however, difficulties hinder the construction of a

stemma of manuscripts. The simple example given above as-
sumes that the different lines of descent have remained independent of one another. But a disturbing element enters when
mixture has occurred, that is, when a copyist has had two or
more manuscripts before him and has followed sometimes one,
sometimes the other; or, as sometimes happened, when a scribe
copied a manuscript from one exemplar and corrected it against
another. To the extent that manuscripts have a 'mixed' ancestry,
the genealogical relations among them become progressively
more complex and obscure to the investigator.[1]

II. REACTIONS AGAINST CLASSICAL TEXTUAL CRITICISM

I. JOSEPH BÉDIER

During the twentieth century the genealogical method has
come under attack from several quarters; some scholars have
rejected it entirely, while others have restricted its application
to a narrow and limited area. One of the former is Joseph Bédier,
an editor of several medieval French documents. It was while
preparing his edition of *Le Lai de l'Ombre par Jean Renart* (Paris,
1913), so Bédier declared, that he became distrustful of the
genealogical method, (1) because in practice it has almost always
resulted in the construction of a tree with two branches of
witnesses (a circumstance which Bédier viewed with cynical
suspicion, suggesting that editors have deliberately forced the
evidence into a stereotyped pattern), and (2) because one can
often argue well for several different stemmata of classification
of manuscripts. His own method was to choose what seems to be
the best manuscript, making the choice on the basis of grammar,
coherent sense, simple and regular orthography, and then to use
the other manuscripts eclectically in correcting sporadic readings in the manuscript accepted as primary.[2]

---

[1] Genealogical mixture is widespread in the textual transmission of most Latin
patristic literature; see the sane and balanced account in Maurice Bévenot, S.J.,
The Tradition of Manuscripts: a Study in the Transmission of St. Cyprian's Treatises
(Oxford, 1961). For the special problems which confront the editor of Greek
patristic documents, see Herbert Musurillo's discussion of 'Some Textual Problems
in the Editing of the Greek Fathers', in *Texte und Untersuchungen*, lxxviii (1961),
pp. 85–96.

[2] Besides the preface in his 1913 edition, see Bédier's fuller exposition in 'La
Tradition manuscrite du *Lai de l'Ombre*: Réflexions sur l'art d'éditer les anciens
textes', *Romania*, liv (1928), pp. 161–96, 321–56.

Among New Testament scholars who have come under the influence of Bédier's scepticism of the value of the genealogical method are Léon Vaganay and Ernest Cadman Colwell. The former roundly asserted that 'applied to New Testament texts this system is useless'.[1] The latter more cautiously declared that 'the genealogical method is not of primary importance. . . . It can chart the history of transmission in an area narrowly limited in time and space. . . . But in the larger area where the larger questions are settled, it still has to demonstrate its value for the reconstruction of the original text of the Greek New Testament.'[2]

In evaluating the justice of Bédier's attack on the genealogical method, it ought to be pointed out that a much more innocent explanation lies behind the circumstance that almost all stemmata result in two branches than the imputation of deliberate suppression or distortion of evidence. From the standpoint of mathematics, as Maas observes, 'We must remind ourselves that of the twenty-two types of stemma possible where three witnesses exist, only one has three branches.'[3]

Bédier's second criticism of Lachmannian methodology possesses a semblance of justification only when one treats manuscripts as though they were fixed entities, as unchanging as a printed book. On the contrary, after a manuscript was copied, it continued to live and was subject to modifications— as the numerous erasures, corrections, additions, glosses, and remarks by readers entered in the margins testify. One must therefore take into account what may be called the successive 'stages of manuscripts',[4] as well as the possibility of multiple parentage.

The disconcerting ambiguity arising from the construction of equally cogent classifications of the same manuscripts need not result in abandoning the Lachmannian method altogether.

[1] Léon Vaganay, *Initiation à la critique textuelle néotestamentaire* (Paris, 1934), p. 60; Eng. trans., p. 71.

[2] E. C. Colwell, 'Genealogical Method: its Achievements and its Limitations', *Journal of Biblical Literature*, lxvi (1947), p. 132. See also his article, 'The Significance of Grouping of New Testament Manuscripts', *New Testament Studies*, iv (1958), pp. 73–92.

[3] Maas, op. cit., p. 48.

[4] For a discussion of the implications of such alterations, marking successive stages in the history of the transmission of a treatise, see Jean Irigoin, 'Stemmas bifides et états des manuscrits', *Revue de philologie*, lxxx (1954), pp. 211–17.

Faced with a number of manuscripts which have a mixed ancestry, the textual critic may well adopt a compromise between the purely eclectic method advocated by Bédier and the rigid genealogical procedure of classical text criticism. Suppose that there are five manuscripts, A, B, C, D, and E, the lineage of which is not clear; we cannot say, for example, that A B C form one family, descended from a common ancestor, while D E form another. A comparison discloses, however, that certain characteristic readings are common to the group A B C, but are not present in D and E. This evidence shows that, so far as these readings are concerned, some manuscript with such characteristic readings was one member in the ancestry common to A, B, and C, though that ancestry may in other respects be mixed.

One may conclude, therefore, that, despite the presence of a large amount of mixture in the ancestry of New Testament manuscripts, it will be advantageous for the textual critic to search out the broad features of more or less closely related groups of manuscripts. Such a process discloses that in general the Koine (or Byzantine) text of the New Testament is secondary, being characterized by the features which Hort delineated with classic vividness (see pp. 131–2 above). Moreover, major dislocations common to the members of smaller groups of manuscripts prove both the existence of such groups and their ultimate derivation from a common archetype which had suffered such dislocations (as, for example, the position of the *pericope de adultera* after Luke xxi. 38 in fam. 13).[1]

2. ALBERT C. CLARK

One of the axioms of classical textual criticism is *brevior lectio potior*, that is, the shorter of two readings is probably original. This principle, which has been accepted as generally valid by both classical and Biblical scholars, was challenged in 1914 by Albert C. Clark in his inaugural lecture as Corpus Professor of

---

[1] Although the presence of mixture to a greater or less extent in New Testament manuscripts makes it impossible to draw up precise genealogical stemmata, the mixture itself carries with it compensatory benefits. As Zuntz has pointed out (*Classica et Mediaevalia*, iii [1940], p. 24), the more widely that cross-fertilization of manuscripts has taken place, the more improbable it is that any old reading, true or false, could have entirely disappeared.

Latin in the University of Oxford.[1] Clark's researches in the manuscripts of Cicero's orations led him to believe that accidental omission was a much more common fault than deliberate interpolation by scribes. Four years later Clark published a lengthy treatise on *The Descent of Manuscripts* (Oxford, 1918), in which he showed that many omissions in classical texts involve multiples of the number of letters in an average line of script. Of two forms of text, one longer and one shorter, the latter can almost always be explained as the result of a scribe's omitting one or more lines of his exemplar. As Clark put it, 'A text is like a traveller who goes from one inn to another, losing an article of luggage at each halt.'[2]

Clark applied his principle, *longior lectio potior*, to the text of the Gospels and Acts,[3] with the result that the Western form of text, being in general the longer text, came off much better than it had at the hands of Westcott and Hort. If Hort could see no good in the Western text, Clark could see none in the Neutral text, which he regarded as the result of accidental omissions of multiples of lines of average length.

Clark's theory of accidental scribal omissions was criticized on several scores by such eminent textual scholars as Sanday, Souter, and Kenyon. The latter pointed out,[4] for example, that (1) variation in the length of lines in manuscripts makes the method of counting letters unreliable except for very short passages; (2) accidental omissions would not account for the regular correspondence of the omissions with breaks in the sense; (3) most of the variants involve, not omission, but differences in wording; and (4) such narrow columns as Clark's theory necessitates are exceedingly rare in the early papyri (an argument that has become the stronger as more and more early papyri with relatively wide columns have come to light). Furthermore, the circumstances of the transmission of the Gospel accounts were quite different from those of Cicero's Verrine orations. The Church preserved many traditions of the deeds and sayings of

[1] Albert C. Clark, *Recent Developments in Textual Criticism*, an Inaugural Lecture delivered before the University on 6 June 1914 (Oxford, 1914).
[2] *Journal of Theological Studies*, xvi (1915), p. 233.
[3] Albert C. Clark, *The Primitive Text of the Gospels and Acts* (Oxford, 1914).
[4] F. C. Kenyon, *The Text of the Greek Bible* (London, 1937), p. 231, and 'The Western Text in the Gospels and the Acts', *Proceedings of the British Academy*, xxiv (1938), pp. 287–315.

Christ which had not been included in the Gospels (cf. John xxi. 25). It would be natural for these to slip into the text of the Gospels, either from the margins of other manuscripts or from the living memory of the Church.

In a subsequent study of the Western text of the Acts, Clark returned to the controversy.[1] This time he practically abandoned the theory of accidental omission and revived the suggestion proposed in the seventeenth century by Jean Leclerc, namely that Luke had himself produced two editions of Acts. This hypothesis shifts the inquiry from scribal transmission to deliberate editorial alteration on the part of the author or editor, and its validity must be tested on grounds other than those of textual criticism alone. The only comment which needs to be made here is that a comparison of the trends in the textual criticism of the *Iliad* and the *Mahābhārata*, two great national epics the transmission of which reveals certain parallels to the transmission of the Gospels, is instructive for the New Testament scholar. Textual critics of both these corpora of quasi-religious literature are convinced that they are growing texts, and that no scribe deliberately excised any considerable portion of either poem.[2]

III. STATISTICAL METHODS OF TEXTUAL CRITICISM

I. DOM HENRI QUENTIN

Several scholars have attempted to replace (or at least to supplement) the genealogical method by means of a purely statistical analysis of variant readings. In his investigation of the transmission of the Latin Vulgate of the Old Testament, Dom Henri Quentin devised his so-called Rule of Iron (*règle de fer*), according to which he submitted all variants to a rigidly mechanical method. Here is his own brief account of the process:

At the very first I reject all thought of the primitive reading. I know neither errors, nor common faults, nor good readings nor bad, but only different forms of the text. Then, by a method resting upon the rigorous use of statistics, I discriminate family from family,

---

[1] Albert C. Clark, *The Acts of the Apostles* (Oxford, 1933).

[2] For a survey of the trends of textual scholarship in the editing of the *Iliad* and the *Mahābhārata*, reference may be made to B. M. Metzger, *Chapters in the History of New Testament Textual Criticism* (Leiden and Grand Rapids, 1963), pp. 142–54.

classify the manuscripts composing each family, and finally classify the families themselves. From this classification results a critical canon that lays down an iron rule in the establishing of a text, and using this, I can reconstruct the archetype, which is the nearest form of text to the original that we can reach with extant manuscripts. Then, but only then, I allow myself to think of the original. I examine the text from that point of view, and where the archetype is obviously faulty, I correct it by using the resources of internal criticism; always, however, taking care to indicate with a conventional sign that, at such and such a point, I have departed from the text resulting from the application of the critical canon.[1]

For the statistical examination of readings (at this stage he does not call them variants) Quentin devised an ingenious method which he called 'comparison by threes' (*comparaison à trois*). It aims at finding for every possible triad among the manuscripts of a text the one manuscript which is mediator between the other two. In order to determine whether in a given triad of manuscripts, as A, B, and C, any one is mediator between the other two, we merely count the agreements of A B against C, of A C against B, and of B C against A. If the figure for any of these relations is zero, the isolated manuscript is mediator between those against which it is opposed. Thus if we find that A C < B = 0 (which is to be read, 'A and C have no common deviation against B'), then B is mediator between A and C. This statistical examination, according to Quentin, gives clues for the grouping of manuscripts within a family, and, thanks to the overlapping of certain triads (those composed of manuscripts from different families), also for the relationship of larger groups.

Through this method Quentin sought to reduce to three the basic manuscripts of the Vulgate from which the others are derived and which ought to make possible the reconstruction of the archetype. He was inclined to place this archetype about 100 or 150 years after St. Jerome. For the Octateuch Quentin

---

[1] Dom Henri Quentin, *Essais de critique textuelle* (Paris, 1926), p. 37. This volume as well as Quentin's earlier *Mémoire sur l'établissement du texte de la Vulgate* (Rome and Paris, 1922) aroused a good deal of controversy; for a bibliography of appraisals of the method, see Paul Collomp, *La Critique des textes* (Paris, 1931), pp. 72 f., to which may be added J. Burke Severs, 'Quentin's Theory of Textual Criticism', *English Institute Annual, 1941* (New York, 1942), pp. 65–93. One of the most trenchant criticisms is that of E. K. Rand in the *Harvard Theological Review*, xvii (1924), pp. 197–264. See below, p. 271.

chose codex Turonensis of the Spanish group of manuscripts, codex Ottobonianus of the Theodulfian group, and codex Amiatinus of the pre-Alcuin group. Of these three he regarded the Tours manuscript, which contains the Pentateuch in a hand of the sixth or seventh century, as the best.

The obvious criticism of the method as a whole is that it is too cumbersome to apply to a text which is of any considerable length and which is preserved in many manuscripts. In the former case obviously a selection must be made of sample passages. Quentin himself based his recension of the Octateuch on the evidence derived from no more than ninety-one groups of variants that were taken from eight sample chapters (one from each book). But such a procedure is open to the objection that the investigator has arbitrarily selected his evidence. Dom John Chapman, who examined some 2,000 variants from Genesis and Exodus, came to conclusions which are generally inconsistent with those of Quentin.[1] Furthermore, a purely mechanical examination of agreements of two manuscripts against a third must be checked by an examination of the nature of the relations which produce zeros—for the same omission by homoeoteleuton may occur independently in the copying of two unrelated manuscripts. It is significant that Quentin's successors in the Benedictine project of editing the Vulgate Bible could not be persuaded to carry on his method beyond the first three books of the Old Testament, which Quentin himself had edited.[2]

2. SIR WALTER W. GREG, ARCHIBALD A. HILL, AND VINTON A. DEARING

Another proposal to edit texts by means of statistical analyses of variant readings was developed by Sir Walter W. Greg, a specialist in Middle English. While studying the relationships of manuscripts of the Chester miracle plays, Greg drew up a system which he called *The Calculus of Variants: an Essay on Textual Criticism* (Oxford, 1927). Like Quentin, Greg believed that it is possible to investigate the stemma of manuscripts without inquiring into the question of the originality and non-originality

---

[1] Dom John Chapman, *Revue Bénédictine*, xxvii (1925), pp. 6–46, 365–403.

[2] The Benedictine edition bears the title *Biblia sacra iuxta latinam vulgatam editionem*. For a description of the project, located at the newly founded Abbey of St. Jerome (Monastero San Girolamo) on the Janiculum Hill in Rome, see J. O. Smit, *De Vulgaat* (Roermond, 1948).

of variant readings, operating simply on the basis of variational groups exhibited by the extant manuscripts. Using only logical deduction, Greg constructed an elaborate calculus of the possibilities of relationship among witnesses. Though his discussion is burdened by a needless proliferation of pseudo-mathematical symbols, Greg's volume is basically sound in theory.

There is, however, a wide gap between Greg's theoretical consideration of the subject and the practical application of his principles to actual textual problems. In an attempt to lay down orderly and consistent rules for dealing with problems which Greg had deemed insoluble by logical methods, Archibald A. Hill developed what he called 'Some Postulates for Distributional Study of Texts'.[1] One of these postulates is the principle of simplicity, which Hill invokes in weighing the assumptions implied in alternate stemmata when there is more than one possible interpretation of the data.

Adopting a distinction made by several scholars[2] between a distributional relationship among manuscripts (that having to do with a theoretical analysis of the statistics of combinations of manuscripts which share variant readings) and a bibliographical relationship among manuscripts (that having to do with the actual chronological and genealogical filiation of manuscripts), Hill goes so far as to declare:

> A tree [i.e. stemma] is a description of the relationship of readings found in manuscripts, and ought never to be understood as a statement that *A* was copied from *B*. It merely states that the readings now found in *A* are derivable from readings now found in *B*, after examination of all the extant evidence. . . . I am labouring the point, since students seem sometimes unnecessarily timid in the face of external evidence, particularly of chronology. . . . Actually an editor who has derived *A* from *B* should be quite unmoved by external evidence that *B* is on twentieth century paper, while *A* is on mediaeval vellum.[3]

To a scholar trained in the classical tradition, such a doctrinaire approach to the problems of textual criticism appears to

---

[1] Published in *Studies in Bibliography: Papers of the Bibliographical Society of the University of Virginia*, iii (1950–1), pp. 63–95.

[2] e.g. Edwin Wolf 2nd, ' "If Shadows be a Picture's Excellence": an Experiment in Critical Bibliography', *Publications of the Modern Language Association of America*, lxiii (1948), pp. 831–57; cf. W. W. Greg, 'Bibliography—An Apologia', *Library*, 4th ser., xiii (1932), pp. 113–43.   [3] Op. cit., pp. 84 f.

be tantamount to saying that when theories and facts disagree,
so much the worse for the facts!

The most recent development of the theoretical and practical implications of Greg's calculus is found in the publications
of Vinton A. Dearing, Associate Professor of English in the
University of California at Los Angeles. Besides serving as textual editor of the California edition of the works of John Dry-
den (1956–), Dearing prepared a handbook of textual criticism
setting forth a synthesis of Quentin's principle of mediators
with Greg's calculus and Hill's principle of simplicity. In his preface Dearing candidly acknowledges:

> My method will not appeal at once to those who feel that 'common
> sense' is a sufficient guide to textual matters, or to those who are
> familiar with other methods. It is difficult to accept a new method
> for doing what is obvious or what an older method will do just as
> well. But any method is necessarily homogeneous. Because the older
> methods defy extension or development, a more comprehensive
> method necessarily presents alternate solutions to familiar problems.
> My method for the first time distinguishes the text conveyed by the
> manuscript—a mental phenomenon—from the manuscript convey-
> ing the text—a physical phenomenon.[1]

Confronted with these preliminary remarks, the reader is
likely to pursue the subject with mixed feelings of curiosity and
scepticism.

Besides setting forth a good deal of general textual methodology, ranging from how to record variant readings to the possibilities of using punched cards and computing machines for
statistical analysis and comparison of manuscripts in textual
criticism, Dearing deals with several text-critical problems, including an analysis of the Greek text of Paul's Epistle to Philemon—the end for which, so the author states, the volume was
initially designed. As regards the textual evidence of Philemon,
Dearing confines his attention to the ten uncial manuscripts
cited by Tischendorf in his eighth edition.[2] These ten manuscripts present fourteen different 'states' of text, inasmuch as
four of them contain later scribal alterations. After tabulating

---

[1] Vinton A. Dearing, *A Manual of Textual Analysis* (Berkeley and Los Angeles,
1959), pp. viii f.
[2] Dearing takes no account of the variant readings from forty-two minuscule
manuscripts cited by Tischendorf for Philemon.

all the different combinations of states of manuscripts which support the variant readings, the author constructs what he calls a textual scheme, concluding that the text of the ancestor of the fourteen states of the manuscripts can be established 'when D* or E* or both agree with $\aleph^c$ or P and when $\aleph^c$ and P agree together'.[1] On the basis of such a purely mathematical methodology in dealing with the evidence, Dearing declares that in his opinion Tischendorf's text agrees with the hypothetical ancestor except that the latter read Χριστὸν Ἰησοῦν in verse 6, δεσμοῖς μου in verse 10, δέ σοι (without καί) in verse 11, σὺ δὲ αὐτόν and σπλάγχνα, προσλάβου in verse 12, and ἀμήν in verse 25.

The New Testament textual critic will doubtless find Dearing's application of the statistical method to the Greek text of Philemon an interesting experiment, but he may well wonder whether the results are worth the effort to achieve them, particularly in view of Dearing's repeated declaration that he has been concerned to construct a textual, not a bibliographical, scheme.[2] That is, Dearing moves in the realm of 'states' of manuscripts, and his findings may or may not coincide with the actual chronological descent of the manuscripts.

By way of concluding his discussion of the variants selected from Tischendorf's apparatus, Dearing writes: 'In time the full collations necessary for a more final analysis will be available, and the necessary mechanical aids to calculation will have been

---

[1] Dearing, op. cit., p. 93.

[2] Dearing's distinction between bibliographical and textual stemmata (compare Hill's distinction between distributional and bibliographical trees, p. 166 above) can be illustrated by the following example: 'Suppose that manuscript B has been copied from manuscript A without verbal alteration, and that manuscript C has been copied from A with some verbal variants. Now, there are two ways of interpreting the relationship of C to B. From a purely mechanical point of view, C does not in any sense derive from B, since both derive independently from A. On the other hand, the *readings* of C could be said to derive from those of B. Moreover, if only B and C are extant, the textual critic may be unable to distinguish B from A, and he may find it convenient, as well as harmless, to assume that B *is* A and therefore an ancestor of C. The first point of view Mr. Dearing labels "bibliographical", the second "textual". In somewhat the way mathematical laws are used in physics, this distinction permits the critic to work out a stemmatic diagram on the abstract "textual" level before returning to the factual "bibliographical" level for final establishment of text. Such procedure should be valid if there is no attempt to draw unjustified "bibliographical" inferences from "textual" assumptions' (from David M. Vieth's review of Dearing's *Manual* in *Journal of English and Germanic Philology*, lix [1960], p. 556). Cf. Dearing's subsequent study, 'Some Notes on Genealogical Methods in Textual Criticism', *Novum Testamentum*, ix (1967), pp. 278–97.

provided. That happy day, it is to be hoped, is not far in the future.'[1] The present writer confesses that he does not share such sanguine expectations of benefits to be derived from what Dearing regards as 'necessary mechanical aids'. A mechanical procedure which dispenses with the subjective element in criticism reminds one of George Foot Moore's trenchant remark that 'the methodical elimination of the element of human intelligence can hardly be the ideal of science'.[2] Though computing machines may conceivably be useful in 'remembering' the statistical details of variant readings, it is not likely that they will replace the use of rational critical processes in evaluating 'good' and 'bad' readings.[3]

IV. LOCAL TEXTS AND ANCIENT EDITIONS

During the past generation a British churchman and an Italian classicist made significant contributions to textual criticism. Though their areas of interest were widely different, in some respects the methods which the two scholars proposed are similar.

1. BURNETT HILLMAN STREETER

In 1924 Canon Streeter published a volume on *The Four Gospels, a Study of Origins*, in which solid scholarship is combined with a fertile imagination and an engaging literary style.

---

[1] Op. cit., p. 93. For a description of the use of mechanical aids in textual editing, see the pamphlet entitled *Methods of Textual Editing*, a paper delivered by Vinton A. Dearing at a Seminar on Bibliography held at the Clark Library, 12 May 1962 (University of California, Los Angeles), pp. 18 ff. Cf. also John William Ellison, 'The Use of Electric Computers in the Study of the Greek New Testament Text' (Unpublished Diss., Harvard University, 1957). See below, p. 271.

[2] Moore's preface to Henry St. John Thackeray's *Josephus, the Man and the Historian* (New York, 1929), p. v.

[3] One of the curiosities of statistical pseudo-scholarship (which need not be dignified beyond this notice in a footnote) is Ivan Panin's *The New Testament in the Original Greek, the Text Established by Means of Bible Numerics*, privately printed by John Johnson at the University Press, Oxford, 1934. Panin prepared his edition by making such alterations in Westcott and Hort's text as he thought were justified on the basis of 'Bible Numerics', a system which he says he discovered in 1890. According to this 'method' the editor gives preference to that variant reading which yields the greatest number of multiples of 7, 11, 15, 23, &c., in the number of vowels, consonants, syllables, parts of speech, &c., in a given verse or pericope. For a refutation of the system (if refutation be deemed necessary!), see Oswald T. Allis, *Bible Numerics* (Chicago, 1944), and, more briefly, J. Oliver Buswell, 'Bible Numerics—the True and the False', *Moody Monthly*, xxxii (1932), pp. 530-1, and 'Notes on Open Letters', *Sunday School Times*, lxxxiv (1942), pp. 1058, 1072-3.

Building on Westcott and Hort's classic work, Streeter refined their methodology in the light of the acquisition of new manuscript evidence since 1881. Adopting an idea which Hug had first developed, Streeter emphasized the importance of isolating the forms of text which were current at the great centres of ancient Christianity. By means of evidence derived from quotations in the writings of early Church Fathers, he isolated and identified the characteristic forms of New Testament text which had developed at the principal sees of the ancient Church. By about A.D. 200 these local texts had reached (so Streeter believed) their maximum divergence, a divergence which is reflected in the earliest Syriac, Latin, and Coptic versions. It is probable that the oldest forms of these three versions were derived respectively from the Greek texts current in Antioch, Rome, and Alexandria.

Besides these three forms of text, Streeter's analysis of the evidence of codex Koridethi (*Θ*) and some of the writings of Origen and Eusebius led him to postulate the existence of a so-called Caesarean text of the Gospels, to which fam. 1 and fam. 13 also belong. Streeter combined into one text-type, which he designated the Alexandrian, the witnesses that Westcott and Hort had assigned to their Neutral and Alexandrian groups. He agreed with Westcott and Hort that the Syrian text, which he renamed the Byzantine text, arose during the fourth century through the recensional activity of Lucian of Antioch and was adopted by about 380 at Constantinople. This text became the prevailing ecclesiastical form of the New Testament throughout the Greek-speaking world, and eventually constituted the basis of the Textus Receptus. Therefore readings later than the fifth century, Streeter argued, can be ignored except when they differ from the prevailing Byzantine text. On the other hand, because it is possible that an ancient form of text may have been preserved at a relatively late date in a locality cut off from the main stream of Christianity, the precedence of manuscripts depends not so much on their age as on their pedigree.

The relationship between the local texts used in the five Churches of Alexandria, Caesarea, Antioch, Italy and Gaul, and Carthage stands in a graded series corresponding to their geographical propinquity around the eastern Mediterranean world. Streeter sets forth this point as follows:

Each member of the series has many readings peculiar to itself, but each is related to its next-door neighbour far more closely than to remoter members of the series. Thus B (Alexandria) has much in common with *fam. Θ* (Caesarea); *fam. Θ* shares many striking readings with Syr. S. (Antioch); Syr. S. in turn has contacts with D *b a* (Italy-Gaul); and, following round the circle to the point from which we started, *k* (Carthage) is in a sense a half-way house between D *b a* and B (Alexandria again).[1]

Figs. 3 and 4 reproduce a stemma and a chart from Streeter's volume, showing the relationship of the several local texts and the chief witnesses which support each.

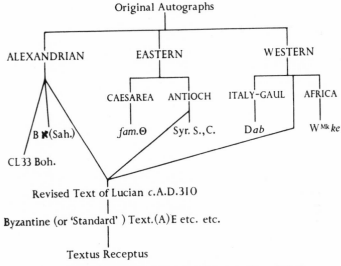

FIG. 3. Stemma Illustrating Streeter's Theory of Local Texts
(from B. H. Streeter, *The Four Gospels*, p. 26)

Some of the practical conclusions which follow from the acceptance of Streeter's theory of local texts include the following, which are set forth in his own words.

(*a*) The textual critic, in weighing the amount of external evidence in favour of any reading, should consider primarily, not the number or the age of the manuscripts which support it, but the number and geographical distribution of the ancient local texts in which it can be traced.

[1] B. H. Streeter, *The Four Gospels*, p. 106.

	ALEXANDRIA.	ANTIOCH.	CAESAREA.	ITALY AND GAUL.	CARTHAGE.
Primary Authority	B	Syr. S.	Θ 565$^{Mk.}$	D	k$^{Mk.\ Mt.}$
Secondary do.	א L Sah. Boh.	Syr. C.	1 &c. 13 &c. 28 700 (W$^{Mk.}$) Old Georgian	b *a*	(W$^{Mk.}$) *e*
Tertiary do.	C, 33, W$^{Lk.Jn.}$ Δ$^{Mk.}$ Ψ$^{Mk.}$ *Frags.:* T$^{Lk.Jn.}$ Z$^{Mt.}$ Ξ$^{Lk.}$	Syr. Pesh. (Arm.)	1424 &c. 544 N-Σ-O Φ 157	*ff*^{2} h$^{Mt.}$ *i r* c$^{Mt.Jn.}$ *Frag.:* n (cf. *a*)	c$^{Mk.\ Lk.}$
Supplementary	579$^{Mk.Lk.Jn.}$ 892 1241 א	Syr. Hcl. Syr. Hier.	U Λ 1071 1604 Old Arm.	*ff, g, l, q* (?) *f*	*m*
Patristic	Origen A.D. 230 Cyril Alex. 430		Origen A.D. 240 Eusebius 325	Tatian 170 Irenaeus 185	Cyprian 250

1 &c. = 1—22—118—131—209—872$^{Mk.}$—1278—1582—2193.   13 &c. = 13—69—124—230—346—543—788—826—828—983—1689—1709.

1424 &c. = 28 MSS., including M, cited by Soden as I$^{\Phi}$.   Byzantine Text: S V Ω; E F G H; (A, K Π, Y); (Γ); (W$^{Mk.}$).

Mixed Frags. P Q R$^{Lk.}$ *N.B.*—1 &c. = *fam.* 1 = Sod. I^{η}; 13 &c. = *fam.* 13 = Sod. I^{ι}. Sod. I^{a} misleadingly includes D with Θ, 28, 544, 565, 700.

FIG. 4. Chart of Witnesses and the Local Texts
(from B. H. Streeter, *The Four Gospels*, p. 108)

(*b*) It follows that manuscripts should be cited, not in alphabetical or numerical order, but in groups corresponding to the local texts which they represent. When at least three of the leading representatives of any local text support a reading, very little is gained by citing additional evidence of manuscripts which normally support the *same* local text.[1]

(*c*) Though on minor points of reading absolute certainty may often be unattainable, a text of the Gospels can be reached, the freedom of which from serious modification or interpolation is guaranteed by the concurrence of different lines of ancient and independent evidence.[2]

2. GIORGIO PASQUALI

In 1932 the learned Italian classicist, Giorgio Pasquali, published a monumental discussion of problems involved in the editing of ancient Greek and Latin authors.[3] The author, who had previously devoted more than forty pages to a review of Paul Maas's *Textkritik*, a succinctly written treatise of eighteen pages,[4] casts his net wide and illustrates his arguments by thousands of references to ancient authors and modern editors. Despite Pasquali's almost exclusive preoccupation with non-Biblical texts, the New Testament scholar will find that more than one suggestion in the volume bears indirectly upon his own special problems. Some of the points which Pasquali makes are the following:[5]

(*a*) The medieval manuscripts of Greek and Latin authors often go back, directly or indirectly, to ancient editions that already differed among themselves.

(*b*) Coincidence in obvious errors or in 'trivializzazioni' does not prove relationship between manuscripts. Furthermore, in general the coincidence of readings in diverse witnesses need not prove relationship, because original readings can be preserved independently in several branches of the tradition.

(*c*) For Latin authors, whose manuscript tradition is much richer than that of most Greek authors, a *codex recentior* is not

---

[1] B. H. Streeter, op. cit., p. 78.'   [2] Ibid., p. 148.
[3] Giorgio Pasquali, *Storia della tradizione e critica del testo* (Florence, 1934; 2nd ed., 1952).
[4] The review appeared in *Gnomon*, v (1929), pp. 417–35, 498–521.
[5] Pasquali sets them forth conveniently in the preface of his volume, pp. xv ff.

necessarily a *codex deterior*. The authority of a witness is independent of its antiquity.

(*d*) The collations of classical authors made by humanist scholars of the Renaissance, as well as the editions printed at that time, rest in part upon manuscripts which are now lost. Therefore a unique variant in a Renaissance text is not always to be credited to the ingenuity of contemporary editors, but may go back to very ancient times.

(*e*) Arbitrary modifications introduced by a scribe into a manuscript may cause us to doubt the value of the whole, but they do not entitle us *a priori* to neglect its authority at other points, on the pretext that it is merely an interpolated manuscript.

(*f*) There is a widespread prejudice which believes that the transmission of manuscripts has been purely mechanical, the work of 'stupid' scribes who transcribed without thinking. There were other scribes, however, who embellished, simplified, and adapted or even collated texts with other documents. A conjecture which is palaeographically justified may enable us to recover, in the case of mechanical transmission, the original reading. On the other hand, in an 'open' recension where 'intelligent' scribes have intervened, internal criticism plays a much more important role in the proposing of emendations.

(*g*) There is a widespread prejudice which believes that the transmission of texts is solely 'vertical' and in chronological sequence; in some cases, however, it has taken place also on a horizontal or transverse plane. The collation of a manuscript with other manuscripts besides the one which served as the exemplar has introduced readings from one branch into another, thus diversifying and contaminating the text.

(*h*) In general linguistics it is commonly acknowledged that the most ancient stages of a phenomenon are preserved best in the peripheral zones of the area of their dispersion, and the coincidence of two forms current in regions far removed from the centre and from each other constitutes a presumption in favour of their antiquity. In the same way the coincidence of particular readings in manuscripts of divergent origin often proves their originality.

In these paragraphs, it will have been observed, Pasquali enunciates principles new and old. Without referring to Streeter's theory of 'local texts' of the New Testament, he suggests that something similar may have occurred in the case of several ancient classical authors. Furthermore, he is inclined to think that, at least as regards the Homeric tradition, Byzantine manuscripts (which may go back to ancient editions) can be relied upon to preserve a text of more value than that contained in papyri, which, though earlier, represent an uncontrolled 'wild' text.

Perhaps one of the more significant points in Pasquali's volume which may aid the New Testament critic is his reference to what is popularly called 'linguistic geography' (the final item mentioned above). The research of Bartoli and other scholars[1] on the diffusion of dialectal forms of speech has not a little to teach the textual critic concerning the somewhat related problems of the dissemination of variant readings.

V. ECLECTICISM, OR 'RATIONAL CRITICISM'

Dissatisfied with the results achieved by weighing the external evidence for variant readings in terms of support from individual manuscripts or families of manuscripts and local texts, several scholars have directed primary attention to the individual variants themselves in an effort to find which will account best for the rise of the others. This process has been given various names. It has been called eclecticism,[2] because in its application the textual critic pays less attention to questions of date and families of manuscripts than to internal or contextual considerations. Consequently the editor of a text follows now one and now another set of witnesses in accord with what is deemed to be the author's style or the exigencies of transcriptional hazards. The ultimate disregard for the external evidence of variants is to be seen in several of Paul Mazon's editions of the Greek classics, where the apparatus supplies only the variants without mentioning the identity of the witnesses which support them.[3]

---

[1] Matteo Bartoli, *Introduzione alla neolinguistica* (Geneva, 1925), and *Saggi di linguistica spaziale* (Turin, 1945). Several atlases of dialects have been or are in the process of being compiled; for a list, see Jos. Schrijnen, *Essai de bibliographie de géographie linguistique générale* (Nimègue, 1933), and for a recently published atlas, see K. Heeroma's *Taalatlas van Oost-Nederland en aangrenzende gebieden* (Assen, 1957-).

[2] e.g. by G. D. Kilpatrick, *Journal of Theological Studies*, xliv (1943), p. 36 ('rigorous eclecticism'), and ibid. xlv (1944), p. 65 ('impartial eclecticism'). See below, p. 271.

[3] Cf. A. Dain's comments on 'Olympian indifference' to what is regarded as 'useless erudition' (*Les Manuscrits* [Paris, 1949], p. 161; rev. ed. [1964], p. 175).

Another descriptive name which has been given to this procedure of handling the textual evidence is rational criticism.[1] The
use of the adjective 'rational' in this connexion is not intended
to suggest that all other methods of criticism are irrational,
but that the critic is concerned primarily with finding plausible
reasons based on internal considerations to justify in each case
his choice of one reading as original and the others as secondary.

It will be understood that almost all textual critics have paid
attention to aspects of rational criticism. Certain scholars,
however, have given primary and sometimes exclusive consideration to the style of the author and the demands of the
context. Such, for example, was the method which Bernhard
Weiss followed in preparing his edition of the Greek Testament
(see pp. 137 f. above). Likewise C. H. Turner, having made a
thorough study of Marcan usage, reconstructed the Greek text
of the first chapter of Mark in accord with stylistic considerations.[2] One of the conclusions to which Turner's investigations
led him was the need to show greater respect for Western
readings, though they may be supported by only a few witnesses
(for instance, by D and one of the three leading Old Latin manuscripts, *k* or *e* or *a*).[3]

More recently several scholars have examined the text of
certain other New Testament books in the light of rational
criticism. For the Pauline Epistles, and especially for 1 Corinthians and Hebrews, the lively and learned Schweich Lectures
delivered in 1946 by Günther Zuntz have much to teach the
student regarding text-critical method.[4] As regards the Book of

---

[1] M.-J. Lagrange uses this term in the title of his monumental volume, *Critique
textuelle*; ii, *La Critique rationnelle* (Paris, 1935), though in practice he frequently
pays more attention to external evidence than one would have thought likely.

[2] C. H. Turner, 'A Textual Commentary on Mark 1', *Journal of Theological
Studies*, xxviii (1926–7), pp. 145–58, and 'Marcan Usage: Notes, Critical and Exegetical, on the Second Gospel', ibid. xxv (1923–4), pp. 377–86; xxvi (1924–5), pp. 12–
20, 145–56, 225–40, 337–46; xxvii (1925–6), pp. 58–62; xxviii (1926–7), pp. 9–30,
349–62.

[3] See his article, 'Western Readings in the Second Half of St. Mark's Gospel',
Journal of Theological Studies, xxix (1927–8), pp. 1–16, and 'The Textual Criticism
of the New Testament', in *A New Commentary on Holy Scripture . . .*, ed. by Charles
Gore *et al.* (London, 1928), pp. 718–29. For adumbrations of this point of view,
compare Turner's earlier article, 'New Testament, Text of', in *The Illustrated Bible
Dictionary*, ed. by William C. Piercy (New York, 1908), pp. 585–96.

[4] G. Zuntz, *The Text of the Epistles: a Disquisition upon the* Corpus Paulinum
(London, 1953).

certain chapter a given manuscript agrees with, say, B and ℵ ten times in differing from the Textus Receptus; for if B and ℵ should also, in that chapter, differ from the Textus Receptus in ninety other instances, the Alexandrian element in the given manuscript would be slight indeed.

In order to provide a more exact method of analysis of manuscript relationships, as long ago as 1911 E. A. Hutton proposed the use of what he called 'Triple Readings' in the analysis of textual affinities.[1] Selecting a list of readings in which the Alexandrian, Western, and Syrian (Byzantine) authorities are divided, he urged that henceforth all manuscripts be analysed by determining the number of agreements with each of these three textual types.

With the multiplication of the number of identifiable textual groups, it is desirable to seek a higher degree of precision than Hutton's method permits. E. C. Colwell, with the assistance of M. M. Parvis, elaborated what is called the method of Multiple Readings in determining the relationship of manuscripts. A Multiple Reading is defined as

one in which the minimum support for each of at least three variant forms of the text is either one of the major strands of the tradition, or the support of a previously established group (such as Family 1, Family Π, the Ferrar Group, K¹, Kⁱ, Kʳ), or the support of some one of the ancient versions (such as af, it, syˢ, syᶜ, bo or sa), or the support of some single manuscript of an admittedly distinctive character (such as D).[2]

Colwell applied these specifications for Multiple Readings to a sample section of text extending from John i. 1 to iv. 40, and found twenty-two instances of Multiple Readings. By tabulating the number of agreements of a newly found manuscript with the several witnesses at those passages which involve Multiple Readings, one will learn something of the textual complexion of that manuscript.

[1] Edward Ardron Hutton, *An Atlas of Textual Criticism, being an Attempt to Show the Mutual Relationship of the Authorities for the Text of the New Testament up to about 1000 A.D.* (Cambridge, 1911).

[2] E. C. Colwell, 'Method in Locating a Newly-discovered Manuscript within the Manuscript Tradition of the Greek New Testament', *Studia Evangelica . . .*, ed. by Kurt Aland *et al.* (= *Texte und Untersuchungen*, lxxiii, Berlin, 1959), p. 759; cf. also C. D. Dicks, *Journal of Biblical Literature*, lxvii (1948), pp. 366–8.

Revelation, one of the most valuable sections of Josef Schmid's extensive monograph on the history of the Greek text of the Apocalypse is his chapter dealing with the bearing of the linguistic usage of the book on the textual evaluation of variant readings.[1]

Turner's reliance on stylistic criteria in making textual decisions has been revived by George D. Kilpatrick of Queen's College, Oxford. Portions of his research into questions of lexical and grammatical usage of authors of the New Testament have been published in several periodicals,[2] and his text-critical conclusions are finding expression in the fascicles of *A Greek–English Diglot for the Use of Translators*, issued for private circulation by the British and Foreign Bible Society (*Mark*, 1958; *Matthew*, 1959; *John*, 1960; *The General Letters*, 1961; *Luke*, 1962).[3] Of two or more variant readings, Kilpatrick usually prefers that one which accords with what is deemed to be the author's style, irrespective of the date and nature of the external evidence supporting the reading. In matters on which no firm decision can be made concerning the author's style, he often appeals to the criterion of Atticism, which became one of the dominant tendencies in literary circles during the first and second Christian centuries. He argues that scribes in the second century introduced many Atticisms into the text of the New Testament.[4] Of two readings, therefore, one of which conforms to Attic canons and the other does not, he is inclined to accept the non-Attic reading, even though no early manuscript evidence may support it. In order to justify his general disregard for the age and quality of external evidence, Kilpatrick declares that by about A.D. 200 the great majority of the deliberate changes had been introduced into the textual stream, and that thereafter scribes transmitted the several forms of text with great fidelity. Thus, though a variant reading may happen to be preserved only in a late minuscule manuscript, if it is in harmony with what is taken to

[1] Josef Schmid, *Studien zur Geschichte des griechischen Apokalypse-Textes; ii, Die alten Stämme* (Munich, 1955), pp. 173–251.

[2] G. D. Kilpatrick, 'Some Notes on Marcan Usage', *Bible Translator*, vii (1956), pp. 2–9, 51–56, 146; 'Some Notes on Johannine Usage', ibid. xi (1960), pp. 173–7; and 'διαλέγεσθαι and διαλογίζεσθαι in the New Testament', *Journal of Theological Studies*, N.S., xi (1960), pp. 338–40.   [3] See below, p. 271.

[4] See Kilpatrick's article, 'Atticism and the Text of the Greek New Testament', in *Neutestamentliche Aufsätze: Festschrift für Prof. Josef Schmid* (Regensburg, 1963), pp. 125–37; compare also his comments in *Göttingische gelehrte Anzeigen*, ccxv (1963), pp. 14 ff. See below, p. 271.

be the author's style or reflects a non-Atticistic tendency, Kilpatrick is disposed to regard it as original.

The extent to which Kilpatrick is prepared to go in adopting readings which have the most meagre external support, if he is convinced that internal considerations require it, may be illustrated by the following readings in the *Greek–English Diglot*:

Matt. xx. 30 ἔκραζον is supported by 118 209 Syr[c, pal].
Matt. xxii. 1 omit εἶπεν with E Syr[p].
Matt. xxii. 7 ἀκούσας δὲ ὁ βασιλεὺς ἐκεῖνος is supported by 33.
Mark v. 11 τὰ ὄρη is supported by 372 485 Syr[s].
Mark ix. 17 ἀποκριθεὶς αὐτῷ is supported by C.
Mark xiv. 6 εἰς ἐμέ is supported by 517 579 *l*251 Syr[s, p] Eth.
Mark xiv. 31 ἐλάλει μᾶλλον is supported by 574 and *k*.
Luke ix. 51 ἐστήριζεν is supported by 1241.
John xix. 35 ἀληθής is supported by ℵ 124 Chr.
Jas. ii. 18 ἔργων τὴν πίστιν μου is supported by Syr[h].
1 Pet. ii. 11 ἀπέχεσθαι ὑμᾶς is supported by Vulg Cyp.
2 John, vs. 8 πλήρης is supported by L Dam.

By way of summary, it is obvious that there is much to commend the practice of a judicious eclecticism in text criticism, for no one manuscript and no one family preserves the original text in its entirety. And certainly the critic must always take into account what is or is not the usage of a given author, for, as A. E. Housman once expressed it in a pithy epigram: 'The indulgence of love for one manuscript and dislike for another inevitably begets indifference to the author himself.'[1] At the same time, however, the weaknesses inherent in the method should not be overlooked. Statistics regarding an author's usage are sometimes derived from concordances which are based on editions of the Greek Testament that contain, in some passages, quite indefensible readings. Furthermore, even if evidence regarding an author's usage has been sifted critically, its significance for the passage at hand must be weighed in the light of two possibilities: (*a*) an author may on occasion vary his usage, and (*b*) a scribe who was aware of the author's prevailing usage may have altered a reading in order to bring it into harmony with that usage.

One may conclude, therefore, that although considerations of the literary usage of a New Testament author will be of con-

[1] In Housman's edition of Lucan's *Bellum civile* (Oxford, 1926), p. vi.

siderable value to the textual critic, it must not be made th primary criterion in the evaluation of variant readings to th virtual neglect of external evidence. Furthermore, to appl rigorously considerations based on the Atticistic revival durin the early Christian centuries is to be in danger of disregardin the operation of other literary and stylistic tendencies that also influenced the Koine during the same period, some of which were deliberately anti-Atticistic.[1]

VI. METHODS OF DETERMINING FAMILY RELATIONSHIPS AMONG MANUSCRIPTS

Obviously the most satisfying method of locating a newly discovered manuscript within the manuscript tradition of the New Testament is to compare it with each and all previously known manuscripts. This procedure, however, entails such an enormous amount of labour, out of all proportion to the importance of the results, that scholars are content to make analyses on a selective basis. Sometimes the manuscript is compared with individual manuscripts which are typical of several families or types of text. The disadvantage of this procedure is that it ignores a large part of the evidence, and consequently one's conclusions may be upset when comparison is made with additional manuscripts.

More often the manuscript is collated against the Textus Receptus and then the variants are analysed in terms of agreement with a large number of manuscripts whose readings have been reported in various *apparatus critici*. Such a method of comparison, however, is scarcely more satisfactory than the other, for it, too, omits a significant portion of the evidence, namely those readings which the manuscript shares with the Textus Receptus. Furthermore, analyses of a text in terms of differences from the Textus Receptus are of little value when no control has been provided. Thus it is quite deceptive to know only that in a

[1] See, for example, the references under 'Antiatticismus' in Wilhelm Schmid's *Der Atticismus in seinen Hauptvertretern* (Stuttgart, 1887–96), and compare Rademacher's warning against undue reliance upon statistical considerations in judging the literary style of an author in a period when quite opposite influences cut across one another; Ludwig Radermacher, *Koine* (= *Sitzungsberichte der Akademie der Wissenschaften in Wien*, Phil.-hist. Kl., ccxxiv, 5. Abhandlung, 1947), pp. 61 f.

The limitation of this method, at least as applied to the sample from John, is that test passages are relatively few in number in comparison with the extent of text investigated. It is conceivable that a given manuscript may agree consistently with a particular type of text in most of the twenty-two passages in the 152 verses covered by John i. 1 to iv. 40, but may disagree with that text-type in a significant number of readings in the remaining 130 verses not represented by Multiple Readings.

It will be apparent from the criticisms levelled at each of the methods mentioned above that no single method thus far devised is entirely satisfactory in determining the textual complexion of a New Testament manuscript. The area tested must be large enough to be representative of the whole. At the same time the method must be sensitive enough to disclose whether various sections of a manuscript have been transcribed from exemplars of diverse text-types. It has been suggested elsewhere by the present writer that in analysing the textual complexion of lectionaries, which are normally collated against the Textus Receptus, it is necessary to have a control to determine precisely what percentage of Alexandrian, Western, and Caesarean deviations from the Textus Receptus are present in sample lections.[1] Furthermore, in all analyses the textual critic must give attention to the problem which arises when one attempts to assess the quality as well as the quantity of variants. The possibility that chance and not genealogical descent may account for the agreement of manuscripts in certain small variations—such as the presence or absence of the article with a proper name, or the aorist for the imperfect tense, and vice versa—has not been sufficiently taken into account.[2]

---

[1] This method entails first the construction in a sample passage of a 'pure' Alexandrian text, a 'pure' Western text, a 'pure' Caesarean text, a 'pure' text of fam. 13, &c., and then the collation of each of these 'pure' texts against the Textus Receptus. By comparing the total number of variants from the Textus Receptus in each of these 'pure' texts with the number of variants which are present also in the Lectionary text, one can determine with precision the degrees of relationship. For an example of the application of this method of textual analysis, reference may be made to the present writer's monograph, *The Saturday and Sunday Lessons from Luke in the Greek Gospel Lectionary* (Chicago, 1944), pp. 24 ff.

[2] See, for example, the discussion of 'Quantità e qualità delle varianti', in Paolo Sacchi, *Alle origini del Nuovo Testamento: Saggio per la storia della tradizione e la critica del testo* (Firenze, 1956), pp. 86 ff. See below, p. 272.

VII. CONJECTURAL EMENDATION

The classical method of textual criticism regularly involves, as was mentioned at the beginning of this chapter, the exercise of conjectural emendation. If the only reading, or each of several variant readings, which the documents of a text supply is impossible or incomprehensible, the editor's only remaining resource is to conjecture what the original reading must have been.

A typical emendation involves the removal of an anomaly. It must not be overlooked, however, that though some anomalies are the result of corruption in the transmission of the text, other anomalies may have been either intended or tolerated by the author himself.[1] Before resorting to conjectural emendation, therefore, the critic must be so thoroughly acquainted with the style and thought of his author that he cannot but judge a certain anomaly to be foreign to the author's intention.

This aspect of criticism has at times been carried to absurd extremes. In his later work Richard Bentley, for example, largely disregarded the evidence of manuscripts in determining the correct readings, and depended chiefly upon his own instinctive feeling as to what an author must have written. He justified such a procedure in the magisterial phrase, *nobis et ratio et res ipsa centum codicibus potiores sunt*, which may be rendered 'for me both reason and the subject-matter are worth more than a hundred manuscripts'. In following this bold principle he did much that was rash and indefensible as well as much that is brilliant and convincing. The *reductio ad absurdum* of such a subjective method is found in Bentley's edition of Milton's *Paradise Lost*, in which he offers more than 800 emendations, restoring what in his opinion Milton must have really said (or meant to say) while dictating the poem to his daughters.[2]

Before a conjecture can be regarded as even probable, it must satisfy the two primary tests which are customarily applied in evaluating variant readings in manuscripts: (1) it must be intrinsically suitable, and (2) it must be such as to account for the corrupt reading or readings in the transmitted text. There

---

[1] For a discussion of the paradoxical possibility of a textual critic's 'improving' on the original, see G. Zuntz's article on 1 Cor. vi. 5 entitled 'The Critic Correcting the Author', *Philologus*, xcix (1955), pp. 295–303.

[2] See James Henry Monk, *The Life of Richard Bentley, D.D.*, 2nd ed., ii (London, 1833), pp. 309–23, and Richard C. Jebb, *Bentley* (London, 1889), pp. 180–91.

is, however, an important difference between the method of applying these tests to a conjectural emendation, and that of applying them to variants in manuscripts. We accept the variant which best satisfies the tests; but we require of a successful conjecture that it shall satisfy them absolutely well. The conjecture does not rise from a certain level of probability ('a happy guess') to the level of certainty, or approximate certainty, unless its fitness is exact and perfect. The only criterion of a successful conjecture is that it shall approve itself as inevitable. Lacking inevitability, it remains doubtful.

An example from English literature will illustrate the wide differences of merit among proposed conjectures.[1] Since the early printers in England were often foreigners, who made quite as bad mistakes as their predecessors the scribes, the text of Shakespeare contains almost as many problem passages as that of Aeschylus. In the folio editions of *Henry V*, Act II, scene iii, the hostess says of the dying Falstaff, 'his nose was as sharp as a pen and a table of Green Fields'. The words 'a table of Green Fields', which appear with trifling variations of spelling in the folio editions but which are omitted in the quarto editions, have been the subject of numerous conjectural emendations. Pope suggested (perhaps ironically) that this was a stage direction to bring in one of Greenfield's tables, Greenfield being supposed to be the furniture-dealer who supplied props for Shakespeare's theatre. Collier proposed 'on a table of green frieze', and another critic suggested 'or as stubble on shorn fields'. The conjecture which today is adopted by editors is 'and a' babbled of green fields', being a modification by Theobald of a happy proposal made by an anonymous annotator who corrected 'a table' to 'a' talked'.[2]

The fault most often committed in the use of conjectural

[1] This example is taken nearly verbatim from James Gow's *Companion to School Classics*, 2nd ed. (London, 1889), pp. 65 f. See below, p. 272.

[2] Several passages in Shakespeare are corrupt beyond the ingenuity of palaeographer and textual critic to propose a cure. Apart from lucky coincidence, what lay behind the hodgepodge of nonsense set by the compositor of the first quarto of *King Lear* in III. iv. 118 ff. is probably unattainable: 'swithald footed thrice the old a nellthu night more and her nine fold bid her, O light and her troth plight and arint thee, with arint thee.' On the special problems involved in the textual criticism of Shakespeare's works, see Madeleine Doran, 'An Evaluation of Evidence in Shakespearean Textual Criticism', *English Institute Annual, 1941* (New York, 1942), pp. 95–114, and F. P. Wilson, 'Shakespeare and the "New Bibliography" ', in *The Bibliographical Society, 1892–1942, Studies in Retrospect* (London, 1945), pp. 133–4.

emendation has been to use it prematurely. Corruptions in the Greek and Latin classics (including the New Testament) have frequently been assumed without adequate reason—as though, indeed, for the mere sake of showing off one's cleverness in proposing an alternative reading. This 'itch for emending' (*pruritus emendandi*) has resulted in the accumulation of literally thousands of proposed alterations of passages in the New Testament. Those which William Bowyer assembled in the eighteenth century (see p. 116 above) were greatly augmented in the latter part of the nineteenth century by a spate of articles and books published in Holland by W. C. van Manen, W. H. van der Sande Bakhuyzen, D. Harting, S. S. de Koe, H. Franssen, J. M. S. Baljon, J. H. A. Michelsen, J. Cramer, and others.[1]

In their edition of the Greek New Testament Westcott and Hort mark with obeli about sixty passages which they (or one of them) suspect involve a 'primitive error', that is, an error older than the extant witnesses, for the removal of which one is confined to conjectural emendation.[2] According to Schmiedel,[3] the editions of Tregelles, Tischendorf, and Weiss contain only one conjecture

---

[1] For the titles of these works, see Eberhard Nestle's bibliographical list in *Urtext und Übersetzungen der Bibel* (Leipzig, 1897), pp. 55–56 (being a reprint of his article 'Bibeltext und Bibelübersetzungen' in Herzog–Hauck's *Realencyklopädie für protestantische Theologie und Kirche*, 3te Aufl.). In the twentieth century the Dutch philologist, I. I. Hartman, maintained that most errors in the transmission of the classics are non-mechanical and therefore inexplicable, and that, therefore, the editor of a text is permitted to abandon manuscript evidence whenever in his opinion this is demanded by the content; see Hartman's article, 'Ars critica, quid sibi habeat propositum et qua utatur ratione', in *Mnemosyne*, N.S., xlviii (1920), pp. 227–38. For a rebuttal of Hartman's argument, see A. Damsté, 'De arte critica', ibid., pp. 424–33, and for several discussions of the proper limitations of conjectural emendation, see the appendix added to the second edition of Pasquali's *Storia della tradizione e critica del testo*, entitled 'Congettura e probabilità diplomatica', pp. 481–6, Paul van den Ven, 'Erreurs de méthode dans la correction conjecturale des textes byzantins', in *Byzantion*, xxiv (1954), pp. 19–45, and the sane remarks by Ludwig Bieler in his stimulating essay, 'The Grammarian's Craft', in *Folia: Studies in the Christian Perpetuation of the Classics*, x (1956), pp. 3–42, especially pp. 26 ff. See below, p. 272.

[2] The following are the passages where Westcott and Hort suspected the presence of a 'primitive error': Matt. xxi. 28 ff.; xxviii. 7; Mark iv. 28; Luke xi. 35; John iv. 1; vi. 4; viii. 9; Acts iv. 25; vii. 46; xii. 25; xiii. 32, 43; xvi. 12; xix. 40; xx. 28; xxv. 13; Rom. i. 32; iv. 12; v. 6; vii. 2; xiii. 3; xv. 32; 1 Cor. xii. 2; 2 Cor. iii. 3, 17; vii. 8; xii. 7; Gal. v. 1; Col. ii. 2, 18, 23; 2 Thess. i. 10; 1 Tim. iv. 3; vi. 7; 2 Tim. i. 13; Philem., vs. 9; Heb. iv. 2; x. 1; xi. 4, 37; xii. 11; xiii. 21; 1 Pet. i. 7; iii. 21; 2 Pet. iii. 10, 12; 1 John v. 10; Jude, vss. 1, 5, 22 f.; Rev. i. 20; ii. 12, 13; iii. 1, 7, 14; ix. 10; xi. 3; xiii. 10, 15, 16; xviii. 12; xix. 13.

[3] Paul W. Schmiedel in *Festgabe Adolf Kaegi von Schülern und Freunden dargebracht zum 30. September 1919* (Frauenfeld, 1919), p. 179.

each: Tregelles at 1 Pet. iii. 7 margin; Tischendorf at Heb. xi. 37; and Weiss at Rev. xviii. 14. The apparatus of the twenty-fourth edition of Nestle's Greek New Testament includes from various sources about 200 conjectures, 90 of which are identified by the name of the scholar who first suggested them.

One must admit the theoretical legitimacy of applying to the New Testament a process which has so often been found essential in the restoration of the right text in classical authors. On the other hand, the amount of evidence for the text of the New Testament, whether derived from manuscripts, early versions, or patristic quotations, is so much greater than that available for any ancient classical author that the necessity of resorting to emendation is reduced to the smallest dimensions.[1] It is perhaps chiefly in the Catholic Epistles and the Apocalypse, where the early manuscript evidence is more limited than for any other part of the New Testament, that the need for attempting conjectural emendation may arise with any degree of urgency.

[1] Of all the emendations proposed for the New Testament perhaps the one which has enjoyed the widest favour is the suggestion that the name 'Enoch' has fallen out of the text of 1 Pet. iii. 19, '. . . [the spirit] in which he [Christ or Enoch?] went and preached to the spirits in prison'. Since 1772, when Bowyer included this emendation in the second edition of his *Critical Conjectures*, down to the present, a large number of scholars have given it their approval, including James Moffatt and Edgar J. Goodspeed, both of whom introduced it into the text of their translations of the New Testament. (For the history of this conjecture and a list of scholars who have adopted it, see B. M. Metzger in *Journal of Religion*, xxxii [1952], pp. 256 f.)

What shall be said of this conjecture? Admittedly the precise meaning of 1 Pet. iii. 19 in the generally received text is difficult to ascertain and a great number of interpretations have been proposed, and admittedly the proposed emendation is attractive palaeographically (ἐν ᾧ καί and Ἐνώχ in uncial script are remarkably similar: ΕΝωΚΑΙ [ΕΝωΧ]). Nevertheless, since the introduction of a new subject ('Enoch') into vs. 19 disturbs an otherwise smooth context and breaks the continuity of the argument, the emendation cannot be accepted—for an emendation that introduces fresh difficulties stands self-condemned.

VII

The Causes of Error in the Transmission of the Text of the New Testament

As the physician must make a correct diagnosis of a disease before attempting to effect its cure, so the textual critic must be aware of the several kinds of injuries and dangers to which a text transmitted by handwriting is liable to be exposed before he can rectify the errors. In fact, it is important to see not only what *might* happen, but also what *has* happened in the copying of manuscripts. No systematic attempt is made in this chapter to evaluate the relative worth of the variant readings; the purpose is to describe and classify the phenomena rather than at this point to prescribe the remedy.[1]

I. UNINTENTIONAL CHANGES

1. ERRORS ARISING FROM FAULTY EYESIGHT

(*a*) The scribe who was afflicted with astigmatism found it difficult to distinguish between Greek letters which resemble one another, particularly when the previous copyist had not

---

[1] For a discussion of the subject from a different point of view, see John W. Burgon's *The Causes of the Corruption of the Traditional Text of the Holy Gospels*, ed. by Edward Miller (London, 1896). A suggestive analysis of the origin of errors in terms of the several stages involved in the process of copying is given by Eugene Vinaver in his 'Principles of Textual Emendation', *Studies in French Language and Mediaeval Literature Presented to Prof. Mildred K. Pope* (Manchester, 1939), pp. 351–69; cf. also J. Andrieu, 'Pour l'explication psychologique des fautes de copiste', *Revue des études latines*, xxviii (1950), pp. 279–92. For a consideration of the origin of transcriptional errors in the copying of the Chinese classics, reference may be made to two publications (in Chinese) by Wang Shu-min, professor at the National University of Taiwan: one is an article on 'Rules of Textual Criticism' in vol. xxiii (2) (1952) of the *Bulletin of the Institute of History and Philology of Academia Sinica* (my information comes from the *Newsletter* of the American Council of Learned Societies, v (2) [1954], pp. 57 f.); the other is a volume of 422 pages entitled *The Textual Criticism of the Chinese Classics* (Nankang, 1959). According to information kindly supplied me by Mr. Andrew T. L. Kuo, in the latter the author analyses 122 examples of text-critical problems arising from faulty transcription and deliberate alterations. See below, p. 272.

written with care. Thus in uncial script the sigma (which was customarily made as a lunar sigma), the epsilon, the theta, and the omicron (C, ϵ, Θ, O) were sometimes confused. For example, in Acts xx. 35 three minuscule manuscripts (614, 1611, and 2138) read κοπιῶντα ἔδει instead of κοπιῶντας δεῖ, an error which goes back to an uncial ancestor written in *scriptio continua*. In 1 Tim. iii. 16 the earlier manuscripts read OC ('he who') while many of the later manuscripts read $\overline{\Theta C}$ (the usual contraction for θεός, 'God'). The letters gamma, pi, and tau (Γ, Π, T) were liable to be confused, particularly if the cross-bar on the first and last letters were carelessly drawn, or if the right leg of the pi were too short. Thus in 2 Pet. ii. 13 some manuscripts read $\text{A}\Gamma\text{A}\Pi\text{A}IC$ ('love feasts') and others read $\text{A}\Pi\text{A}T\text{A}IC$ ('deceptions'). If two lambdas were written too close together they could be taken as the letter mu, as has happened at Rom. vi. 5, where most manuscripts have $\text{A}\Lambda\Lambda\text{A}$ ('but') but others have $\text{A}M\text{A}$ ('together'). If a lambda is followed too closely by an iota the combination may look like the letter nu (ΛI and N). Thus in the manuscripts of 2 Pet. ii. 18 $O\Lambda I\Gamma\omega C$ ('scarcely') alternates with $ONT\omega C$ ('really'), where the tau and the gamma are also confused. Sometimes Δ and Λ were mistaken for each other, as in Acts xv. 40, where $E\Pi I\Lambda E\Xi\text{A}MENOC$ ('having chosen') appears in codex Bezae as $E\Pi I\Delta E\Xi\text{A}MENOC$ ('having received').

In the generally accepted text of 1 Cor. xii. 13 Paul declares: 'By one Spirit we were all baptized into one body ... and all were made to drink of one Spirit.' Several witnesses, however, conclude the statement thus: '... all were made to drink of one drink', a variant which arose when scribes misread the letters $\overline{\Pi M\text{A}}$ (the usual contraction of the word πνεῦμα) as $\Pi OM\text{A}$ ('drink'). Since the word καί was sometimes abbreviated K, a kappa with a heavy dot of ink at the end of the lower diagonal line might be taken as the syllable καί. This has in fact happened at Rom. xii. 11, where the curious variant, 'serving the time' (τῷ καιρῷ δουλεύοντες), arose from the true text, 'serving the Lord' (τῷ κυρίῳ δουλεύοντες), because a scribe took the contraction of the word κυρίῳ ($\overline{K\omega}$) as $\text{K}P\omega$.

The examples cited above involve the confusion of similar-appearing letters in uncial script, used in the production of manuscripts down to the ninth century. It is scarcely necessary to consider similarities of letters in the subsequent minuscule script, for the overwhelming proportion of variant readings originated prior to the period of the minuscule manuscripts.

As was mentioned in the first chapter (see pp. 8–9 above), in antiquity non-literary, everyday documents were customarily written in a cursive hand in which most of the letters were formed without lifting the pen, and abbreviations were freely used. Whether any of the books of the Greek Bible ever circulated in cursive, or semi-cursive, script is an important question to which different answers have been given. Wikenhauser, following Roller, argues that it is unlikely that the original texts of the New Testament books were written in cursive script, because the rough surface of papyrus made it difficult to use that form of writing.[1] On the other hand, Nau pointed out that in the books of Chronicles codex Vaticanus contains certain permutations of the letters mu, nu, and beta which cannot be explained in terms of confusion of uncial script, in which these three letters are very different from one another, but which are readily explainable in cursive script, where they resemble each other closely. For example, the permutation of μ and ν in 2 Chron. xvi. 7, $A\nu\alpha\mu\epsilon\iota$ for $A\nu\alpha\nu\epsilon\iota$; xvii. 8, $M\alpha\nu\theta\alpha\nu\iota\alpha s$ and $I\omega\rho\alpha\nu$ for $N\alpha\nu\theta\alpha\nu\iota\alpha s$ and $I\omega\rho\alpha\mu$; xxxi. 12–13, $X\omega\mu\epsilon\nu\iota\alpha s$ and $M\alpha\epsilon\theta$ for $X\omega\nu\epsilon\nu\iota\alpha s$ and $N\alpha\epsilon\theta$; the permutation of β and ν in 2 Chron. xvii. 8, $T\omega\beta\alpha\delta\omega\beta\epsilon\iota\alpha$ for $T\omega\beta\alpha\delta\omega\nu\epsilon\iota\alpha$; the permutation of β and μ in 2 Chron. xxi. 10, $\Lambda o\mu\nu\alpha$ for $\Lambda o\beta\nu\alpha$; xxxvi. 2, $A\beta\epsilon\iota\tau\alpha\lambda$ for $A\mu\epsilon\iota\tau\alpha\lambda$.[2]

Another example of a Biblical manuscript which undoubtedly goes back to a cursive ancestor is the Berlin fragment of Genesis, a papyrus copy in semi-cursive script dating from the third century A.D. From a study of a wide variety of scribal errors in the text, the editors conclude that one or more ancestors were written in a typical cursive hand.[3]

---

[1] Alfred Wikenhauser, *New Testament Introduction* (New York, 1958), p. 67.

[2] See F. Nau in *Revue de l'orient chrétien*, xvi (1911), pp. 428–9.

[3] See the list of scribal errors collected by Henry A. Sanders and Carl Schmidt, *The Minor Prophets in the Freer Collection and the Berlin Fragment of Genesis* (New York, 1927), pp. 244–6. See below, p. 272.

For examples of variant readings in codex Bezae which may have arisen in a cursive ancestor, see Paul Glaue's lists in *Zeitschrift für die neutestamentliche Wissenschaft*, xlv (1954), pp. 92–94.

It is possible that $\mathfrak{P}^{75}$ had a cursive ancestor, for in Luke xvi. 19 the name of the Rich Man is ($\dot{o}\nu\dot{o}\mu\alpha\tau\iota$) $N\epsilon\nu\eta s$, which is thought to stand by haplography for ($\dot{o}\nu\dot{o}\mu\alpha\tau\iota$) $N\iota\nu\epsilon\nu\eta s$. Now, though the similarity of $\tau\iota$ and $\nu\iota$ is not close when written in uncials, in some forms of first-century cursive script the syllable $\tau\iota$ could have been very (*b*) When two lines in the exemplar from which the scribe was making a copy happened to end with the same word or words, or even sometimes with the same syllable, his eye might wander from the first to the second, accidentally omitting the whole passage lying between them. Thus is to be explained the curious reading at John xvii. 15 in codex Vaticanus, which lacks the words which are enclosed in square brackets: 'I do not pray that thou shouldst take them from the [world, but that thou shouldst keep them from the] evil one.' In the exemplar from which the scribe of this manuscript was copying, the Greek text probably stood in the following arrangement:

$$\ldots\ldots\ldots a\mathring{v}\tau o\mathring{v}s\ \mathring{\epsilon}\kappa\ \tau o\hat{v}$$
$$\kappa\acute{o}\sigma\mu ov\ldots\ldots\ldots\ldots$$
$$\ldots\ldots\ldots a\mathring{v}\tau o\mathring{v}s\ \mathring{\epsilon}\kappa\ \tau o\hat{v}$$
$$\pi o\nu\eta\rho o\hat{v}\ldots\ldots\ldots\ldots$$

After the scribe had copied the first line, his eye returned, not to the beginning of line 2, but to the beginning of line 4. Such an error is called *parablepsis* (a looking by the side),[1] and is facilitated by *homoeoteleuton* (a similar ending of lines).

Many other examples of omission, called haplography, occur in a wide variety of manuscripts. For example, the whole verse at Luke x. 32 is lacking in $\aleph$ because the sentence ends with the same verb ($\mathring{a}\nu\tau\iota\pi a\rho\hat{\eta}\lambda\theta\epsilon\nu$) as the previous sentence (vs. 31). Codex Alexandrinus omits the entire verse at 1 Cor. ix. 2, which ends with the same four words ($\mathring{v}\mu\epsilon\hat{\imath}s\ \mathring{\epsilon}\sigma\tau\epsilon\ \mathring{\epsilon}\nu\ \kappa\nu\rho\acute{\iota}\omega$) as the previous verse. Since the last five words in Luke xiv. 26 and in 27 are exactly the same ($o\mathring{v}\ \delta\acute{v}\nu a\tau a\iota\ \epsilon\mathring{\imath}\nu a\acute{\iota}\ \mu ov\ \mu a\theta\eta\tau\acute{\eta}s$), it is easy to account for the accidental omission of verse 27 in more than a dozen different manuscripts. The words of 1 John ii. 23, 'He who confesses the Son has the Father also', fell out of the later manuscripts (on which the King James version depends) because of the presence of $\tau\grave{o}\nu\ \pi a\tau\acute{\epsilon}\rho a\ \mathring{\epsilon}\chi\epsilon\iota$ in adjacent clauses. Other interesting cases of error arising from homoeoteleuton are found

---

easily confused with the letter ν; for examples, see E. M. Thompson, *Handbook of Greek and Latin Palæography* (New York, 1893), chart facing p. 148, and L. Gonzaga da Fonseca, *Epitome introductionis in palaeographiam graecam* (*biblicam*), ed. altera (Rome, 1944), pp. 85, 94 f.

[1] On the possibility of the scribe's eye wandering to a different column of the exemplar, see the examples cited by J. Rendel Harris in the *American Journal of Philology*, vi (1885), pp. 25–40.

in various manuscripts at Luke v. 26; xi. 32; xii. 9; and Rev. ix. 2–3.

Sometimes the eye of the scribe picked up the same word or group of words a second time and as a result copied twice what should have appeared only once (this kind of error is called dittography). In Acts xix. 34 the cry of the mob, 'Great is Artemis of the Ephesians', is given twice in codex Vaticanus. Again, instead of the generally accepted text of Acts xxvii. 37, 'We were in all two hundred and seventy-six ($\overline{\cos}$)[1] persons in the ship (ἐν τῷ πλοίῳ)', codex Vaticanus and the Sahidic version read '. . . about seventy-six (ὡς $\overline{os}$) . . .'. The difference in Greek is slight (ΠΛΟΙΩ$\overline{\cos}$ and ΠΛΟΙωω$\overline{\cos}$).

2. ERRORS ARISING FROM FAULTY HEARING

When scribes made copies from dictation, or even when a solitary scribe in his own cell pronounced to himself the words which he was transcribing, confusion would sometimes arise over words having the same pronunciation as others, but differing in spelling (as the English words 'there' and 'their' or 'grate' and 'great'). During the early centuries of the Christian era certain vowels and diphthongs of the Greek language lost their distinctive sounds and came to be pronounced alike, as they are today in modern Greek. The confusion between ω and o was common, accounting for such variants as ἔχωμεν and ἔχομεν in Rom. v. 1, and ὧδε and ὅδε in Luke xvi. 25.

The diphthong αι and the vowel ε came to be pronounced alike (with a short ĕ sound). As a result the second person plural ending -σθε sounded the same as the ending of the middle and passive infinitive -σθαι, accounting for the variants ἔρχεσθαι and ἔρχεσθε in Luke xiv. 17, ζηλοῦσθε and ζηλοῦσθαι in Gal. iv. 18, and similarly in many other passages. Sometimes the change of vowels resulted in an entirely different word. Thus in Matt. xi.16

---

[1] After the second century B.C. the letters of the Greek alphabet served as numerals. In addition to the twenty-four letters of the alphabet, three obsolete signs were also employed: the digamma (ϝ) or stigma (ς) for 6, the koppa (ϙ or ϛ) for 90, and the sampi (ϡ) for 900. The first nine letters of the alphabet stand for units, the second nine for tens, the third nine for hundreds: α′ = 1, β′ = 2, γ′ = 3, δ′ = 4, ε′ = 5, ϝ′ or ς′ = 6, ζ′ = 7, η′ = 8, θ′ = 9, ι′ = 10 (ια′ = 11, ιβ′ = 12, &c.), κ′ = 20 (κα′ = 21, &c.), λ′ = 30, μ′ = 40, ν′ = 50, ξ′ = 60, ο′ = 70, π′ = 80, ϙ′ or ϛ′ = 90, ρ′ = 100, σ′ = 200, τ′ = 300, υ′ = 400, φ′ = 500, χ′ = 600, ψ′ = 700, ω′ = 800, ϡ′ = 900, ͵α = 1,000, ͵β = 2,000, ͵γ = 3,000, &c.

ἑτέροις ('others') in some manuscripts varies with ἑταίροις ('comrades') in other manuscripts.

The pronunciation of ου and of υ was sometimes indistinguishable, and accounts for the variation in Rev. i. 5. The translators of the King James version followed a text of this verse which had λούσαντι ('Unto him that loved us, and *washed* us from our sins in his own blood'), whereas the text used by modern translators reads the verb λύσαντι ('. . . and *freed* us from . . .'), which is found in the earlier Greek manuscripts.

In Koine Greek the vowels η, ι, and υ, the diphthongs ει, οι, and υι, and the improper diphthong ῃ came to be pronounced alike, all of them sounding like *ēē* in English 'feet'. It is not surprising that one of the commonest kinds of scribal confusion involves the substitution of these seven vowels or diphthongs for one another. This kind of error, which is commonly called itacism, accounts for several extremely odd mistakes present in otherwise good manuscripts. For example, in 1 Cor. xv. 54 the statement 'Death is swallowed up in victory (νῖκος)' appears in 𝔭⁴⁶ and B as 'Death is swallowed up in conflict (νεῖκος)'. According to the vision of the Seer on Patmos, around God's throne in heaven was 'a rainbow (ἶρις) that looked like an emerald' (Rev. iv. 3). In ℵ, A, and other witnesses one finds the similarly pronounced word 'priests' (ἱερεῖς)!

In view of the ever-present possibility of committing itacism, it is not surprising that the evidence for the Greek personal pronouns varies widely in New Testament manuscripts (as ἡμεῖς/ ὑμεῖς, ἡμῖν/ὑμῖν, and ἡμᾶς/ὑμᾶς). Problems arise especially in the epistolary literature. Did John write his First Letter 'that our (ἡμῶν) joy may be complete' or 'that your (ὑμῶν) joy may be complete'? Does Paul include himself with his readers at Gal. iv. 28 by using ἡμεῖς, or did he write ὑμεῖς? Whichever reading is judged to be original, it is easy to see how the other arose. In the five chapters of 1 Peter the manuscripts contain at least seven instances of such an interchange of personal pronouns (i. 3, 12; ii. 21 [twice]; iii. 18, 21; v. 10). Occasionally a confusion of personal pronouns took place that produced virtual nonsense in the context; Paul's solemn statement in 2 Thess. ii. 14, 'He called you (ὑμᾶς) through our gospel, so that you may obtain the glory of our Lord Jesus Christ', reads in manuscripts A B D*, &c., 'He called us (ἡμᾶς) through our gospel . . .'. So widespread is this kind of scribal error that the testimony of even the best manuscripts respecting personal pronouns is liable to suspicion, and one's decision between such variant readings must turn upon considerations of fitness in the context.

Besides eliminating differences in the pronunciation of certain vowel sounds, later Greek ceased to give the rough breathing a distinctive force. Manuscripts which have rough and smooth breathing marks often use them most arbitrarily, so that αὐτοῦ varies with αὑτοῦ, ἕστηκεν (perfect tense of ἵστημι) varies with ἔστηκεν (imperfect tense of στήκω), εἷς with εἰς, and other similar pairs of words.[1]

In addition to confusion of vowels which sounded alike, certain consonants are occasionally interchanged, as in Matt. ii. 6 ἐκ σοῦ ('from you') becomes ἐξ οὗ ('from whom') in ℵ[c] (cf. also Matt. xxi. 19 and Mark xi. 14). In the same category belong instances of confusion between forms of verbs spelled with a single or double consonant (e.g. the present and the second aorist stems, ἔμελλεν and ἔμελεν, in John xii. 6) and the confusion of different words altogether (e.g. ἐγεννήθησαν and ἐγενήθησαν in John i. 13). Somewhat similar are the readings in 1 Thess. ii. 7, where the pronunciation of ἐγενήθημεν ἤπιοι ('we were gentle') is almost indistinguishable from ἐγενήθημεν νήπιοι ('we were babes', see pp. 230–3 below).

A curious interchange of consonants has taken place at Rev. xv. 6, where the description of the seven angels as 'robed in pure bright linen' (λίνον) becomes 'robed in pure bright stone' (λίθον) in several early manuscripts (including A C and codices of the Vulgate). At Heb. iv. 11 the scribe of codex Claromontanus wrote ἀληθείας ('truth') for ἀπειθείας ('disobedience'), with quite disastrous results to the sense!

3. ERRORS OF THE MIND

The category of errors of the mind includes those variations which seem to have arisen while the copyist was holding a clause or a sequence of letters in his (somewhat treacherous) memory between the glance at the manuscript to be copied and the writing down of what he saw there. In this way one must

[1] For other examples, with references to specific New Testament manuscripts, see Blass–Debrunner–Funk, *A Greek Grammar of the New Testament and Other Early Christian Literature* (Chicago, [1961]), § 14.

account for the origin of a multitude of changes involving the substitution of synonyms, variation in the order of words, and the transposition of letters.

(*a*) The substitution of synonyms may be illustrated by the following examples: εἶπεν for ἔφη; ἐκ for ἀπό, and the reverse; εὐθύς for εὐθέως, and the reverse; ὅτι for διότι; περί for ὑπέρ, and the reverse; ὀμμάτων for ὀφθαλμῶν.

(*b*) Variations in the sequence of words is a common phenomenon; thus the three words πάντες καὶ ἐβαπτίζοντο in Mark i. 5 also appear in the order καὶ ἐβαπτίζοντο πάντες as well as καὶ πάντες ἐβαπτίζοντο.

(*c*) The transposition of letters within a word sometimes results in the formation of a different word, as ἔλαβον in Mark xiv. 65, becomes ἔβαλον in some manuscripts (and ἔβαλλον in other manuscripts). Such alterations of letters sometimes produce utter nonsense; at John v. 39, where Jesus speaks of the Scriptures as 'they that bear witness (αἱ μαρτυροῦσαι) concerning me', the scribe of codex Bezae wrote 'they are sinning (ἁμαρτά-νουσαι) concerning me'!

(*d*) The assimilation of the wording of one passage to the slightly different wording in a parallel passage, which may have been better known to the scribe, accounts for many alterations in the Synoptic Gospels. Thus at Matt. xix. 17 the reading of the earlier manuscripts, 'Why do you ask me about what is good? One there is who is good', is changed in later manuscripts to agree with the form of Jesus' words as reported in Mark x. 17 and Luke xviii. 18, 'Why do you call me good? No one is good but God alone.' (The King James translators followed the later form of text in Matthew.) More than once in the Epistles to the Colossians and to the Ephesians scribes have introduced into passages of one Epistle words and phrases which properly belong to parallel passages in the other. Thus, to the statement in Col. i. 14, 'in whom we have redemption, the forgiveness of sins', a few later Greek manuscripts add the words 'through his blood', a phrase derived from the parallel in Eph. i. 7. (Here again the King James version follows the secondary form of text.)

4. ERRORS OF JUDGEMENT

Though perhaps several of the following examples might be classified below under the category of deliberate changes introduced for doctrinal reasons, it is possible to regard them as unintentional errors committed by well-meaning but sometimes stupid or sleepy scribes.

Words and notes standing in the margin of the older copy were occasionally incorporated into the text of the new manuscript. Since the margin was used for glosses (that is, synonyms of hard words in the text) as well as corrections, it must have often been most perplexing to a scribe to decide what to do with a marginal note. It was easiest to solve his doubt by putting the note into the text which he was copying. Thus it is probable that what was originally a marginal comment explaining the moving of the water in the pool at Bethesda (John v. 7) was incorporated into the text of John v. 3b–4 (see the King James version for the addition). Again, it is altogether likely that the clause in later manuscripts at Rom. viii. 1, 'who walk not according to the flesh but according to the spirit', was originally an explanatory note (perhaps derived from vs. 4) defining 'those who are in Christ Jesus'. As was mentioned in Chapter I, some manuscripts are provided with marginal helps designed to assist the reader of the fixed Scripture lessons appointed by the ecclesiastical calendar (the Lectionary). As a result, lectionary formulas, such as εἶπεν ὁ κύριος, occasionally crept into the text of certain non-lectionary manuscripts (e.g. at Matt. xxv. 31 and Luke vii. 31).[1]

Other errors originated, not because of the exercise of faulty judgement, but from the lack of judgement altogether. Only heedlessness to a degree that passes comprehension can account for some of the absurdities perpetrated by witless scribes. For example, after εἰς τοὺς ἁγίους of 2 Cor. viii. 4 a good many minuscule manuscripts have added the gloss δέξασθαι ἡμᾶς. It appears that a scribe of one of these manuscripts wrote in the margin beside δέξασθαι ἡμᾶς the comment ἐν πολλοῖς τῶν ἀντιγράφων οὕτως εὕρηται ('it is found thus in many of the copies'). Then the scribe of a subsequent manuscript (cited by Bengel, ad loc.) incorporated this comment on the gloss directly in his text as though it were part of the apostle Paul's instructions to the Corinthians!

What is perhaps the most atrocious of all scribal blunders is

---

[1] For other examples of influence from lectionaries, reference may be made to the present writer's monograph, *The Saturday and Sunday Lessons from Luke in the Greek Gospel Lectionary* (Chicago, 1944), pp. 14–17.

contained in the fourteenth-century codex 109. This manuscript of the Four Gospels, now in the British Museum, was transcribed from a copy which must have had Luke's genealogy of Jesus (iii. 23–38) in two columns of twenty-eight lines to the column. Instead of transcribing the text by following the columns in succession, the scribe of 109 copied the genealogy by following the lines across the two columns.[1] As a result, not only is almost everyone made the son of the wrong father, but, because the names apparently did not fill the last column of the exemplar, the name of God now stands within the list instead of at its close (it should end, of course, '. . . Adam, the son of God'). In this manuscript God is actually said to have been the son of Aram, and the source of the whole race is not God but Phares!

II. INTENTIONAL CHANGES[2]

Odd though it may seem, scribes who thought were more dangerous than those who wished merely to be faithful in copying what lay before them. Many of the alterations which may be classified as intentional were no doubt introduced in good faith by copyists who believed that they were correcting an error or infelicity of language which had previously crept into the sacred text and needed to be rectified.[3] A later scribe might even reintroduce an erroneous reading that had been previously corrected. For example, in the margin of codex Vaticanus at Heb.

[1] For a description of other manuscripts in which the Lucan genealogy of Jesus is confused to a greater or less extent, see Jacob Geerlings, *Family Π in Luke* (*Studies and Documents*, xxii, Salt Lake City, 1962), pp. 127–37.

[2] For other discussions of this subject, see Eric L. Titus, *The Motivation of Changes made in the New Testament Text by Justin Martyr and Clement of Alexandria: a Study in the Origin of New Testament Variation* (Unpublished Diss., University of Chicago, 1942); C. S. C. Williams, *Alterations to the Text of the Synoptic Gospels and Acts* (Oxford, 1951); Leon E. Wright, *Alterations of the Words of Jesus as Quoted in the Literature of the Second Century* (Cambridge, Massachusetts, 1952); E. W. Saunders, 'Studies in Doctrinal Influence on the Byzantine Text of the Gospels', *Journal of Biblical Literature*, lxxi (1952), pp. 85–92; K. W. Clark, 'Textual Criticism and Doctrine', *Studia Paulina in honorem Johannis de Zwaan* (Haarlem, 1953), pp. 52–65; Eric Fascher, *Textgeschichte als hermeneutisches Problem* (Halle/S., 1953); and Manfred Karnetzki, 'Textgeschichte als Überlieferungsgeschichte', *Zeitschrift für die neutestamentliche Wissenschaft*, xlvii (1956), pp. 170–180.

[3] Jerome complained of the copyists who 'write down not what they find but what they think is the meaning; and while they attempt to rectify the errors of others, they merely expose their own' (*scribunt non quod inveniunt, sed quod intellegunt; et dum alienos errores emendare nituntur, ostendunt suos*), *Epist.* lxxi. 5, *Ad Lucinum* (Migne, *P.L.* xxii. 671; *C.S.E.L.* lv, pp. 5 f.). For other patristic references to the incompetence of some copyists, see pp. 72 and 152 above.

i. 3 there is a curiously indignant note by a rather recent scribe[1] who restored the original reading of the codex, φανερῶν, for which a corrector had substituted the usual reading, φέρων: 'Fool and knave, can't you leave the old reading alone and not alter it!' (ἀμαθέστατε καὶ κακέ, ἄφες τὸν παλαιόν, μὴ μεταποίει).

Andrew of Caesarea in Cappadocia, in his commentary on the Book of Revelation,[2] written about the year 600, expressly applied the curse recorded in Rev. xxii. 18–19 to those *litterati* who considered that Attic usage[3] and a strictly logical train of thought were more worthy of respect and more to be admired (ἀξιοπιστότερα καὶ σεμνότερα) than the peculiarities of Biblical language. What Andrew refers to is illustrated by an anecdote told by Sozomen, a fifth-century lawyer of Constantinople who wrote a history of the Church. He relates that at an assembly of Cypriot bishops about the year 350, one Triphyllios of Ledra, a man of culture and eloquence, was addressing the assembly, and in quoting the text, 'Rise, take up your bed and walk', substituted the more refined Attic Greek word σκίμπους for the colloquial Koine word κράββατος ('pallet') used in John v. 8. Whereupon a certain Bishop Spyridon sprang up and indignantly called to him before the whole assembly, 'Are you, then, better than he [Jesus] who uttered the word κράββατος, that you are ashamed to use his word?'[4] Despite the vigilance of ecclesiastics of Bishop Spyridon's temperament, it is apparent from even a casual examination of a critical apparatus that scribes, offended by real or imagined errors of spelling, grammar, and historical fact, deliberately introduced changes into what they were transcribing.

I. CHANGES INVOLVING SPELLING AND GRAMMAR

The Book of Revelation, with its frequent Semitisms and solecisms, afforded many temptations to style-conscious scribes. It

---

[1] The scribe was perhaps of the thirteenth century; see below, p. 272.

[2] Josef Schmid, *Studien zur Geschichte des griechischen Apokalypse-Textes; i, Der Apokalypse-Kommentar des Andreas von Kaisareia* (Munich, 1955), p. 262, ll. 3–12.

[3] Cf. Wilhelm Michaelis, 'Der Attizismus und das Neue Testament', *Zeitschrift für die neutestamentliche Wissenschaft*, xxii (1923), pp. 91–121, and G. D. Kilpatrick, 'Atticism and the Text of the Greek New Testament', *Neutestamentliche Aufsätze: Festschrift für Prof. Josef Schmid* (Regensburg, 1963), pp. 125–37.

[4] Sozomen, *Hist. Eccl.* i. 11. Eusebius tells us that Tatian ventured to paraphrase certain words of the apostle Paul 'as though improving their style' (ὡς ἐπιδιορθούμενον αὐτῶν τῆς φράσεως σύνταξιν), *Hist. Eccl.* iv. xxxix. 6.

is not difficult to imagine, for example, that the use of the nominative case after the preposition ἀπό (in the stereotyped expression, ἀπὸ ὁ ὢν καὶ ὁ ἦν καὶ ὁ ἐρχόμενος, Rev. i. 4) would grate on the sensibilities of Greek copyists, and that consequently they would insert after ἀπό either τοῦ, or θεοῦ, or κυρίου in order to alleviate the syntax. As a matter of fact, all three of these attempts to patch up the grammar are represented today in one or more manuscripts.

The use of καί joining the finite verb ἐποίησεν in Rev. i. 6 to the participles in vs. 5 strains the rules of Greek concord beyond the breaking-point; scribes mended the syntax by changing the indicative to another participle (ποιήσαντι). The genitive case of πεπυρωμένης in Rev. i. 15, which agrees with nothing in its clause, was altered by some scribes to the dative and by others to the nominative, either of which construes grammatically with the rest of the sentence. In Rev. ii. 20 ἡ λέγουσα, a pendent nominative, was emended to τὴν λέγουσαν, which stands in apposition to the immediately preceding words, τὴν γυναῖκα Ἰεζάβελ.

2. HARMONISTIC CORRUPTIONS

Some harmonistic alterations originated unintentionally (examples are given in section I. 3 (*d*) above); others were made quite deliberately. Since monks usually knew by heart extensive portions of the Scriptures (see p. 87 above), the temptation to harmonize discordant parallels or quotations would be strong in proportion to the degree of the copyist's familiarity with other parts of the Bible. The words which belong in John xix. 20, 'It was written in Hebrew, in Latin, and in Greek', have been introduced into the text of many manuscripts at Luke xxiii. 38. The shorter form of the Lord's Prayer in Luke xi. 2–4 ('Father, hallowed be thy name. Thy kingdom come. Give us each day our daily bread; and forgive us our sins, for we ourselves forgive every one who is indebted to us; and lead us not into temptation') was assimilated in many copies of Luke to agree with the more familiar, longer form in Matt. vi. 9–13. At Acts ix. 5–6 the words spoken to Paul at his conversion are conformed in some manuscripts to agree with the parallel account in xxvi. 14–15. Frequently Old Testament quotations are enlarged from the Old Testament context, or are made to conform more closely to the Septuagint wording. For example, the clause in the King James version at Matt. xv. 8, '[This people] draweth nigh unto me with their mouth'—a clause which is not found in the earlier manuscripts of Matthew—was introduced into later manuscripts by conscientious scribes who compared the quotation with the fuller form in the Septuagint of Isa. xxix. 13. The earlier manuscripts of John ii. 17 quote Ps. lxix. 9 in the form 'Zeal for thy house will consume (καταφάγεται) me'. Since, however, the current Septuagint text of this Psalm reads the aorist form (κατέφαγε), later scribes conformed the Johannine quotation to the text of the Septuagint. At Rom. xiii. 9 Paul's reference to four of the Ten Commandments is expanded in some manuscripts by the addition of another, 'You shall not bear false witness.' At Heb. xii. 20 a few witnesses extend the quotation from Exod. xix. 13, 'If even a beast touches the mountain, it shall be stoned', by adding the words that follow in Exodus, 'or thrust through with a dart' (as the King James version renders it).

3. ADDITION OF NATURAL COMPLEMENTS AND SIMILAR ADJUNCTS

The work of copyists in the amplifying and rounding off of phrases is apparent in many passages. Not a few scribes supposed that something is lacking in the statement in Matt. ix. 13, 'For I came not to call the righteous, but sinners', and added the words 'unto repentance' (from Luke v. 32). So, too, many a copyist found it hard to let 'the chief priests' pass without adding 'the scribes' (e.g. Matt. xxvi. 3), or 'scribes' without 'Pharisees' (e.g. Matt. xxvii. 41); or to copy out the phrase, 'Your Father who sees in secret will reward you' (Matt. vi. 4, 6), without adding the word 'openly'.

Col. i. 23 contains an interesting example illustrating how scribes succumbed to the temptation of enhancing the dignity of the apostle Paul. In this verse the author warns the Colossians against shifting from the hope of the gospel, which 'has been preached to every creature under heaven and of which I, Paul, became a minister'. The word διάκονος, which means literally one who serves, a minister, also came to be used for a lower order of the ministry ('deacon'). Perhaps thinking that such a rank was less than appropriate for the great apostle to the Gentiles, the scribes of ℵ* and P changed διάκονος to κῆρυξ καὶ ἀπόστολος, while A and Syr^h ^mg read all three nouns ('of which I, Paul, became a herald and apostle and minister'). MS. 81 reads διάκονος καὶ ἀπόστολος, and the Ethiopic prefers κῆρυξ καὶ διάκονος. Here the shorter, less spectacular reading is obviously original.

A good example of a growing text is found in Gal. vi. 17, where the earliest form of the text is that preserved in 𝔭⁴⁶ B A C* *f*, 'I bear on my body the marks of Jesus'. Pious scribes could not resist the temptation to embroider the simple and unadorned Ἰησοῦ with various additions, producing κυρίου Ἰησοῦ, as in C³ D^c E K L and many other witnesses; κυρίου Ἰησοῦ Χριστοῦ, in ℵ d e Augustine; and κυρίου ἡμῶν Ἰησοῦ Χριστοῦ, in D^gr* G Syr^p Goth Chrysostom, Victorinus, Epiphanius.

4. CLEARING UP HISTORICAL AND GEOGRAPHICAL DIFFI-CULTIES

In the earlier manuscripts of Mark i. 2 the composite quotation from Malachi (iii. 1) and from Isaiah (xl. 3) is introduced by the formula, 'As it is written in Isaiah the prophet'. Later scribes, sensing that this involves a difficulty, replaced ἐν τῷ Ἡσαΐα τῷ προφήτῃ with the general statement ἐν τοῖς προφήταις. Since the quotation which Matthew (xxvii. 9) attributes to the prophet Jeremiah actually comes from Zechariah (xi. 12 f.), it is not surprising that some scribes sought to mend the error, either by substituting the correct name or by omitting the name altogether. A few scribes attempted to harmonize the Johannine account of the chronology of the Passion with that in Mark by changing 'sixth hour' of John xix. 14 to 'third hour' (which appears in Mark xv. 25). At John i. 28 Origen[1] altered Βηθανίᾳ to Βηθαβαρᾷ in order to remove what he regarded as a geographical difficulty, and this reading is extant today in MSS. Π Ψ 33 69 and many others, including those which lie behind the King James version. The statement in Mark viii. 31, that 'the Son of man must suffer many things . . . and be killed and after three days (μετὰ τρεῖς ἡμέρας) rise again', seems to involve a chronological difficulty, and some copyists changed the phrase to the more familiar expression, 'on the third day' (τῇ τρίτῃ ἡμέρᾳ).

---

[1] *Comm. in Joan.* ii. 19 (13) (*G.C.S.*, Origenes, iv. 76. 23–24, ed. Klostermann).

The author of the Epistle to the Hebrews places the golden altar of incense in the Holy of Holies (Heb. ix. 4), which is contrary to the Old Testament description of the Tabernacle (Exod. xxx. 1–6). The scribe of codex Vaticanus and the translator of the Ethiopic version correct the account by transferring the words to ix. 2, where the furniture of the Holy Place is itemized.

5. CONFLATION OF READINGS

What would a conscientious scribe do when he found that the same passage was given differently in two or more manuscripts which he had before him? Rather than make a choice between them and copy only one of the two variant readings (with the attendant possibility of omitting the genuine reading), most scribes incorporated both readings in the new copy which they were transcribing. This produced what is called a conflation of readings, and is characteristic of the later, Byzantine type of text. For example, in some early manuscripts the Gospel according to Luke closes with the statement that the disciples 'were continually in the temple blessing God', while others read 'were continually in the temple praising God'. Rather than discriminate between the two, later scribes decided that it was safest to put the two together, and so they invented the reading 'were continually in the temple praising and blessing God'.

In the early manuscripts at Mark xiii. 11 Jesus counsels his followers not to be 'anxious beforehand' ($\pi\rho o\mu\epsilon\rho\iota\mu\nu\hat{a}\tau\epsilon$) what they should say when persecuted. Other manuscripts of Mark read 'do not practise beforehand' ($\pi\rho o\mu\epsilon\lambda\epsilon\tau\hat{a}\tau\epsilon$), which is the expression used also in the Lucan parallel (xxi. 14). Rather than choose between these two verbs, a good many copyists of Mark gave their readers the benefit of both. In Acts xx. 28 the two earlier readings, 'church of God' and 'church of the Lord', are conflated in later manuscripts, producing 'the church of the Lord and God'.

Occasionally conflate readings appear even in early manuscripts. For example, codex Vaticanus is alone in reading $\kappa\alpha\lambda\acute{\epsilon}\sigma\alpha\nu\tau\iota$ $\kappa\alpha\grave{\iota}$ $\acute{\iota}\kappa\alpha\nu\acute{\omega}\sigma\alpha\nu\tau\iota$ at Col. i. 12, whereas all the other manuscripts have one or the other participle.

6. ALTERATIONS MADE BECAUSE OF DOCTRINAL CONSIDERATIONS

The number of deliberate alterations made in the interests of doctrine is difficult to assess. Irenaeus, Clement of Alexandria, Tertullian, Eusebius, and many other Church Fathers accused the heretics of corrupting the Scriptures in order to have support for their special views.[1] In the mid-second century Marcion expunged his copies of the Gospel according to Luke of all references to the Jewish background of Jesus. Tatian's Harmony of the Gospels contains several textual alterations which lent support to ascetic or encratite views.

Even within the pale of the Church one party often accused another of altering the text of the Scriptures. Ambrosiaster, the fourth-century Roman commentator on the Pauline Epistles, believed that where the Greek manuscripts differed on any important point from the Latin manuscripts which he was accustomed to use, the Greeks 'with their presumptuous frivolity' had smuggled in the corrupt reading. In revising the Old Latin text of the Gospels, St. Jerome was apprehensive lest he be censured for making even slight alterations in the interest of accuracy—a fear that events proved to be well founded!

The manuscripts of the New Testament preserve traces of two kinds of dogmatic alterations: those which involve the elimination or alteration of what was regarded as doctrinally unacceptable or inconvenient, and those which introduce into the Scriptures 'proof' for a favourite theological tenet or practice.

In transcribing the prologue to the Third Gospel, the scribes of several Old Latin manuscripts as well as the Gothic version

---

[1] See August Bludau, *Die Schriftfälschungen der Häretiker: ein Beitrag zur Textkritik der Bibel* (Münster/W., 1925). Such changes prove that the autographs of the books of the New Testament were no longer in existence, otherwise an appeal would have been made directly to them. Their early loss is not surprising, for during persecutions the toll taken by imperial edicts aiming to destroy all copies of the sacred books of Christians must have been heavy. Furthermore, simply the ordinary wear and tear of the fragile papyrus, on which at least the shorter Epistles of the New Testament had been written (see the reference to χάρτης in 2 John, vs. 12), would account for their early dissolution. It is not difficult to imagine what would happen in the course of time to one much-handled manuscript, passing from reader to reader, perhaps from church to church (see Col. iv. 16), and suffering damage from the fingers of eager if devout readers as well as from climatic changes. (On Peter of Alexandria's reference to the original copy of John's Gospel preserved at Ephesus [Migne, *P.G.* xviii. 517], see Juan Leal, 'El autógrafo de IV Evangelio …', *Estudios eclesiásticos*, xxxiv [1960], pp. 895-905.) See below, p. 273.

obviously thought that the Evangelist should have referred to divine approval of his decision to compose a Gospel, and so to Luke's statement (i. 3), 'It seemed good to me . . . to write an orderly account . . .', they added after 'me' the words 'and to the Holy Spirit'. The addition imitates the text of Acts xv. 28, which reads, 'For it has seemed good to the Holy Spirit and to us . . .'.

The inconsistency between Jesus' declaration in John vii. 8, 'I am not going up to the feast, for my time has not yet fully come', and the statement two verses later, 'But after his brothers had gone up to the feast, then he also went up, not publicly but in private' (a discrepancy which Porphyry[1] seized upon to accuse Jesus of 'inconstantia ac mutatio'), led some scribes to change οὐκ to οὔπω ('I am *not yet* going up . . .'). Jesus' statement, 'But of that day and hour no one knows, not even the angels of heaven, nor the Son, but the Father only' (Matt. xxiv. 36 and Mark xiii. 32), was unacceptable to scribes who could not reconcile Jesus' ignorance with his divinity, and who saved the situation by simply omitting the phrase οὐδὲ ὁ υἱός.

In Luke xxiii. 32 the text of 𝔭75 ℵ B reads ῍Ηγοντο δὲ καὶ ἕτεροι κακοῦργοι δύο σὺν αὐτῷ ἀναιρεθῆναι ('And also other criminals, two, were led away with him to be crucified'). To avoid the implication that Jesus was also a criminal, most Greek witnesses have changed the sequence of words to . . . ἕτεροι δύο κακοῦργοι . . ., which has the effect of subordinating the word κακοῦργοι ('And also two others, criminals, were led away with him to be crucified'). Two Old Latin manuscripts (*c* and *e*), the Sinaitic Syriac, and the Sahidic version solve the difficulty in another way—they leave the word ἕτεροι untranslated.

An interesting variant reading, reflecting a certain delicate perception of what was deemed to be a more fitting expression, is found in one manuscript of the Palestinian Syriac lectionary at Matt. xii. 36; instead of the generally received logion of Jesus, 'I tell you, on the day of judgement men will render account for every careless word they utter', the scribe of codex c wrote '. . . men will render account for every good word they do not utter'.

In Luke ii there are several references to Joseph and Mary which, in the ordinary text, doubtless appeared to some persons

---

[1] Quoted by Jerome, *Dialogus contra Pelagianos*, ii. 17 (Migne, *P.L.* xxiii. 578 f.).

in the early Church to require rephrasing in order to safeguard the virgin birth of Jesus. In ii. 41 and 43 instead of the words 'his parents' (οἱ γονεῖς αὐτοῦ) some manuscripts read 'Joseph and Mary'. In ii. 33 and 48 certain witnesses alter the reference to Jesus' father either by substituting the name Joseph (as in vs. 33) or by omitting it altogether (as in vs. 48).

In view of the increasing emphasis on asceticism in the early Church and the corresponding insistence upon fasting as an obligation laid on all Christians, it is not surprising that monks, in their work of transcribing manuscripts, should have introduced several references to fasting, particularly in connexion with prayer. This has happened in numerous manuscripts at Mark ix. 29, Acts x. 30, and 1 Cor. vii. 5. In Rom. xiv. 17, where the kingdom of God is said to be not eating and drinking, 'but righteousness and peace and joy in the Holy Spirit', codex 4 inserts after 'righteousness' the words 'and asceticism' (καὶ ἄσκησις). Such interpolations abound in chapter vii of 1 Corinthians.

7. ADDITION OF MISCELLANEOUS DETAILS

In Matt. i. 8 codex Bezae and the Curetonian Syriac insert several additional Old Testament names in Jesus' genealogy, thereby destroying the Evangelist's intended pattern of fourteen generations (i. 17). Besides the instances of agrapha contained in certain manuscripts at Luke vi. 4 and Matt. xx. 28 (see p. 50 above), there is a curious expansion of Jesus' words to Peter in a twelfth- or thirteenth-century minuscule codex of the Gospels (no. 713) at Matt. xvii. 26. The passage runs as follows (the addition is in italics):

Jesus spoke to him, saying, 'What do you think, Simon? From whom do kings of the earth take toll or tribute? From their sons or from aliens?' And when he said, 'From aliens', Jesus said to him, 'Then are the sons free?' *Simon said, 'Yes.' Jesus says to him, 'Then you also must give, as being an alien to them.* But, not to give offence to them, go to the sea and cast a hook, &c.'

It is noteworthy that this expansion, preserved in a late Greek manuscript, was apparently known in the second or third century, for it is witnessed by Ephraem's commentary on Tatian's Diatessaron as well as the Arabic form of the Diatessaron.[1]

[1] For a discussion of the reading, see J. Rendel Harris, 'The First Tatian Reading in the Greek New Testament', *Expositor*, 8th ser., xxiii (1922), pp. 120–9.

Two late minuscule manuscripts of the Book of Acts (614 and 2147) describe the Philippian jailor as ὁ πιστὸς Στεφανᾶς (Acts xvi. 27). Codices 181 and 460 identify the members of 'the household of Onesiphorus', to whom the writer of 2 Tim. iv. 19 sends greetings; in accord with the apocryphal Acts of Paul and Thecla they are said to be 'Lectra, his wife, and Simaeas and Zeno, his sons'.

In the Vulgate at Phil. iv. 3 the words γνήσιε σύζυγε ('true yokefellow') are appropriately rendered by the Latin *germane compar*. Curiously enough, the Greek text of the bilingual manuscripts F and G make the adjective *germane* into a proper name, reading γνήσιε Γέρμανε σύζυγε!

The threefold sanctus, ἅγιος, ἅγιος, ἅγιος, sung by the four living creatures before the throne of God (Rev. iv. 8), is expanded in various manuscripts; according to Hoskier's collations, one or more manuscripts have ἅγιος four times, six times, seven times, eight times (ℵ*), nine times (B and eighty other manuscripts), and even thirteen times (MS. 2000).

According to a scribal addition in the margin of codex S, the name of Cleopas' companion on the Emmaus road (Luke xxiv. 18) was Simon (ὁ μετὰ τοῦ Κλεωπᾶ πορευόμενος Σίμων ἦν, οὐχ ὁ Πέτρος ἀλλ' ὁ ἕτερος). The margin of codex V has the note, 'The one with Cleopas was Nathanael, as the great Epiphanios said in the *Panarion*. Cleopas was a cousin of the Saviour, the second bishop of Jerusalem.'

A number of interesting expansions appear in manuscripts of the early versions. An apocryphal addition in two Old Latin manuscripts (*a* and *g*[1]) states that when Jesus 'was baptized, a tremendous light flashed forth from the water, so that all who were present feared' (Matt. iii. 15). Another Old Latin manuscript (*k*) amplifies Mark's account of the resurrection of Jesus by adding at xvi. 3:

Suddenly at the third hour of the day[1] there was darkness throughout the whole circuit of the land, and angels descended from heaven, and he rose[1] in the brightness of the living God, [and] at once they ascended with him, and immediately there was light. Then they [the women] drew near to the tomb.

The natural curiosity of readers regarding the identity of

[1] The text at this point is not grammatical; the English renders the general sense.

persons that are referred to without being named in the New Testament prompted scribes to supply proper names. The Sahidic version gives the name Nineveh to the anonymous Rich Man of Luke xvi. 19, as does also the recently discovered 𝔭[75] (see p. 42 above). The two robbers who were crucified on either side of Jesus are variously named in Old Latin manuscripts:[1]

		Right-hand	Left-hand
Codex *c*	Matt. xxvii. 38	Zoatham	Camma
	Mark xv. 27	Zoathan	Chammatha
		?Right-hand	*?Left-hand*
Codex *l*	Luke xxiii. 32	Joathas	Maggatras
Codex *r*	Luke xxiii. 32	....	Capnatas

The titles of the books of the New Testament were the objects of a good deal of elaboration by scribes. It will be obvious that titles of, for example, Paul's Epistles were not needed until the apostle's correspondence had been collected into one corpus. The earliest titles were short and to the point. Later scribes, however, were not content with a bare and unadorned title; they embroidered it in ways they thought to be in accord with the position and reputation of the author. Thus in ℵ and C the Book of Revelation is entitled simply Ἀποκάλυψις Ἰωάννου. Later manuscripts describe John as 'the divine' (i.e. 'the theologian', Ἀποκάλυψις Ἰωάννου τοῦ θεολόγου, MSS. 35, 69, 498, 1957). Others expand by prefixing 'saint' to the name (ἁγίου Ἰωάννου, MSS. 1, 2015, 2020, &c.), and still others add 'the Evangelist' and/or 'the apostle'. The longest and most fulsome title is that found in a manuscript at Mount Athos (Hoskier's 236; Greg. 1775): 'The Revelation of the all-glorious Evangelist, bosom friend [of Jesus], virgin, beloved to Christ, John the theologian, son of Salome and Zebedee, but adopted son of Mary the Mother of God, and Son of Thunder' (Ἡ ἀποκάλυψις τοῦ πανενδόξου εὐαγγελιστοῦ, ἐπιστηθίου φίλου, παρθένου, ἠγαπημένου τῷ Χριστῷ, Ἰωάννου τοῦ θεολόγου, υἱοῦ Σαλώμης καὶ Ζεβεδαίου, θετοῦ δὲ υἱοῦ τῆς θεοτόκου Μαρίας, καὶ υἱοῦ βροντῆς). The only designation which the scribe omits (probably by accident!) is 'apostle'.

Other scribal additions which eventually found their way into the King James version are the subscriptions that are

[1] See J. Rendel Harris, 'On Certain Obscure Names in the New Testament', *Expositor*, 6th ser., i (1900), pp. 161–77, and 'A Further Note on the Names of the Two Robbers in the Gospel', ibid., pp. 304–8.

appended to the Pauline Epistles, giving information regarding the traditional place from which each was sent, as well as in some cases what was believed to be the name of the amanuensis or of the messenger who was to carry the Epistle.

Lest the foregoing examples of alterations should give the impression that scribes were altogether wilful and capricious in transmitting ancient copies of the New Testament, it ought to be noted that other evidence points to the careful and pains-taking work on the part of many faithful copyists. There are, for example, instances of difficult readings which have been trans-mitted with scrupulous fidelity. Thus ἦλθεν at Gal. ii. 12 yields no good sense and can scarcely be the form intended by the author. Nevertheless, the scribes of the earliest manuscripts (in-cluding 𝔭⁴⁶ ℵ B D* G *al*) refrained from correcting it to ἦλθον. Another instance of a manifestly erroneous reading is εἴ τις σπλάγχνα καὶ οἰκτιρμοί at Phil. ii. 1, which could have arisen when the original amanuensis misunderstood Paul's pronun-ciation of εἴ τι σπλάγχνα . . . . However the solecism may have originated, the significant point is that all uncials and most minus-cules have transmitted it with conscientious exactness.

Even in incidental details one observes the faithfulness of scribes. For example, the scribe of codex Vaticanus copied quite mechanically the section numbers which run in one series throughout the corpus of the Pauline Epistles, even though this series had been drawn up when the Epistle to the Hebrews stood between Galatians and Ephesians and is therefore not suitable for the present sequence of the Epistles in Vaticanus.[1] These examples of dogged fidelity on the part of scribes could be multiplied, and serve to counterbalance, to some extent, the impression which this chapter may otherwise make upon the beginner in New Testament textual criticism.[2]

[1] See p. 48 above.

[2] For other examples of the faithfulness of scribes, see B. Blumenkranz, 'Fidélité du scribe', *Revue du Moyen Âge*, viii (1952), pp. 323–6, and H. J. Vogels, ' "Librarii dormitantes": Aus der Überlieferung des Ambrosiaster-Kommentars zu den Paulinischen Briefen', *Sacris Erudiri: Jaarboek voor Godsdienstwetenschappen*, viii (1956), pp. 5–13.

VIII

The Practice of New Testament
Textual Criticism

I. BASIC CRITERIA FOR THE EVALUATION OF VARIANT READINGS

Perhaps the most basic criterion for the evaluation of variant readings is the simple maxim 'choose the reading which best explains the origin of the others'. We all follow this common-sense criterion when confronted with errors and 'variant readings' in modern printed books. For example, two editions of John Bunyan's classic, *The Pilgrim's Progress*, diverge in the story of Christian's finding and using a key by which he was able to make his escape from Doubting Castle. One edition reads 'The lock went desperately hard', while another reads 'The lock went damnable hard.' Which is the original reading and which has been altered? Did Bunyan write 'desperately' and a modern editor change it to 'damnable' for some inexplicable reason? Or did Bunyan write 'damnable' (using the word in its non-profane sense) and someone subsequently alter it in order to remove what was deemed to be an offensive expression? There can surely be no doubt what the answer is.[1]

Another criterion which we instinctively recognize to be basic is that the reconstruction of the history of a variant reading is prerequisite to forming a judgement about it. For example, in the earlier printings of the second edition of the unabridged *Webster's New International Dictionary of the English Language* (Springfield, 1934) there stands the entry:

> **dord** (dôrd), *n.*   *Physics & Chem.*   Density.

Now, it is a fact that there is no English word 'dord'; its presence

---

[1] The example given above has been simplified; at least three different modifications of the original reading have been introduced by editors or printers. Besides 'desperately hard' the present writer has seen copies which read 'extremely hard' and 'very hard'; for the authentic text, reference may be made to James B. Wharey's collation of the first eleven editions of *The Pilgrim's Progress* (Oxford, 1928), all of which read 'damnable hard'.

in this venerable dictionary is the result of what may be called an accidental 'scribal error'. As was acknowledged later by the publishers, the entry originated in the confusion of the abbreviation, given both as a lower-case letter and an upper-case letter, of the word 'density', and was intended to stand thus:

d. or **D.,**   *Physics & Chem.*   Density.

Not noticing the periods, someone took the collocation of letters as a word and called it a noun. The remarkable thing is that the error escaped detection for more than a decade, during which the volume was reprinted several times.

Another example of a clerical mistake, this one occurring in the highly esteemed *Who's Who in America*, arose because of incompetent judgement. The first time that the biography of Thomas Mann appeared in this distinguished cyclopedia of famous persons, he was given, quite gratuitously, a middle name. In the volume for 1939 the entry reads, in bold-face type, 'Mann, Thomas Schriftst'; in subsequent volumes, however, 'Schriftst' is lacking. Which form of the name is correct? An examination of the volume *Wer Ist's*, which is the German counterpart of *Who's Who*, discloses that 'Schriftst.' is the customary abbreviation of the German word for 'author' (*Schriftsteller*). Obviously someone who prepared the biographical sketch for the American volume mistakenly took the abbreviation of Mann's occupation to be his middle name.

The two criteria mentioned earlier are capable of very wide application, and include by implication a great many other subsidiary criteria. It will be useful, however, to specify in more precise detail the various considerations which scholars take into account in evaluating variant readings of New Testament witnesses. It is usual to classify these criteria in terms of (1) External Evidence and (2) Internal Evidence; the latter involves what Hort termed Transcriptional Probabilities and Intrinsic Probabilities. (Here the student should re-read the account of the principles underlying Westcott and Hort's edition, pp. 129–35 above, as well as the summary of B. H. Streeter's subsequent contributions to textual theory, pp. 169–73 above.) The following is a list of the chief considerations which the textual critic takes into account when evaluating variant readings in the New Testament.

An outline of basic criteria and considerations to be taken into account in evaluating variant readings

I. EXTERNAL EVIDENCE, involving considerations bearing upon:

(1) The date of the witness. (Of even greater importance than the age of the document itself is the date of the type of text which it embodies. The evidence of some minuscule manuscripts (e.g. 33, 81, and 1739) is of greater value than that of some of the later or secondary uncials.)

(2) The geographical distribution of the witnesses that agree in supporting a variant. (One must be certain, however, that geographically remote witnesses are really independent of one another. Agreements, for example, between Old Latin and Old Syriac witnesses may be due to influence from Tatian's Diatessaron.)

(3) The genealogical relationship of texts and families of witnesses. (Witnesses are to be weighed rather than counted. Furthermore, since the relative weight of the several kinds of evidence differs for different kinds of variants, there can be no merely mechanical evaluation of the evidence.)

II. INTERNAL EVIDENCE, involving two kinds of probabilities:

A. Transcriptional Probabilities depend upon considerations of palaeographical details and the habits of scribes. Thus:

(1) In general the more difficult reading is to be preferred, particularly when the sense appears on the surface to be erroneous, but on more mature consideration proves itself to be correct. (Here 'more difficult' means 'more difficult to the scribe', who would be tempted to make an emendation. The characteristic of most scribal emendations is their superficiality, often combining 'the appearance of improvement with the absence of its reality' [Westcott–Hort, ii, p. 27]. Obviously the category 'more difficult reading' is relative, and a point is sometimes reached when a reading must be judged to be so difficult that it can have arisen only by accident in transcription.)

(2) In general the shorter reading is to be preferred, except where (*a*) parablepsis arising from homoeoteleuton may have occurred; or where (*b*) the scribe may have omitted material which he deemed to be (i) superfluous, (ii) harsh, or (iii) contrary to pious belief, liturgical usage, or ascetical practice.

(Compare Griesbach's fuller statement of this criterion, p. 120 above.)

(3) Since scribes would frequently bring divergent passages into harmony with one another, in parallel passages (whether involving quotations from the Old Testament or different accounts of the same event or narrative) that reading is to be preferred which stands in verbal dissidence with the other.

(4) Scribes would sometimes (*a*) replace an unfamiliar word with a more familiar synonym, (*b*) alter a less refined grammatical form or less elegant lexical expression in accord with Atticizing preferences, or (*c*) add pronouns, conjunctions, and expletives to make a smooth text.

B. Intrinsic Probabilities depend upon considerations of what the author was more likely to have written, taking into account:

(1) the style and vocabulary of the author throughout the book,

(2) the immediate context,

(3) harmony with the usage of the author elsewhere, and, in the Gospels,

(4) the Aramaic background of the teaching of Jesus,

(5) the priority of the Gospel according to Mark, and

(6) the influence of the Christian community upon the formulation and transmission of the passage in question.

Not all of these criteria are applicable in every case. The critic must know when it is appropriate to give primary consideration to one type of evidence and not to another. Since textual criticism is an art as well as a science, it is understandable that in some cases different scholars will come to different evaluations of the significance of the evidence. This divergence is almost inevitable when, as sometimes happens, the evidence is so divided that, for example, the more difficult reading is found only in the later witnesses, or the longer reading is found only in the earlier witnesses.

One of the perennial dangers which confront scholars in every discipline is the tendency to become one-sided and to oversimplify their analysis and resolution of quite disparate questions. In textual criticism this tendency can be observed when a scholar, becoming enamoured of a single method or criterion of textual analysis, applies it more or less indiscriminately to a wide variety of problems. For example, at the beginning of the twentieth century Adalbert Merx devoted three learned volumes to the attempt to prove that the Western text is closest to the original, and that its best representative is the Sinaitic Syriac palimpsest.[1] Nearly half a century ago Adolf von Harnack, believing that the principles of New Testament criticism needed to be revised, suggested that the Latin Vulgate had been largely overlooked in the arsenal of the critic's tools.[2] Though it may well be that some scholars had not given due consideration to Jerome's contributions to textual criticism, Harnack's proposal to accord the Vulgate text a preponderant weight in the evaluation of variant readings found many adverse critics, including several Roman Catholic scholars.[3] Similarly, von Soden's extravagant estimate of the influence which Marcion and Tatian exerted upon the text of the New Testament and A. C. Clark's repeated appeal to the longer text are generally regarded today as warnings against a one-sided and unwarranted over-simplification of the evidence.[4]

II. THE PROCESS OF EVALUATING VARIANT READINGS

To teach another how to become a textual critic is like teaching another how to become a poet. The fundamental principles and criteria can be set forth and certain processes can be described, but the appropriate application of these in individual

---

[1] Adalbert Merx, *Die vier kanonischen Evangelien nach ihrem ältesten bekannten Texte . . .; 2ter Theil, Erläuterungen* (Berlin, 1902, 1905, 1911).

[2] Adolf von Harnack, *Zur Revision der Prinzipien der neutestamentlichen Textkritik: die Bedeutung der Vulgata für den Text der katholischen Briefe und der Anteil des Hieronymus an dem Übersetzungswerk* (= *Beiträge zur Einleitung in das Neue Testament*, 7. Teil; Leipzig, 1916), and 'Studien zur Vulgata des Hebräerbriefs' in *Sitzungsberichte der Preussischen Akademie*, 1920, pp. 179–201 (= *Studien zur Geschichte des Neuen Testaments und der Alten Kirche*, i, ed. by Hans Lietzmann [Berlin, 1931], pp. 191–234).

[3] See, for example, Michael Hetzenauer, *De recognitione principiorum criticae textus Novi Testamenti secundum Adolfum de Harnack* (Ratisbonae, 1921; reprinted from *Lateranum*, 1920, no. 2), and J. Belser, 'Zur Textkritik der Schriften des Johannes', *Theologische Quartalschrift*, xcviii (1916), pp. 145–84.

[4] Housman poked fun at this type of textual critic. 'We must have', he wrote, 'no favourite method. An emendator with one method is as foolish a sight as a doctor with one drug. The scribes knew and cared no more about us and our tastes than diseases care about the tastes of doctors; they made mistakes not of one sort but of all sorts, and the remedies must be of all sorts too' (A. E. Housman, ed., *M. Manilii Astronomicon, liber primus* [Cambridge, 1903], pp. liii f.).

cases rests upon the student's own sagacity and insight. With this caveat in mind, the beginner will know how to estimate the following simplified description of text-critical methodology.

As a preliminary step in analysing and evaluating the evidence found in a critical apparatus, the several variant readings should be set down in a list, each with its supporting witnesses. This will help one to see clearly the point at issue, and whether the documents have two principal readings or more.

In the evaluation of the evidence the student should begin with external considerations, asking himself which reading is supported by the earliest manuscripts and by the earliest type of text. Readings which are early and are supported by witnesses from a wide geographical area have a certain initial presumption in their favour. On the other hand, readings which are supported by only Koine or Byzantine witnesses (Hort's Syrian group) may be set aside as almost certainly secondary.[1] The reason that justifies one in discarding the Koine type of text is that it is based on the recension prepared near the close of the third century by Lucian of Antioch, or some of his associates, who deliberately combined elements from earlier types of text. Despite the fact that it appears in a large majority of Greek manuscripts (for it was adopted, with subsequent modifications, as the received text of the Greek Orthodox Church), the abundance of witnesses numerically counts for nothing in view of the secondary origin of the text-type as a whole.

To facilitate the process of ascertaining which types of text support the several variant readings, the student should become thoroughly familiar with the following tables of witnesses. One must beware, however, of supposing that these text-types are static and exactly defined entities; on the contrary, each text-type involves a process[2] of textual development which, though distinctive and characteristic as a whole, cannot be isolated within precisely determined boundaries.

[1] Theoretically it is possible that the Koine text may preserve an early reading which was lost from the other types of text, but such instances are extremely rare (one example is discussed on pp. 238–9 below). For a survey of previous evaluations of such readings, see the chapter on the Lucianic Recension in B. M. Metzger, *Chapters in the History of New Testament Textual Criticism* (Leiden and Grand Rapids, 1963), pp. 1–41. See below, p. 273.

[2] Cf. E. C. Colwell's discussion of 'The Origin of Texttypes of New Testament Manuscripts', *Early Christian Origins: Studies in honor of Harold R. Willoughby*, ed. by Allen Wikgren (Chicago, 1961), pp. 128–38, especially pp. 136 f.

KOINE OR BYZANTINE WITNESSES

Gospels: A E F G H K P S V W (in Matt. and Luke viii. 13–
xxiv. 53) *ΠΨ* (in Luke and John) *Ω* and most minuscules.
Acts: Hᵃ Lᵃᵖ Pᵃ 049 and most minuscules.
Epistles: Lᵃᵖ 049 and most minuscules.
Revelation: 046 051 052 and many minuscules.[1]

PRE-KOINE TYPES OF TEXT

The forms of text which antedate the Koine or Byzantine text
include the Western group of texts, the so-called Caesarean text,
and the Alexandrian (Hort's 'Neutral') text.[2]

The Western group of texts

Though some have held that the Western text was the deliberate creation of an individual or several individuals who
revised an earlier text,[3] most scholars do not find this type of
text homogeneous enough to be called a textual recension; it
is usually considered to be the result of an undisciplined and
'wild' growth of manuscript tradition and translational activity.

The Western type of text can be traced back to a very early
date, for it was used by Marcion (and probably Tatian),
Irenaeus, Tertullian, and Cyprian. Its most important witnesses
are codex Bezae and the Old Latin manuscripts, all of which
are characterized by longer or shorter additions and by certain
striking omissions. So-called 'Western' texts of the Gospels,
Acts, and Pauline Epistles circulated widely,[4] not only in North

[1] The Byzantine text of the Book of Revelation is less homogeneous than it is in
other books of the New Testament, for the Greek Orthodox Church has never included readings from the Apocalypse in its lectionary system—a system which
exerted a stabilizing influence on the Byzantine text of other books of the New
Testament.

[2] For fuller descriptions of each of these three pre-Koine types of text, as well as
lists of witnesses that support each type in the several natural divisions of the New
Testament (Gospels, Acts, Pauline Epistles, Catholic Epistles, and Revelation),
see M.-J. Lagrange, *Critique textuelle*; ii, *La Critique rationnelle* (Paris, 1935). Somewhat different lists are given in the preface of August Merk's *Novum Testamentum
graece et latine*, 8th ed. (Rome, 1957).

[3] So, for example, James Hardy Ropes, *The Text of Acts* (= *The Beginnings of
Christianity*, Part I, vol. iii; London, 1926), pp. viii ff., and W. H. P. Hatch, *The
'Western' Text of the Gospels* (Evanston, 1937). Ropes suggests that the preparation
of the Western text was involved in the work of forming the primitive canon of the
New Testament.

[4] The Catholic Epistles and the Book of Revelation seem not to have existed in a
characteristically Western form of text.

Africa, Italy, and Gaul (which are geographically 'Western'), but also in Egypt[1] and (in somewhat different text-forms) in the East. These latter text-forms are represented by the Sinaitic and Curetonian manuscripts of the Old Syriac, by many of the marginal notes in the Harclean Syriac, and perhaps by the Palestinian Syriac.

Westcott and Hort regarded the Western text as almost totally corrupt and accepted as original in it only what they called 'Western non-interpolations'. As was mentioned above, subsequent scholars (e.g. Merx and A. C. Clark) reacted against this one-sided view with an equally one-sided preference for the Western text. Today such extreme positions for and against Western forms of text find little favour, for most textual scholars recognize that all of the pre-Koine forms of text deserve a hearing, and that any one of them may preserve original readings which have been lost to the other text-types.

WESTERN WITNESSES

Gospels: D W (in Mark i. 1–v. 30) 0171, the Old Latin; Syr^s and Syr^c (in part), early Latin Fathers, Tatian's Diatessaron.

Acts: $\mathfrak{p}^{29}$ $\mathfrak{p}^{38}$ $\mathfrak{p}^{48}$ D 383 614 Syr$^{h\ mg}$, early Latin Fathers, the Commentary of Ephraem (preserved in Armenian).

Pauline Epistles: the Greek–Latin bilinguals D^p E^p F^p G^p; Greek Fathers to the end of the third century; the Old Latin and early Latin Fathers; Syrian Fathers to about A.D. 450.

The Caesarean text and its witnesses

B. H. Streeter identified the text that Origen used at Caesarea and associated it with the text in Θ, fam. 1, fam. 13, and other witnesses. Subsequent investigations by Lake, Blake, and New showed that the Caesarean text probably originated in Egypt and was brought by Origen to Caesarea, from where it was carried to Jerusalem (a number of Caesarean witnesses contain the so-called 'Jerusalem colophon'; see the description of

---

[1] Evidence for the presence of the Western text in Egypt is found chiefly in several papyri (e.g. $\mathfrak{p}^{29}$, $\mathfrak{p}^{38}$, and $\mathfrak{p}^{48}$). The common opinion that Clement of Alexandria was accustomed to use a Western form of text (a view based on P. M. Barnard, *The Biblical Text of Clement of Alexandria* [*Texts and Studies*, v. 5; Cambridge, 1899]) must now be modified in the light of further research by R. J. Swanson (*The Gospel Text of Clement of Alexandria* [Unpublished Diss., Yale University, 1956]), who finds that in the *Stromata* Clement's quotations of Matthew and John are twice as often from the Egyptian (= Alexandrian) text as from the Western text.

codex 157 in Chapter II above), to the Armenians (who had a colony in Jerusalem at a very early date), and thence to the Georgians (codex Koridethi belongs to Georgia).

The special character of the Caesarean text is its distinctive mixture of Western readings and Alexandrian readings. According to Lagrange, evidently its maker knew both and made a kind of compromise; in substance he followed the Alexandrian text while retaining any Western readings which did not seem too improbable, for the latter text was widely current, although the former was the better. One may also observe a certain striving after elegance, and thus consideration for the needs of the Church.[1]

According to more recent investigations made by Ayuso and others,[2] it is necessary to distinguish two stages in the development of the Caesarean text (at least for Mark). The Old Egyptian text which Origen brought with him to Caesarea may be called the pre-Caesarean text. This is preserved in $\mathfrak{p}^{45}$, W (in Mark v. 31–xvi. 20), fam. 1, fam. 13, 28, and many Greek lectionaries. At Caesarea and in its subsequent development, the pre-Caesarean text took on the form to which we are led back by the common evidence of Θ, 565, and 700, many of the citations of Origen and Eusebius, and the Old Armenian and Old Georgian versions (this form is the Caesarean text proper). There also seems to be some degree of affinity between the Old Syriac (Syr[s, c]) and the Caesarean text. In short, the Caesarean text appears to be the most mixed and the least homogeneous of any of the groups which can be classified as distinct text-types.

The Alexandrian text

It is widely agreed that the Alexandrian text was prepared by skilful editors, trained in the scholarly traditions of Alexandria.[3] The text on which they relied must have already been an ancient text in all important points. Until recently the two chief witnesses to this form of text were B and ℵ, dating from about the

---

[1] M.-J. Lagrange, *La Critique textuelle; ii, La Critique rationnelle* (Paris, 1935), pp. 163 ff.

[2] For a survey of the history of the investigation of the Caesarean text, see pp. 42–71 of the volume mentioned in n. 1 on p. 212 above. See below, p. 273.

[3] See G. Zuntz, *The Text of the Epistles, a Disquisition upon the* Corpus Paulinum (London, 1953), pp. 272–6.

middle of the fourth century. With the discovery, however, of
$\mathfrak{p}^{66}$ and $\mathfrak{p}^{75}$, both dating from about the end of the second or
the beginning of the third century,[1] proof is now available that
Hort's 'Neutral' text goes back to an archetype which must be
put early in the second century.[2] This earlier form of the Alexandrian text, which may be called the proto-Alexandrian text,
is generally shorter than the text presented in any of the other
forms, the Western being the longest. Furthermore, the proto-
Alexandrian text appears not to have undergone the systematic
grammatical and stylistic polishing that was given to other
texts, including the later form of the Alexandrian text itself.

Though most scholars have abandoned Hort's optimistic view
that codex Vaticanus (B) contains the original text almost unchanged except for slips of the pen, they are still inclined to
regard the Alexandrian text as on the whole the best ancient
recension and the one most nearly approximating the original.

ALEXANDRIAN WITNESSES

(1) Proto-Alexandrian:

$\mathfrak{p}^{45}$ (in Acts) $\mathfrak{p}^{46}$ $\mathfrak{p}^{66}$ $\mathfrak{p}^{75}$ $\aleph$ B Sahidic (in part), Clement of
Alexandria, Origen (in part), and most of the papyrus
fragments with Pauline text.

(2) Later Alexandrian:

(C) L T W (in Luke i. 1–viii. 12 and John) (X) Z $\varDelta$ (in
Mark) $\varXi$ $\varPsi$ (in Mark; partially in Luke and John) 33
579 892 1241 Bohairic.
Acts: $\mathfrak{p}^{50}$ A (C) $\varPsi$ 33 81 104 326.
Pauline Epistles: A (C) H[p] I $\varPsi$ 33 81 104 326 1739.
Catholic Epistles: $\mathfrak{p}^{20}$ $\mathfrak{p}^{23}$ A (C) $\varPsi$ 33 81 104 326 1739.
Revelation: A (C) 1006 1611 1854 2053 2344; less good $\mathfrak{p}^{47}$ $\aleph$

After having ascertained the text-types represented by the
evidence supporting each of the variant readings under examination, the student should draw a tentative conclusion as to the
preferred reading on the basis of considerations bearing on the
age of the manuscripts, the geographical spread of the witnesses

---

[1] Herbert Hunger, however, dates $\mathfrak{p}^{66}$ earlier in the second century; see n. 1 on
p. 40 above.   [2] See below, p. 273.

which join in support of a given reading, and the textual types to which they belong. Due appreciation of the implications of genealogical relationship among manuscripts prevents one from favouring a reading merely because a large number of witnesses may support it.

The next step in the process of evaluating variant readings is to appeal to internal evidence, beginning with transcriptional probabilities. Which reading is the more difficult—that is, more difficult to the scribe? Other things being equal, the reading which puzzled the scribe is most likely to be correct. On the other hand, there is a point at which what is relatively difficult becomes absolutely difficult, and therefore impossible to be regarded as original.

Some readings were favoured by scribes because they supported current beliefs and practices in their part of the Christian world. Hence the textual critic will need to have the fullest knowledge of the development of Christian doctrine and cultus, as well as all the heretical aberrations in the early Church. It goes without saying that acquaintance with palaeographical features of uncial and minuscule hands, along with a knowledge of dialectical variations in Greek orthography and syntax, will often suggest the correct evaluation of a variant reading. When dealing with a passage in the Synoptic Gospels it is necessary to examine the evidence of parallel passages. The harmonization of the Evangelists is by definition a secondary procedure; therefore the supreme rule for editors of the text is to give each Gospel its own proper character. This means that ordinarily the reading which differs from a parallel passage (particularly when the evidence for the reading of the parallel is firm) should be preferred. Likewise, in instances of quotations from the Old Testament, the text and apparatus of the Septuagint must be consulted. Since scribes tended to make New Testament quotations conform to the text of the Septuagint, readings which diverge from the Old Testament should not be rejected without the most careful consideration.

Finally, the student may appeal to intrinsic probability. The reading deemed original should be in harmony with the author's style and usage elsewhere. Since, however, it is conceivable that several variant readings may fulfil this requirement, the textual critic should be guided more by negative judgements delivered by intrinsic evidence than by positive judgements. The appropriate question to ask is whether intrinsic evidence *opposes* the conclusion commended by genealogical considerations, the geographical distribution of witnesses, and transcriptional probabilities.

Sometimes it happens that the only reading which seems to be in harmony with the author's usage elsewhere is supported by the poorest external evidence. In such cases the decision of the textual critic will be made in accord with his general philosophy of textual methodology. It is probably safest for the beginner to rely upon the weight of external evidence rather than upon what may be an imperfect knowledge of the author's usage.

In the course of time the student will observe that generally the reading which is supported by a combination of Alexandrian and Western witnesses is superior to any other reading. There is, however, an exception to this observation; in the Pauline Epistles the combination of B D G is ordinarily not of great weight. The reason for this is that though B is purely Alexandrian in the Gospels, in the Pauline Epistles it has a certain Western element. Hence the combination of B plus one or more Western witnesses in Paul may mean only the addition of one Western witness to others of the same class.

The combination of Western and Caesarean witnesses does not usually possess exceptional weight, for the Caesarean text was probably formed from a base which had Western affiliations.

In the evaluation of readings which are supported by only one class of witnesses, the student will probably find that true readings survive frequently in the Alexandrian text alone, less frequently in the Western group alone, and very rarely only in Caesarean witnesses. As a rule of thumb, the beginner may ordinarily follow the Alexandrian text except in the case of readings contrary to the criteria which are responsible for its being given preference in general. Such a procedure, however, must not be allowed to degenerate into merely looking for the reading which is supported by B and ℵ (or even by B alone, as Hort was accused of doing); in every instance a full and careful evaluation is to be made of all the variant readings in the light of both transcriptional and intrinsic probabilities. The possibility must always be kept open that the original reading has been preserved alone in any one group of manuscripts, even, in extremely rare instances, in the Koine or Byzantine text.

It remains now to put into practice these principles. Lest, however, the student imagine that the procedures of criticism are stereotyped and doctrinaire, this section may be concluded on a lighter vein with a quotation from a scintillating essay on textual criticism by A. E. Housman:

> Textual criticism is not a branch of mathematics, nor indeed an exact science at all. It deals with a matter not rigid and constant, like lines and numbers, but fluid and variable; namely the frailties and aberrations of the human mind, and of its insubordinate servants, the human fingers. It is therefore not susceptible of hard-and-fast rules. It would be much easier if it were; and that is why people try to pretend that it is, or at least behave as if they thought so. Of course you can have hard-and-fast rules if you like, but then you will have false rules, and they will lead you wrong; because their simplicity will render them inapplicable to problems which are not simple, but complicated by the play of personality. A textual critic engaged upon his business is not at all like Newton investigating the motions of the planets: he is much more like a dog hunting for fleas. If a dog hunted for fleas on mathematical principles, basing his researches on statistics of area and population, he would never catch a flea except by accident. They require to be treated as individuals; and every problem which presents itself to the textual critic must be regarded as possibly unique.[1]

III. THE TEXTUAL ANALYSIS OF SELECTED PASSAGES

The following passages have been chosen in order to provide illustrative examples of various kinds of text-critical problems. To prevent monotony in the exposition and to emphasize that no one stereotyped method of textual analysis is suited to all problems, the presentation of the kinds and nature of the evidence will be varied in sequence and in development of argument. The discussion begins with relatively simple problems, for which one can usually find clear and unambiguous solutions, and concludes with more complex problems, where the probabilities are much more evenly divided and where the

[1] A. E. Housman, 'The Application of Thought to Textual Criticism', *Proceedings of the Classical Association, August, 1921*, xviii (London, 1922), pp. 68–69. (This essay is now more widely available in John Carter's edition of several of Housman's critical writings, entitled *Selected Prose* [Cambridge, 1961], pp. 131–50.)

critic must sometimes be content with choosing the least unsatisfactory reading, or even with admitting that he has no clear basis for choice at all.

It is customary in a critical apparatus to use abbreviations of certain Latin words as a concise and 'international' working language. The following are in general use:

pc (*pauci*)	=	a few other manuscripts
al (*alii*)	=	other manuscripts
pm (*permulti*)	=	very many other manuscripts
pl (*plerique*)	=	most other manuscripts
rell (*reliqui*)	=	the remaining witnesses
vid (*videtur*)	=	as it seems, apparently
omn (*omnes*)	=	all manuscripts
codd (*codices*)	=	manuscripts of a version or Church Father as distinguished from the edition
ap (*apud*)	=	in the writings of, on the authority of (e.g. Papias ap Eusebius)
pt (*partim*)	=	divided evidence (e.g. Orig[pt] signifies that Origen is inconsistent in his quotations of the same passage)
2/4	=	divided evidence (e.g. Orig 2/4 signifies that in two cases out of four quotations of the same passage Origen supports a given reading)

An asterisk (*) placed after the siglum of a manuscript indicates that the manuscript at the passage referred to has been corrected and that the original reading is being cited; a superior letter ([c]) placed after the siglum indicates that the corrected reading is being cited. Sometimes the work of more than one corrector can be differentiated (for the several ways in which such information is cited, see the descriptions of codex Sinaiticus, p. 46 above, and codex Ephraemi, p. 49 above). When the siglum of a manuscript is enclosed within parentheses, this signifies that the manuscript supports the chief point of the variant reading but differs in minor respects.

In this connexion a warning may not be out of place: in some *apparatus critici* of the New Testament the sigla of uncial manuscripts are often cited without the superior letter (or the inferior numeral) that serves to distinguish certain manuscripts from others designated by the same siglum. Thus D *simpliciter* often stands for codex Claromontanus (instead of D^p [or D₂]) as well as for codex Bezae. In such instances one must be alert to distinguish between the two manuscripts by observing whether the variant reading occurs in the Gospels or Acts (in this case D = codex Bezae), or whether the variant occurs in the Pauline Epistles (in this case D = codex Claromontanus). In the following textual analyses the witness's siglum with the superior letter (when this is appropriate) will be used in accord with the descriptions of manuscripts given above in Chapter II: that is to say, the superior letter ᵃ after a siglum indicates a manuscript that contains the Acts and the Catholic Epistles, ᵖ indicates the Pauline Epistles, and ʳ the Book of Revelation.

In the King James version of Acts vi. 8 Stephen is described as 'full of faith and power' (πλήρης πίστεως καὶ δυνάμεως), whereas in the Revised Standard Version and the New English Bible he is said to be 'full of grace and power' (πλήρης χάριτος καὶ δυνάμεως). The difference in the English versions represents not variant renderings of the same Greek word but variant readings in the basic Greek text. The textual evidence, which involves four variant readings, is as follows:

(1) 'grace' (χάριτος) is read by 𝔭⁷⁴ ℵ A B D, more than twenty minuscule manuscripts, the Vulgate, Sahidic, Bohairic, Syriac^p, Armenian, and Ethiopic (the last reads χάριτος θεοῦ).

(2) 'faith' (πίστεως) is read by H^a P^a, many minuscule manuscripts, Syriac^h, and Chrysostom.

(3) 'grace and faith' (χάριτος καὶ πίστεως) is read by E^a.

(4) 'faith and grace of the Spirit' (πίστεως καὶ χάριτος πνεύματος) is read by Ψ.

Of these four variant readings it is obvious that either the first two are independent abridgements of the longer readings, or the third and fourth readings have arisen from combining the elements of the first two. Considerations of both external evidence and internal probability unite to demonstrate that readings (3) and (4) are secondary, being alternative conflations of the other two. Reading (3) is supported by the uncial manuscript.E^a, which dates from the sixth century and is one of the earliest representatives of the Koine or Byzantine type of text in Acts. Reading (4) is supported by the uncial manuscript Ψ, which dates from the eighth or ninth century and has a mixed type of text in Acts. Transcriptional considerations lead one to conclude that both (3) and (4) presuppose the priority of the other two readings, for it is easier to believe that a scribe, knowing the existence of readings (1) and (2), decided to join them, lest the copy which he was writing lose one or the other, than to believe that two scribes independently took offence at the longer reading and that each chose to perpetuate half of it in his copy. Thus external evidence, which is meagre in extent and relatively late in date, and transcriptional probabilities unite against the originality of readings (3) and (4).

Variant reading (2) is supported by two uncial manuscripts, Hª of the ninth century and Pª of the tenth century, both representative of the Koine or Byzantine type of text. The majority of the minuscule manuscripts join these two uncial witnesses. The earliest witness to reading (2) is Chrysostom, who died A.D. 407.

Variant reading (1) is supported by a wide variety of witnesses, including representatives of the major pre-Koine types of text. Codices Sinaiticus and Vaticanus, both of the fourth century, are the earliest and best uncial representatives in Acts of the Alexandrian type of text. Codex Bezae, of the fifth or sixth century, is the chief Greek representative of the Western group of witnesses. Codex Alexandrinus, of the fifth century, and 𝔓⁷⁴, dating from about the seventh century, have a mixed type of text. The evidence of the early versions, including the Latin, Syriac, Coptic, and Armenian, reflect the wide geographical area over which the reading was accepted. The external evidence in support of reading (1) is, therefore, far superior in point of age and diversity of text-type to that supporting reading (2).

Internal probabilities likewise favour reading (1). If the account originally stated that Stephen was 'full of faith', there is no discernible reason why a scribe should alter it to 'full of grace'. On the other hand, in view of the statement made three verses earlier that Stephen was a man 'full of faith and the Holy Spirit' (vs. 5), it is easy to understand that in transcribing the later statement in verse 8 copyists would be likely, either consciously or unconsciously, to substitute πίστεως, which they recalled from the earlier passage, for the correct reading χάριτος. The presence of πνεύματος in reading (4) is to be explained in the same way.

Thus the converging of several strands of evidence, both external and internal, leads one to the firm conclusion that the author of Acts vi. 8 wrote πλήρης χάριτος καὶ δυνάμεως.

Not a few New Testament manuscripts incorporate here and there interesting details, some of which may be historically correct. The story of the woman taken in adultery, for example, has all the earmarks of historical veracity; no ascetically minded monk would have invented a narrative which closes with what seems to be only a mild rebuke on Jesus' part: 'Neither do I condemn you; go, and do not sin again.' At the same time the pericope, which is usually printed as John vii. 53–viii. 11, must be judged to be an intrusion into the Fourth Gospel.

The account is lacking in the best Greek manuscripts: it is absent from 𝔓66 𝔓75 ℵ B L N T W X Δ Θ Ψ 33 157 565 892 1241 fam. 1424, &c. Codices A and C are defective at this point, but it is highly probable that neither contained the section, for there would not have been space enough on the missing leaves to include it along with the rest of the text. The Old Syriac (Syrs, c) and the Arabic form of Tatian's Diatessaron betray no knowledge of the passage, nor is it contained in the best manuscripts of the Peshitta. Likewise the old Coptic Churches did not include it in their Bible, for the Sahidic, the sub-Achmimic, and the older Bohairic manuscripts lack it. Some Armenian manuscripts as well as the Old Georgian version omit it. In the West the passage is absent from the Gothic version and from several Old Latin manuscripts (a f l*q).

Even more significant is the fact that no Greek Church Father for a thousand years after Christ refers to the pericope, including even those who, like Origen, Chrysostom, and Nonnus (in his metrical paraphrase), dealt with the entire Gospel verse by verse. Euthymius Zigabenus, who lived in the first part of the twelfth century, is the first Greek writer to comment on the passage, and even he declares that the accurate copies of the Gospel do not contain it.

When one adds to this impressive and diversified list of external evidence the consideration that the style and vocabulary of the pericope differ markedly from the rest of the Fourth Gospel, and that it interrupts the sequence of vii. 52 and viii. 12 f., the case against its being of Johannine authorship appears to be conclusive.

The earliest Greek manuscript known to contain the passage is codex Bezae, of the fifth or sixth century, which is joined by several Old Latin manuscripts (*b c e ff² j*). The pericope is obviously a piece of floating tradition which circulated in certain parts of the Western Church. It was subsequently inserted into various manuscripts at various places. Most scribes thought that it would interrupt John's narrative least if it were inserted after vii. 52 (D E F G H K M S U *Γ Λ Π* 28 579 700 1579, &c.). Others placed it after vii. 36 (MS. 225) or after xxi. 24 (fam. 1 1076 1570 1582). The revision of the Old Georgian version, made in the eleventh century by George the Athonite, contains the passage after vii. 44. The scribe of an ancestor of fam. 13 inserted it in another Gospel altogether, after Luke xxi. 38. Significantly enough, in many of the manuscripts which contain the passage it is marked with an obelus (as, for example, in S) or an asterisk (as, for example, in E M *Λ*), indicating that, though the scribes of these manuscripts included the account, they were aware that it lacked satisfactory credentials.

A few of the manuscripts which report the incident also include an interesting expansion at the close of viii. 8. More than one reader of the statement that Jesus 'bent down and wrote with his finger on the ground' must have wondered what it was that the Lord wrote. An unknown copyist satisfied this natural curiosity by adding the words, 'the sins of each of them'.[1]

The best disposition to make of the pericope as a whole is doubtless to print it at the close of the Fourth Gospel, with a footnote advising the reader that the text of the pericope has no fixed place in the ancient witnesses.[2]

An interesting example of several different attempts to clarify a comment made by the Fourth Evangelist, which was felt to be open to misinterpretation, is found in John vii. 37–39:

[1] See David C. Voss, 'The Sins of Each One of Them', *Anglican Theological Review*, xv (1933), pp. 321–3.

[2] For a discussion of the origin of the pericope and the problem of why it was so late in being incorporated into the canonical text, see Harald Riesenfeld, 'Perikopen de adultera i den fornkyrkliga traditionen', *Svensk exegetisk årsbok*, xvii (1953), pp. 106–18. See below, p. 273.

On the last day of the feast, the great day, Jesus stood up and proclaimed, 'If any one thirst, let him come to me and drink. He who believes in me, as the scripture has said, "Out of his heart shall flow rivers of living water".' Now this he said about the Spirit, which those who believed in him were to receive; for as yet the Spirit had not been given, because Jesus was not yet glorified.

In the final sentence the clause 'for as yet the Spirit had not been given' (οὔπω γὰρ ἦν πνεῦμα δεδομένον) appears in seven different forms:

(1) πνεῦμα 𝔭⁶⁶ᶜ 𝔭⁷⁵ ℵ K T Θ Π Ψ 1079 1546 Copᵇᵒ Arm.

(2) πνεῦμα ἅγιον 𝔭⁶⁶* L W X Γ Δ Λ 28 33 565 700.

(3) πνεῦμα ἅγιον ἐπ' αὐτοῖς D ƒ Goth.

(4) πνεῦμα δεδομένον a b c e ff² g l Vulg Syrˢ, ᶜ, ᵖ Eusebius.

(5) πνεῦμα ἅγιον δεδομένον B 053 1230 e q Syrᵖᵃˡ, ʰ.

(6) 'for they had not yet received [the] Spirit' Copˢᵃʰ, ˢᵘᵇ⁻ᵃᶜʰ·

(7) 'for the Holy Spirit had not yet come' Eth.

A little reflection will make it obvious that the reading which explains the rise of all the others is (1) πνεῦμα. Many scribes were doubtless perplexed by the bare and ambiguous statement 'for as yet the Spirit was not, because Jesus was not yet glorified'. Lest this be taken to affirm that the Spirit was not yet in existence prior to Jesus' glorification, modifications were introduced to relieve the difficulty. Several Western witnesses (D ƒ Goth) read (3), 'for the Holy Spirit was not yet in them'. Other witnesses add the verb 'given' (as in readings 4 and 5), or 'received' (reading 6), or 'come' (reading 7).

The introduction of the adjective ἅγιον (readings 2, 3, and 5) is a most natural kind of addition that many scribes would make independently of one another. (The correction found in 𝔭⁶⁶, deleting ἅγιον, is in keeping with the observed vigilance of this scribe in correcting his own inadvertent errors.) It is noteworthy that in this case codex Vaticanus is doubly in error (5), having added both ἅγιον and a predicate verb.

The evidence for (2) can be joined to that of (1) in respect of resisting the temptation to add a predicate verb. There is thus a very widespread and diversified constellation of witnesses in support of the more difficult and shorter reading. It can scarcely be doubted, therefore, that the original text had simply οὔπω γὰρ ἦν πνεῦμα.[1]

---

[1] This is the text lying behind the King James version, the Revised Version of

How did Mark end his Gospel? Unfortunately, we do not know; the most that can be said is that four different endings are current among the manuscripts, but that probably none of them represents what Mark originally intended to stand as the close of his Gospel. These four endings may be called the short ending, the intermediate ending, the long ending, and the long ending expanded. The evidence for each of them is as follows:

(1) The last twelve verses of Mark (xvi. 9–20) are lacking in the two earliest parchment codices, B and ℵ, in the Old Latin manuscript *k*, the Sinaitic Syriac, many manuscripts of the Old Armenian version, the Adysh and Opiza manuscripts of the Old Georgian version, and a number of manuscripts of the Ethiopic version. Clement of Alexandria, Origen, and Ammonius show no knowledge of the existence of these verses; other Church Fathers state that the section is absent from Greek copies of Mark known to them (e.g. Jerome, *Epist.* cxx. 3, *ad Hedibiam*, 'Almost all the Greek copies do not have this concluding portion'). The original form of the Eusebian sections makes no provision for numbering sections after xvi. 8. Not a few manuscripts which contain the passage have scholia stating that older Greek copies lack it (so, for example, MSS. 1, 20, 22, &c.), and in other witnesses the passage is marked with asterisks or obeli, the conventional sigla used by scribes to indicate a spurious addition to a literary document.

(2) The intermediate ending ('But they reported briefly to Peter and those with him all that they had been told. And after this Jesus himself sent out by means of them, from east to west, the sacred and imperishable proclamation of eternal salvation') is present in several uncial manuscripts of the seventh, eighth, and ninth centuries (L Ψ 099 0112), as well as in a few minuscule manuscripts (274[mg] [see Plate XI] 579), and several ancient versions (*k* Syr[h mg] Coptic[pt] Eth[codd]).[1]

(3) The long ending, so familiar through the King James version and other translations of the Textus Receptus, is present

1881, and the American Standard Version of 1901, all of which use italics to show what the translators added for the sake of English readers: '. . . was not yet *given*'. Since neither the Revised Standard Version nor the New English Bible employs italics in this way, the inclusion of the verb 'given' in these two versions is to be accounted for either as the result of licence in translation or the choice of what appears to be a secondary variant reading as the basic text.

[1] For detailed evidence of the Coptic versions, see P. E. Kahle, *Journal of Theological Studies*, N.S., ii (1951), pp. 49–57.

in the vast number of witnesses (including several which also contain the intermediate ending), namely A C D L W Θ, most of the later uncials, the great majority of the minuscules, most of the Old Latin witnesses, the Vulgate, Syr[c, p], and Coptic[pt]. It is probable that Justin Martyr at the middle of the second century knew this ending; in any case Tatian, his disciple, included it in his Diatessaron.

(4) The long ending in an expanded form existed, so Jerome tells us, in Greek copies current in his day, and since the discovery of W earlier this century we now have the Greek text of this expansion (for a translation of the addition after vs. 14, see p. 57 above).

None of these four endings commends itself as original. The obvious and pervasive apocryphal flavour of the expansion in (4), as well as the extremely limited basis of evidence supporting it, condemns it as a totally secondary accretion.

The long ending (3), though present in a variety of witnesses, some of them ancient, must also be judged by internal evidence to be secondary. For example, the presence of seventeen non-Marcan words or words used in a non-Marcan sense; the lack of a smooth juncture between verses 8 and 9 (the subject in vs. 8 is the women, whereas Jesus is the presumed subject in vs. 9); and the way in which Mary is identified in verse 9 even though she has been mentioned previously (vs. 1)—all these features indicate that the section was added by someone who knew a form of Mark which ended abruptly with verse 8 and who wished to provide a more appropriate conclusion. An Armenian manuscript of the Gospels, copied A.D. 989 (see Plate XIV*b*), contains a brief rubric of two words in the space at the end of the last line of verse 8 and before the last twelve verses, namely *Ariston eritsou* ('of the Presbyter Ariston'). Many have interpreted this as a reference to Aristion, a contemporary of Papias in the early second century and traditionally a disciple of John the Apostle. But the probability that an Armenian rubricator would have access to historically valuable tradition on this point is almost nil, especially if, as has been argued, the rubric was added in the thirteenth or fourteenth century.[1]

The internal evidence of the so-called intermediate ending (2) is decidedly against its being genuine. Besides containing a high

[1] So Joseph Schäfers in *Biblische Zeitschrift*, xiii (1915), pp. 24–25.

percentage of non-Marcan words, its rhetorical tone differs totally from the simple style of Mark's Gospel. The mouth-filling phrase at the close ('the sacred and imperishable message of eternal salvation') betrays the hand of a later Greek theologian.

Thus we are left with the short ending, witnessed by the earliest Greek, versional, and patristic evidence. Both external and internal considerations lead one to conclude that the original text of the Second Gospel, as known today, closes at xvi. 8. But did Mark intend to conclude his Gospel with the melancholy statement that the women were afraid (ἐφοβοῦντο γάρ)? Despite the arguments which several modern scholars have urged in support of such a view,[1] the present writer cannot believe that the note of fear would have been regarded as an appropriate conclusion to an account of the Evangel, or Good News. Furthermore, from a stylistic point of view, to terminate a Greek sentence with the word γάρ is most unusual and exceedingly rare—only a relatively few examples have been found throughout all the vast range of Greek literary works, and no instance has been found where γάρ stands at the end of a book. Moreover, it is possible that in verse 8 Mark uses the verb ἐφοβοῦντο to mean 'they were afraid of' (as he does in four of the other occurrences of this verb in his Gospel). In that case obviously something is needed to finish the sentence.

It appears, therefore, that ἐφοβοῦντο γάρ of Mark xvi. 8 does not represent what Mark intended to stand at the end of his Gospel. Whether he was interrupted while writing and subsequently prevented (perhaps by death) from finishing his literary work, or whether the last leaf of the original copy was accidentally lost before other copies had been made, we do not know. All that is known is that more than one person in the early Church sensed that the Gospel is a torso and tried in various ways to provide a more or less appropriate conclusion.[2]

---

[1] e.g. J. M. Creed, *Journal of Theological Studies*, xxxi (1932), pp. 175–80; Ernst Lohmeyer, *Das Evangelium des Markus* (Göttingen, 1937), pp. 356–60; N. B. Stonehouse, *The Witness of Matthew and Mark to Christ* (Philadelphia, 1944), pp. 86–118; A. M. Farrer, *The Glass of Vision* (London, 1948), pp. 136–46; R. H. Lightfoot, *The Gospel Message of St. Mark* (Oxford, 1950), pp. 80–97, 106–16.

[2] Almost all textual studies and critical commentaries on the Gospel according to Mark agree that the last twelve verses cannot be regarded as Marcan; typical is the monograph by Clarence R. Williams, *The Appendices to the Gospel according to*

It should not be overlooked that the text-critical analysis of the endings of Mark's Gospel has an important bearing on the historical and literary source criticism of the Gospels. Since Mark was not responsible for the composition of the last twelve verses of the generally current form of his Gospel, and since they undoubtedly had been attached to the Gospel before the Church recognized the fourfold Gospels as canonical, it follows that the New Testament contains not four but five evangelic accounts of events subsequent to the Resurrection of Christ.

In contrast with the length of the preceding textual variant, embracing twelve verses, one or two variant readings will now be examined which involve the presence or absence of a single letter.

The Greek text which lies behind the traditional words of the angelic chorus at the birth of Jesus ('Glory to God in the highest, and on earth peace, good will toward men', Luke ii. 14, King James version) differs by only the letter sigma from the Greek text which lies behind the same verse in the Revised Standard Version ('Glory to God in the highest, and on earth peace among men with whom he is well pleased!'). In the former case the King James translators followed the Textus Receptus, which reads εὐδοκία, supported by E F G H L S U V Θ Ξ Ω, many minuscules, the Syriac, Bohairic, and Georgian versions, Tatian, and Eusebius. In the latter case the Revisers followed a Greek text which reads the genitive case, εὐδοκίας, supported by B* ℵ* A D W 28, the Old Latin, Jerome's Vulgate, the Gothic, the Sahidic, Irenaeus, Cyril of Jerusalem, and the Latin Fathers.

Mark: a Study in Textual Transmission (= *Transactions of the Connecticut Academy of Arts and Sciences*, vol. xviii; New Haven, 1915).

In the last century two major attempts were made to defend the genuineness of the long ending; namely John W. Burgon's *The Last Twelve Verses of the Gospel according to St. Mark Vindicated* . . . (London, 1871; reprinted 1959), and J. P. P. Martin's *Introduction à la critique textuelle du Nouveau Testament: Partie pratique*, vol. ii (Paris, 1884). The most recent effort to rehabilitate this position was made by M. van der Valk in his 'Observations on Mark 16, 9–20 in Relation to St. Mark's Gospel', published in *Humanitas*, N.S., vi–vii (Instituto de estudos clássicos, Faculdade de letras da Universidade de Coimbra, 1958), pp. 52–95. This essay is a singular exhibition of how not to practise textual criticism! Omitting entirely all consideration of the external evidence of manuscripts, van der Valk concentrates on more or less irrelevant and speculative considerations in order to arrive at what appears to be a predetermined conclusion. See below, p. 273.

It will be observed that the earliest Greek manuscripts of both the Alexandrian and Western groups are joined by significant versional and patristic evidence in support of εὐδοκίας, proving that this reading was widely disseminated in the West and was known in Upper Egypt and in Palestine as well. On the other hand, the nominative form of the word was also widely read, being current in Syria, in Egypt around the delta, at Caesarea (Θ, Eusebius), and dating from as early as the second century (Tatian). On the whole, the external evidence appears to favour the genitive case, for the combination of B ℵ W with D and the Old Latin outweighs the external support for the nominative case. Internal considerations confirm this judgement, for in the context the genitive case is the more difficult to construe and therefore would be more likely to be altered to the nominative than vice versa. Furthermore, consideration of intrinsic suitability corroborates the other evidence, for the expression 'men of [his, i.e. God's] good will [or favour]' is a perfectly good Semitic construction, appearing several times in the Hebrew hymns discovered at Qumran,[1] and thus is entirely congruous with the Semitic cast of the first two chapters of Luke.

Luke ii. 14, therefore, involves a twofold strophe ('glory . . . peace'), and not a threefold strophe ('glory . . . peace . . . good will', all in the nominative). The sense is that the birth of the Messiah, the Lord (vs. 11), is the occasion for the ascription of glory to God in highest heaven and the enjoyment of peace on earth among men of God's good will, i.e. those persons on whom his favour rests, chosen to be the recipients of the gift of his Messiah.

Another interesting variant reading which arises from the presence or absence of a single Greek letter is found in 1 Thess. ii. 7. Here the reading is either 'we were gentle (ἤπιοι) among you, like a nurse taking care of her children', or 'we were babes (νήπιοι) among you, like a nurse taking care of her children'. The word ἤπιοι is supported by ℵ^c A C^b D^{p(c)} K^p L^p P^p 33 Syr^{p, h}, Sahidic, Armenian, Clement 2/2, Origen 3/4, Chrysostom,

---

[1] See Claus-Hunno Hunzinger, 'Neues Licht auf Lc. 2. 14', *Zeitschrift für die neutestamentliche Wissenschaft*, xliv (1952–3), pp. 85–90; id., 'Ein weiterer Beleg zu Lc. 2. 14 ἄνθρωποι εὐδοκίας', ibid. xlix (1958), pp. 129–31, and cf. Ernest Vogt, ' "Peace among Men of God's Good Pleasure" Lk. 2. 14', in *The Scrolls and the New Testament*, ed. by K. Stendahl (New York, 1957), pp. 114–17. See below, p. 273.

Theodore of Mopsuestia; the word νήπιοι is supported by 𝔭⁶⁵ ℵ* B C* Dᵖ* Fᵖ Gᵖ I, Old Latin, Vulgate, Bohairic, Ethiopic, Origenˡᵃᵗ, Ephraem, Cyril, Jerome, Augustine, and Ambrosiaster.

It is easy to see how each of these variant readings may have arisen, for the word which precedes the variant is ἐγενήθημεν. When the text was copied by dictation, the pronunciation of ἐγενήθημεν ἤπιοι would be almost indistinguishable from ἐγενήθημεν νήπιοι, and vice versa. Likewise when the words stand in uncial script, ΕΓΕΝΗΘΗΜΕΝΝΗΠΙΟΙ is very like ΕΓΕΝΗΘΗΜΕΝΗΠΙΟΙ, and vice versa. Furthermore, it must be remembered that N at the end of a line was frequently indicated merely by a stroke above the preceding letter, thus: ΕΓΕΝΗΘΗΜΕ̄.

It is less easy to decide in which direction the change went. On the one hand, the weight and diversity of external evidence are clearly in favour of νήπιοι, which is supported by the earliest form of the Alexandrian text (𝔭⁶⁵ [third century], ℵ*, and B), the Western text (D* and Old Latin), as well as a wide variety of Versions and Fathers. Such a constellation of witnesses led Lachmann, Westcott–Hort, Zimmer,[1] and Bover to print νήπιοι in their text, a choice favoured also by such commentators as Lightfoot, Findlay (doubtfully), Wohlenberg, Frame, and Milligan (doubtfully).

On the other hand, Paul's violent transition in the same sentence from a reference to himself as a babe to the thought of his serving as a mother-nurse has seemed to most editors and commentators to be little short of absurdity, and therefore Tregelles, Tischendorf, Alford, Weiss, von Soden, Merk, and Vogels follow the Textus Receptus and print ἤπιοι, a reading which is supported by Bornemann, von Dobschütz, Moffatt, Dibelius, Lemonnyer, Vosté, Neil, and Rigaux, and is adopted by the translators of the Revised Standard Version and the New English Bible.

Those who are impressed by the external evidence supporting νήπιοι attempt to alleviate the difficulty in sense that this word introduces by pointing to the earlier context (vss. 3–6), where

---

[1] Besides his monograph on *Der Text der Thessalonicherbriefe* (Quedlinburg, 1893), Friedrich Zimmer supported his view in his contribution to Bernhard Weiss's Festschrift, *Theologische Studien* (Göttingen, 1897), pp. 248–73, especially pp. 264–9.

Paul speaks not of his gentleness but of his unselfish love. He defends himself against the charge, not of being harsh, but of using flattery to gain an unfair advantage. He suggests his lack of guile and childlike innocence, so it is argued, by calling himself a 'babe'. The word for 'babe' by association brings with it the idea of a 'nurse', and, with his characteristic rapidity of thought, Paul inverts the metaphor and now refers to himself as a mother-nurse. Such an inversion of metaphor—a Christian teacher being first compared to the child and then to the mother—is quite in the apostle's manner; e.g., in Gal. iv. 19 the sudden shift in metaphor is even more startling ('My little children, with whom I am again in travail until Christ be formed in you!'). It is also significant that twelve of the sixteen cases of νήπιος in the New Testament are found in Paul (including Eph. iv. 14), whereas ἤπιος appears elsewhere in the Greek Bible only in 2 Tim. ii. 24.

Not all of these arguments in favour of νήπιοι, however, are as significant as they may seem to be at first sight. Whatever may be said of the more remote context, in the immediate context 'gentle' is certainly the appropriate antithesis to what Paul has just disclaimed in verse 6b, namely the assertion of his apostolic dignity or authority, while in connexion with the following clauses it is immeasurably preferable to 'babes'. Furthermore, though it is true that Paul uses νήπιος frequently, it must not be overlooked that he never refers to himself as a babe, but always applies it to his converts. Moreover, it is certainly not without importance that at 2 Tim. ii. 24 more than one scribe succumbed to the temptation to substitute the more familiar word, νήπιος, for the true text ἤπιος (so the Greek text of the four manuscripts Dᴾ* Eᴾ* Fᴾ Gᴾ and the Ethiopic).[1]

By way of striking a balance in the arguments *pro et contra*, it appears that here internal considerations should be allowed to take precedence over external evidence. Since νήπιοι, which is by far the more common word in the New Testament, could so easily have been introduced by carrying over the final ν of the preceding word, and since the violence done to the sense when νήπιοι is read appears to be intolerable, one is entitled to apply Daniel Mace's crisp dictum that no manuscript is so old as

---

[1] The opposite error of writing ἤπιος for νήπιος also occurs sporadically in individual manuscripts, namely in A at Eph. iv. 14 and in 33 at Heb. v. 33.

common sense, and to make a tentative decision in favour of ἤπιοι.

A knowledge of Hebrew and especially of Aramaic will occasionally throw light upon a variant reading in the Gospels. For example, the words of Jesus in Mark xiv. 25, 'Truly I say to you, I shall not drink again of the fruit of the vine until that day when I drink it new in the kingdom of God', are transmitted in three different forms. The text which lies behind the English versions is (1) οὐκέτι οὐ μὴ πίω, supported by A B Δ, most minuscules, b ff² i l q r², Vulg, Syrˢ, ᵖ, ʰ, Sah, Geo, (Arm). There are, however, two other readings: (2) οὐ μὴ πίω, supported by ℵ C (D) L W 471 892 1342 c k, Vulg (1 MS.), Boh, Eth; and (3) οὐ μὴ προσθῶ πιεῖν (πεῖν), supported by D Θ 565 a f Arm. (Θ reads οὐκέτι οὐ μὴ προσθῶμεν πιεῖν.)

The third reading, found in Western and Caesarean witnesses, involves a Semitic idiom, meaning literally, 'I shall not add to drink . . .'. This idiom appears frequently in the Septuagint, which has more than 100 examples of προστιθέναι (προστίθεσθαι) for the Hebraic הוֹסִיף (with an infinitive), meaning πάλιν. It appears that the Eucharistic words of Jesus, which were undoubtedly spoken in Aramaic or Hebrew to the apostles, have been preserved in literalistic fashion in the third variant reading, whereas the other two readings provide alternative interpretations of the meaning, expressed in more idiomatic Greek. (The second reading, in fact, can be called a misinterpretation, for it omits the idea expressed by 'again'.) Whether the idiom which is preserved in the third variant reading is to be considered original to Mark's Gospel (as Wellhausen[1] suggested), or whether it is a secondary Biblicism in imitation of the Septuagint (as Schürmann[2] argues), or whether it discloses influence from extra-canonical reports of Jesus' Eucharistic words (as Jeremias,[3] following Black,[4] prefers), it is in any case a most

---

[1] Julius Wellhausen, *Einleitung in die drei ersten Evangelien*, 2te Aufl. (Berlin, 1911), p. 9.

[2] Heinz Schürmann, *Der Paschamahlbericht Lk. 22, (7–14) 15–18* (Münster/W., 1953), p. 35, Anm. 154.

[3] Joachim Jeremias, *Die Abendmahlsworte Jesu*, 3te Aufl. (Göttingen, 1960), pp. 174 f.; Eng. trans., *The Eucharistic Words of Jesus* (London, 1966), p. 183.

[4] Matthew Black, *An Aramaic Approach to the Gospels and Acts*, 2nd ed. (Oxford, 1954), pp. 214 f.; 3rd ed. (1967), pp. 279 f.

noteworthy variant reading which is eminently suitable in the context.

Màny scholars[1] have given attention to the textual problem found in Acts xx. 28, the report of Paul's farewell address to the Ephesian elders: 'Take heed to yourselves and to all the flock, in which the Holy Spirit has made you guardians, to feed the church of... which he obtained with his own blood.' Should the ellipsis be filled with the words 'the Lord' or 'God'?

The external evidence is as follows:

(1) θεοῦ ℵ B 218 257 383 459 614 917 1175 1522 1611 1758 2138 2298, *al*, Vulg, Syr^h, Basil, Ambrose, Epiphanius, Cyril of Alexandria.

(2) κυρίου 𝔭74 A C* D E^a Ψ 33 181 209 307 337 429 431 436 610 623 1739 1891, *gig*, Sah, Boh, Syr^h mg, Arm, Irenaeus^lat, Didymus, Lucifer.

(3) κυρίου καὶ θεοῦ C^3 H^a L^a P^a, more than 100 minuscules, Old Slavonic, Theophylact.

(4) θεοῦ καὶ κυρίου 47.

(5) κυρίου θεοῦ 3 95**.

(6) Χριστοῦ Syr^codd, Apost. Const., Athanasius^codd.

(7) Ἰησοῦ Χριστοῦ m.

Of these seven readings, obviously only the first two merit any attention, for (6) and (7) are insufficiently supported, and the rest are conflations of κυρίου and θεοῦ in various combinations preserved in Byzantine texts.

On the basis of external evidence it is difficult to decide which of the first two readings is original. Palaeographically the difference concerns only a single letter: $\overline{KY}$ and $\overline{ΘY}$. Each is supported by early and diversified witnesses. Perhaps the most that can be said is that θεοῦ is the Alexandrian reading and κυρίου is supported by typical Western documents. One must rely chiefly on considerations of internal probabilities in reaching a decision.

---

[1] See, for example, Ezra Abbot, 'On the Reading "Church of God", Acts xx. 28', *Bibliotheca Sacra*, xxxiii (1876), pp. 313–52 (reprinted in the volume *The Authorship of the Fourth Gospel and Other Critical Essays* [Boston, 1888], pp. 294–331), Charles F. De Vine, 'The "Blood of God" in Acts 20:28', *Catholic Biblical Quarterly*, ix (1947), pp. 381–408, as well as critical commentaries on the passage and the discussion by Hort in *The New Testament in the Original Greek*, [ii,] *Appendix*, pp. 98–100.

The phrase ἐκκλησία κυρίου occurs seven times in the Septuagint but nowhere else in the New Testament. On the other hand, ἐκκλησία τοῦ θεοῦ appears with moderate frequency (eleven times) in the Epistles traditionally ascribed to Paul and nowhere else in the New Testament. (The expression αἱ ἐκκλησίαι πᾶσαι τοῦ Χριστοῦ occurs once in Rom. xvi. 16.) It is possible, therefore, that a scribe, finding θεοῦ in his exemplar, was influenced by Old Testament usage and altered it to κυρίου. On the other hand, it is also possible that a scribe, influenced by Pauline usage, changed κυρίου of his exemplar to θεοῦ.

Two considerations which, in the opinion of the present writer, tip the scales in favour of the originality of the reading θεοῦ are the following:

(*a*) It is undeniable that θεοῦ is the more difficult reading. The following clause refers to the church 'which he obtained διὰ τοῦ αἵματος τοῦ ἰδίου'. If this is taken in its usual sense ('with his own blood'), the scribe might well raise the question, Does God have blood?, and thus be led to change θεοῦ to κυρίου. On the other hand, if κυρίου were the original reading, there is nothing unusual in the context which would cause a scribe to introduce the more difficult θεοῦ.

(*b*) The other consideration asks which reading is more likely to have been altered during the Arian controversy that raged over the Person of Christ. In this connexion Alford's reasoning still seems to be cogent. He writes:

> If the passage is of such a nature that, whichever reading is adopted, the orthodox meaning is legitimate, but the adoption of the stronger orthodox reading is absolutely incompatible with the heretical meaning,—then it is probable that such stronger orthodox reading was the original. For while the heretics would be certain [the present writer would prefer to say 'tempted'] to annul the expression offensive to them and substitute the weaker one, the orthodox, on the above hypothesis, would have originally no motive for alteration.[1]

In paragraph (*a*) above it was implied that διὰ τοῦ αἵματος τοῦ ἰδίου could have a meaning other than its usual one ('with his own blood'); this other meaning, which may have been in the mind of the writer of Acts, is 'with the blood of his Own'.

[1] Henry Alford, *The Greek Testament*, new ed., i (Boston, 1881), p. 83 of the prolegomena, n. 1.

(It is not necessary to suppose, with Hort, that υἱοῦ may have dropped out after τοῦ ἰδίου, though palaeographically such an omission would have been easy.) This absolute use of the singular number of ἴδιος, which is otherwise unknown in the New Testament, is found occasionally in the Greek papyri as a term of endearment referring to near relatives.[1] It is possible, therefore, that 'his Own' (ὁ ἴδιος) was a title which early Christians gave to Jesus, comparable with 'the Beloved' (ὁ ἀγαπητός); compare Rom. viii. 32, where Paul refers to God 'who did not spare τοῦ ἰδίου υἱοῦ' in a context that clearly alludes to Gen. xxii. 16, where the Septuagint has τοῦ ἀγαπητοῦ υἱοῦ.

In conclusion, whatever may be thought of the slight possibility that τοῦ ἰδίου is used here as the equivalent of τοῦ ἰδίου υἱοῦ, it appears that the reading θεοῦ was more likely to have been altered to κυρίου than vice versa, and it is therefore to be regarded as the original.[2]

Of all the letters attributed to Paul, his letter to the Colossians contains proportionately the greatest number of textual problems. The close of Col. ii. 2 presents what is, at first, a bewildering variety of readings; the manuscripts present fifteen different conclusions of the phrase εἰς ἐπίγνωσιν τοῦ μυστηρίου . . . ('to the knowledge of the mystery of . . .'):

A (1)   τοῦ θεοῦ Χριστοῦ 𝔭46 B and Hilary of Poitiers.
  (2)   τοῦ θεοῦ Hᵖ Pᵖ 69 424** 436 462 1912, Sahidic^Beatty MS.
  (3)   τοῦ Χριστοῦ 1462.
  (4)   τοῦ θεοῦ ὅ ἐστιν Χριστός Dᵖ* d e, Augustine.
  (5)   τοῦ θεοῦ ὅ ἐστιν περὶ Χριστοῦ Ethiopic.
  (6)   τοῦ θεοῦ τοῦ ἐν Χριστῷ 33, Clement.
  (7)   τοῦ θεοῦ τοῦ ἐν Χριστῷ Ἰησοῦ Armenian.
  (8)   τοῦ θεοῦ καὶ Χριστοῦ Cyril of Alexandria.
B (9)   τοῦ θεοῦ πατρὸς Χριστοῦ ℵ* 216 440.

---

[1] James Hope Moulton, *A Grammar of New Testament Greek*, i, *Prolegomena*, 3rd ed. (Edinburgh, 1908), p. 90.

[2] The reading θεοῦ is preferred by Westcott–Hort, Weiss, Vogels, Merk, Bover, Harnack (*Beiträge*, iv, p. 330), Jackson and Lake (in *Beginnings of Christianity*), G. H. C. Macgregor (in *Interpreter's Bible*), F. F. Bruce (*Acts*), C. S. C. Williams (in Harper's [= Black's] *New Testament Commentaries*), and De Vine (op. cit.).

The reading κυρίου is preferred by Tischendorf, Abbot, von Soden, Ropes, the Revised Standard Version, and the New English Bible.

(10) τοῦ θεοῦ πατρὸς τοῦ Χριστοῦ A C 4, Sahidic, Bohairic.

(11) τοῦ θεοῦ καὶ πατρὸς τοῦ Χριστοῦ ℵ[c], Syr[h].

(12) τοῦ θεοῦ πατρὸς καὶ τοῦ Χριστοῦ 441 1908, Syr[p], Chrysostom.

(13) τοῦ θεοῦ πατρὸς καὶ τοῦ Χριστοῦ Ἰησοῦ Vulgate, Bohairic[codd], Pelagius.

(14) τοῦ θεοῦ πατρὸς καὶ τοῦ κυρίου ἡμῶν Χριστοῦ Ἰησοῦ 1 Vulgate MS.

(15) τοῦ θεοῦ καὶ πατρὸς καὶ τοῦ Χριστοῦ D[p(c)] E[p] K[p] L[p], most minuscules, Theodoret, &c.

Of all these variant readings the one which has been placed first is to be preferred on the basis of both external and internal considerations. Externally, it is supported by the earliest and best Greek manuscripts; internally, the difficulty of interpreting the meaning of the expression τοῦ μυστηρίου τοῦ θεοῦ Χριστοῦ has led to the multiplication of scribal attempts to clarify the sense. An obviously popular expedient was the insertion of the word πατρός; this addition appears in seven of the variant readings (those grouped under *B*). The insertion of the article before Χριστοῦ (readings 10–15) is plainly in the interest of making the expression parallel with τοῦ θεοῦ. The reading placed last in the list (it lies behind the rendering of the King James version, 'the mystery of God, and of the Father, and of Christ'), though supported by the largest number of witnesses, is also the weakest, for it is a conflation of the two types of amelioration represented in (11) and (12).

If reading (9) were original, then the rise of all eight readings grouped under *A* is inexplicable, for why should πατρός have fallen out? On the contrary, πατρός was inserted in order to clarify the syntactical relation between θεοῦ and Χριστοῦ (for reading (1) could mean 'the knowledge of the mystery of God Christ', or 'the knowledge of the mystery of God's Christ', or 'the knowledge of God's mystery, of Christ'). Besides the insertion of πατρός (readings 9–15) several other attempts were made to explain the relationship of Χριστοῦ to θεοῦ (4, 5, 6, 7, 8). The scribes responsible for readings (2) and (3) sought to relieve the difficulty by the elimination of one or the other of the two genitives—and in support of (3) the scribe could point to Eph. iii. 4 as a precedent (τῷ μυστηρίῳ τοῦ Χριστοῦ). Reading (4) gives what must be the right sense, suggesting that in reading (1) the word Χριστοῦ is explanatory of τοῦ μυστηρίου τοῦ θεοῦ. Perhaps in dictating the Epistle the author separated the word Χριστοῦ from the preceding phrase by a slight pause for breath, which can be represented in modern printing by a comma. Thus it is possible to explain the origin of all the other readings on the assumption that reading (1) is original, but this reading cannot be explained as derivative from any of them. Since the external support of (.1) is of the best, both as regards age and character, one must conclude that τοῦ θεοῦ Χριστοῦ is the earliest attainable form of text preserved among the extant witnesses.[1]

As was remarked earlier, the harmonization of the Evangelists, whether done by scribes deliberately or unconsciously, is by definition a secondary process. Therefore the supreme rule for editors of the text is to give each Gospel its own proper character. Of many, many examples which might be cited as illustrations of this basic principle, the following has been chosen in order to show that on very rare occasions the correct reading may be preserved alone in the Koine or Byzantine text.

If one were to take into consideration only the external evidence in support of ἀρχιερεῖς in Luke xx. 1 ('the chief priests and the scribes with the elders came up . . .'), there would appear to be no doubt whatever concerning its originality—the diversity and the antiquity of the witnesses are most impressive, and the support for the variant reading ἱερεῖς appears to be negligible. Thus:

(1) ἀρχιερεῖς ℵ B C D L M N Q R Θ Ψ, fam. 1, fam. 13, fam. 1424, 33 157 579 892 1071 1604, Old Lat, Vulg, Syr, Sah, Boh, Arm, Geo, Eth, Diatess[Arab, Ital(Ven),] [Dutch(Liège)].

(2) ἱερεῖς A E G H K S U V W Γ Δ Λ Π, many minuscules, Goth.

When one looks at a harmony of the Gospels, however, he discovers that the parallels to this account (Matt. xxi. 23 and Mark xi. 27) refer to 'the chief priests' in company with scribes and/or elders, with no fluctuation in the manuscript evidence.

[1] The caution with which the conclusion is expressed is in deference to those who, like F. W. Beare in the *Interpreter's Bible*, ad loc., think that the difficult expression τοῦ θεοῦ Χριστοῦ is too difficult for the author to have written, and that some primitive error must lie behind the earliest attainable text.

Furthermore, a concordance provides the information that the same kind of stereotyped formula appears nearly fifty times throughout the Gospels and Acts, and in no case has ἱερεῖς replaced ἀρχιερεῖς.

In the passage under consideration there is no discernible motive for altering 'chief priests' to 'priests', whereas the influence of the stereotyped phrase containing ἀρχιερεῖς would have been felt independently by scribes of manuscripts in every textual tradition. One must conclude, therefore, that Tischendorf and von Soden are correct in printing ἱερεῖς in Luke xx. 1, and that Westcott–Hort, Weiss, Vogels, Merk, Bover, Nestle, and the British and Foreign Bible Society's text of 1958 are wrong in preferring ἀρχιερεῖς.[1]

There are other instances besides Luke xx. 1 where it has happened that almost all of the 'good' manuscripts are in error and the correct reading is preserved in 'inferior' witnesses. Thus at Matt. xii. 47 the best Alexandrian witnesses (B ℵ*), joining with representatives of the Western group (*ff*[1] *k* Syr[s, c]), are convicted of having accidentally omitted a whole verse. Verse 47 closes with the same word as verse 46, and the eyes of copyists have chanced to wander from the end of one to the end of the other.

In Heb. vii. 1 the relative pronoun ὅς, which is not suited to the syntax of the sentence, is supported by ℵ A B D[p] I K[p] 33 *al.* The grammatically correct ὁ is witnessed by 𝔭46 C* and the Koine group of manuscripts. In this case one can see how the primitive error entered both the Alexandrian and Western traditions, for the following word begins with the letter sigma (συναντήσας), and so the correct ὁ came to be pronounced and spelled ὅς.

Occasionally considerations relating to intrinsic evidence will cast a decisive vote in the face of what appears to be overwhelming external testimony. The generally received text of Matt. xxii. 34–35 reads 'But when the Pharisees heard that he [Jesus] had silenced the Sadducees, they came together. And

---

[1] For another discussion of this passage, see Heinrich Greeven's comments in *New Testament Studies*, vi (1960), pp. 295 f., where he comes to the same conclusion as that adopted here.

one of them, a lawyer, asked him a question, to test him.' This all seems straightforward enough and quite unexceptional. There are, however, a few witnesses which omit νομικός ('a lawyer') at verse 35, namely fam. 1, *e*, Syr^s, Arm, Geo, and Origen according to Rufinus' Latin translation. Normally this evidence, comprising only part of the Caesarean text with some versional support, would not be regarded as especially weighty. In this case, however, internal considerations of the most compelling kind make it altogether likely that all of the uncials and almost all the minuscules are wrong in reading νομικός. In the first place, except for this passage, it is Luke alone of the four Evangelists who employs the word νομικός; the usual word in Matthew for one concerned with the Mosaic law is γραμματεύς, a word which appears frequently in all three Synoptic Gospels. In the second place, an examination of a harmony of the Gospels discloses that in the parallel passage Luke reads 'And behold, a lawyer stood up to put him [Jesus] to the test . . .' (x. 25). There is no reason why scribes should have omitted νομικός from Matt. xxii. 35, but there would have been a strong temptation to add such a circumstantial detail from the parallel account in Luke. Despite, therefore, the rather limited range of evidence in support of the shorter text, it appears that νομικός is an intrusion into the text of Matt. xxii. 35.

In 1 Thess. iii. 2, 'We sent Timothy, our brother and . . . in the gospel of Christ, to establish you in your faith and to exhort you', the word or words after 'our brother and' have been transmitted in five different forms. They are the following:

(1) 'God's fellow worker' (συνεργὸν τοῦ θεοῦ, D^p* 33 *d e*, Pelagius, Ambrosiaster, pseudo-Hieronymus).

(2) 'fellow worker' (συνεργόν, B, Ephraem (as it seems)).[1]

(3) 'God's servant' (διάκονον τοῦ θεοῦ, ℵ A P^p 424**, Goth, Boh, Arm, Syr^h, Eth, Basil, Theod. Mops.^{lat}).

(4) 'servant and God's fellow worker' (διάκονον καὶ συνεργὸν τοῦ θεοῦ, F^p G^p).

(5) 'God's servant and our fellow worker' (διάκονον τοῦ θεοῦ καὶ συνεργὸν ἡμῶν, D^{p(c)} K^p L^p Syr^p, most minuscules, Chrysostom, Theodoret).

---

[1] See Joseph Molitor, *Der Paulustext des hl. Ephräm aus seinem armenisch erhaltenen Paulinenkommentar* . . . (Rome, 1938), p. 112.

The reading placed last in the list, though supported by the great majority of witnesses, is obviously a secondary reading that was formed by joining readings (3) and (2) with the addition of the word ἡμῶν. This conflate reading, so typical of the Koine type of text, lies behind the rendering of the verse in the King James version.

The fourth reading is also a type of conflated reading. The reviser has rather mechanically combined readings (3) and (1), writing the qualifying genitive τοῦ θεοῦ only once. The external support for this variant is of little value, for the two bilingual manuscripts F and G are so closely related to each other as to constitute but one witness, and this witness belongs to a secondary stratum of the Western type of text. We are left therefore with readings (1), (2), and (3); which of these gave rise to the others? It is difficult to answer this question with assurance, for, as it happens, more or less compelling reasons can be found for preferring each of the three readings as the original—reasons which led Bover and the translators of the New English Bible to adopt (1), Weiss to adopt (2), and Tischendorf, Westcott–Hort, von Soden, Vogels, Merk, and the Revised Standard Version to adopt (3). Arguments which support each of these choices involve the following considerations.

The second reading, συνεργόν, can scarcely be original, for then one would have no adequate explanation for the addition of τοῦ θεοῦ, producing reading (1), or its alteration to διάκονον with the addition of τοῦ θεοῦ, producing reading (3).

It cannot be disputed that the third reading, 'God's servant', is attested by several excellent Alexandrian witnesses as well as by representatives of widely diversified versions. But the expression is both so clear and so rich that, if original, no one would have felt the need of altering it. The same cannot be said of the first reading in the list, for the application to Timothy of the expression 'God's fellow worker' may have offended the scrupulous. How can any man (so some may have reasoned) be given so exalted a title, least of all a young convert who was merely assisting Paul? Two courses were open to those who wished to soften the idea: by suppressing τοῦ θεοῦ, Timothy becomes Paul's fellow worker (reading 2), in accord with his designation in Rom. xvi. 21; or by keeping τοῦ θεοῦ and substituting διάκονον for συνεργόν, Timothy is again described (reading 3) in typically Pauline language (Rom. xiii. 4; 2 Cor. vi. 4). Thus it would appear that reading (1) συνεργὸν τοῦ θεοῦ is original, for it explains the origin of the others.

On the other hand, however, one's confidence in the preceding arguments may well be weakened by a second review of the evidence. Those who are moved chiefly by considerations based on external evidence will certainly not be impressed by the combination of Dᵖ*, 33, *d*, *e*, Pelagius, Ambrosiaster, and pseudo-Hieronymus. Furthermore, the argument which was used above to discredit the originality of the reading συνεργὸν τοῦ θεοῦ, namely that it would have offended the scrupulous, becomes less cogent when one observes that a similar expression in 1 Cor. iii. 9 (θεοῦ γάρ ἐσμεν συνεργοί) has occasioned no textual variation in any known witness. Furthermore, the generally acknowledged tendency of Western texts to substitute synonyms and near-synonyms suggests that reading (1) arose as a scribal alteration of (3).

The chief weakness, however, of the argument in favour of the originality of reading (3) is the absence of any good reason to account for the deletion of τοῦ θεοῦ to produce the second reading. Weiss therefore argues that the simplest explanation to account for the rise of the many forms of the text is to regard συνεργόν of B as the original, of which all the others are modifications.[1]

In making an assessment of the weight of the argument supporting each of the variant readings, one will do well to exercise great caution. According to Lachmann the degree of certitude or probability attaching to any particular variant may be assessed as certain, almost certain, probable, doubtful, very doubtful, or nil. In this case, whatever choice is made among the three chief variants, every candid critic must acknowledge the strength of the arguments supporting the other two.

Another example where violent conflict between external and internal evidence makes it impossible to come to a confident decision among variant readings is found in Acts xii. 25. The natural impression which one gets when reading the section xi. 27 to xiii. 1 is that xi. 30 refers to the arrival of Paul and

---

[1] B. Weiss, *Textkritik der paulinischen Briefe* (= *Texte und Untersuchungen*, xiv (3); Leipzig, 1896), pp. 13 f. It is significant that in this case Westcott and Hort did not see fit to follow their favourite manuscript.

Barnabas at Jerusalem and that xii. 25 ought to tell of their departure from Jerusalem. There is, however, early and rather widespread support for the almost impossible reading εἰς Ἰερουσαλήμ (ℵ B Hᵃ Lᵃ Pᵃ 81, &c., Syrʰ ᵐᵍ, 1 Sah MS.,¹ Ethʳᵒ). The other readings are ἐξ Ἰερουσαλήμ (A 33 547 913 1739 1891, Sah, Boh, Arm) and ἀπὸ Ἰερουσαλήμ (D 181 431 614, &c., *gig*, Vulg; Syrᵖ witnesses to either ἐξ or ἀπό).

All the canons of textual criticism favour the more difficult reading εἰς, supported as it is by the earliest and best manuscripts; but the sense of the context cries out for a preposition that means 'from'.² Was εἰς a primitive corruption which later scribes attempted to correct by altering it to ἐξ or ἀπό? Here one must acknowledge that he simply does not know what the author originally wrote.³

Does Luke say that Jesus sent out seventy or seventy-two disciples (Luke x. 1, 17)? The evidence is as follows:

ἑβδομήκοντα is supported by 𝔓⁴⁵ (extant for vs. 17 only)⁴ ℵ A C L W Δ Θ Λ Ξ, fam. 1, fam. 13, most minuscules, *f q i*

---

¹ This Sahidic manuscript is B.M. Or. 7594, thought by some to date from the fourth century; see n. 1 on p. 79 above.

² According to the *addenda* to Tischendorf's 8th ed. (as reported in Gregory's *Prolegomena*, p. 1281), the scribe of B had begun to write ἀπό, but then changed it to εἰς.

³ Hort (*Appendix*, p. 94) suggested that the passage be emended by transposing the order of the words, thus separating εἰς Ἰερουσαλήμ from ὑπέστρεψαν and ranging it with what follows (ὑπέστρεψαν τὴν εἰς Ἰερουσαλὴμ πληρώσαντες διακονίαν, 'they returned, having fulfilled their ministry at Jerusalem'). More recently Dom J. Dupont concluded a lengthy examination of the verse by suggesting that the preposition εἰς be retained and the difficulty in sense be alleviated by punctuating with a comma after the main verb (ὑπέστρεψαν, εἰς Ἰερουσαλὴμ πληρώσαντες τὴν διακονίαν); see his article, 'La Mission de Paul "à Jérusalem" (Actes xii. 25)', *Novum Testamentum*, i (1956), pp. 275–303.

⁴ F. G. Kenyon erroneously reported the evidence of 𝔓⁴⁵ as supporting the numeral 72 (ο̄β̄). The present writer has examined this passage in 𝔓⁴⁵ under natural and artificial light, and has assured himself that the Greek character which follows the omicron is nothing but a *diple*, or space-filler (>), which scribes used occasionally in order to bring an otherwise short line even with the right-hand margin of the column. In fact, by consulting Kenyon's volume of plates of 𝔓⁴⁵ anyone can see the similarity between the disputed character and the *diple* which appears on the same folio near the top of the column. For a fuller discussion of the reading of 𝔓⁴⁵, including C. H. Roberts's view that the numeral is 76 (ο̄ϛ̄), see B. M. Metzger, 'Seventy or Seventy-two Disciples?', in *New Testament Studies*, v (1959), pp. 299–306, on the basis of which the citation of the evidence of 𝔓⁴⁵ was corrected in the 1960 edition of Nestle's Greek Testament. Other editions of the Greek Testament continue to repeat the error in Kenyon's edition of 𝔓⁴⁵.

(extant for vs. 1 only), Syr[c (vs. 17), p, h, pal], Cop[boh], Goth, Iren, Tert, Clem, Orig, Eus, Ambr, Jerome.

ἑβδομήκοντα δύο is supported by 𝔭[75] B D M (vs. 1 only) 0181 (vs. 1 only) *a b c d l r*[2], Vulg, Syr[s, c (vs. 1), h mg (vs. 17)], Cop[sah], Georg[1, 2], Diatess[Dutch Pers Ital], Orig, Ephr, Aug, Ambrst.

The external evidence is almost evenly divided; the chief representatives of the Alexandrian and the Western groups, with most of the Old Latin and the Sinaitic Syriac, support the numeral seventy-two. On the other hand, other Alexandrian evidence of relatively great weight (ℵ L Δ Λ Ξ) as well as Caesarean witnesses (𝔭[45], fam. 1, fam. 13) join in support of the numeral seventy.

The factors bearing upon the evaluation of internal evidence, whether involving transcriptional or intrinsic probabilities, are singularly elusive. It is likely that in most of the early manuscripts (as in 𝔭[45] and 𝔭[75]) the numeral was written with letters of the alphabet (either $\overline{o\beta}$ or $\overline{o}$). It was easy, therefore, for either number to be accidentally altered to the other. If the variation was made deliberately, one can imagine that an Alexandrian scribe with a mathematical penchant altered seventy to seventy-two for the sake of what he may have regarded as scholarly symmetry. On the other hand, if the alteration was made unwittingly, it is perhaps more likely that the precise number should be transformed into the round number seventy than that the 'solemn' number seventy should be transformed into seventy-two.

Those who transmitted the account prior to its inclusion in Luke x may have wished to convey a symbolic meaning in the number of the disciples, and it is easy to find parallels in Jewish antiquities for either seventy or seventy-two. Seventy elders were appointed by Moses to assist him (Num. xi. 16–17, 24–25); there were seventy sons of Jerubbaal (Judges ix. 2), seventy sons of Ahab (2 Kings x. 1), and seventy priests of Bel (Bel and Dragon, vs. 10).

On the other hand, according to the Letter of Aristeas (§§ 46–50) seventy-two elders (six from each of the twelve tribes) were chosen in order to prepare a Greek translation of the Torah (the Septuagint), and in 3 Enoch the number of princes of kingdoms on high is seventy-two, corresponding to the seventy-two languages of the world (xvii. 8; cf. xviii. 2 f., xxx. 2).[1]

---

[1] For many other examples from Jewish antiquities involving seventy and seventy-two, see the article referred to in the previous footnote.

It is, however, exceedingly difficult to ascertain what symbolism is intended in Luke's account. On the one hand, if the mission of this group of disciples is to be understood as a mission to Israel, the number may have been chosen as a multiple of the twelve tribes of Israel. On the other hand, since several New Testament writers presuppose a parallel between Jesus and Moses,[1] it may be that this group of Jesus' disciples is intended to correspond to the seventy elders who assisted Moses. So evenly balanced are these two possibilities that it is hazardous to dogmatize as to which is more probable.

A total appraisal of both external and internal evidence bearing on these variant readings must remain indecisive. Though the reading 'seventy-two' is supported by a combination of early witnesses that normally carries a high degree of conviction of originality, yet the diversity of witnesses which read 'seventy' is so weighty and internal considerations are so evenly balanced that the textual critic must simply acknowledge his inability to decide with assurance between the two. If one is editing the Greek text of Luke perhaps the least unsatisfactory resolution of the dilemma is to have recourse to brackets (which are always a tacit confession of the editor's uncertainty) and to print ἑβδομήκοντα [δύο].

The passages discussed above will suffice as specimens illustrating the wide variety of considerations which one must take into account when evaluating variant readings. In addition to solving such problems individually as they occur in the text, an editor of the Greek Testament is confronted with still others arising from the diversity of usage and authorship within the New Testament as a whole. How far, for example, should he attempt to standardize first aorist endings on second aorist stems? Shall he reproduce in his edition divergencies between two or more authors in the spelling of the same proper name? Or, even within the same book, is it permissible to vary the spelling of a proper name? For example, shall he print the title of Paul's Epistle to the Colossians *ΠΡΟΣ ΚΟΛΑΣΣΑΕΙΣ* (with 𝔭⁴⁶ A B* I Kᴾ and many manuscripts), as the Textus Receptus, Lachmann, and Westcott and Hort do, but spell the

---

[1] See J. Jeremias in Kittel, *Theologisches Wörterbuch zum Neuen Testament*, iv, pp. 871–8.

name of the city in Col. i. 2 Κολοσσαῖς (with 𝔭⁴⁶ ℵ [A has a lacuna] B Dᵖ Eᵖ Fᵖ Gᵖ Lᵖ, &c.)? It will be understood that it is far easier to ask such questions than to answer them.

By way of conclusion, let it be emphasized again that no single manuscript and no one group of manuscripts exists which the textual critic may follow mechanically. All known witnesses of the New Testament are to a greater or less extent mixed texts, and even the earliest manuscripts are not free from egregious errors. Although in very many cases the textual critic is able to ascertain without residual doubt which reading must have stood in the original, there are not a few other cases where he can come only to a tentative decision based on an equivocal balancing of probabilities. Occasionally none of the variant readings will commend itself as original, and he will be compelled either to choose the reading which he judges to be the least unsatisfactory or to indulge in conjectural emendation. In textual criticism, as in other areas of historical research, one must seek not only to learn what can be known, but also to become aware of what, because of conflicting witnesses, cannot be known.

APPENDIX

Check-list of the Greek Papyri of the New Testament

THE following list supplies a brief conspectus of basic information concerning (*a*) the contents of each papyrus document of the Greek New Testament; (*b*) the latest opinion regarding its approximate date,[1] given by century in Roman numerals; (*c*) the present location of the papyrus; (*d*) the bibliographical reference to the *editio princeps* of the papyrus; and (*e*) the text-type or family to which the papyrus has been thought to belong. (In some cases too little text has been preserved to warrant making a judgement concerning textual affinities.)

All of the papyri are in codex-form except 𝔓¹², 𝔓¹³, 𝔓¹⁸, and 𝔓⁴³ (?) which are fragments from rolls. (See below, p. 273.)

Abbreviations

P.Oxy. = B. P. Grenfell and A. S. Hunt, *The Oxyrhynchus Papyri*,
i– (London, 1898–).

P.S.I. = *Pubblicazioni della Società Italiana, Papiri Greci e Latini*.

Sanz = Peter Sanz, *Griechische literarische Papyri christlichen Inhalts*,
i (Vienna, 1946).

𝔓¹ (*a*) Matt. i. 1–9, 12, 14–20, 23; (*b*) III; (*c*) Philadelphia, University of Pennsylvania Museum, no. E 2746; (*d*) P.Oxy. i, pp. 4–7, no. 2; (*e*) Alexandrian text.

𝔓² (*a*) John xii. 12–15; (*b*) VI; (*c*) Florence, Museo Archeologico, Inv. no. 7134; (*d*) E. Pistelli in *Studi religiosi*, vi (1906), pp. 129–30; (*e*) mixed text.

𝔓³ (*a*) Luke vii. 36–45; x. 38–42; (*b*) VI/VII; (*c*) Vienna, Österreichische Nationalbibliothek, Sammlung Papyrus Erzherzog Rainer, no. G 2323; (*d*) K. Wessely in *Wiener Studien*, iv (1882), pp. 198–9, 211–14; vii (1885), pp. 69–70; and J. N. Birdsall, ibid., lxxvi (1963), pp. 163–4; (*e*) Alexandrian text.

[1] The dates are those suggested by the following palaeographers who based their judgements upon a comprehensive evaluation of all the New Testament Greek papyri: Herbert Hunger of Vienna, Karl Preisendanz of Heidelberg, C. H. Roberts of Oxford, the late Wilhelm Schubart of Halle, and T. C. Skeat of London (see Kurt Aland, *New Testament Studies*, ix [1963], pp. 303–16).

𝔓⁴ (*a*) Luke i. 58–59, 62–ii. 1, 6–7; iii. 8–38; iv. 2, 29–32, 34–35; v. 3–8, 30–38; vi. 1–16; (*b*) III; (*c*) Paris, Bibliothèque Nationale, no. Gr. 1120, suppl. 2°; (*d*) M.-J. Lagrange, *Critique textuelle*, pp. 119–23; cf. Jean Merell, *Revue biblique*, xlvii (1938), pp. 5–22; (*e*) Alexandrian text.

𝔓⁵ (*a*) John i. 23–31, 33–41; xvi. 14–30; xx. 11–17, 19–20, 22–25; (*b*) III; (*c*) London, British Museum, P. 782 and P. 2484; (*d*) P.Oxy. ii, pp. 1–8, no. 208, and P.Oxy. xv, pp. 8–12, no. 1781; (*e*) Western text.

𝔓⁶ (*a*) John x. 1–2, 4–7, 9–10; xi. 1–8, 45–52; (*b*) IV; (*c*) Strasbourg, Bibliothèque de la Université, 351ʳ, 335ᵛ, 379, 381, 383, 384 copt.; (*d*) F. Rösch, *Bruchstücke des I. Clemensbriefes nach dem achmimischen Papyrus der Strassburger Universitäts- und Landesbibliothek* (Strassburg, 1910), pp. 119–22, 131–4, 143–8; (*e*) agrees with B and Θ.

𝔓⁷ (*a*) Luke iv. 1–2; (*b*) V; (*c*) now lost; was in Kiev, library of the Ukrainian Academy of Sciences; (*d*) C. R. Gregory, *Textkritik des Neuen Testamentes*, iii, p. 1086, and K. Aland in *New Testament Studies*, iii (1957), pp. 262–4.

𝔓⁸ (*a*) Acts iv. 31–37; v. 2–9; vi. 1–6, 8–15; (*b*) IV; (*c*) now lost; was in Berlin, Staatliche Museen, P. 8683; (*d*) C. R. Gregory, *Textkritik des Neuen Testamentes*, iii, pp. 1086–90; (*e*) mixture of Alexandrian and Western texts.

𝔓⁹ (*a*) 1 John iv. 11–12, 14–17; (*b*) III; (*c*) Cambridge, Massachusetts, Harvard University, Semitic Museum, no. 3736; (*d*) P.Oxy. iii, pp. 2–3, no. 402.

𝔓¹⁰ (*a*) Rom. i. 1–7; (*b*) IV; (*c*) Cambridge, Massachusetts, Harvard University, Semitic Museum, no. 2218; (*d*) P.Oxy. ii, pp. 8–9, no. 209; (*e*) Alexandrian text.

𝔓¹¹ (*a*) 1 Cor. i. 17–23; ii. 9–12, 14; iii. 1–3, 5–6; iv. 3–v. 5, 7–8; vi. 5–7, 11–18; vii. 3–6, 10–14; (*b*) VII; (*c*) Leningrad, State Public Library; (*d*) Tischendorf in *Verhandlungen der 25. Versammlung der deutschen Philologen und Schulmänner in Halle* (Leipzig, 1868), pp. 44–45, and K. Aland in *New Testament Studies*, iii (1957), pp. 268–78; (*e*) Alexandrian text.

𝔓¹² (*a*) Heb. i. 1; (*b*) end of III; (*c*) New York, Pierpont Morgan Library, no. G. 3; (*d*) Grenfell and Hunt in *The Amherst Papyri*, i (London, 1900), pp. 30–31.

𝔓¹³ (*a*) Heb. ii. 14–v. 5; x. 8–22, 29–xii. 17; (*b*) III/IV (perhaps first half of fourth century); (*c*) London, British Museum, P. 1532 (verso), and Florence, Biblioteca Medicea Laurenziana;

(*d*) P.Oxy. iv, pp. 36–48, no. 657; and *P.S.I.* xii (1951), pp. 209–10, no. 1292; (*e*) Alexandrian text.

𝔭¹⁴   (*a*) 1 Cor. i. 25–27; ii. 6–8; iii. 8–10, 20; (*b*) v (?); (*c*) Mount Sinai, St. Catharine's Monastery, no. 14; (*d*) J. Rendel Harris, *Biblical Fragments from Mount Sinai* (London, 1890), pp. xiii, 54–56; (*e*) Alexandrian text.

𝔭¹⁵   (*a*) 1 Cor. vii. 18–viii. 4; (*b*) iii; (*c*) Cairo, Museum of Antiquities, no. 47423; (*d*) P.Oxy. vii, pp. 4–8, no. 1008; (*e*) Alexandrian text.

𝔭¹⁶   (*a*) Phil. iii. 9–17; iv. 2–8; (*b*) iii/iv; (*c*) Cairo, Museum of Antiquities, no. 47424; (*d*) P.Oxy. vii, pp. 8–11, no. 1009; (*e*) Alexandrian text.

𝔭¹⁷   (*a*) Heb. ix. 12–19; (*b*) iv; (*c*) Cambridge, England, University Library, gr. theol. f. 13 (P), Add. 5893; (*d*) P.Oxy. viii, pp. 11–13, no. 1078; (*e*) mixed text.

𝔭¹⁸   (*a*) Rev. i. 4–7; (*b*) iii/iv; (*c*) London, British Museum, P. 2053 (verso); (*d*) P.Oxy. viii, pp. 13–14, no. 1079; (*e*) agrees with ℵ, A, and C.

𝔭¹⁹   (*a*) Matt. x. 32–xi. 5; (*b*) iv/v; (*c*) Oxford, Bodleian Library, MS. Gr. bibl. d. 6 (P.); (*d*) P.Oxy. ix, pp. 7–9, no. 1170; (*e*) mixed text, chiefly Western.

𝔭²⁰   (*a*) Jas. ii. 19–iii. 2, 4–9; (*b*) iii; (*c*) Princeton, New Jersey, University Library, Classical Seminary AM 4117 (15); (*d*) P.Oxy. ix, pp. 9–11, no. 1171; (*e*) Alexandrian text.

𝔭²¹   (*a*) Matt. xii. 24–26, 31–33; (*b*) iv/v; (*c*) Allentown, Pennsylvania, Library of Muhlenberg College, Theol. pap. 3; (*d*) P.Oxy. x, pp. 12–14, no. 1227; (*e*) agrees with D and ℵ^corr.

𝔭²²   (*a*) John xv. 25–27; xvi. 1–2, 21–32; (*b*) iii; (*c*) Glasgow, University Library, MS. 2–x. 1; (*d*) P.Oxy. x, pp. 14–16, no. 1228; (*e*) mixed text, agrees partly with ℵ^corr and partly with D.

𝔭²³   (*a*) Jas. i. 10–12, 15–18; (*b*) beginning of iii; (*c*) Urbana, Illinois, University of Illinois, Classical Archaeological and Art Museum, G. P. 1229; (*d*) P.Oxy. x, pp. 16–18, no. 1229; (*e*) Alexandrian.

𝔭²⁴   (*a*) Rev. v. 5–8; vi. 5–8; (*b*) iv; (*c*) Newton Center, Massachusetts, Library of Andover Newton Theological School; (*d*) P.Oxy. x, pp. 18–19, no. 1230; (*e*) agrees with ℵ.

𝔭²⁵   (*a*) Matt. xviii. 32–34; xix. 1–3, 5–7, 9–10; (*b*) end of iv; (*c*) now lost; was in Berlin, Staatliche Museen, P. 16388; (*d*) Otto Stegmüller in *Zeitschrift für die neutestamentliche Wissenschaft*, xxxvii (1938), pp. 223–9; (*e*) Western text.

𝔭²⁶   (*a*) Rom. i. 1–16; (*b*) *c.* 600; (*c*) Dallas, Texas, Southern Methodist University, Lane Museum; (*d*) P.Oxy. xi, pp. 6–9, no. 1354; (*e*) agrees with A and ℵ.

𝔭²⁷   (*a*) Rom. viii. 12–22, 24–27, 33–39; ix. 1–3, 5–9; (*b*) III; (*c*) Cambridge, England, University Library, Add. MS. 7211; (*d*) P.Oxy. xi, pp. 9–12, no. 1355; (*e*) chiefly Alexandrian text, but with Western readings.

𝔭²⁸   (*a*) John vi. 8–12, 17–22; (*b*) III; (*c*) Berkeley, California, Library of Pacific School of Religion, Pap. 2; (*d*) P.Oxy. xiii, pp. 8–10, no. 1596; (*e*) Alexandrian text.

𝔭²⁹   (*a*) Acts xxvi. 7–8, 20; (*b*) III; (*c*) Oxford, Bodleian Library, MS. Gr. bibl. g. 4 (P.); (*d*) P.Oxy. xiii, pp. 10–12, no. 1597; (*e*) Western text (?).

𝔭³⁰   (*a*) 1 Thess. iv. 13, 16–18; v. 3, 8–10, 12–18, 26–28; 2 Thess. i. 1–2; (*b*) III; (*c*) Ghent, University Library, U. Lib. P. 61; (*d*) P.Oxy. xiii, pp. 12–14, no. 1598; (*e*) mixed text.

𝔭³¹   (*a*) Rom. xii. 3–8; (*b*) VII; (*c*) Manchester, England, John Rylands Library, P. Ryl. 4; (*d*) A. S. Hunt, *Catalogue of Greek Papyri in the John Rylands Library*, i (Manchester, 1911), p. 9; (*e*) agrees with ℵ.

𝔭³²   (*a*) Titus i. 11–15; ii. 3–8; (*b*) *c.* 200; (*c*) Manchester, England, John Rylands Library, P. Ryl. 5; (*d*) A. S. Hunt, *Catalogue of Greek Papyri in the John Rylands Library*, i (Manchester, 1911), pp. 10–11; (*e*) agrees with ℵ, also with F and G.

𝔭³³   (*a*) Acts xv. 22–24, 27–32; (*b*) VI; (*c*) Vienna, Österreichische Nationalbibliothek, no. 190; (*d*) C. Wessely, *Studien zur Palaeographie und Papyruskunde*, xii (1914), p. 245; (*e*) chiefly Alexandrian text.

𝔭³⁴   (*a*) 1 Cor. xvi. 4–7, 10; 2 Cor. v. 18–21; x. 13–14; xi. 2, 4, 6–7; (*b*) VII; (*c*) Vienna, Österreichische Nationalbibliothek, no. 191; (*d*) C. Wessely, *Studien zur Palaeographie und Papyruskunde*, xii (1914), p. 246; (*e*) Alexandrian text.

𝔭³⁵   (*a*) Matt. xxv. 12–15, 20–23; (*b*) IV (?); (*c*) Florence, Biblioteca Medicea Laurenziana; (*d*) *P.S.I.* i (1912), pp. 1–2; (*e*) mixed text (Alexandrian and Western).

𝔭³⁶   (*a*) John iii. 14–18, 31–32; (*b*) VI; (*c*) Florence, Biblioteca Medicea Laurenziana; (*d*) *P.S.I.* i (1912), pp. 5–6; (*e*) mixed text (Western and Alexandrian).

𝔭³⁷ (*a*) Matt. xxvi. 19–52; (*b*) iii/iv; (*c*) Ann Arbor, Michigan, University of Michigan Library, Invent. no. 1570; (*d*) H. A. Sanders in *Harvard Theological Review*, xix (1926), pp. 215–26, and in *Michigan Papyri*, pp. 9–14; (*e*) Caesarean text.

𝔭³⁸ (*a*) Acts xviii. 27–xix. 6, 12–16; (*b*) *c.* 300; (*c*) Ann Arbor, Michigan, University of Michigan Library, Invent. no. 1571; (*d*) H. A. Sanders in *Harvard Theological Review*, xx (1927), pp. 1–19, and in *Michigan Papyri*, pp. 14–19; (*e*) Western text.

𝔭³⁹ (*a*) John viii. 14–22; (*b*) iii; (*c*) Chester, Pennsylvania, Crozer Theological Seminary Library, no. 8864; (*d*) P.Oxy. xv, pp. 7–8, no. 1780; (*e*) Alexandrian text.

𝔭⁴⁰ (*a*) Rom. i. 24–27, 31–ii. 3; iii. 21–iv. 8; vi. 4–5, 16; ix. 17, 27; (*b*) iii; (*c*) Heidelberg, Universitätsbibliothek, Inv. Pap. graec. 45; (*d*) F. Bilabel, *Griechische Papyri* (Heidelberg, 1924), pp. 28–31 (= *Veröffentlichungen aus den Badischen Papyrus-Sammlungen*, iv, pp. 124–7); (*e*) Alexandrian text.

𝔭⁴¹ (*a*) Acts xvii. 28–xviii. 2, 24–25, 27; xix. 1–4, 6–8, 13–16, 18–19; xx. 9–13, 15–16, 22–24, 26–28, 35–38; xxi. 1–4; xxii. 11–14, 16–17; (*b*) viii; (*c*) Vienna, Österreichische Nationalbibliothek, Pap. K. 7541–8; (*d*) C. Wessely, *Studien zur Palaeographie und Papyruskunde*, xv (1914), pp. 107–18; (*e*) Western text.

𝔭⁴² (*a*) Luke i. 54–55; ii. 29–32; (*b*) vii/viii; (*c*) Vienna, Österreichische Nationalbibliothek, KG 8706; (*d*) Walter Till and Peter Sanz, *Eine griechisch-koptische Odenhandschrift* (= *Monumenta biblica et ecclesiastica*, v; Rome, 1939), p. 112; (*e*) agrees with A.

𝔭⁴³ (*a*) Rev. ii. 12–13; xv. 8–xvi. 2; (*b*) vi/vii; (*c*) London, British Museum, Pap. 2241; (*c*) W. E. Crum and H. I. Bell, *Wadi Sarga: Coptic and Greek Texts* (Copenhagen, 1922), pp. 43–45; (*e*) chiefly Alexandrian text.

𝔭⁴⁴ (*a*) Matt. xvii. 1–3, 6–7; xviii. 15–17, 19; xxv. 8–10; John x. 8–14; ix. 3–4; xii. 16–18 [in this order]; (*b*) vi/vii; (*c*) New York, Metropolitan Museum of Art, Inv. 14-1-527; (*d*) H. G. Evelyn White, *The Monastery of Epiphanius at Thebes*, ii (New York, 1926), pp. 120–1, 301; (*e*) Alexandrian text.

𝔭⁴⁵ (*a*) Matt. xx. 24–32; xxi. 13–19; xxv. 41–46; xxvi. 1–39; Mark iv. 36–40; v. 15–26, 38–vi. 3, 16–25, 36–50; vii. 3–15, 25–viii. 1, 10–26, 34–ix. 8, 18–31; xi. 27–33; xii. 1, 5–8, 13–19, 24–28; Luke vi. 31–41, 45–vii. 7; ix. 26–41, 45–x. 1, 6–22,

26–xi. 1, 6–25, 28–46, 50–xii. 12, 18–37, 42–xiii. 1, 6–24, 29–
xiv. 10, 17–33; John x. 7–25, 31–xi. 10, 18–36, 43–57; Acts
iv. 27–36; v. 10–20, 30–39; vi. 7–vii. 2, 10–21, 32–41, 52–viii. 1,
14–25, 34–ix. 6, 16–27, 35–x. 2, 10–23, 31–41; xi. 2–14, 24–xii.
5, 13–22; xiii. 6–16, 25–36, 46–xiv. 3, 15–23; xv. 2–7, 19–26,
38–xvi. 4, 15–21, 32–40; xvii. 9–17; (*b*) III; (*c*) Dublin, Chester
Beatty Museum; and Vienna, Österreichische Nationalbibliothek, P. Gr. Vind. 31974; (*d*)F. G. Kenyon, *The Chester Beatty
Biblical Papyri*, fasc. ii, *Gospels and Acts* (London, 1933), and
Hans Gerstinger in *Aegyptus*, xiii (1933), pp. 67–72; (*e*) partly
Alexandrian, partly Western (pre-Caesarean) text.

$\mathfrak{p}^{46}$ (*a*) Rom. v. 17–vi. 3, 5–14; viii. 15–25, 27–35, 37–ix. 32;
x. 1–xi. 22, 24–33, 35–xiv. 8, 9–xv. 9 (fragmentary), 11–33;
xvi. 1–23, 25–27; Heb., 1 and 2 Cor., Eph., Gal., Phil., Col.
(all with lacunae); 1 Thess. i. 1, 9–10; ii. 1–3; v. 5–9, 23–28;
(*b*) *c*. 200; (*c*) Dublin, Chester Beatty Museum, and Ann Arbor,
Michigan, University of Michigan Library, Invent. no. 6238;
(*d*) F. G. Kenyon, *The Chester Beatty Biblical Papyri*, fasc. iii
(London, 1934), and fasc. iii Supplement (London, 1936), and
H. A. Sanders, *A Third-century Papyrus Codex of the Epistles of Paul*
(Ann Arbor, 1935); (*e*) Alexandrian text.

$\mathfrak{p}^{47}$ (*a*) Rev. ix. 10–xvii. 2 (with small lacunae); (*b*) end of III;
(*c*) Dublin, Chester Beatty Museum; (*d*) F. G. Kenyon, *The
Chester Beatty Biblical Papyri*, fasc. iii (London, 1934); (*e*) agrees
with A, C, and א.

$\mathfrak{p}^{48}$ (*a*) Acts xxiii. 11–17, 23–29; (*b*) end of III; (*c*) Florence, Museo Medicea Laurenziana; (*d*) *P.S.I.* x (1932), pp. 112–18;
(*e*) Western text.

$\mathfrak{p}^{49}$ (*a*) Eph. iv. 16–29, 31–v. 13; (*b*) end of III; (*c*) New Haven,
Connecticut, Yale University Library, P. 415; (*d*) W. H. P.
Hatch and C. B. Welles, *Harvard Theological Review*, li (1958),
pp. 33–35; (*e*) Alexandrian text.

$\mathfrak{p}^{50}$ (*a*) Acts viii. 26–32; x. 26–31; (*b*) IV/V; (*c*) New Haven, Connecticut, Yale University Library, P. 1543; (*d*) C. H. Kraeling
in *Quantulacumque*, Festschrift for Kirsopp Lake (London,
1937), pp. 163–72; (*e*) agrees chiefly with B.

$\mathfrak{p}^{51}$ (*a*) Gal. i. 2–10, 13, 16–20; (*b*) *c*. 400; (*c*) London, British
Museum; (*d*) P.Oxy. xviii, pp. 1–3, no. 2157; (*e*) partly
Alexandrian, partly eclectic text.

𝔭⁵²   (*a*) John xviii. 31–33, 37–38; (*b*) beginning of II; (*c*) Manchester, John Rylands Library, P. Ryl. Gr. 457; (*d*) C. H. Roberts, *An Unpublished Fragment of the Fourth Gospel in the John Rylands Library* (Manchester, 1935); (*e*) Alexandrian text.

𝔭⁵³   (*a*) Matt. xxvi. 29–40; Acts ix. 33–38, 40–x. 1; (*b*) III; (*c*) Ann Arbor, Michigan, University of Michigan Library, Invent. no. 6652; (*d*) H. A. Sanders in *Quantulacumque*, Festschrift for Kirsopp Lake (London, 1937), pp. 151–61; (*e*) Egyptian mixed text.

𝔭⁵⁴   (*a*) Jas. ii. 16–18, 22–26; iii. 2–4; (*b*) V/VI; (*c*) Princeton, New Jersey, Princeton University Library, Garrett Depos. 7742; (*d*) E. H. Kase, Jr., *Papyri in the Princeton University Collections*, ii (Princeton, 1936), pp. 1–3; (*e*) agrees with B, ℵ, and C.

𝔭⁵⁵   (*a*) John i. 31–33, 35–38, on upper portion of page, *hermeneia* below (as 𝔭⁵⁹ and 𝔭⁶⁰); (*b*) VI/VII; (*c*) Vienna, Österreichische Nationalbibliothek, P. Gr. Vind. 26214; (*d*) Sanz, pp. 58–59; (*e*) Alexandrian text.

𝔭⁵⁶   (*a*) Acts i. 1, 4–5, 7, 10–11; (*b*) V/VI; (*c*) Vienna, Österreichische Nationalbibliothek, P. Gr. Vind. 19918; (*d*) Sanz, pp. 65–66; (*e*) Alexandrian text.

𝔭⁵⁷   (*a*) Acts iv. 36–v. 2, 8–10; (*b*) IV/V; (*c*) Vienna, Österreichische Nationalbibliothek, P. Gr. Vind. 26020; (*d*) Sanz, pp. 61–67; (*e*) Alexandrian text.

𝔭⁵⁸   (*a*) Acts vii. 6–10, 13–18; (*b*) VI; (*c*) Vienna, Österreichische Nationalbibliothek, P. Gr. Vind. 17973, 36133⁵⁴, and 35831; (*d*) Sanz, pp. 67–68; (*e*) Alexandrian, agreeing partly with *I*-text.

𝔭⁵⁹   (*a*) John i. 26, 28, 48, 51; ii. 15–16; xi. 40 52: xii. 25, 29, 31, 35; xvii. 24–26; xviii. 1–2, 16–17, 22; xxi. 7, 12–13, 15, 17–20, 23, on upper portion of page, *hermeneia* below (as 𝔭⁵⁵ and 𝔭⁶⁰); (*b*) VII; (*c*) New York, New York University, Washington Square College of Arts and Sciences, Department of Classics, P. Colt. 3; (*d*) Lionel Casson and E. L. Hettich, *Excavations at Nessana*, ii (Princeton, 1950), pp. 79–93.

𝔭⁶⁰   (*a*) John xvi. 29–xix. 26 with lacunae (probably contained *hermeneia*, as 𝔭⁵⁵ and 𝔭⁵⁹); (*b*) VII; (*c*) New York, New York University, Washington Square College of Arts and Sciences, Department of Classics, P. Colt. 4; (*d*) Lionel Casson and E. L. Hettich, *Excavations at Nessana*, ii (Princeton, 1950), pp. 94–111; (*e*) Alexandrian text.

𝔭⁶¹ (*a*) Rom. xvi. 23, 25–27; 1 Cor. i. 1–2, 4–6; v. 1–3, 5–6, 9–13; Phil. iii. 5–9, 12–16; Col. i. 3–7, 9–13; iv. 15; 1 Thess. i. 2–3; Titus iii. 1–5, 8–11, 14–15; Philem., vss. 4–7; (*b*) *c.* 700; (*c*) New York, New York University, Washington Square College of Arts and Sciences, Department of Classics, P. Colt. 5; (*d*) Lionel Casson and E. L. Hettich, *Excavations at Nessana*, ii (Princeton, 1950), pp. 112–22; (*e*) probably Egyptian.

𝔭⁶² (*a*) Matt. xi. 25–30; (*b*) IV; (*c*) Oslo, University Library; (*d*) Leiv Amundsen in *Symbolae Osloenses*, xxiv (1945), pp. 121–40; (*e*) Alexandrian text.

𝔭⁶³ (*a*) John iii. 14–18; iv. 9–10; (*b*) *c.* 500; (*c*) Berlin, Staatliche Museen; (*d*) Otto Stegmüller in *Biblica*, xxxiv (1953), pp. 13–22.

𝔭⁶⁴ (*a*) Matt. xxvi. 7, 10, 14–15, 22–23, 31–33; (*b*) *c.* 200; (*c*) Oxford, Magdalen College Library; (*d*) Colin Roberts in *Harvard Theological Review*, xlvi (1953), pp. 233–7.

𝔭⁶⁵ (*a*) 1 Thess. i. 3–10; ii. 1, 6–13; (*b*) III; (*c*) Florence, Biblioteca Medicea Laurenziana; (*d*) *P.S.I.* xiv (1957), pp. 5–7; (*e*) Alexandrian text.

𝔭⁶⁶ John i. 1–vi. 11, 35–xiv. 26, and fragments of xiv. 29–xxi. 9; (*b*) *c.* 200; (*c*) Cologny/Genève, Bibliothèque Bodmer; (*d*) V. Martin, *Papyrus Bodmer II: Évangile de Jean*, chs. 1–14 (Bibliotheca Bodmeriana, 1956); *Supplément, Évangile de Jean*, chs. 14–21 (Bibliotheca Bodmeriana, 1958); nouvelle éd., V. Martin et J. W. B. Barns (1962); (*e*) mixed text.

𝔭⁶⁷ Matt. iii. 9, 15; v. 20–22, 25–28; (*b*) *c.* 200; (*c*) Barcelona, Fundación San Lucas Evangelista, P. Barc. 1; (*d*) P. Roca-Puig, *Un papiro griego del evangelio de San Mateo* (Barcelona, 1956); 2nd ed., with a Note by Colin [H.] Roberts (1962); (*e*) agrees with ℵ.

𝔭⁶⁸ (*a*) 1 Cor. iv. 12–17, 19–21; v. 1–3; (*b*) VII (?); (*c*) Leningrad, State Public Library, Gr. 258; (*d*) K. Aland in *New Testament Studies*, iii (1957), pp. 266–9; (*e*) agrees with the Textus Receptus against the Alexandrian text.

𝔭⁶⁹ Luke xxii. 41, 45–48, 58–61; (*b*) III; (*c*) place (?); (*d*) P.Oxy. xxiv, pp. 1–4, no. 2383; (*e*) mixed text.

𝔭⁷⁰ (*a*) Matt. xi. 26–27; xii. 4–5; (*b*) III; (*c*) place (?); (*d*) P.Oxy. xxiv, pp. 4–5, no. 2384.

𝔭⁷¹ Matt. xix. 10–11, 17–18; (*b*) IV; (*c*) place (?); (*d*) P.Oxy. xxiv, pp. 5–6, no. 2385; (*e*) agrees with B.

𝔓⁷² Jude, 1 Pet., 2 Pet.; (b) III/IV; (c) Cologny/Genève, Bibliothèque Bodmer; (d) M. Testuz, *Papyrus Bodmer VII–IX* (Bibliotheca Bodermeriana, 1959); (e) mixed text.

𝔓⁷³ (a) Matt. xxv. 43; xxvi. 2–3; (b) —; (c) Cologny/Genève, Bibliothèque Bodmer; (d) not yet published.

𝔓⁷⁴ (a) Acts i. 2–5, 7–11, 13–15, 18–19, 22–25; ii. 2–4, 6–iii. 26; iv. 2–6, 8–27, 29–xxvii. 25, 27–xxviii. 31 ; Jas. i. 1–6, 8–19, 21–23, 25, 27–ii. 15, 18–22, 25–iii. 1, 5–6, 10–12, 14, 17–iv. 8, 11–14; v. 1–3, 7–9, 12–14, 19–20; 1 Pet. i. 1–2, 7–8, 12–13, 19–20, 25; ii. 7, 11–12, 18, 24; iii. 4–5; 2 Pet. ii. 21; iii. 4, 11, 16; 1 John i. 1, 6; ii. 1–2, 7, 13–14, 18–19, 25–26; iii. 1–2, 8, 14, 19–20; iv. 1, 6–7, 12, 16–17; v. 3–4, 10, 17; 2 John, vss. 1, 6–7, 12–13; 3 John, vss. 6, 12; Jude, vss. 3, 7, 12, 18, 24–25; (b) VII; (c) Cologny/ Genève, Bibliothèque Bodmer; (d) Rodolphe Kasser, *Papyrus Bodmer XVII* (Bibliotheca Bodmeriana, 1961); (e) agrees frequently with A.

𝔓⁷⁵ (a) Luke iii. 18–22, 33–iv. 2, 34–v. 10, 37–vi. 4, 10–vii. 32, 35–43, 46–xviii. 18; xxii. 4–xxiv. 53; John i. 1–xiii. 10; xiv. 8–xv. 8 (with lacunae); (b) beginning of III; (c) Cologny/Genève, Bibliothèque Bodmer; (d) Victor Martin and Rodolphe Kasser, *Papyrus Bodmer XIV–XV* (Bibliotheca Bodmeriana, 1961); (e) agrees with B.

𝔓⁷⁶ (a) John iv. 9, 12; (b) VI; (c) Vienna, Österreichische Nationalbibliothek, P. Gr. Vind. 36102; (d) Herbert Hunger, *Biblos: Österreichische Zeitschrift für Buch- und Bibliothekswesen*, viii (1959), pp. 7–12.

In addition to the 76 papyri described above, according to a preliminary announcement[1] official numbers have been assigned to five more Greek papyri of the New Testament: 𝔓⁷⁷ and 𝔓⁷⁸ are included in vol. xxxiii of the Oxyrhynchus Papyri, 𝔓⁷⁹ is in the National Museum at Berlin,[2] and 𝔓⁸⁰ and 𝔓⁸¹ (tentative numbers) are among the documents found at Khirbet Mird. Still to be assigned an official number is a fourth-century fragment of 1 Pet. ii. 20–iii. 12, published as no. 2 in the series *Papyrologica Castroctaviana*, edited by José O'Callaghan.[3]

[1] Kurt Aland, *Studien zur Überlieferung des Neuen Testaments und seines Textes* (Berlin, 1967), p. 91, Anm. 2.

[2] This is presumably the leaf, acquired in 1877–91 by the Library (No. 6774), which has now been published by Kurt Treu ('Neue neutestamentliche Fragmente der Berliner Papyrussammlung', *Archiv für Papyrusforschung*, xviii (1966), pp. 37 f., with a Plate.

[3] Serbio Daris, *Un nuovo frammento della Prima Lettera di Pietro* (Barcelona, 1967), with a Plate.

Scraps of New Testament papyri, apparently regarded as too insignificant to merit the assignment of official numbers, include the following: a sixth-century fragment containing 2 Cor. x. 4 and 1 Thess. v. 8,[1] a third-century leaf from a miniature codex containing some words of the Lord's Prayer (Matt. vi. 10 f.),[2] and a fragment preserving a verse of the Gospel of John (iii. 34).[3]

The following lists of numerals indicate the distribution of the papyri by book in the New Testament:

Matthew: 1, 19, 21, 25, 35, 37, 44, 45, 53, 62, 64, 67, 70, 71, 73.
Mark: 45.
Luke: 3, 4, 7, 42, 45, 69, 75.
John: 2, 5, 6, 22, 28, 36, 39, 44, 45, 52, 55, 59, 60, 63, 66, 75, 76.
Acts: 8, 29, 33, 38, 41, 45, 48, 50, 53, 56, 57, 58, 74.
Romans: 10, 26, 27, 31, 40, 46, 61.
1 Corinthians: 11, 14, 15, 34, 46, 61, 68.
2 Corinthians: 34, 46.
Galatians: 46, 51.
Ephesians: 46, 49.
Philippians: 16, 46, 61.
Colossians: 46, 61.
1 Thessalonians: 30, 46, 61, 65.
2 Thessalonians: 30.
Titus: 32, 61.
Philemon: 61.
Hebrews: 12, 13, 17, 46.
James: 20, 23, 54, 74.
1 Peter: 72, 74.
2 Peter: 72, 74.
1 John: 9, 74.
2 John: 74.
3 John: 74.
Jude: 72, 74.
Revelation: 18, 24, 43, 47.

---

[1] Herbert Hunger, 'Zwei unbekannte neutestamentliche Papyrusfragmente der Österreichisches Nationalbibliothek', *Biblos*, viii (1959), pp. 7-12. It may be mentioned that the other fragment referred to in the title of the article has been assigned the number 𝔭76.

[2] Edited by J. W. B. Barns, in Barns and H. Zilliacus, *The Antinoopolis Papyri*, Part II (London, 1960), pp. 6-7; cf. Ernst Bammel, 'Ein neuer Vater-Unser-Text', *Zeitschrift für die neutestamentliche Wissenschaft*, lii (1961), pp. 280-1, and 'A New Text of the Lord's Prayer', *Expository Times*, lxxiii (1961-2), p. 54.

[3] R. Roca-Puig, 'Un papir grec de l'Evangeli de S. Joan a Barcelona (P. Barc. nº 83)', *Analecta sacra Tarraconensia*, xxxvii (1964), pp. 353-5.

Bibliography

THE following is a chronological list of introductions to New Testament textual criticism. In addition to these volumes many dictionaries of the Bible, introductions to the New Testament, and histories of the English Bible contain brief surveys of the subject. For bibliography on special points of New Testament textual criticism, reference may be made to monographs mentioned in the appropriate sections above, as well as to two other publications by the present writer, namely *Annotated Bibliography of the Textual Criticism of the New Testament, 1914–1939* (Copenhagen, 1955), and *Chapters in the History of New Testament Textual Criticism* (Leiden and Grand Rapids, 1963).

J. I. DOEDES, *Verhandeling over de tekstkritiek des Nieuwen Verbonds* (Teyler's godgeleerd Genootschap, deel xxxiv), Haarlem, 1844, 481 pp.

J. SCOTT PORTER, *Principles of Textual Criticism with their Application to Old and New Testaments* . . ., London, 1848, 515 pp.

THOMAS SHELDON GREEN, *A Course of Developed Criticism on Passages of the New Testament Materially Affected by Various Readings*, London, 1856, 192 pp.

SAMUEL PRIDEAUX TREGELLES, *Introduction to the Textual Criticism of the New Testament*; being vol. iv of Thomas Hartwell Horne's *An Introduction to the Critical Study and Knowledge of the Holy Scriptures*, 10th ed., London, 1856; 13th ed., 1872, 402 pp.

F. H. A. SCRIVENER, *A Plain Introduction to the Criticism of the New Testament*, London, 1861, 490 pp.; 2nd ed., Cambridge, 1874, 607 pp.; 3rd ed., 1883, 712 pp.; 4th ed., 2 vols., edited by Edward Miller, London, 1894, 418, 428 pp.

C. E. HAMMOND, *Outlines of Textual Criticism applied to the New Testament*, Oxford, 1872, 138 pp.; 6th ed., revised, 1902, 179 pp.

WILLIAM MILLIGAN and ALEXANDER ROBERTS, *The Words of the New Testament, as Altered by Transmission and Ascertained by Modern Criticism*, Edinburgh, 1873, 262 pp.

FREDERIC GARDINER, *Principles of Textual Criticism; with a Graphic Table of Uncials*, reprinted from *Bibliotheca Sacra*, xxxii (1875), pp. 209–65.

F. H. SCRIVENER, *Six Lectures on the Text of the New Testament and the Ancient Manuscripts which contain it, chiefly addressed to those who do not read Greek*, Cambridge and London, 1875, 216 pp.

THOMAS RAWSON BIRKS, *Essay on the Right Estimation of Manuscript Evidence in the Text of the New Testament*, London, 1878, 128 pp.

BROOKE FOSS WESTCOTT and FENTON JOHN ANTHONY HORT, *The New Testament in the Original Greek*, [ii], *Introduction* [and] *Appendix*, Cambridge and London, 1881, 324, 188 pp.; 2nd ed., 1896, 330, 180 pp.

J. P. P. MARTIN, *Introduction à la critique textuelle du Nouveau Testament: Partie théorique*, Paris, *c.* 1883, 712 pp.; *Partie pratique*, 5 vols., Paris, *c.* 1883–6, 327, 554, 512, 549, 248 pp.

PHILIP SCHAFF, *A Companion to the Greek Testament and the English Version*, New York, 1883, 616 pp.; 3rd ed., revised, 1889, 618 pp.

FR. SCHJØTT, 'Det ny Testamentes Texthistorie i de tre første Aarhundreder', *Teologisk Tidsskrift for den danske Folkekirke*, i (1884), pp. 343–92; 'De nytestamentlige Uncialhaandskrifter', ibid., vi (1889), pp. 432–57, 500–55.

EDWARD MILLER, *A Guide to the Textual Criticism of the New Testament*, London, 1886, 147 pp.

BENJAMIN B. WARFIELD, *An Introduction to the Textual Criticism of the New Testament*, London, 1886, 225 pp.

CASPAR RENÉ GREGORY, *Prolegomena*, being vol. iii of Tischendorf's *Novum Testamentum Graece*, ed. octava critica maior, Leipzig, 1884–94, 1426 pp.

ARNOLD RÜEGG, *Die neutestàmentliche Textkritik seit Lachmann; ein Versuch zur Orientierung*, Zurich, 1892, 97 pp. (with a list of N.T. MSS., their editors, and collators).

EBERHARD NESTLE, *Einführung in das griechische Neue Testament*, Göttingen, 1897, 129 pp.; 2te Aufl., 1899, 288 pp.; 3te Aufl., 1909, 298 pp.; Eng. trans. from 2nd German ed. by William Eadie, *Introduction to the Textual Criticism of the Greek New Testament*, London, 1901, 351 pp.

CHARLES F. SITTERLY, *Praxis in Manuscripts of the Greek Testament*, New York, 1898; 4th ed. = part 3 of *The Canon, Text and Manuscripts of the New Testament*, New York and Cincinnati, 1914, 126 pp.

MATHEUS LUNDBORG, *Nya Testamentets text, dess historia och kritiska behandling i allmänna grunddrag*, Lund, 1899, 406 pp.

MARVIN R. VINCENT, *A History of the Textual Criticism of the New Testament*, New York, 1899, 185 pp.

KIRSOPP LAKE, *The Text of the New Testament*, Oxford, 1900, 104 pp.; 6th ed., revised by Silva New, 1928, 104 pp.

FREDERIC G. KENYON, *Handbook to the Textual Criticism of the New Testament*, London, 1901, 321 pp.; 2nd ed., 1912, 381 pp.

RUDOLF KNOPF, *Der Text des Neuen Testaments*, Giessen, 1906, 48 pp.

AUGUST POTT, *Der Text des Neuen Testaments nach seiner geschichtlichen Entwicklung*, Leipzig, 1906, 108 pp.; 2te Aufl., 1919, 116 pp.

CASPAR RENÉ GREGORY, *Canon and Text of the New Testament*, New York, 1907, pp. 297–539.

——*Textkritik des Neuen Testamentes*, 3 vols., Leipzig, 1900–9, 1486 pp.

HERMANN FREIHERR VON SODEN, *Die Schriften des Neuen Testaments in ihrer ältesten erreichbaren Textgestalt*, I. Teil, *Untersuchungen*, i. Abteilung, *Die Textzeugen*, Berlin, 1902, 704 pp.; ii. Abteilung, *Die Textformen*, A. *Die Evangelien*, 1907, pp. 705–1520; iii. Abteilung, *Die Textformen*, B. *Der Apostolos mit Apokalypse*, 1910, pp. 1521–2203.

JENS STUB IRGENS, *De trykte græske Nye Testamenters historie tilligemed en indledning dertil og et anhang*, Kristiania, 1907, 196 pp.

ERNEST JACQUIER, *Le Nouveau Testament dans l'église chrétienne. II. Le Texte du Nouveau Testament*, Paris, 1913, 535 pp.

ALEXANDER SOUTER, *The Text and Canon of the New Testament*, London, 1913, pp. 1–145; revised by C. S. C. Williams, 1954, pp. 1–133.

P. G. GROENEN, *Algemeene inleiding tot de Heilige Schrift. II. Geschiedenis van den tekst*, Leiden, 1917, 375 pp.

ERNST VON DOBSCHÜTZ, *Eberhard Nestle's Einführung in das griechische Neue Testament*, 4te Aufl. völlig umgearbeitet, Göttingen, 1923, 160 pp.

HEINRICH JOSEPH VOGELS, *Handbuch der Textkritik des Neuen Testaments*, Münster/W., 1923, 255 pp.; 2et Aufl., Bonn, 1955, 236 pp.

A. T. ROBERTSON, *An Introduction to the Textual Criticism of the New Testament*, New York, 1925, 300 pp.; 2nd ed., 1928, 300 pp.

GIUSEPPE SACCO, *La Koinè del Nuovo Testamento e la trasmissione del sacro testo*, Rome, 1928, pp. 151–327.

ERNST NACHMANSON, *Nya Testamentet, en översikt av dess yttre historia*, Stockholm, 1931, 164 pp.

LÉON VAGANAY, *Initiation à la critique textuelle néotestamentaire*, Paris, 1934, 188 pp.; Eng. trans., *An Introduction to the Textual Criticism of the New Testament*, London, 1937, 208 pp.

M.-J. LAGRANGE, *Introduction à l'étude du Nouveau Testament; deuxième partie, Critique textuelle. II. La Critique rationnelle*, Paris, 1935, 685 pp.

EUGÈNE MERCIER, *Le Texte du Nouveau Testament*, Lausanne, 1935, 127 pp.

AUGUSTE HOLLARD, *Histoire du texte du Nouveau Testament*, Paris, 1936, 80 pp.

FREDERIC G. KENYON, *The Text of the Greek Bible: a Students' Handbook*, London, 1937, 264 pp.; 2nd ed., 1949, 264 pp.; German trans. by Hans Bolewski, *Der Text der griechischen Bibel: ein Lehrbuch*, Göttingen, 1952, 166 pp.; 2te Aufl., überarbeitet und ergänzt von A. W. Adams, mit einer Tabelle zur Textgeschichte des Neuen Testaments von Ferdinand Hahn, 1961, 200 pp.

R. WEHNER, *Nya Testamentets grundtext genom seklerna*, Stockholm, 1943, 34 pp.

JOHANNES SUNDWALL, *Nya Testaments urtext*, Abo, 1946, 104 pp.

ERNEST CADMAN COLWELL, *What is the Best New Testament?* Chicago 1952, 127 pp.

PAOLO SACCHI, *Alle origini del Nuovo Testamento: Saggio per la storia della tradizione e la critica del testo*, Firenze, 1956, 178 pp.

L. D. TWILLEY, *The Origin and Transmission of the New Testament: a Short Introduction*, Edinburgh, 1957, pp. 36–63.

JEAN DUPLACY, *Où en est la critique textuelle du Nouveau Testament?* Paris, 1959, 103 pp.

A. IVANOV, "Tekstual'nye pamyatniki svyashchennykh novozavetnykh pisanii', *Bogoslovskie trudy*, i (1959 [1960]), pp. 53–83.

VINCENT TAYLOR, *The Text of the New Testament: a Short Introduction*, London and New York, 1961, 113 pp.

TOSHIO HIRUNUMA, *New Testament Textual Criticism* (in Japanese), Tokyo, 1962, 192 pp.

J. HAROLD GREENLEE, *An Introduction to New Testament Textual Criticism*, Grand Rapids, 1964, 160 pp.

BRUCE M. METZGER, *Der Text des Neuen Testaments; Einführung in die neutestamentliche Textkritik*, Stuttgart, 1966, 272 pp. (a translation of the first edition of the present work).

HAROLD K. MOULTON, *Papyrus, Parchment and Print; the Story of how the New Testament Text has reached us* (World Christian Books no. 57), London, 1967, 77 pp.

Additional Notes

FOR THE SECOND EDITION

p. 3, *n.* 1. For further bibliography on Greek palaeography see Alphonse Dain, 'Paléographie grecque', in *L'Histoire et ses méthodes*, ed. by Charles Samaran (Paris, 1961), pp. 532–52, and Jean Irigoin, 'Les manuscrits grecs, 1931–1960', *Lustrum*, vii (1962 [1963]), pp. 5–93.

p. 5, *line* 10. Concerning parchment, see Karl J. Lüthi, *Das Pergament, seine Geschichte, seine Anwendung* (= *Bibliothek des Schweizerischen Gutenbergmuseums*, vol. vi; Bern, 1938), and concerning papyrus see José O'Callaghan, 'El papiro en el lenguaje de los Padres latinos . . . III. El papiro, como planta, en la Biblia: sus alegorías', *Studia papyrologica. Revista Española de papirología*, i (1962), pp. 105–19. For a general introduction to the study of Greek papyri, see Eric G. Turner's recently published volume entitled *Greek Papyri, An Introduction* (Oxford and Princeton, 1967).

p. 5, *n.* 1. See also W. E. Engelkes, *Het Grieksche boek in voor-Alexandrijnschen tijd* (Diss.; Amsterdam, 1926); E. G. Turner, *Athenian Books in the Fifth and Fourth Centuries* B.C. (Inaugural Lecture, University College; London, 1952); A. F. Norman, 'The Book Trade in Fourth-Century Antioch', *Journal of Hellenic Studies*, lxxx (1960), pp. 122–6; and Tönnes Kleberg, *Bokhandel och bokförlag i antiken* (Stockholm, [1962]). The last mentioned has a good bibliography.

p. 6, *n.* 1. For a different view see Saul Lieberman, 'Jewish and Christian Codices', *Hellenism in Jewish Palestine* (New York, 1950), pp. 203 ff., who suggests that 'the first Jewish Christians, such as Matthew and Mark, would follow the accepted Jewish practice and put down their ὑπομνήματα in codices' (p. 205), for codices or notebooks were regarded as 'the most suitable way of indicating that they were writing the Oral Law for private, or unofficial use, and not for publication' (ibid.). Cf. also C. H. Roberts, 'P. Yale 1 and the Early Christian Book', *Essays in Honor of C. Bradford Welles* (= *American Studies in Papyrology*, vol. i; New Haven, 1966), pp. 25–29.

p. 8, *n.* 2. . . . For descriptions of Greek manuscripts copied between A.D. 1200 and 1400, see Alexander Turyn, *Codices Graeci Vaticani saeculis XIII et XIV scripti annorumque notis instructi* (Vatican City, 1965).

p. 12, *n.* 1. Concerning Latin palimpsest manuscripts, see E. A. Lowe, 'Codices rescripti; a List of the Oldest Latin Palimpsests with Stray Observations on their Origin', *Mélanges Eugène Tisserant*, vol. v (Vatican City, 1964), pp. 67–113.

For an example of a multiple palimpsest which, according to A. S. Atiya, has five layers (early Kufic, over pre-Kufic Naskh, over Greek uncials [a portion of I Cor. in lectionary form, dating from the late sixth or early seventh century], over Syriac [relatively late], over Syriac ['portions of the Gospels of St. Matthew, St. John, and especially St. Mark, which [have] a considerable number of signific. nt variants from the Peshitta text'); see his article 'Codex Arabicus (Sinai Arabic MS. No. 514)', in *Homage to a Bookman; Essays on Manuscripts, Books and Printing Written for Hans P. Kraus* . . . (Berlin, 1967), pp. 75–84.

p. 13, *n.* 3. See also W. B. Sedgwick, 'Reading and ·Writing in Classical Antiquity', *Contemporary Review*, cxxxv (January–June 1929), pp. 93 f.

p. 17, *n.* 2. For a revised and enlarged form of the present writer's paper, 'When did Scribes Begin to Use Writing Desks?', see his *Historical and Literary Studies, Pagan, Jewish, and Christian* (Leiden and Grand Rapids, 1968), chap. xii. For further discussion of the furniture found in the so-called Scriptorium at Qumran, see K. W. Clark, 'The Posture of the Ancient Scribe', *The Biblical Archaeologist*, xxvi (1963), pp. 63–72.

p. 23, *n.* 1. Cf. also H. K. McArthur, 'The Earliest Divisions of the Gospels', *Studia Evangelica*, iii, ed. by F. L. Cross (= *Texte und Untersuchungen*, lxxxviii; Berlin, 1964), pp. 266–72. (See also the literature mentioned below in the addendum to p. 104.)

p. 24, *n.* 2. For further investigation see Carl Nordenfalk, 'The Apostolic Canon Tables', *Gazette des beaux-arts*, lxii (1963), pp. 17–34, and H. K. McArthur, 'The Eusebian Sections and Canons', *Catholic Biblical Quarterly*, xxvii (1965), pp. 250–6.

p. 25, *n.* 1. For an extended discussion of the Eusebian Canon Tables, see Eb. Nestle, 'Die Eusebianische Evangelien-Synopse', *Neue kirchliche Zeitschrift*, xix (1908), pp. 40–51, 93–114, and 219–32.

p. 30, *n.* 2. Cf. Ewald Jammers, *Tafeln zur Neumenschrift, mit einer Einführung* (Tutzing, 1965).

p. 31, *n.* 1. See also H. Greeven, 'Die Textgestalt der Evangelienlektionare', *Theologische Literaturzeitung*, lxxvi (1951), cols. 513–22, and Allen Wikgren, 'Chicago Studies in the Greek Lectionary of the New Testament', in *Biblical and Patristic Studies in Memory of Robert Pierce Casey*, ed. by J. N. Birdsall and R. W. Thomson (Freiburg, 1963), pp. 96–121.

p. 32, *line* 5 *from bottom*. The statistics are given by Kurt Aland in his *Studien zur Überlieferung des Neuen Testaments und seines Textes* (Berlin, 1967), p. 207.

p. 33, *n.* 1. The most recently published fascicle in the Chicago series is the Princeton dissertation of Ray Harms, *The Matthean Weekday Lessons in the Greek Gospel Lectionary* (Chicago, 1966). For a survey of the work done at the

University of Chicago on Greek lectionaries, see Wikgren's article cited above in the addendum to p. 31, n. 1. The dissertation of Ronald E. Cocroft, *A Study of the Pauline Lessons in the Matthean Section of the Greek Lectionary* (Library of Princeton Theological Seminary, 1967), is scheduled for publication in the series *Studies and Documents* (Salt Lake City, 1968).

p. 33, n. 2. For an enlarged edition of the papyrus fever amulet see the present writer's *Literary and Historical Studies, Pagan, Jewish, and Christian* (Leiden and Grand Rapids, 1968), pp. 104–10.

p. 34, n. 1. For popular accounts concerning the transmission of the ancient classics, see Frederic George Kenyon, 'The Lineage of the Classics', *Harper's Monthly Magazine*, cv (June–November 1902), pp. 335–41, and Ernst von Dobschütz, 'Homer und die Bibel, eine überlieferungsgeschichtliche Vergleichung', *Neue Jahrbücher für Wissenschaft und Jugendbildung*, i (1925), pp. 331 ff.

p. 38, n. 1. Sir Frederic G. Kenyon re-edited the thirty leaves of the portion in the possession of the University of Michigan, along with ten leaves which he had previously edited, to which were added forty-six newly acquired leaves of the same codex, in Fasciculus iii Supplement, Pauline Epistles, of *The Chester Beatty Biblical Papyri* (London, 1936).

p. 40, n. 2. For further studies of 𝔓⁶⁶ see J. N. Birdsall, *The Bodmer Papyrus of the Gospel of John* (London, 1960); M.-E. Boismard in *Revue Biblique*, lxx (1963), pp. 120–37; G. D. Fee, 'The Corrections of Papyrus Bodmer II and Early Textual Transmission', *Novum Testamentum*, vii (1965), pp. 247–57; Miguel Balgué in *Studia papyrologica*, iv (1965), pp. 76–89; E. C. Colwell, 'Scribal Habits in Early Papyri; a Study in the Corruption of the Text', in *The Bible in Modern Scholarship*, ed. by J. Philip Hyatt (Nashville, 1965), pp. 370–89; and E. F. Rhodes, 'The Corrections of Papyrus Bodmer II', *New Testament Studies*, xiv (1967–8), pp. 271–81.

p. 41, line 7. For further studies of 𝔓⁷² see Éd. Massaux, 'Le texte de la Iᵃ Petri du Papyrus Bodmer VIII (𝔓⁷²)', *Ephemerides theologicae Lovanienses*, xxxix (1963), pp. 616–71; M. A. King, 'Notes on the Bodmer Manuscripts', *Bibliotheca Sacra*, cxxi (1964), pp. 54–57; F. W. Beare, 'The Text of I Peter in the Bodmer Papyrus (𝔓⁷²)', in *Studia Evangelica*, iii, ed. by F. L. Cross (= *Texte und Untersuchungen*, lxxxviii; Berlin, 1964), pp. 263–5; J. D. Quinn, 'Notes on the Text of 𝔓⁷²', *Catholic Biblical Quarterly*, xxvii (1965), pp. 241–9; and Sakae Kubo, 𝔓⁷² *and the Codex Vaticanus* (= *Studies and Documents*, xxvii; Salt Lake City, 1965), who concludes that, 'exclusive of singular variants, 𝔓⁷² has as a whole a text superior to that of B' (p. 152). In Jude its text has been described as 'wild' and analogous to the Western or Bezan text of the Gospels and Acts; so Éd. Massaux, 'Le texte de l'Épître de Jude du Papyrus Bodmer VII', in *Scrinium Lovaniense. Mélanges historiques Étienne Van Cauwenberg* (Louvain, 1961), pp. 108–25.

p. 41, line 15. According to Philippe-H. Menoud, in Acts 𝔓⁷⁴ agrees more frequently with ℵ and A than with B, especially as to order of words; it supports no truly Western reading ('Papyrus Bodmer XVII', *Revue de théologie et de philosophie*, 3ᵉ sér., xii (1962), pp. 112–16).

p. 41, *line* 6 *from bottom*. For further studies of 𝔭⁷⁵ see C. L. Porter, 'Papyrus Bodmer XV (P75) and the Text of Codex Vaticanus', *Journal of Biblical Literature*, lxxxi (1962), pp. 363–76; Kurt Aland, 'Neue neutestamentliche Papyri', *New Testament Studies*, xi (1964–5), pp. 5–21, and xii (1965–6), pp. 195–210 (reprinted, with additions, in Aland's *Studien zur Überlieferung des Neuen Testaments und seines Textes* [Berlin, 1967], pp. 155–72); and especially Carlo M. Martini, S.J., *Il problema della recensionalità del codice B alla luce del papiro Bodmer XIV* (Rome, 1966).

p. 45, *n.* 2. See also Christian Tindall, *Contributions to the Statistical Study of the Codex Sinaiticus* (Edinburgh, 1961).

p. 47, *line* 8. H. Nordberg finds that codex Alexandrinus agrees with the dominant type of text represented in the biblical quotations made by St. Athanasius ('The Bible Text of St. Athanasius', *Arctos, acta philologica Fennica*, N.S. iii [1962], pp. 119–41).

p. 47, *line* 21. In 1965 the New Testament portion of codex Vaticanus was photographically reproduced by order of Pope Paul VI and copies were presented to the members and observers of the Vatican Council II. The title-page reads as follows: τα ιερα βιβλια | Codex Vaticanus graecus | 1209. | Phototypice expressus | iussu | Pauli PP VI | Pontificis Maximi | *H KAINH ΔIAΘHKH.* | In Civitate Vaticana | 1965. The several forms of the edition contain also a second title-page, as well as an Introduction of 21 pages (signed by Mgr. Paul Canart and Carlo M. Martini, S.J.) in English, French, German, Italian, or Spanish.

p. 49, *n.* 2. In the opinion of Hermann J. Frede, however, codex Bezae dates from the fourth century (see his *Altlateinische Paulus-Handschriften* [Freiburg, 1964], p. 18, Anm. 4).

p. 50, *n.* 2. The book of Acts according to codex Bezae was translated by Fr. A. Bornemann in his *Acta Apostolorum ab Sancto Luca conscripta ad Codicis Cantabrigiensis . . .* (Grossenhain, 1848).

p. 51, *n.* 2. Codex Claromontanus is dated by Frede in the fifth century; see addendum to p. 49, n. 2, above.

p. 52, *line* 4. On codex E, see Russell Champlin, *Family E and its Allies in Matthew* (= *Studies and Documents*, xxviii; Salt Lake City, 1967), and Jacob Geerlings, *Family E and its Allies in Mark* (= *Studies and Documents*, xxxi; Salt Lake City, 1968).

p. 59, *line* 17. On the textual affinities of codex Petropolitanus, see Silva Lake, *Family Π and the Codex Alexandrinus; The Text According to Mark* (=

Studies and Documents, v; London, 1937); Jacob Geerlings, *Family Π in Luke* (= *Studies and Documents*, xxii; Salt Lake City, 1962); idem, *Family Π in John* (= *Studies and Documents*, xxiii; Salt Lake City, 1963); and Russell Champlin, *Family Π in Matthew* (= *Studies and Documents*, xxiv; Salt Lake City, 1964).

p. 62, *n*. 1. See also Jacob Geerlings, *The Lectionary Text of Family 13 According to Cod Vat Gr 1217* (*Gregory 547*) [The Farrer Lectionary] (= *Studies and Documents*, xv; Salt Lake City, 1959); idem, *Family 13. The Farrer Group. The Text According to Matthew* (= *Studies and Documents*, xix; Salt Lake City, 1964); idem, *Family 13* (*The Farrer Group*). *The Text According to Luke* (= *Studies and Documents*, xx; 1961); idem, *Family 13* (*The Farrer Group*). *The Text According to John.* (= *Studies and Documents*, xxi; 1962).

p. 62, *n*. 3. See also M. R. James, *The Wanderings and Homes of Manuscripts* (London, 1919), pp. 17 f. Concerning the scribe Emmanuel, see H. L. Gray, 'Greek Visitors to England in 1455–1456', in *Anniversary Essays in Mediaeval History*, by Students of Charles Homer Haskins (Boston and New York, 1919), pp. 81–116, especially 105 ff.

p. 67, *n*. 1. For diminutive Greek and Coptic manuscripts see W. H. Willis in *Classical, Mediaeval and Renaissance Studies in Honor of Berthold Louis Ullman*, ed. by Charles Henderson, Jr., i (Rome, 1964), p. 270, n. 1.

p. 67, *n*. 2. See also the present writer's articles, 'A Survey of Recent Research on the Ancient Versions of the New Testament', in *New Testament Studies*, ii (1955–6), pp. 1–16; 'The Early Versions of the New Testament', in *Peake's Commentary on the Bible*, ed. by M. Black and H. H. Rowley (London, 1962), pp. 671–5; 'Versions, Ancient', in *The Interpreter's Dictionary of the Bible*, iv (New York, 1962), pp. 749–60; and 'Recent Contributions to the Study of the Ancient Versions of the New Testament', in *The Bible in Modern Scholarship*, ed. by J. P. Hyatt (Nashville, 1965), pp. 347–69.

p. 68, *n*. 1. See also Allen Wikgren, 'The Use of the Versions in New Testament Textual Criticism', *Journal of Biblical Literature*, lxvii (1948), pp. 135–41.

p. 71, *last line*. For a convenient scriptural list indexing the several publications containing portions of the Palestinian Syriac version, see Fr. Schulthess, *Lexicon Syropalaestinum* (Berlin, 1903), pp. vii–xvi. For additions to the list in the book of Acts, see Charles Perrot, 'Un fragment christo-palestinien découvert à Khirbet Mird (Actes des Apôtres, x, 28–29; 32–41)', *Revue Biblique*, lxx (1963), pp. 506–55, especially 544. For Syriac manuscripts in general, see James T. Clemons, 'A Checklist of Syriac Manuscripts in the United States and Canada', *Orientalia Christiana Periodica*, xxxii (1966), pp. 224–51, 478–522.

p. 72, *line* 11. For a rich bibliographical survey see M. Bogaert, 'Bulletin de la Bible latine', *Revue Bénédictine*, lxxiv–lxxv (1964–5), pp. [1]–[72].

p. 75, *line* 5 *from bottom*. See also Hermann J. Frede, *Altlateinische Paulus-Handschriften* (Freiburg, 1964), and Walter Thiele, *Die lateinischen Texte des 1. Petrusbriefes* (Freiburg, 1965).

p. 76, *line* 26. According to Westcott and Hort (*The New Testament in the Original Greek*; [ii], *Introduction* [*and*] *Appendix* [Cambridge, 1881], p. 152), 'the text of A in several books agrees with the Latin Vulgate in so many peculiar readings devoid of Old Latin attestation as to leave little doubt that a Greek MS. largely employed by Jerome in his revision of the Latin version must have had to a great extent a common original with A'. Wordsworth and White concluded (*Nouum Testamentum Latine*, i [Oxford, 1889–1898], pp. 655–72) that Jerome used a type of text represented today by B, ℵ, and L. According to von Soden (*Die Schriften des Neuen Testaments*, I. iii [Berlin, 1910], pp. 1544–72) Jerome followed a type of Greek text which was similar to the archetype of the three great recensions, *I, H,* and *K*. H. J. Vogels rejected the conclusions of all his predecessors and held that Jerome utilized what modern scholars call the Koine type of Greek text (*Vulgatastudien. Die Evangelien der Vulgata untersucht auf ihre lateinische und griechische Vorlage* [Münster i. W., 1928], pp. 55–80). In a review of Vogel's monograph, F. C. Burkitt criticized the author for exaggerating the influence of the Koine type of text upon the Vulgate, and suggested that it is 'more likely that he [Jerome] had at least two MSS., one of which was mainly *H*[*esychian*] and the other (or others) mainly *K*[*oine*], and that in important cases . . . he made an eclectic choice between them' (*Journal of Theological Studies*, xxx [1929], p. 412). Lagrange also believed that Jerome had availed himself of more than one type of Greek text, but thought that, besides codices resembling A and B, he was influenced by the type of text represented in ℵ even more than by that in A (*Critique textuelle*; ii, *La Critique rationnelle* [Paris, 1935], pp. 287 ff.).

With regard to the Acts of the Apostles, Wordsworth and White (op. cit., ii [Oxford, 1905], pp. x–xiii) collected a series of readings which they interpreted as showing that Jerome's Greek text differed somewhat from any that is known today. After a close scrutiny of these readings, J. H. Ropes rejected their conclusion, holding that the Vulgate text of Acts is substantially the translation of the Old Uncial text of the general type of B, ℵ, A, C, 81, and that of these five manuscripts, it agrees most often with A, but also preserves a certain number of Western readings derived from the Old Latin (*The Text of Acts* [London, 1926], p. cxxvi; cf. also Ropes and W. H. P. Hatch, 'The Vulgate, Peshitto, Sahidic, and Bohairic Versions of Acts and the Greek MSS.', *Harvard Theological Review*, xxi [1928], pp. 69–95, especially 73 ff.).

As concerns the textual complexion of the Pauline Epistles in the Latin Vulgate, according to Lagrange (op. cit., pp. 501 and 509), Jerome seems to have reacted against the predominance of the Western type of reading.

For a survey of research on the Vulgate text of the Catholic Epistles since the publication of Harnack's monograph, *Zur Revision der Prinzipien der neutestamentlichen Textkritik; die Bedeutung der Vulgata für den Text der katholischen Briefe* (Leipzig, 1916), reference may be made to the present writer's contribution to *New Testament Manuscript Studies*, ed. by M. M.

Parvis and A. P. Wikgren (Chicago, 1950), pp. 59 f.; cf. also Walter Thiele's *Wortschatzuntersuchungen zu den lateinischen Texten der Johannesbriefe* (Freiburg, 1958).

As for the text of the Apocalypse, H. J. Vogels has shown the resemblance of the Latin Vulgate to codex Sinaiticus (*Untersuchungen zur Geschichte des lateinischen Apokalypseübersetzung* [Düsseldorf, 1920], pp. 19 ff.), although, strangely enough, he refuses to admit that Jerome based his work on this type of text, holding instead that the ancestors of Sinaiticus were influenced by the Old Latin (for a refutation of the latter view, see Lagrange, op. cit., pp. 609 ff., who argues that not only was the Old Latin base of the Vulgate related to that of the Old Uncials, but also that as far as Jerome revised the text of the Apocalypse—the amount of revision has been disputed—it was still further in the direction of the Old Uncials). The Vulgate therefore possesses no little importance in the textual criticism of the book of Revelation.

p. 77, line 20. In the Pauline Epistles the text of the Book of Armagh is predominantly Old Latin, with only a small number of Vulgate readings.

p. 78, line 30. On the Sixtine edition of the Vulgate Bible see Paul M. Baumgarten, *Die Vulgata Sixtina von 1590 und ihre Einführungsbulle, Aktenstücke und Untersuchungen* (Münster/W., 1911).

p. 81, line 4 from bottom. An important Coptic witness (copied at the end of the fourth or the beginning of the fifth century) to the Western text of Acts is described by the late T. C. Petersen in a preliminary article entitled, 'An Early Manuscript of Acts; an Unrevised Version of the Ancient so-called Western Text', *Catholic Biblical Quarterly*, xxvi (1964), pp. 225–41; see also E. J. Epp, 'Coptic Manuscript G67 and the Rôle of Codex Bezae as a Western Witness in Acts', *Journal of Biblical Literature*, lxxxv (1966), pp. 197–212.

On Greek and Coptic bilingual manuscripts of the New Testament see Kurt Treu, 'Griechisch-koptische Bilinguen des Neuen Testaments', in *Koptologische Studien in den DDR* (= *Wissenschaftliche Zeitschrift der Martin-Luther-Universität*, Halle–Wittenberg, 1965 [appeared 1966]), pp. 95–124.

For the Gospel of John in Coptic, see R. Kasser, *L'Évangile selon saint Jean et les versions coptes* (Neuchâtel, 1966).

For the Acts of the Apostles, see Anton Joussen's (unpublished) dissertation at the University of Bonn entitled *Die koptischen Versionen der Apostelgeschichte (Kritik und Wertung)* (Bonn, 1963 [Vorwort dated 13 June 1959]). Joussen's conclusions include the following: '(1) The Greek text presupposed by the Sahidic and Bohairic (Fayyumic) belongs to that type represented chiefly in ℵ and B; (2) Both [Coptic] versions presuppose a Greek text that must have contained a mass of Western readings; (3) The recognition that the Sahidic and also the Bohairic contain a not inconsiderable number of variants which occur elsewhere only in Latin and Syriac witnesses shows (as Zahn pointed out, *Urausgabe*, p. 225) that these translations have carried over a not insignificant influence from the same type of Greek text which the Coptic versions have followed' (pp. 216 f.).

For 1 Peter, William H. Willis has announced the preparation of a critical edition of that book in Sahidic (see the *Yearbook* of the American Philosophical Society for 1963 [Philadelphia, 1964], pp. 627 f.); cf. also Willis's article, 'An Unrecognized Fragment of First Peter in Coptic', in *Classical, Mediaeval and Renaissance Studies in Honor of Berthold Louis Ullman*, ed. by Charles Henderson, Jr., i (Rome, 1964), pp. 265–71.

p. 83, *line 6 from bottom.* The ancestry of the Old Georgian version has been disputed (for a survey of earlier opinions see the present writer's discussion in *New Testament Manuscript Studies*, ed. by M. M. Parvis and A. P. Wikgren [Chicago, 1950], pp. 41 ff.). According to recent scholars, it was translated from an Armenian version that preserved certain Syriacisms; see Arthur Vööbus, *Early Versions of the New Testament* (Stockholm, 1954), pp. 187–96, and Joseph Molitor, 'Die Bedeutung der altgeorgischen Bibel für die neutestamentliche Textkritik', *Biblische Zeitschrift*, n.F. iv (1960), pp. 39–53; 'Zur armenischen Vorlage der altgeorgischen Version des 1. Johannesbriefes', *Handes Amsorya*, lxxv (1961), cols. 415–29; 'Die syrische Grundlage der altgeorgischen Evangelienübersetzung nach Aussage ihrer Harmonismen', *Bedi Kartlisa (Revue de Kartvélologie)*, xiii–xiv, No. 41–42 (1962), pp. 98–105; 'Die Eigennamen in der Johannes-Apokalypse des Euthymius', ibid., xvii–xviii, No. 45–46 (1964), pp. 127–31; 'Syrische Lesarten im altgeorgischen Tetraevangelium', ibid., xix–xx, No. 48–49 (1965), pp. 112–18; and 'Neuere Ergebnisse zur Textgeschichte des georgischen Neuen Testamentes', ibid., xxi–xxii, No. 50–51 (1966), pp. 111–20.

p. 84, *line 10.* Other monographs and editions include Ilia Abuladze, *The Acts of the Apostles according to the Old Manuscripts* (in Georgian; Tiflis, 1950); K'et'evan Lort'k'ip'anidze, *The Georgian Versions of the Catholic Epistles according to Manuscripts of the 10th to 14th Centuries* (in Georgian; Tiflis, 1956), translated into Latin by Joseph Molitor in *Oriens Christianus*, xlix (1965), pp. 1–17; l (1966), pp. 37–45; and Ilia Imnaišvili, *The Apocalypse of John and its Commentary* [i.e., the Commentary of Andrew of Caesarea] (in Georgian; Tiflis, 1961), translated into Latin by Joseph Molitor in *Oriens Christianus*, l (1966), pp. 1–12 (continued). For the Gospels see J. Molitor, *Synopsis latina Evangeliorum Ibericorum antiquissimorum secundum Matthaeum, Marcum, Lucam*, desumpta e codicibus Adysh, Opiza, Tbeth necnon e fragmentis biblicis et patristicis quae dicuntur Chanmeti et Haemeti (Louvain, 1965).

p. 85, *n.* 2. A preliminary analysis of the textual affinities of the Nubian version (so far as it has been preserved) was made by the present writer in a paper entitled, 'The Christianization of Nubia and the Old Nubian Version of the New Testament', in *Studia Patristica*, vii, ed. by F. L. Cross (= *Texte und Untersuchungen*, xcix; Berlin, 1965), pp. 531–42, and reprinted in his *Historical and Literary Studies, Pagan, Jewish, and Christian* (Leiden and Grand Rapids, 1968), pp. 112–22.

p. 86, *n.* 1. On the Anglo-Saxon version, see M. C. Morrell, *A Manual of Old English Biblical Materials* (Knoxville, 1965).

p. 90, *n.* 1. The Dura fragment of the Diatessaron was re-edited, with a few minor alterations, by C. Bradford Welles, *et al.*, in *The Parchments and Papyri* (= *The Excavations at Dura-Europos* . . ., *Final Report*, vol. v, part 1; New Haven, 1959), pp. 73–74.

p. 91, *n.* 2. Cf. also Louis Leloir, 'Divergences entre l'original syriaque et la version arménienne du commentaire d'Éphrem sur le Diatessaron', in *Mélanges Eugène Tisserant*, ii (Città del Vaticano, 1964), pp. 303–31.

p. 92, *n.* 1. Cf. also the present writer's survey of Tatianic studies in the chapter entitled, 'Recent Contributions to the Study of the Ancient Versions of the New Testament', in *The Bible in Modern Scholarship*, ed. by J. P. Hyatt (Nashville, 1965), pp. 352 ff.

p. 95, *n.* 2. See also R. P. Breaden, 'A Colophon of Interest in the Early Printing of Greek', *Bulletin of the New York Public Library*, l (1946), pp. 471–5.

p. 99, *line* 9. Most of the manuscripts that Erasmus used in the preparation of his editions of the New Testament came from the collection of manuscripts that had been bequeathed in 1443 to the Dominican monastery at Basle by John Stojković of Ragusa, one of the cardinals created by the Anti-Pope, Felix V; cf. Aloysius Krchňák, *De vita et operibus Ioannis de Ragusia* (= *Lateranum*, N.S. xxvi, 2–3; Rome, 1960), and R. W. Hunt, 'Greek Manuscripts in the Bodleian Library from the Collection of John Stojković of Ragusa', in *Studia Patristica*, vol. vii, part 1, ed. by F. L. Cross (= *Texte und Untersuchungen*, xcii; Berlin, 1966), pp. 75–82. See also Bo Reicke, 'Erasmus und die neutestamentliche Textgeschichte', *Theologische Zeitschrift*, xxii (1966), pp. 254–65, who discusses the several Greek manuscripts, now in the University Library at Basle, used by Erasmus for his first edition of the Greek New Testament.

p. 100, *n.* 2. Bornkamm's view is upheld by Heinz Bluhm in his study, *Martin Luther, Creative Translator* (St. Louis, 1965), p. 75.

On the question of Calvin's interest in textual criticism of the New Testament, see T. H. L. Parker, 'The Sources of the Text of Calvin's New Testament', *Zeitschrift für Kirchengeschichte*, 4te Folge, x (= lxxiii) (1962), pp. 277–98. In a Postscript Parker states, 'I have since investigated the Greek text behind Calvin's Latin. It is clear that he did not confine himself to any one printed edition of the Greek New Testament. I am also more ready to believe that he made use of Greek manuscripts at first hand' (p. 298).

p. 102, *n.* 2. The Holy Office declared subsequently (2 June 1927) that its decree was not intended to hinder Catholic scholars from thoroughly investigating the matter and from espousing an opinion contrary to the authenticity of the passage, provided that they profess themselves ready to stand by the judgement of the Church; see H. Denzinger and K. Rahner, *Enchiridion symbolorum*, 28th ed. (Freiburg i. Br., 1952), no. 2198, and *Enchiridion biblicum*, 3rd ed. (Naples and Rome, 1956), no. 136.

p. 102, *n.* 3. From the standpoint of the Greek Orthodox Church, see the defence of the genuineness of the passage by Panagotes Ch. Demetropoulos, ʿΗ γνησιότης τοῦ χωρίου I ʾΙωάν. 5.7 β – 8α περὶ τῶν ἐν τῷ οὐρανῷ μαρτύρων, in *Actes du XIIᵉ Congrès international d'Études byzantines*, Ochride, 10–16 septembre 1961, tom. ii (Belgrade, 1964), pp. 429–38.

In connexion with the history of the discussion of the passage it deserves to be mentioned that Sir Isaac Newton wrote at length concerning the evidence supporting the passage (which he regarded as spurious) in a letter to a friend dated 14 Nov. 1690; see *The Correspondence of Isaac Newton*, ed. by H. W. Turnbull, iii (Cambridge, 1961), pp. 83–109.

p. 104, *line 8 from bottom*. For wide-ranging information concerning verse-division in the New Testament, see William Wright's article on 'Verse' in the first edition (the article is shortened in later editions) of John Kitto's *Cyclopædia of Biblical Literature*, ii (London, 1845; New York, 1846), pp. 905–14, supplemented by Wright's articles in *The Christian Remembrancer*, n.s. iii (January–June 1842), pp. 455–69, 672–90. For a list of differences in verse-division among about fifty editions of the Greek New Testament, see Ezra Abbot's excursus in Caspar René Gregory's *Prolegomena*, being vol. iii of Tischendorf's *Novum Testamentum Graece*, 8th ed., part 1 (Leipzig, 1884), pp. 167–82, reprinted in English in Abbot's posthumously published volume entitled, *The Authorship of the Fourth Gospel and Other Critical Essays* (Boston, 1888), pp. 464–77.

p. 121, *n.* 1. Griesbach was also criticized by Frederick Nolan in his two volumes entitled, *An Inquiry into the Integrity of the Greek Vulgate, or Received Text, of the New Testament; in which the Greek Manuscripts are newly Classed, the Integrity of the Authorised* [English] *Text Vindicated, and the Various Readings Traced to their Origin* (London, 1815), and *Supplement to an Inquiry* . . . (London, 1830).

p. 126, *n.* 1. For a more recent assessment of Lachmann and his work, see Sebastiano Timpanaro, *La genesi del metodo del Lachmann* (Florence, 1963).

p. 136, *line* 6. Essentially the same point of view is expressed in the defence of the Byzantine text-type of the New Testament by A. Ivanov of the Moscow Theological Academy in a series of articles published in *Zhurnal Moskovskoi Patriarchii* (1954–56) and summarized by Robert P. Casey in 'A Russian Orthodox View of New Testament Textual Criticism', *Theology*, lx (1957), pp. 50–54.

p. 139, *n.* 1. For more extensive statistics concerning a comparison of several modern critical editions of the Greek New Testament, see Kurt Aland, *Studien zur Überlieferung des Neuen Testaments und seines Textes* (Berlin, 1967), pp. 59–80.

p. 154, *n.* 3. See also M.-J. Lagrange, 'La critique textuelle avant le concile de Trente', *Revue Thomiste*, xxxix. 2 (1934–5), pp. 400–9 (= Lagrange's *Critique textuelle*; ii, *La Critique rationnelle* [Paris, 1935], pp. 294–301).

p. 156, *n.* 1. For other treatises on textual criticism see V. Coulton, *Essai sur la méthode de la critique conjecturale appliquée au texte d'Aristophane* (Paris, 1933); Gilbert J. Garraghan, S.J., *A Guide to Historical Method*, ed. by Jean Delanglez, S.J. (New York, 1946), pp. 215–31; *Studien zur Textgeschichte und Textkritik*, ed. Hellfried Dahlmann and Reinhold Merkelbach (Köln and Opladen, 1959); Franz Wieacker, *Textstufen klassischer Juristen* (= *Abhandlungen der Akademie der Wissenschaften in Göttingen*, philol.-hist. Kl., Dritte Folge, Nr. 45; Göttingen, 1960); G. Thomson, 'Method in Textual Criticism. A Tribute to Walter Headlam (1866–1908)', *Eirene, Studia Graeca et Latina*, i (1960), pp. 51–60; Robert Marichal, 'La critique des textes', in *L'Histoire et des méthodes*, ed. by Charles Samaran (Paris, 1961), pp. 1247–1366; Herbert Hunger, Otto Stegmüller, *et al.*, *Geschichte der Textüberlieferung der antiken und mittelalterlichen Literatur*; Band I, *Überlieferung der antiken Literatur* (Zürich, 1961); B. A. von Groningen, *Traité d'histoire et de critique des textes grecs* (= *Verhandelingen der koninklijke Nederlandse Akademie van Wetenschappen*, Afd. Letterkunde, N.R., Deel lxx, no. 2; Amsterdam, 1963); D. S. Likhachev, *Tekstologiya; Kratkii ocherk* (Moscow–Leningrad, 1964); and G. Zuntz, *An Inquiry into the Transmission of the Plays of Euripides* (Cambridge, 1965).

p. 164, *n.* 1. See also P. S. Coculesco, 'Sur les méthodes de critique textuelle du type Lachmann–Quentin', *Grai și suflet*, iv (Bucharest, 1929–30), pp. 97–107, and W. P. Shepard, 'Recent Theories of Textual Criticism', *Modern Philology*, xxviii (1930), pp. 129–41.

p. 169, *n.* 1. Cf. also Jack Burch, 'The Use of a Computor in New Testament Text Criticism', *Restoration Quarterly*, viii (1965), pp. 119–25, based upon Burch's (unpublished) thesis entitled *A Critical Study of the Greek Text of Second Timothy as Seen in Selected Uncial, Cursive and Lectionary Manuscripts*, 2 vols. (Library of Abilene Christian College, Texas, 1963).

p. 175, *n.* 2. For an example of the application of such eclecticism, see Kilpatrick's chapter entitled, 'An Eclectic Study of the Text of Acts', in *Biblical and Patristic Studies in Memory of Robert Pierce Casey*, ed. by J. N. Birdsall and R. W. Thomson (Freiburg, 1963), pp. 64–77.

p. 177, *n.* 3. Since 1962 there have appeared the fascicles entitled *The Pastoral Letters and Hebrews* (1963), and *Romans and 1 and 2 Corinthians* (1964). According to H. K. Moulton, the chief criticisms that have been levelled against Kilpatrick's text in the Diglot fascicles are: '(1) There has been rather too rigid a reliance on word order . . . ; (2) There has been too great a dependence on the early versions as against the great uncials . . . ; and (3) As a result of these two, and other, considerations the choice of reading has been eclectic to the extent that the normal rules of manuscript evidence have taken a very secondary place' ('The Present State of New Testament Textual Criticism', *The Bible Translator*, xvi [1965], p. 196).

p. 177, *n.* 4. Cf. also Kilpatrick's contributions, 'The Greek New Testament Text of Today and the *Textus Receptus*', in *The New Testament in History and Contemporary Perspectives; Essays in Memory of G. H. C. Macgregor*, ed. by H. Anderson and W. Barclay (Oxford, 1965), pp. 189–208; and 'Style and

Text in the Greek New Testament', in *Studies in the History and Text of the New Testament in Honor of Kenneth Willis Clark*, ed. by Boyd L. Daniels and M. Jack Suggs (= *Studies and Documents*, xxix; Salt Lake City, 1967), pp. 153–60.

p. 181, *n.* 2. For other studies of the significance of quantitative and qualitative analyses of relationships among manuscripts, see J. Fourquet, 'Fautes communes ou innovations communes', *Romania*, lxx (1948–9), pp. 85–95; E. F. Hills, 'The Inter-Relationship of the Caesarean Manuscripts', *Journal of Biblical Literature*, lxviii (1949), pp. 141–59; E. C. Colwell and E. W. Tune, 'The Quantitative Relationships between MS. Text-Types', in *Biblical and Patristic Studies in Memory of Robert Pierce Casey*, ed. by J. N. Birdsall and R. W. Thomson (Freiburg, 1963), pp. 25–32; E. C. Colwell, 'Variant Readings: Classification and Use', *Journal of Biblical Literature*, lxxxiii (1964), pp. 253–61; and E. C. Colwell, 'External Evidence and New Testament Textual Criticism', in *Studies in the History and Text of the New Testament in Honor of Kenneth Willis Clark*, ed. by Boyd L. Daniels and M. Jack Suggs (= *Studies and Documents*, xxix; Salt Lake City, 1967), pp. 1–12. For what is described as a rapid method of ascertaining the relationships among manuscripts of the later text-types, see Eldon Jay Epp, 'The Claremont Profile-Method for Grouping New Testament Minuscule Manuscripts', ibid., pp. 27–38.

p. 183, *n.* 1. For other examples see Fredson Bowers, *Bibliography and Textual Criticism* (Oxford, 1964), pp. 54 f.

p. 184, *n.* 1. Cf. also C. Könnecke, *Emendationen zu Stellen des Neuen Testaments* (= *Beiträge zur Förderung christlicher Theologie*, xii, 1; Gütersloh, 1908).

p. 186, *n.* 1. Cf. also H. C. Youtie, *The Textual Criticism of Documentary Papyri*, *Prolegomena* (= Bulletin Supplement no. 6, Institute of Classical Studies, University of London; 1958), and E. C. Colwell, 'Scribal Habits in Early Papyri: A Study in the Corruption of the Text', in *The Bible in Modern Scholarship*, ed. by J. P. Hyatt (Nashville, 1965), pp. 370–89.

For problems concerning the correct text of Lincoln's Gettysburg Address (of which several slightly different copies are extant), see William E. Barton, *Lincoln at Gettysburg; What He Intended to Say; What He Said; What He Was Reported to Have Said; What He Wished He Had Said* (Indianapolis, 1930).

p. 188, *n.* 3. For a list of errors made by modern editors in deciphering Greek papyri, see Youtie, op. cit. (see addendum to p. 186, n. 1 above), and his essay, 'The Papyrologist: Artificer of Fact', *Greek, Roman, and Byzantine Studies*, iv (1963), pp. 19–32.

p. 196, *n.* 1. The date is that suggested by Tischendorf, 8th ed., in loc. Tischendorf is in error in reading τό, for τόν clearly stands in the gloss; see the plate reproducing the folio of codex Vaticanus in H. J. Vogels, *Codicum Novi Testamenti specimina* (Bonn, 1927).

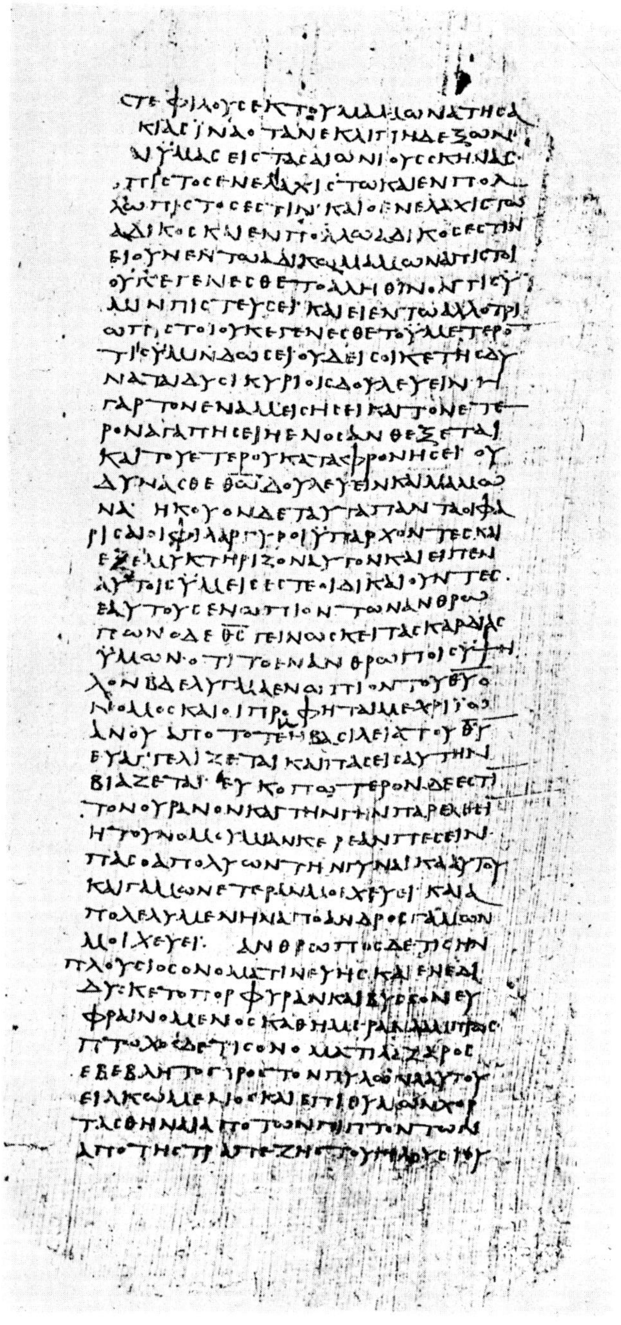

PLATE III

Bodmer Papyrus XIV (p75, about A.D. 175–225), Cologny/Geneva.
Luke xvi. 9–21 (the name of the Rich Man is given in line 8 from the
bottom; see p. 42). Actual size 10⅜ in. × 5⅛ in.

PLATE IV

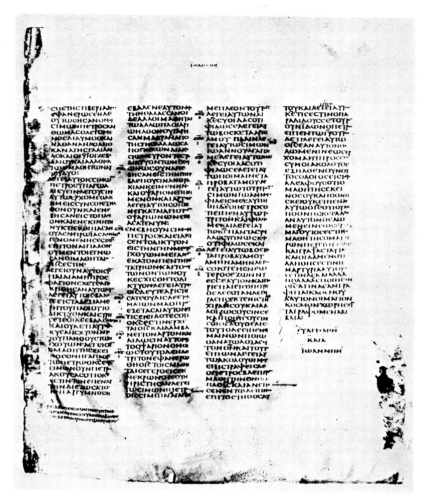

Codex Sinaiticus (ℵ, iv cent.), British Museum, London; last folio of the Gospel according to John (see p. 46), John xxi. 1–25. Actual size 14⅞ in. × 13½ in.

PLATE V

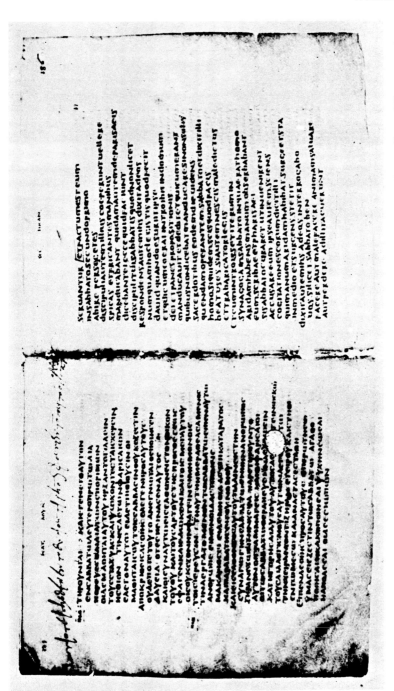

Codex Bezae (D, v or vi cent.), University Library, Cambridge; Luke v. 38–vi. 9 (with an agraphon of Jesus, lines 16 ff.; see p. 50).
Actual size 10 in. × 8⅜ in.

PLATE VI

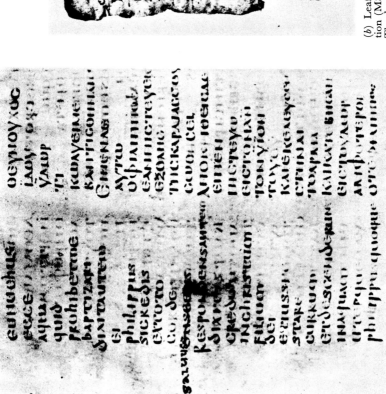

(b) Leaf from a pocket-sized copy of the Book of Revelation (MS. no. 0169, iv cent.), Speer Library, Princeton Theological Seminary, Princeton, New Jersey; Rev. iii. 19–iv. 1 (see p. 67). Actual size 3¾ in. × 2⅞ in.

(a) Codex Laudianus 35 (Eᵃ, vi or vii cent.), Bodleian Library, Oxford; Acts viii. 36–38 (the earliest known witness to vs. 37; see p. 52). Actual size 10¾ in. × 8⅜ in.

Codex Rossanensis (Σ, vi cent.), in the Archives of the Archiepiscopal Curia, Rossano, Calabria; folio 8ᵛ (Muñoz), Christ and Barabbas before Pilate (with the court stenographer standing by the table; see pp. 17 and 59). Actual size 11⅝ in. × 9⅝ in.

PLATE VIII

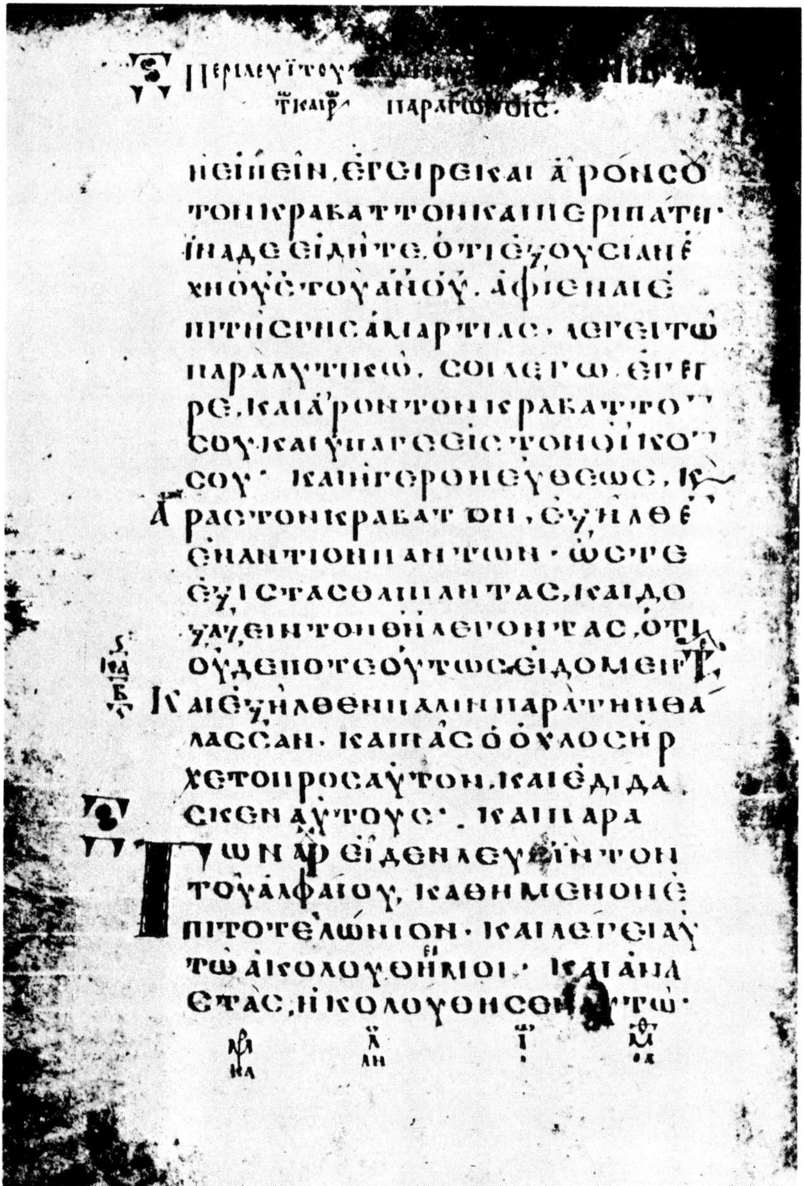

Codex Basiliensis (E, viii cent.), University Library, Basle; Mark ii. 9–14 (with *titlos*, lectionary equipment, and Eusebian canon numerals; see pp. 23, 25, 30, and 52). Actual size 9 in. × 6½ in.

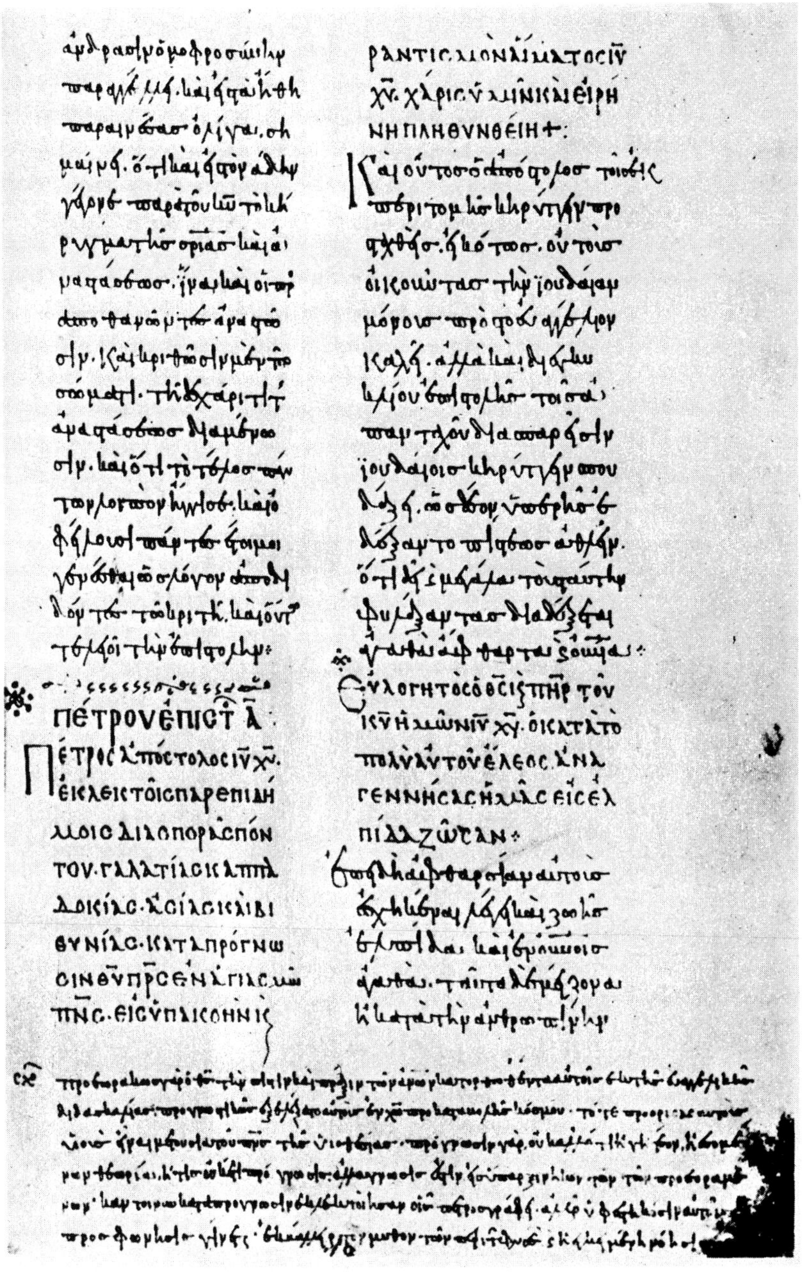

PLATE IX

Codex Mosquensis (K^ap, ix or x cent.), State Historical Museum, Moscow; 1 Pet. i. 1–2 and 3, with commentary and scholia (see pp. 27 and 54). Actual size 13¼ in. × 9⅜ in.

PLATE X

Greek Gospel Lectionary 562 (written, according to a colophon, in the city of Capua, A.D. 991), in the Vatican Library, Rome; John xix. 10–16 and Matt. xxvii. 3–5 (see pp. 30 f.). Actual size 9⅞ in. × 7⅛ in.

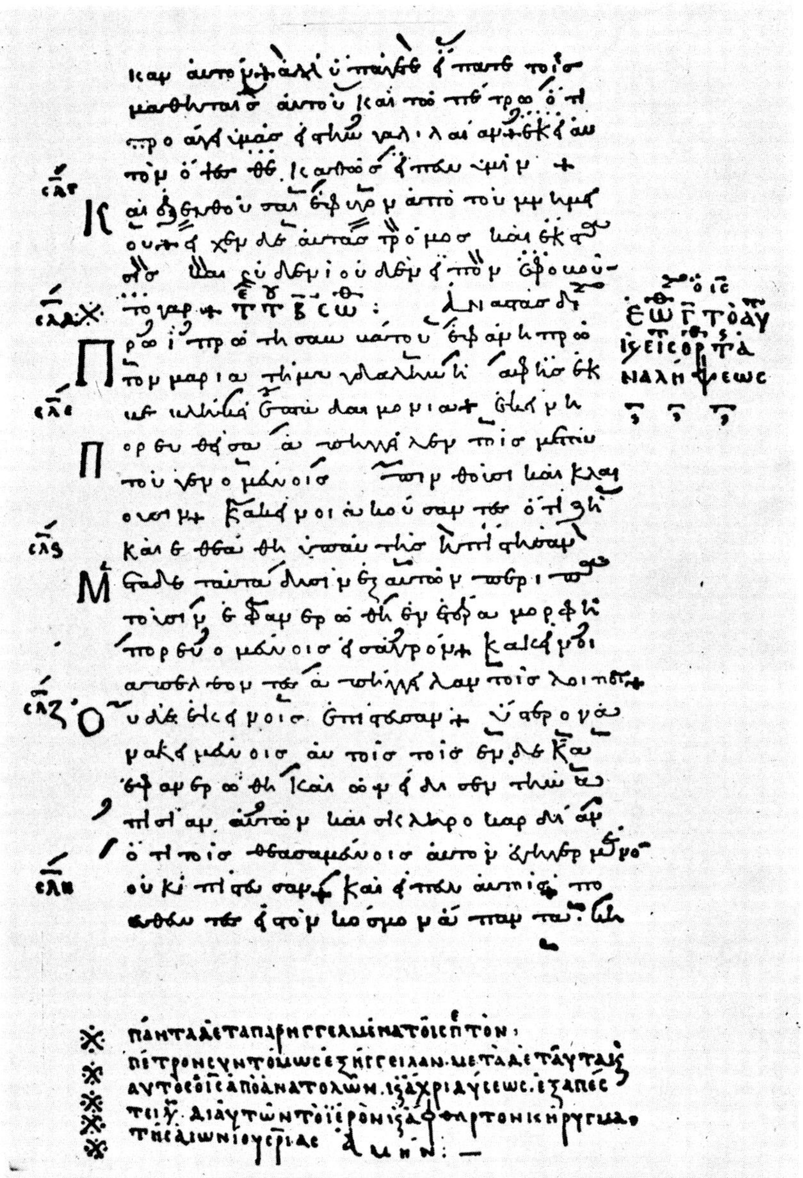

PLATE XI

Greek Gospel MS. 274 (x cent.), Bibliothèque Nationale, Paris; Mark xvi. 6–20 and the intermediate ending of Mark (see pp. 30 and 226). Actual size 9⅜ in. × 6½ in.

PLATE XII

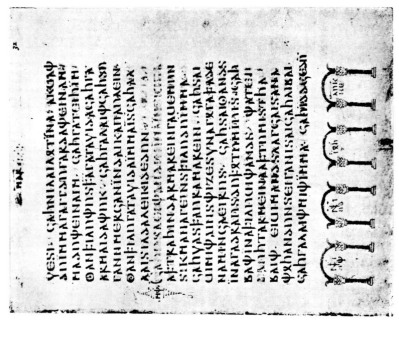

(a) Curetonian Syriac MS. (early v cent.), British Museum, London (see pp. 68–69); John vi. 30–41 (with headline and corrections). Actual size 11¼ in.×9 in.

(b) Gothic codex Argenteus (v or vi cent.), University Library, Uppsala (see pp. 25 and 82); Mark v. 18–24. Actual size 9¼ in.×7½ in.

PLATE XIII

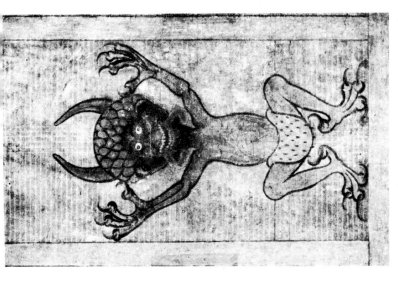

(a) Codex Sangallensis (Δ, ix cent.), Monastery of St. Gall, Switzerland; Greek text with Latin interlinear; Luke ii. 51–iii. 7 (see p. 58). Actual size 8⅞ in. × 7⅛ in.

(b) Codex Gigas (A.D. 1204–30), Royal Library, Stockholm, sometimes called the 'Djävulsbibeln' because of this picture on folio 290 (see pp. 67 and 74 f.). Actual size 36 in. × 20 in.

PLATE XIV

(*a*) Chester Beatty Coptic (Sahidic) MS. B (about
A.D. 600), Chester Beatty Museum, Dublin; John i. 1–10
(see p. 80). Actual size 4¾ in. × 4 in.

(*b*) Armenian Gospel MS. 229 of the Patriarchal Library of Etchmiadzin (dated A.D. 989),
now in the State Repository of Manuscripts, Erevan; mention of Ariston the Presbyter,
col. b, between lines 6 and 7 opposite decorative boss (see p. 227). Actual size of entire
folio 13⅜ in. × 10¾ in. (plate reproduces lower three-quarters of folio 110ᵛ)

PLATE XV

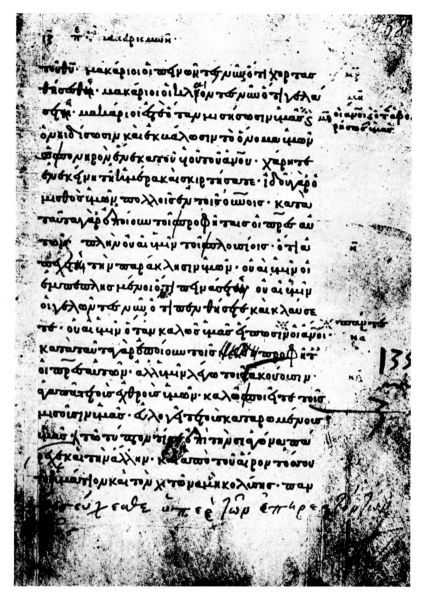

Greek Gospel MS. 2 (xii cent.), University Library, Basle; Luke vi. 20–30; one of the inferior manuscripts used by Erasmus for his first edition of the Greek New Testament (see pp. 98–100), with his corrections and annotations for the printer (e.g. in lines 8 and 9 an oblique stroke separates the definite article from the following word, and in the lower margin is Erasmus' addition of προσεύχεσθε ὑπὲρ τῶν ἐπηρεαζόντων ὑμᾶς, which the scribe had accidentally omitted from the text of vs. 28, third line from the bottom). Actual size 7¾ in. × 6 in.

PLATE XVI

αὐτῶν ἐν ἑαυτοῖς ἀπολαμβάνοντες. καὶ καθὼς οὐκ ἐδοκίμασαν τὸν θεὸν ἔχειν ἐν ἐπιγνώσει παρέδωκεν αὐτοὺς ὁ θεὸς εἰς ἀδόκιμον νοῦν, ποιεῖν τὰ μὴ καθήκοντα, πεπληρωμένους πάσῃ ἀδικίᾳ, πορνείᾳ, πονηρίᾳ, πλεονεξίᾳ, κακίᾳ, μεστοὺς φθόνου, φόνου, ἔριδος δόλου, κακοηθείας, ψιθυριστάς, καταλάλους, θεοστυγεῖς, ὑβριστάς, ὑπερηφάνους, ἀλαζόνας, ἐφευρετὰς κακῶν, γονεῦσιν ἀπειθεῖς, ἀσυνέτους, ἀσυνθέτους, ἀστόργους, ἀσπόνδους, ἀνελεήμονας. οἵτινες τὸ δικαίωμα τοῦ θεοῦ ἐπιγνόντες, ὅτι οἱ τὰ τοιαῦτα πράσσοντες ἄξιοι θανάτου εἰσίν, οὐ μόνον αὐτὰ ποιοῦσιν, ἀλλὰ καὶ συνευδοκοῦσι τοῖς πράσσουσι. Cap. 2.

Διὸ ἀναπολόγητος εἶ ὦ ἄνθρωπε πᾶς ὁ κρίνων. ἐν ᾧ γὰρ κρίνεις τὸν ἕτερον, σεαυτὸν κατακρίνεις. τὰ γὰρ αὐτὰ πράσσεις ὁ κρίνων. οἴδαμεν δὲ ὅτι τὸ κρίμα τοῦ θεοῦ ἐστὶ κατὰ ἀλήθειαν ἐπὶ τοὺς τὰ τοιαῦτα πράσσοντας. λογίζῃ δὲ τοῦτο ὦ ἄνθρωπε ὁ κρίνων τοὺς τὰ τοιαῦτα πράσσοντας καὶ ποιῶν αὐτά, ὅτι σὺ ἐκφεύξῃ τὸ κρίμα τοῦ θεοῦ. ἢ τοῦ πλούτου τῆς χρηστότητος αὐτοῦ καὶ τῆς ἀνοχῆς καὶ τῆς μακροθυμίας καταφρονεῖς. ἀγνοῶν ὅτι τὸ χρηστὸν τοῦ θεοῦ εἰς μετάνοιάν σε ἄγει. κατὰ δὲ τὴν σκληρότητά σου καὶ ἀμετανόητον καρδίαν θησαυρίζεις σεαυτῷ ὀργὴν ἐν ἡμέρᾳ ὀργῆς καὶ ἀποκαλύψεως καὶ δικαιοκρισίας τοῦ θεοῦ, ὃς ἀποδώσει ἑκάστῳ κατὰ τὰ ἔργα αὐτοῦ. τοῖς μὲν καθ᾽ ὑπομονὴν ἔργου ἀγαθοῦ δόξαν καὶ τιμὴν καὶ ἀφθαρσίαν ἐπιζητοῦσι, ζωὴν αἰώνιον. τοῖς δὲ ἐξ ἐριθείας, καὶ ἀπειθοῦσι μὲν τῇ ἀληθείᾳ, πειθομένοις δὲ τῇ ἀδικίᾳ, θυμὸς καὶ ὀργή. θλῖψις καὶ στενοχωρία ἐπὶ πᾶσαν ψυχὴν ἀνθρώπου τοῦ κατεργαζομένου τὸ κακόν, ἰουδαίου τε πρῶτον καὶ ἕλληνος. δόξα δὲ καὶ τιμὴ καὶ εἰρήνη παντὶ τῷ ἐργαζομένῳ τὸ ἀγαθόν, ἰουδαίῳ τε πρῶτον καὶ ἕλληνι. οὐ γάρ ἐστι προσωποληψία παρὰ τῷ θεῷ. ὅσοι γὰρ ἀνόμως ἥμαρτον, ἀνόμως καὶ ἀπολοῦνται. καὶ ὅσοι ἐν νόμῳ ἥμαρτον, διὰ νόμου κριθήσονται. οὐ γὰρ οἱ ἀκροαταὶ τοῦ νόμου δίκαιοι παρὰ τῷ θεῷ, ἀλλ᾽ οἱ ποιηταὶ τοῦ νόμου δικαιωθήσονται. ὅταν γὰρ ἔθνη τὰ μὴ νόμον ἔχοντα φύσει τὰ τοῦ νόμου ποιῇ, οὗτοι νόμον μὴ ἔχοντες ἑαυτοῖς εἰσὶ νόμος, οἵτινες ἐνδείκνυνται τὸ ἔργον τοῦ νόμου γραπτὸν ἐν ταῖς καρδίαις αὐτῶν, συμμαρτυρούσης αὐτῶν τῆς συνειδήσεως, καὶ μεταξὺ ἀλλήλων τῶν λογισμῶν κατηγορούν-

sui in semetipsis recipientes. Et sicut non probauerunt deum habere in notitia: tradidit illos deus in reprobum sensum: ut faciant ea que non conueniunt: repletos omni iniquitate: malicia: fornicatione: auaricia: nequitia: plenos inuidia: homicidijs: contentione: dolo: malignitate: susurrones: detractores: deo odibiles: contumeliosos: superbos: elatos: inuentores malorum: parentibus non obedientes: insipientes: incompositos: sine affectione: absque federe: sine misericordia. Qui cum iustitiam dei cognouissent: non intellexerunt quoniam qui talia agunt digni sunt morte: non solum qui ea faciunt: sed etiam qui consentiunt facientibus. Cap. 2.

Propter quod inexcusabilis es o homo omnis qui iudicas. In quo enim alterum iudicas teipsum condemnas. Eadem enim agis que iudicas. Scimus enim quoniam iudicium dei est secundum veritatem in eos qui talia agunt. Existimas autem hoc o homo qui iudicas eos qui talia agunt et facis ea: quia tu effugies iudicium dei? An diuitias bonitatis eius et patientie et longanimitatis contemnis? Ignoras quoniam benignitas dei ad penitentiam te adducit? Secundum autem duritiam tuam et impenitens cor thesaurizas tibi iram in die ire et reuelationis iusti iudicij dei: qui reddet vnicuique secundum opera eius. His quidem qui secundum patientiam boni operis gloriam et honorem et incorruptionem querentibus vitam eternam. His autem qui sunt ex contentione et qui non acquiescunt veritati credunt autem iniquitati: ira et indignatio. tribulatio et angustia in omnem animam hominis operantis malum iudei primum et greci. Gloria autem et honor et pax omni operanti bonum: iudeo primum et greco. Non enim est acceptio personarum apud deum. Quicunque enim sine lege peccauerunt: sine lege peribunt. Et quicunque in lege peccauerunt per legem iudicabuntur. Non enim auditores legis iusti sunt apud deum: sed factores legis iustificabuntur. Cum enim gentes que legem non habent naturaliter ea que legis sunt faciunt: eiusmodi legem non habentes ipsi sibi sunt lex: qui ostendunt opus legis scriptum in cordibus suis: testimonium reddente illis conscientia ipsorum: et inter se inuicem cogitationum accusantium

Complutensian Polyglot Bible, vol. v, first printed Greek New Testament (1514), Rom. i. 27–ii. 15 (see pp. 96–98). Actual size 14 in. × 9½ in.

General Index

Index of New Testament Passages